GLOBAL ASIAN AMERICAN POPULAR CULTURES

Global Asian American Popular Cultures

Edited by Shilpa Davé, Leilani Nishime, and Tasha Oren

NEW YORK UNIVERSITY PRESS
New York

NEW YORK UNIVERSITY PRESS

New York
www.nyupress.org

© 2016 by New York University
All rights reserved

References to Internet websites (URLs) were accurate at the time of writing.
Neither the author nor New York University Press is responsible for URLs
that may have expired or changed since the manuscript was prepared.

ISBN: 978-1-4798-6709-7 (hardback)
ISBN: 978-1-4798-1573-9 (paperback)

For Library of Congress Cataloging-in-Publication data, please contact
the Library of Congress.

New York University Press books are printed on acid-free paper,
and their binding materials are chosen for strength and durability.
We strive to use environmentally responsible suppliers and materials
to the greatest extent possible in publishing our books.

Manufactured in the United States of America

10 9 8 7 6 5 4 3 2 1

Also available as an ebook

To our families

CONTENTS

Acknowledgments   xi

Introduction   1
  Shilpa Davé, Leilani Nishime, and Tasha Oren

PART I. STARS AND CELEBRITIES

1. Trans-Pacific Flows: Globalization and Hybridity in Bruce Lee's
   Hong Kong Films   15
   Daryl Joji Maeda

2. "I'm Thankful for Manny": Manny Pacquiao, Pugilistic Nationalism,
   and the Filipina/o Body   27
   Constancio Arnaldo

3. A History of Race and He(te)rosexuality in the Movies:
   James Shigeta's Asian American Male Stardom   46
   Celine Parreñas Shimizu

4. Model Maternity: Amy Chua and Asian American Motherhood   61
   Julia H. Lee

5. YouTube Made the TV Star: KevJumba's Star Appearance on
   The Amazing Race 17   74
   Vincent Pham and Kent A. Ono

6. David Choe's "KOREANS GONE BAD": The LA Riots,
   Comparative Racialization, and Branding a Politics of Deviance   89
   Wendy Sung

PART II. MAKING COMMUNITY

7. From the Mekong to the Merrimack and Back: The Transnational
   Terrains of Cambodian American Rap   107
   Cathy J. Schlund-Vials

8. "You'll Learn Much about Pakistanis from Listening to Radio":
   Pakistani Radio Programming in Houston, Texas   124
   Ahmed Afzal

9. Online Asian American Popular Culture, Digitization, and Museums   139
   Konrad Ng

10. Asian American Food Blogging as Racial Branding: Rewriting the
    Search for Authenticity   151
    Lori Kido Lopez

11. Picturing the Past: Drawing Together Vietnamese American
    Transnational History   165
    Timothy K. August

PART III. WADING IN THE MAINSTREAM

12. Paradise, Hawaiian Style: Tourist Films and the Mixed-Race Utopias
    of U.S. Empire   183
    Camilla Fojas

13. Post-9/11 Global Migration in *Battlestar Galactica*   197
    Leilani Nishime

14. "Did You Think When I Opened My Mouth?" Asian American
    Indie Rock and the Middling Noise of Racialization   214
    Douglas Ishii

15. Winning the Bee: South Asians, Spelling Bee Competitions, and
    American Racial Branding   228
    Shilpa Davé

16. The Blood Sport of Cooking: On Asian American Chefs
    and Television   244
    Tasha Oren

PART IV. MIGRATION AND TRANSNATIONAL POPULAR CULTURE

17. Curry as Code: Food, Race, and Technology   263
    Madhavi Mallapragada

18. Bollywood's 9/11: Terrorism and Muslim Masculinities in Popular
    Hindi Cinema   276
    Deepti Misri

19. Hybrid Hallyu: The African American Music Tradition in K-Pop   290
    Crystal S. Anderson

20. Transnational Beauty Circuits: Asian American Women,
    Technology, and Circle Contact Lenses   304
    Linda Trinh Võ

21. Making Whales out of Peacocks: Virtual Fashion and Asian Female
    Factory Hands   321
    Christopher B. Patterson

22. Failed Returns: The Queer *Balikbayan* in R. Zamora Linmark's
    Leche and Gil Portes's *Miguel/Michelle*   335
    Robert Diaz

    About the Contributors   351
    Index   355

ACKNOWLEDGMENTS

Working on this follow-up collection has been more pleasure than labor, thanks to our outstanding contributors and everyone at NYU Press. We thank them, and our insightful anonymous reviewers, for their hard work, assistance, and, of course, patience.

Shilpa wishes to thank the University of Virginia for its institutional support, Leilani extends thanks to the University of Washington's Department of Communication, and Tasha is grateful for the support of the Center for 21th Century Studies and the University of Wisconsin–Milwaukee. We are lucky to enjoy loving friends and family, the fellowship of wise and helpful colleagues, and the continuous engagement of our wonderful students. We three are honored and thankful for them all, as we are for our own sustaining friendship and the opportunity to work together on this book.

Introduction

SHILPA DAVÉ, LEILANI NISHIME, AND TASHA OREN

When setting out nearly a decade ago to collect and publish our first volume, *East Main Street: Asian American Popular Culture*, we sought to broaden the parameters of what then constituted "Asian American" as a scholarly category.[1] At the time, our argument was that Asian American studies should consider popular culture in its broadest scope, as we called for a multidisciplinary study of Asian American cultural productions as part of a complex conversation with American history, contemporary mainstream culture, and burgeoning digital technologies.

The study of popular culture within Asian American studies has since emerged as a rich, mature, and multifaceted field in which such approaches are hardly novel. Yet scholars must now contend with a media environment that has only grown denser, broader, faster, and more agile. Technologies of production, reception, and content delivery are yet again straining our conventional grasp of popular circulation. The proliferating avenues of media convergence force us to rearticulate the impact of media platforms on the creation of new audiences and textual meanings. The enduring allure of celebrity and the rapid rise and fall of popular trends have only intensified, and their fragmentation across media cultures challenge scholars to divine their significance in more complicated and multivalent ways.

In addition to the always-churning engine of global Hollywood, the increasing reach of an assembled transnational media culture and the growing production of global popular culture in Asia are also reshaping our models of locality, influence, and provenance. These changes have invited new possibilities for envisioning how popular culture and media forms work to simultaneously maintain and shift our understanding of Asian American identity beyond the tropes of immigrant and native. Evolving means of making, interacting with, and consuming media form a complex, even overwhelming, terrain. Trying to track the often ephemeral work of local community formations to share histories in the midst of political and social shifts means that scholars must travel global pathways as migration becomes an ever more formative experience for Asian American communities. It is in the midst of this fully networked and dynamic cultural moment that our current collection sets off to chart a global Asian American popular media culture.

Asian American popular culture is not only on Main Street—as the title of our first collection declared—but also at the crossroads of global and national expressions of culture intersecting with race, gender, class, and religion in multiple arenas of exchange, both cultural and commercial. While Asian Americans have been the subject and object of American popular culture for a long time, the accessibility of culture across national borders and the rapid circulation of cultural "flashpoints"—like K-pop viral YouTube sensation Psy; Jeremy Lin's sudden, and brief, global superstardom; or the current American obsessions with Bollywood and ramen—offer new interesting pathways in conceiving how categories of "Asian" and "Asian American" exist in counterbalance and dependency within global popular culture. The growth in representation, attention, and media access to people of color and recent increases in the outward flow and hybridization of Asian cultural products such as Hallyu, transnational music and dance collaborations, food, gaming, and fashion all present new and expanded horizons for the study of Asian American popular culture in a global context.

Even in the midst of all this change—the rise of new social and media platforms in the early part of the twenty-first century and in the context of a supposed post-racial United States after the 2008 election of President Barack Obama—central questions remain constant in the meeting place of Asian American studies and media studies. How do we engage with culture? How do Asian Americans continue to influence the popular, and what are the limits and distinctions between mainstream and the margins? Asian American popular culture remains a crucial site for understanding how communities share information and how the meanings of mainstream are shaped with technology and inflected by historical representations and categories. Asian American popular culture is also at the crux of global and national trends in media studies because it crosses and collapses boundaries, acting as a lens with which to view the ebbs and flows of transnational influences on global and American cultures.

In *Global Asian American Popular Cultures*, we highlight new approaches to popular culture, both contemporary and historic, that address these global currents from a variety of perspectives. In this volume, we showcase the productive encounter of Asian American studies with the fields of American studies, anthropology, communications, film, history, media, music, literature, museum studies, television studies, sociology, and cultural studies. Speaking to the broadening of Asian American studies, the essays collected here certainly push on geographical and disciplinary borders but also press on conventions of foci and scale. In this, we stake out new approaches to the popular that account for emerging textual fields, global producers and technologies of distribution, transmedial circulation, and transnational mobility in the peripheries as well as in mainstream culture. These interdisciplinary works provide fresh insights to our current global media moment and to Asian American studies as they pose new questions, draw surprising links, and offer fresh methods and possibilities.

Global Asian American Popular Cultures is divided into four parts—"Stars and Celebrities," "Making Community," "Wading in the Mainstream," and "Migration and Transnational Popular Culture"—that organize the essays as a progressive broadening from individuals, to Asian American communities (physical or virtual), to the U.S. mainstream, and to global-scale exchanges. The connections and overlaps between the articles also suggest the necessity of reaching beyond these categories and for presenting a critical perspective that defines Asian American culture—through texts, producers, celebrities, media forms, or audiences—as active, complex, and productively contradictory. In total, *Global Asian American Popular Cultures* offers a select sampling of the best of contemporary Asian American studies but, more important, also signals the field's ongoing collaboration with cultural, media, American, and global studies.

Part I: Stars and Celebrities

As Richard Dyer argues in one of the earliest theoretical analyses of celebrity, stardom is an ideological phenomenon.[2] A celebrity is hardly the sum of an individual's accomplishments; rather, a celebrity must be understood in terms of his or her cultural role. The chapters in Part I take as their focus specific individual stars and celebrities but place their fame within a larger social and historical context to examine what cultural shifts are marked by their rise to stardom, what needs or issues they activate, and how they engage, maintain, or challenge ideological formations. These stars illuminate the structural role of the Asian American public figure in marking the divisions between and among racial, gender, national, and class categories.

While mainstream U.S. media might be more commonly characterized as absent of Asian American stars, this conception of the media landscape evidences a historical amnesia and a narrow vision of what constitutes celebrity. Daisuke Miyao and Hye Seung Chung have written about the early film stardom of Sessue Hayakawa and Philip Ahn,[3] and the original "Dragon Lady" Anna May Wong is almost a cottage industry in academic film history. These early film stars as well as midcentury actors are continually rediscovered by Asian American scholars to remind us of our long, if willfully forgotten, history of contributing to U.S. cultural life. The chapters here include historical figures, but they also make claims to a wide diversity of contemporary celebrity icons. Drawing from sports, publishing, the art world, and video blogs, these authors, like commodity culture more generally, do not discriminate between high and low culture or mainstream and underground celebrity. Instead, they discover how and why certain Asian Americans have gained iconic status in each distinct milieu.

As the field of Asian American studies has increasingly emphasized trans-nationality as a category of analysis, so, too, have studies of Asian American stars begun to trace their paths across national boundaries. In "Trans-Pacific Flows: Globalization and Hybridity in Bruce Lee's Hong Kong Films," Daryl Joji Maeda returns to the most-written-about Asian American star in history. As most of his fans know, Bruce Lee participated in both the Hollywood and Hong Kong entertainment industry. Maeda, however, argues that Lee's transnationality extends beyond his personal biography or the narrative content of his films. By reading the fight scenes in tandem with both biography and narrative, Maeda develops a kinetic analysis of Lee's three Hong Kong films. In each film, the style of fighting responds to Lee's rejection of the strict nationalism of traditional martial arts forms in favor of a progressively more hybrid style. Constancio Arnaldo continues this line of inquiry, albeit with a different methodological approach, in his chapter "'I'm Thankful for Manny': Manny Pacquiao, Pugilistic Nationalism, and the Filipina/o Body." Like Maeda, Arnaldo studies how audiences negotiate diasporic identity through performance spaces and through the physical and masculine body, in this instance the body of Filipino American boxer Manny Pacquiao. Arnaldo reads the gatherings for Pacquiao's fights as ritualized spaces where Filipina/o Americans combine sporting competitions with performances of what it means to be Filipina/o and American. Pacquiao's body becomes a meeting point for narratives of masculinity, colonial history, and the powerful yet vulnerable racialized body.

As Lee's and Pacquiao's fame demonstrate, popular representations of Asian American masculinity, while certainly plagued by stereotypes of passivity and asexuality, have also made room for alternative performances of gender. The chapters by Celine Parreñas Shimizu and Julia Lee bring us additional lenses for understanding the imbrications of race and gender in the making of Asian American celebrity. Shimizu's "A History of Race and He(te)rosexuality in the Movies: James Shigeta's Asian American Male Stardom" takes up the unlikely film career of James Shigeta. His multiple roles in the 1950s as a romantic hero contradict the common lament about the negation of Asian American masculinity in Hollywood film. She reads three of his films—*Walk like a Dragon, Flower Drum Song*, and *Bridge to the Sun*—to argue for the transformative effects of Shigeta's star power and acting ability. In contrast, Amy Chua's celebrity persona, which Julia Lee explores in "Model Maternity: Amy Chua and Asian American Motherhood," may break away from the hypersexualized image of Asian American femininity but replaces it with an equally damaging vision of racialized motherhood. While seeming to be a critique of "Western" motherhood, Chua turns Asian American motherhood, or the "tiger mother" image, into a commodity. This commodified ethnicity builds the cultural capital of Asian Americans through an embrace of a neoliberal vision of racial/ethnic identity.

In the process, Chua differentiates between the "bad" too-Chinese Asian American mother and the "good" upwardly mobile one that commodifies and exploits her difference.

The last two essays look toward the possibilities offered by a new generation of Asian American stars who traverse the traditional barriers of technology, media, and racial identification. These are not conventional stars garnering mainstream media hype; they are celebrities within their own subcultures. Like those more familiar stars, they act out the anxieties and dreams of their fans, managing the contradictions inherent in all ideologies. For many Asian Americans, Kevin Wu is the undisputed star of YouTube. In "YouTube Made the TV Star: KevJumba's Star Appearance on *The Amazing Race 17*," Vincent Pham and Kent Ono trace Wu's movement between his extremely successful video blog to his appearance on reality television to understand the impact of social media and Internet content on the overall condition of Asian Americans. The essay examines Wu's online success to argue that Asian American media convergence of mainstream and online fame risks falling into traditional model minority representations. However, by moving back and forth between his television and YouTube audience, Wu's persona minimizes mainstream media's impact on Asian American representation while still adding to his celebrity capital and retaining his agency over his own online stardom. The section concludes with the controversial figure of "outsider" artist David Choe. Wendy Sung reads the "street" art of David Choe as a problematic response to dominant white and Asian American figurations of the Los Angeles riots in "David Choe's 'KOREANS GONE BAD': The LA Riots, Comparative Racialization, and Branding a Politics of Deviance." Sung illustrates how Choe rejects the black aggressor versus Asian capitalist exploiter storyline of the mainstream press *and* the *sai-e-gu* Asian American victim identity. Instead, Choe's stories of growing up and living in a mixed African American/Asian American community are set alongside stories of black/Asian antagonism. Further, Choe's celebrity persona of macho misogyny functions as an art market branding and a refusal of the politics of respectability—a politics tied to a victim identity and the rhetoric of an idealized racial solidarity. The questions raised by these celebrity-centered studies, about the reverberations of trauma and the ongoing struggle over identity, representation, and community, also occupy the authors included in the next section of the book but scale both up and down from individual to group identity and from fandom to self-defined localities of place and shared experience.

Part II: Making Community

Part I of this collection explores the individual and the exceptional; Part II moves in the opposite direction, toward shared identities formed along national and ethnic lines. If, as we argue in the first section, the star/celebrity facilitates ideology by smoothing over social contradictions and projecting an idealized version of the self, then the chapters in Part II ask how those ideologies might be resisted or reshaped through community identities and histories. The authors examine a variety of forms, from the soundscapes of music and radio, to the exploding possibilities of the Internet, to the unexpected subcultures of graphic novels in order to expand our notions of what it takes to create and maintain community.

While the larger turn toward a neoliberal ethic has permeated almost every facet of everyday life, the authors collected here document the continued importance of community identity and collective action in the face of persistent racism, xenophobia, and the lasting trauma of war. Asian Americans have also long been an integral part of the colorblind and bootstrapping rhetoric that holds Asian Americans up as symbols or models of the insignificance of race, the importance of individual effort in overcoming all obstacles, and the embrace of a neoliberal ethic of opportunity/prosperity. The authors here powerfully counter this narrative with their detailed look at the survival strategies of Asians in the United States. These include narrating a collective history in the face of a willful historical amnesia, using in-reach, lo-fi, and grassroots methods to create cultural identities, and manipulating brand culture to make racialized communities legible. Their creative approaches ask us to rethink how we create community now and in the future.

The first two chapters of "Making Community" investigate sound as the web that holds together a dispersed community. In "From the Mekong to the Merrimack and Back: The Transnational Terrains of Cambodian American Rap," Cathy Schlund-Vials writes about the Cambodian American community and how their experiences of structural inequality from low-skilled or unskilled employment to state deportation are explored in hip-hop. These artists produce and perform critical rhymes about everyday life, racism, xenophobia, and the ongoing War on Terror. As Schlund-Vials writes, "Set against histories of war-driven dislocation and forced relocation, Cambodian American rap determinedly recollects, through lyrics and samples, . . . the Cambodian genocide and its refugee aftermath." Focusing his analysis on production as well as content, Ahmed Afzal follows with an ethnographic study of community formation around the development of local radio. The chapter "'You'll Learn Much about Pakistanis from Listening to Radio': Pakistani Radio Programming in Houston, Texas" contrasts two time periods, the 1970s–1990s and current radio. In the earlier period, characterized by non-profit community-based programming, radio worked to create a cohesive community for its upwardly mobile core audience. Program content emphasized nostalgia for the homeland and worked to bridge ethnic and national boundaries. By contrast, contemporary community radio, much more commercial and sponsored by local businesses, creates niche audiences by addressing specific consumer identities through programming content that stresses difference. Ultimately, the chapter traces the intersection of commerce, culture, and changes in demographics and immigration patterns to understand the formation of diasporic communities.

Afzal argues that the widely dispersed Pakistani population in Houston necessitated the mediation of community through a technology that could reach a wide swath of the Houston suburban landscape. Likewise, the articles by Konrad Ng and Lori Kido Lopez examine the possibilities and limits of computer-mediated communication in building community and marking racialized identities across a scattered population. Ng, the director of the Smithsonian Institution's Asian Pacific American Center from 2011 to 2015, asks what happens to Asian American history and experience as museums move toward digitization. In "Online Asian American Popular Culture, Digitization, and Museums," he argues that digitization has allowed national museums to expand what legitimately counts as national history. Ng presents different examples of case studies of online exhibits such as a comic book rendering of the historical exhibit *I Want the Wide American Earth: An Asian Pacific American Story* and an exhibition of Korean taco food trucks featured in the *Smithsonian Asian-Latino Project*. These examples, as well as other exhibits, connect Asian American community, identity, and history to a national narrative while simultaneously redefining how we create, respond, and develop national narratives. Lopez, in contrast, analyzes Asian American food bloggers who have a much more ambivalent relationship to community identity. "Asian American Food Blogging as Racial Branding: Rewriting the Search for Authenticity" centers on the thriving phenomena of Asian American food blogging and points to the centrality of authenticity as a trope that is both upheld and deconstructed. Lopez finds bloggers' claims of authenticity deployed to legitimate ethnic identity for both authors and their recipes that, in turn, are used primarily as a means of capitalizing on a logic of racial branding. Yet, in the posts and writing that Lopez analyzes, authenticity claims are simultaneously destabilized by bloggers, as their writing often expresses dynamic, transnational identity formations and undermines notions of fixed correspondence between culinary origins, identity, and contemporary cooking practices.

The sensory pleasures of food also subtend the search for community identity we find in Timothy August's study of the graphic novel *Vietnamerica*. In "Picturing the Past: Drawing Together Vietnamese American Transnational History" August explores the generic possibilities of the graphic novel to write and visualize an alternative narrative of Vietnamese Americans. He closely reads the relationship of words to the image to decipher how *Vietnamerica* presents Vietnamese identity as a collective identity and history rather than an individual story. The broad structural and abstracted collective identity described in the book is paradoxically conveyed by an emphasis on the somatic experiences (sound, smell, taste) of a Vietnamese identity. These distinct ways of understanding identity are made whole by the rendering of the protagonist's journey through the genre of the graphic novel.

Part III: Wading in the Mainstream

From Asian American cultural production and articulations of identity and community we turn to the broader frame of definitions of Asian American life and experience within mainstream U.S. culture. The common stereotype of the easy assimilation of Asian model minorities into mainstream culture crumbles under the close scrutiny of these authors. The essays in Part III examine the various strategies and means by which Asian Americans negotiate mainstream presence, neither blending into a "post-racial" media landscape nor standing apart as abject outsiders. By focusing their analysis on Asian Americans and also recentering them from their engagement at the margins of film, television, music, and competition culture, the essays offer nuanced ways of rethinking representations of Asian Americans across media industries.

By grappling with the specific genre of each media form, the authors also ask to what extent cultural frames that define Asian Americans—and the works they produce—have changed in the recent past. Each generic form carries within it a historical, gendered, and geographically specific narrative of our national culture. In both adhering to generic rules in order to tell a legible story and by consciously adjusting and expanding on those generic conventions, these authors probe the boundaries of mainstream media productions from musicals and indie rock to science fiction, spelling bees, and cooking competitions.

Part III opens with Camilla Fojas's account of how the state of Hawaii has come to signify a friendly, multiracial paradise in the popular American imagination. "Paradise, Hawaiian Style: Tourist Films and the Mixed Race Utopias of U.S. Empire" focuses on the role of Hollywood cinemas, namely Elvis Presley's cycle of Hawaiian films of the late 1950s and early 1960s, in shaping the image of Hawai'i for the U.S. imaginary. As Fojas illustrates, the iconic "types" that emerge in these films come to stand in for mainland experiences of Hawai'i—the beach boy, the surfer, the playboy—and function not as hedonistic rebels but as representatives of American enterprising spirit. Fojas further shows how Hollywood and the domestic tourism industry worked together to shape the image of the new state along specific ideological lines as both a tourist destination and a new frontier for expansive economic opportunity, all in a site of racial harmony, contrasting with the racial unrest on the mainland. The next essay steers the conversation of island and mainland racial politics to representations of racial partnerships and interactions in the realm of outer space. In "Post-9/11 Global Migration in *Battlestar Galactica*," Leilani Nishime examines inter- and intraracial relationships in a global context through the interstellar science fiction narrative. Exploring the popular and critically acclaimed sci-fi series *Battlestar Galactica*, Nishime joins other critics in finding this post-9/11 program a particularly rich text for the expression and fantasy resolution of contemporary social and political anxieties. However, while many critics found the show's image of global politics and thematically resonant wartime narrative progressive, Nishime finds that many such storylines are buttressed by troubling depictions of race, gender, and nationality for characters marked as Asian American women. As Nishime argues, both of the primary Asian American characters in the program enact distinctive narratives of assimilation that together work to dislocate global migration from its underpinnings in capital, labor, and politics, posing "successful" cultural citizenship as one achieved at the site of heterosexual domesticity that renounces all transnational attachments.

The next chapter turns from geographically centered narratives of belonging to racial ones taking up Asian Americans who travel and trouble the "middle" space between white and black racial definitions. Douglas Ishii's "'Did You Think When I Opened My Mouth?': Asian American Indie Rock and the Middling Noise of Racialization" explores the idea of "middleness" as a framework to understand the ways in which Asian American indie rock productions and their politics are defined as they challenge the white/anti-black hierarchies of both popular music and indie culture. For Ishii, Asian American indie rock—a central site for negotiating creative labor—is also the locus for the exploration of "racializing capital" and the workings of commerce and agency in the music industry. The final two essays in Part III look to cultural spaces where Asians literally compete to assert their place in relation to the white mainstream. In light of South Asian domination of the National Spelling Bee competition, Shilpa Davé deconstructs the popularity and importance of the spelling bee for South Asian American communities and its implication and deployment in particular models of success in "Winning the Bee: South Asians, Spelling Bee Competitions, and American Racial Branding." As Davé illustrates, the spelling bee is at once a symbolic articulation of mainstream assimilation, a treasured expression of the American dream, and a counterpathway to academic prestige for immigrant children. The spelling bee reads as a cultural narrative about South Asian immigrants' community achievements and yet is also a site where South Asian Americans are celebrated as they embrace market-based and individualistic definitions of success. As Davé shows, competitive spelling bees function as a cultural ritual defined through a symbiotic logic that links South Asian American success to a narrowly delimited performance of identity and also provides an opportunity for redefining community engagements with mainstream expectations. In "The Blood Sport of Cooking: On Asian American Chefs and Television," Tasha Oren traces the histories of Asian American chefs on TV and the development of the television cooking competition from its Japanese origins to its adaptation and massive popularity in the United States. In pairing these two parallel and largely unrelated TV histories, Oren argues that the specific and politically laden history of Asian American food and cooking practices produced discourses about culinary style, tradition, and individual biography. These narratives lend themselves particularly well to the televisual identity-based spectacle that forms the narrative conventions of cooking competitions. Further, as she argues, this logic is also at the heart of the current ascendance of Asian American celebrity chefs in U.S. gastroculture.

Part IV: Migration and Transnational Popular Culture

From anime to the K-pop sensation "Gangnam Style," it is clear that the United States no longer has a stranglehold on global popular culture. While it may now be commonplace to recognize Asia as a major force and source of popular culture, what is less commonly noted or understood is how global culture circulates in multiple and unexpected patterns. Moving beyond the influence of U.S. culture industries on Asia or the popularity of trends originating in Asia, Part IV complicates the movement of culture across borders by emphasizing the ways popular culture is both hybrid and differentially valued within global and local hierarchies. The circulation of cultural narratives, music, and objects is not a neutral process but, as Benjamin Lee and Edward LiPuma suggest, an exchange that is determined and controlled by human and community agency.[4] The articles in this section transition from examining how cultural objects travel to also analyzing and identifying the linkages and structures in transnational and global movements and migrations such as labor, trade, and world economies of consumption. As many of the authors here reveal, the meanings of popular culture are fundamentally unstable and change as culture moves across national and local contexts.

Part IV opens by addressing the circulation of historical and popular touchstone cultural narratives in the twenty-first century, namely, the 9/11 attacks on the World Trade Towers, the ascent of K-pop as a global phenomena, and labor outsourcing in the technology industry. While cultural mobility is often described at the sensual sites of spectacle, sound, or taste, Madhavi Mallapragada's article places an emphasis on the olfactory and shows how discourses over smell facilitate articulations of race, nationalism, immigration, and masculinity. "Curry as Code: Food, Race, and Technology" takes up smell as a racializing trope and a discursive locale from which to explore the representation of Indian immigrant information technology workers. Curry, as Mallapragada argues, "operates as a code—a metaphorical and covert form of representation" that casts Indian immigrants as foreign, unwelcome, and lingering. Negotiations over the shared space of the workplace kitchen thus become clashes over immigration, racialized labor, and cultural politics as curry is both code and a metaphor for the "Indian" body.

The complexities of representing the Indian and South Asian body as a gendered and raced other is further examined by Deepti Misri in "Bollywood's 9/11: Terrorism and Muslim Masculinities in Popular Hindi Cinema." Here Misri explores Indian cinema's foray into post-9/11 narratives from the perspective of immigrant South Asians and South Asian Americans in the United States—a perspective all but absent in Hollywood and independents U.S. films. In her comparison of two popular Bollywood films, *New York* (2009) and *Kurbaan* (2009), Misri reframes discussions of the "good" and "bad" Muslim U.S. citizens in cinematic narrative as she questions the relationship between the state and the normative heterosexual family as the marker of good citizenship. Misri argues it is the failure of the traditional heterosexual family narrative that allows for a patriotic Muslim American story. These and other Bollywood films offer a contrasting historical and cultural narrative of 9/11 that reflect local and global consequences for South Asians and the South Asian diaspora. Cultural negotiations over identity and tradition turn to questions of authenticity and cultural adaptation in the movement from film to music. In "Hybrid Hallyu: The African American Music Tradition in K-Pop," Crystal Anderson explores the inter-racial and inter-cultural influences that complicate national histories and notions of musical authenticity in Afro-Asian K-pop. Anderson traces the history of African Americans in Korean popular music and crossover traditions of hip-hop and rhythm and blues in the music of Psy and Big Mama to propose a counter model of cultural authenticity. This alternative definition of cultural alliance relies less on conventions of cultural identity, politics, or historical legacy and is instead predicated on shared aesthetics of musical form and expression.

The complex network of racial discourses and aesthetics in border-crossing texts is further examined by Linda Trinh Võ in "Transnational Beauty Circuits: Asian American Women, Technology, and Circle Contact Lenses." In this chapter, Võ charts the growing global popularity of cosmetic contact lenses, their marketing, and their signification and popularity among Asian and Asian American young women. As the essay illustrates, this anime-inspired fashion trend links various spheres of global cultural production together: the historical circulation and cross pollination between US and Japanese animation traditions, the evolution of fashion styles as marks of authority and defiance by young women in Japan and Korea, and the harnessing of digital culture by young Asian American women and other minorities to counter their underrepresentation in mainstream commercial beauty culture.

Fashion, commercial circulation, and the virtual pathways between East and West also form the terrain for Christopher Patterson's "Making Whales out of Peacocks: Virtual Fashion and Asian Female Factory Hands." Yet here the author reconfigures notions of consumption, labor, and globalization by exploring how virtual shopping in the play worlds of the videogame intersect with the hard materiality of global labor and the politics of consumption, identity, and power.

Pairing the actual practice of character enhancement and in-game consumption with the geopolitical structures of the gaming industry and its labor divisions, Patterson dismantles the illusion of virtuality. As the essay demonstrates, games like *Guild Wars 2* and *Lord of the Rings Online* construct play environments that actively erase the sweatshops, classed labor practices, and conspicuous consumption that sustain and animate them.

In the final article, Robert Diaz discusses the circulation of cultural commodities and the movement of racialized bodies in narratives of the return to the homeland. He looks to queered homecoming stories to trouble the very notion of cultural authenticity rooted in geography and state politics. "Failed Returns: The Queer *Balikbayan* in R. Zamora Linmark's *Leche* and Gil Portes's *Miguel/Michelle*" sets conventional Filipino nationalist narratives against those of the queer Filipino American returnee, illustrating how the former support essentialist notions of patriotism and justify the exploitation of out-migration labor. As Diaz's analysis reveals, investment in normative nationalist, gendered, and sexual identities undergirds these conventional narratives. In contrast, the "failure" of the returnees and their homecoming confront and speak back to the normalized practices of global labor migration, giving voice to the complexities of postcolonial histories and cultural circulations.

The essays collected here highlight the current diversity in subjects and approaches in research on global Asian American popular culture; together they present important routes for understanding how we make meanings with and through the various realms of the popular, as well as the stakes for Asian American representation and participation within an expanding and volatile media culture.

NOTES

1 Shilpa Davé, Leilani Nishime, and Tasha G. Oren, eds., *East Main Street: Asian American Popular Culture* (New York: NYU Press, 2005).

2 Richard Dyer, *Heavenly Bodies: Film Stars and Society* (New York: Psychology Press, 2004).

3 Daisuke Miyao, *Sessue Hayakawa: Silent Cinema and Transnational Stardom* (Durham, NC: Duke University Press, 2007); Hye Seung Chung, *Hollywood Asian: Philip Ahn and the Politics of Cross-Ethnic Performance* (Philadelphia: Temple University Press, 2006).

4 Benjamin Lee and Edward LiPuma, "Cultures of Circulation: The Imaginations of Modernity," *Public Culture* 14, no. 1 (Winter 2002): 191–213.

PART I

Stars and Celebrities

1

Trans-Pacific Flows

Globalization and Hybridity in Bruce Lee's Hong Kong Films

DARYL JOJI MAEDA

Bruce Lee is often imagined as a martial artist who broke out of Asia to become an international superstar. This narrative obscures the decades-long, if not centuries-long, trans-Pacific flows of peoples and cultures from which Lee emerged and that he addressed in his films and martial arts performances. Instead of understanding Hong Kong as the locality from which Lee escaped to enter the global arena, this chapter argues that the three films he made as an adult in Hong Kong are already thoroughly enmeshed in processes of colonialism, migration, hybridization, and globalization. The historian Penny Von Eschen notes briefly that "Bruce Lee's career was the product of globalization" and illustrates the "multiple global flows" of people, capital, and culture.[1] This chapter goes beyond the social history of Lee and his migrations to consider how his Hong Kong films construct a syncretic aesthetic of martial arts to reject the notion of cultural purity in favor of hybridity and privilege migration and diaspora over settlement and home. In short, it shows how representations of fighting provide visual narratives of cultural mixtures and national crossings.

Bruce Lee's filmic sensibility mirrored his own transnational life. Although his family hailed from Hong Kong, he was born in San Francisco while his father was touring the United States with a Cantonese opera troupe. When he was still an infant, his family returned to Hong Kong, where he grew up and appeared in twenty films as a child actor. He returned to the nation of his birth at the age of eighteen, taught kung fu, and found work in Hollywood, first as Kato in the television series *The Green Hornet* and later in small roles in films and TV shows. He pitched a television show about a Chinese martial artist to Warner Bros. but was bypassed for David Carradine, the white actor who starred as the Shaolin monk Kwai Chang Caine in the *Kung Fu* television series. Convinced that he could never surmount racial prejudice in Hollywood, Lee returned to Hong Kong, where he starred in three films that broke box-office records in Hong Kong and throughout Asia.[2] Becoming the biggest movie star in Asia finally enabled Lee to star in a Hollywood-produced film. *Enter the Dragon* (1973) brought Lee his greatest success in the West, but by the time it was released, he was dead, the victim of sensitivity to a prescription medication, an overdose of illegal drugs, a mob hit, or a mysterious kung fu assassination—depending on which version you find most believable.

Although it might be tempting to treat *Enter the Dragon* as the culmination of Lee's transnational career, his three prior Hong Kong films show how processes of colonialism and globalization can be comprehended through the visual medium of cinematic martial arts. In sequence, these films depict the creation of a diasporic community, contest colonialism through the construction of a hybrid nationalism, and finally deconstruct cultural and national boundaries. This trilogy of sorts contains an arc that points to an increasing ethos of migration and hybridization and may be read as an allegory of the transnational movements and crossings that have characterized the Pacific for over a century.

Diasporic Community in *The Big Boss*

Bruce Lee's first movie with the Hong Kong production company Golden Harvest was *The Big Boss* (1971), which was released in the United States as *Fists of Fury*. In it, he plays Cheng Chao-An, a country bumpkin from China who travels to Thailand to find work. This journey reflects a centuries-old pattern of out-migration from southern China, which has created diasporic communities of ethnic Chinese in nations throughout Southeast Asia. Cheng obtains a job in an ice factory that turns out to be a drug-smuggling operation run by the titular Big Boss. Although he has vowed to his mother not to fight, circumstances eventually force his hands (and feet), and he ends up kicking all kinds of ass. The film explores major themes of loyalty, ambition, romance, and revenge. But most important, for the purposes of this essay, it shows the creation and maintenance of a diasporic community.

The film opens by showing Cheng arriving on a ferryboat and quickly being apprised of the dangers of this new land. The uncle who greets him at the ferry warns, "Life here is very different from back home, so be careful." Uncle's warning proves prophetic, for when they stop at a roadside stand for shaved ice treats, four local thugs accost the pretty female proprietor and a little boy selling rice cakes. Uncle reminds Cheng that he has promised not to fight, pulling out a jade pendant that Cheng wears under his shirt. Throughout the film, this "locket" symbolizes Cheng's promise to his mother to avoid fighting. Fortunately, another man arrives and singlehandedly dispatches all four hoodlums. He turns out to be Cheng's cousin, Hsu Chien, who throughout the film functions as Cheng's alter ego in four ways. First, he is an awesome fighter; second, he resembles Cheng facially; third, he wears dark Chinese garb identical to Cheng's uniform; and finally, he ardently seeks justice for his community.

Hsu Chien leads Cheng and Uncle to a house that stands in stark contrast to the alienation suggested in the opening scene and introduces Cheng to six more male cousins and his sister, Chiao Mei, who eventually becomes Cheng's romantic interest and represents family and community throughout the film. The male cousins live together, working, eating, and sleeping communally and calling each other "brother" at various times to emphasize their close bonds.

Cheng joins his cousins in working at the ice factory, where two cousins accidentally discover the drug-smuggling operation then subsequently disappear. Hsu Chien attempts to find them, confronts the Big Boss, and eventually falls victim himself to the Boss's henchmen. When Cheng and the remaining cousins go on strike to protest the disappearances, the factory manager orders a band of thugs to attack them. Mindful of his promise to his mother, Cheng watches the mayhem wistfully, even while the workers take the brunt of the beatings and his cousins urge him to fight. But when a hoodlum rips the locket off Cheng's chest, the trademark Bruce Lee snarl emerges, he emits a fierce howl, and jumps into the fray. The fight ends with the thugs fleeing from Cheng, but he finds his jade pendant—and his promise—shattered.

Rather than punishing Cheng, the manager promotes him to foreman and takes him to a dinner where he is plied with extravagant food, abundant liquor, and available prostitutes. When Cheng awakes in the morning, he finds a naked woman snuggled up against him, but he dresses quickly, only to bump into Chiao Mei as he scurries out of the brothel. Cheng returns to the factory and orders the laborers to resume working, but they refuse and instead accuse him of selling out. These juxtapositions show that Cheng has betrayed the trust of his surrogate family and strained his ability to belong to the diasporic community that they have built.

Cheng returns to grill the prostitute, who informs him that the factory is a drug-shipping operation. After he leaves, the Boss's son kills the prostitute and kidnaps Chiao Mei to add to his father's harem of drug-addicted prostitutes. Cheng goes to the factory, where he discovers the drugs and Hsu Chien's body encased in the blocks of ice. But as he is processing the information, the Boss's son and a gang of knife-wielding minions attack. In a pitched battle Cheng defeats them and kills the Boss's son. He rushes home only to find all of his male cousins massacred and Chiao Mei missing. The morning finds Cheng sitting beside the river, contemplating the slaughter, as a voiceover externalizes his inner thoughts: "I promised my mother I'd keep out of trouble. . . . If I had any sense, I'd get out of here. If anything happened to me, who would take care of Mom? . . . She's over seventy, but I can't just walk away from this. I just can't do that, I can't." A vision of his slain cousins and Chiao Mei appears in the water as he ponders his old promise to his mother. Torn between the vow made in the homeland and allegiance to his newfound community in a new land, Cheng tosses his packet of belongings into the river. This symbolizes a fundamental break. He is casting aside the things he brought from the motherland and making a new start, declaring that his primary allegiance belongs to the community of expatriates he has joined. He stares heavenward and vows vengeance, an act that will cement his place in the new nation.

In the climactic scene, Cheng runs to the Big Boss's compound where he faces off with a half-dozen guards armed with knives, all of whom are Thai rather than Chinese and clad in gloriously garish 1970s Western-style slacks and shirts, in contrast to Cheng's simple black and white Chinese garb. The fight takes place on a lawn in front of a reflecting pool, behind which is a Thai-style Buddhist shrine, a visual reminder that they are not in China but in a foreign land. After quickly defeating the guards, Cheng takes on the Big Boss himself. Like Cheng, the Boss also wears a collarless, wide-cuffed Chinese coat, and alternating shots of their feet show Cheng and the Boss to be wearing identical dark gray/black flowing Chinese pants and canvas shoes. They match each other unarmed, punch for punch and kick for kick, until the Boss grabs two knives from the fallen guards and begins to get the best of Cheng. During the fight, one of the Boss's prostitutes frees Chiao Mei and urges her to flee. The fight ends when the Boss flings a knife at Cheng, but Cheng kicks it back and buries it in his gut. Cheng thrusts eight fingers deep into the Boss's chest and punches him in the head repeatedly until both collapse, Cheng motionless atop the dead body of the Boss in a symbolic death of his own.

After Cheng finally manages to kill the Boss, Chiao Mei arrives with two cars full of Thai police officers who rush out to capture Cheng. He shakes them off and threatens to fight, but when Chiao Mei cries, "Listen Cheng, give up!" he looks up, as if conscious of his situation for the first time in a sudden rebirth of sorts, and he raises his bloodstained hands to be arrested. The film concludes with the handcuffed Cheng and Chiao Mei walking toward the police cars, flanked by the officers. This ending is unsatisfying in the sense that it presumes that Cheng will have to face trial for murder, but in other ways it represents a new beginning for him. To begin with, when he fights the Big Boss, Cheng takes on his evil doppelgänger. By slaying the Boss, Cheng not only exacts revenge for his cousins but also eliminates his old self. Similarly, Cheng's alter ego Hsu Hsien lies buried in ice. With these symbolic doubles dead, Cheng must build a new identity and self. But what will that identity be? Although the film ends before answering that question definitively, it certainly implies that the new beginning will occur in Thailand with Chiao Mei. Cheng's submission to Thai justice suggests that whatever fate awaits him, he will face it not in China but in this land that will become his new home. Furthermore, Cheng and Chiao Mei walking together arm in arm toward the police car suggests that the two of them will enter the future together and that the family they build will replace the lost diasporic community represented by the cousins. Thus, *The Big Boss* represents how diasporic migrations create new senses of identity and belonging as people leave their homelands behind.

The Globalization of Martial Arts in *Fist of Fury*

Bruce Lee's second film, *Fist of Fury* (1972), came out hot on heels of *The Big Boss*. The two were scheduled for release in the United States close together, and a mix-up resulted in their titles being switched. *The Big Boss* was supposed to be called *The Chinese Connection*, a reference to *The French Connection* (1971), a then-current film about narcotics trafficking, while the title of the second film was mistranslated as *Fists of Fury* (note the pluralization of "fists"). During export or import, the reels were placed in the wrong cans, and the titles were thus swapped, so the first film became known in the U.S. as *Fists of Fury* and second film as *The Chinese Connection* despite having nothing to do with drug smuggling.[3] (In this essay I refer to films by their original titles, simply because they make more sense.) The titling blunder shows how travels across national borders and cultural and linguistic boundaries can deform meanings, but *Fist of Fury* also demonstrates how the transnational migrations can result in wondrous new hybrid forms.

On the surface, the subject matter of *Fist of Fury* appears to be ill suited for exploring the notion of hybridity. Bruce Lee plays Cheng Chao-an, a student of the Jing Wu school of martial arts in early twentieth-century Shanghai. In the film, martial arts provide an arena for contests over national supremacy and expressions of national pride. During this period, China was humiliated by a series of unequal treaties that granted foreign nations, including Japan, extraterritorial rights in China in places such as the International Settlement of Shanghai, where foreigners enjoyed rights over Chinese citizens. In one of the film's most famous scenes, Cheng is denied entrance to a park that features a sign reading "No Dogs and Chinese Allowed".

Historically speaking, the real Jing Wu school was established after the unsuccessful Boxer Rebellion, in which martial fighters tried to oust British imperialists from China. The school was intended to preserve the teaching of various kung fu styles and was thus closely associated with Chinese nationalism.[4] In the film, the leader of the Jing Wu school and Cheng's beloved teacher has been poisoned by Suzuki, the head of a Japanese karate dojo. The Japanese karatekas (practitioners of karate) humiliate the Chinese students, giving them a parchment reading "The Sick Man of Asia" (a derogatory reference to China's state of humiliation in having been carved up by imperial powers) and eventually attack and kill nearly all of the Jing Wu students. Cheng restores their national pride by beating up hordes of Japanese martial artists, tearing the "Sick Man" parchment and forcing two Japanese students to eat it, destroying the "No Dogs and Chinese Allowed" sign, and finally slaying Suzuki. The most straightforward reading of the movie thus focuses on the restoration of Chinese pride in the face of Japanese imperialism. In that vein, the film scholar Stephen Teo contends that Bruce Lee's nationalism may be the most important characteristic of his films, calling him "an ardent nationalist" whose work "stir[s] the hearts of Chinese audiences everywhere, while foreign critics talk of jingoism and chauvinism."[5] Indeed, Hong Kong audiences reportedly erupted in standing ovations when Cheng smashed the racist sign.

A more intriguing story lurks beneath the surface of *Fist of Fury*, one that complicates its seemingly straightforward nationalism with hybridity and transnational crossings. In this film, Bruce Lee introduces the use of nunchaku (also known as nunchuks), a weapon consisting of two rods of hardened wood joined by a short length of chain. The most captivating martial arts sequences occur when Chen showcases the nunchaku, sending them twirling in rapid arcs through the air and striking opponents with lightning quickness. At that time, the nunchaku was a relatively obscure Okinawan weapon, but Lee's dazzling usage made them seem like the coolest thing on earth. Within a few years, nunchaku had become so popular that they were banned as deadly weapons in parts of the United States and in all of Canada and England. The story of how the nunchaku came to play a starring role in this movie demonstrates the transnational flows of martial arts and artists.

Although Bruce Lee studied Wing Chun kung fu in Hong Kong and taught it when he initially returned to the United States, he was a serious student of other martial arts as well. He collected books on many different disciplines and perused them for insights into efficient and effective fighting. In addition to studying books, he worked out with martial arts experts of various disciplines, picking and choosing aspects he found to be effective. Long before the advent of "mixed martial arts," Lee was an ardent advocate of disciplinary mixing. In fact, famously he mocked blind adherence to what he dismissed as the "classical mess" of orthodox kung fu and karate. At the entrance to his kwoon (kung fu studio) in Los Angeles's Chinatown sat a tombstone inscribed with the words, "In Memory of a Once Fluid Man, Crammed and Distorted by the Classical Mess."[6] The inscription encapsulated Lee's conviction that doggedly reproducing the classical forms of kung fu and karate would produce stiff, wooden fighters who would be unable to adapt and change their styles to meet new challenges. Instead, he created Jeet Kune Do, a discipline that stipulated "no style" so that it could adapt to any other style.[7] Lee's eclecticism surely stemmed in part from his performance on a global martial arts stage. Leaving Hong Kong immersed him in transnational currents that intermingled martial arts practitioners and styles to a greater extent than had ever occurred in the history of fighting.

In Los Angeles, Lee met Dan Inosanto, who became a student, friend, and martial arts icon in his own right.[8] The Filipino American Inosanto was an ardent advocate of understanding multiple martial arts forms rather than adhering strictly to any single one, a perspective honed by his experiences in the U.S. Army. As a paratrooper in the elite 101st Airborne Division, Inosanto was stationed at Fort Campbell in Kentucky, where he witnessed the confluence of martial arts styles including boxing, wrestling, karate, and others. He trained with an American karate instructor who had learned his craft as part of the occupation forces in Japan, and the martial arts school at the base featured instruction in Korean, Japanese, and Okinawan disciplines by veterans who had been stationed abroad. The heterogeneity of martial arts at Fort Campbell can be traced to the most belligerent cause of transnational cultural crossings—imperialism, which delivered U.S. armed forces personnel to various points in occupied Asia and reassembled them back home.

After his army discharge, Inosanto moved to Los Angeles, where he studied kenpo karate with the legendary Ed Parker. Parker had learned martial arts in Hawaii, where migrants from Okinawa, Japan, and China were drawn to work the sugar plantations and intermixed their various styles to form kenpo. Thus, like military occupation, labor migration also provided the context for the cross-pollination for martial arts disciplines.

Parker organized the First International Karate Championship, held in Long Beach in the summer of 1964, and asked Inosanto to host a guest who was visiting the tournament but not competing. That guest was Bruce Lee, who was living in Seattle at the time. Inosanto and Lee bonded over their commitment to understanding diverse styles, and Inosanto began training with Lee. Inosanto introduced Lee to a Filipino weapon called as the "tabak toyok," akin to the nunchaku, which Lee understood instinctively despite having no real training. Inosanto believes that Lee's dexterity with the sticks derived from his experience with the épée, a Western fencing sword, which he had learned from his older brother Peter, a champion fencer. He thus extended his knowledge of how to use a long stick in combat to using the nunchaku as a striking instrument.

Tracing Bruce Lee's virtuoso deployment of the nunchaku in *Fist of Fury* shows the importance of transnational cultural flows to the development of his martial artistry. Lee began with training in Wing Chun kung fu and knowledge of long sticks derived from fencing, a British importation to Hong Kong. In the United States, he met and worked out with martial artists whose training derived from Chinese, Okinawan, Japanese, and Filipino disciplines. The forces of British imperialism, in the form of the colonization of Hong Kong, and American imperialism, which resulted in the annexation of Hawaii and permanent military bases in Korea, the Philippines, Okinawa, and Japan, brought all of these styles into conversation and enabled Lee to become the consummate adapter and synthesizer of these forms.

Hybridity in *Way of the Dragon*

Bruce Lee's first two films enjoyed enormous popularity in Hong Kong and throughout Asia. *The Big Boss* became the largest-grossing movie in Hong Kong history, playing seven performances per day in each of sixteen theaters and displacing the former box office champ, *The Sound of Music*.[9] Subsequently, *Fist of Fury* topped *The Big Boss*.[10] This success earned Lee almost total artistic control of his third film, *Way of the Dragon* (1972), which he wrote, directed, choreographed, and co-produced. In this most ambitious of Lee's Hong Kong films, themes of migration and hybridity take center stage. (Because it was released in the United States in 1974, after the Hollywood-produced *Enter the Dragon*, American audiences know it as *Return of the Dragon*). *Way of the Dragon* surpassed both of its predecessors, becoming the first Hong Kong film to gross over $5 million.[11]

Lee plays Tang Lung, who travels from Hong Kong to Rome to aid the owners of a Chinese restaurant: Chen Ching-hua—a lovely damsel in distress—and her Uncle Wang. An Italian mob boss is trying to force them to sell their business by having his thugs harass and drive off potential customers. Although the Chinese cook and waiters try to defend the restaurant, it teeters close to failure. Tang takes on the hoodlums and ultimately faces off with imported mercenaries played by martial arts champions, including karate expert Chuck Norris.

Diaspora constitutes the first major theme of the film. The film's opening credits announce its interest in migration. Wavy lines scroll across the screen from left to right, suggesting flowing water, and a stop-motion animated cutout of a dragon boat and its rowing crew traverse the waters in the opposite direction until it crashes onto a rocky shore and the boat transforms into a dragon. The first scene accentuates the sense of alienation, beginning with a closeup of Tang Lung's face then panning out to reveal him standing in the Rome airport surrounded by Europeans. Tang is wearing charcoal-colored Chinese clothing of loose pants and a collarless, wide-cuffed shirt, while the Europeans are clad in turtlenecks, jeans, polyester shirts, suede jackets, and 1970s suits with wide lapels. An older white woman gapes unblinkingly at Tang from within his personal space as if she has never seen a more curious sight. Other passengers cast more discreet glances at Tang, but it is clear that they, too, see him as an oddity. The scene showcases Lee's acting talent, for he silently conveys his discomfort with uncomfortable swallows, a downcast gaze, cocking of the eyebrow, awkward smiles, and a nervous hand to the face. This is a performance worthy of Buster Keaton or Charlie Chaplin. When Chen arrives to take him home, they drive past the Egyptian obelisk at Piazza del Popolo, the Colosseum, and the Trevi Fountain. This brief jaunt through the city emphasizes Tang's distance from home by firmly placing the narrative among the famous sights of Rome. It also conjures tourism, which involves travel and temporary stays in unfamiliar locales.

In its depiction of a diasporic community, *Way of the Dragon* resembles *The Big Boss*. As in the earlier film, Lee plays an unsophisticated country boy who in this case hails from the New Territories, a rural area of Hong Kong far from the big city. It is obvious that he doesn't belong in Italy: He is suspicious of depositing his meager monetary stash in a bank, unwittingly cavorts with a prostitute, and squats over the toilet Chinese-style instead of sitting on it like a Westerner. Tang's naïveté signals that he is a fish out of water, but all of the Chinese characters (save for the translator, Mr. Ho, whom I will discuss later) form a diasporic community around the restaurant—they are in an alien land far from home, bound together by their common homeland. Uncle Wang expresses this idea when Tang first arrives at the restaurant. After inquiring about Tang's flight from Hong Kong, he sighs wistfully, "It's ages since I was there." For him and the other Chinese characters, Hong Kong is the home to which they intend to return one day.

The film draws distinctions between members of the diasporic community and the people surrounding them through highlighting differences of race, nationality, and martial arts disciplines. Racially, the Chinese restaurant workers stand in contrast to the Italian boss and his thugs, who are both white and black. In addition, the thugs tower over the diminutive Chinese. The national distinction becomes clear when Uncle Wang cautions, "Thugs are safest at home. This is their home. Where we are now, we're all foreigners. All around us is their territory." Finally, the restaurant workers practice the Asian martial arts of karate and kung fu, in contrast to the thugs, who fight as Western boxers.

The first big fight scene begins with an Italian tough guy assuming a three-quarter boxing stance, with left foot forward and left fist high. When a waiter comes at him with a karate approach, the thug knocks him out with a single overhand right. The thugs sneer, "Chinese boxing!" a clear indication that they do not understand the distinction between karate and kung fu, but more important, it establishes a firm hierarchy of West over East. Tang cannot let this stand, so he uses kung fu–style high kicks to knock out the first boxer and then defeats another thug who bobs and weaves in classic boxing style.

In *Fist of Fury*, the triumph of kung fu over karate symbolized the recuperation of Chinese national pride, but *Way of the Dragon* proceeds in a much more complex way, setting up dichotomies only to subvert them. Rather than making simplistic statements of Chinese superiority over Japanese, or Asian superiority over the West, it argues for the power of hybridity and cultural crossings and ultimately demonstrates the untenable nature of binaries.

The first potential dichotomy differentiates between Chinese kung fu and Japanese karate. When Tang first arrives at the restaurant, he observes the waiters practicing karate, which they plan to use to defend themselves against the thugs who are scaring customers away. They scorn "Chinese boxing" (as the movie labels kung fu) as lacking power. Conversely, the cook, who is the only kung fu aficionado, dismisses karate as foreign and therefore uninteresting. After the first fight in which Tang uses kung fu to demolish the Italian boxers, the waiters abandon karate and beg him to teach them the Chinese art. This might be seen as the triumph of kung fu over karate, but Tang insists otherwise. In response to the cook's labeling of karate as "foreign," Tang says, "Foreign or not, if it helps you to look after yourself when you're in a fight, then you should learn to use it. It doesn't matter at all where it comes from." This is not the kung fu versus karate nationalist dichotomy of *Fist of Fury* but, rather, the hybridity that incorporated nunchaku into Lee's choreography in that same film.

The second possible dichotomy could be drawn between the Asians as good guys versus Westerners as villains. At first, the film appears to follow this formula, as the Chinese restaurant workers appear to be innocent victims of the Italian mob boss and his white and black hoods. However, the neat categorization of Asian as good and European as evil falls apart quickly, as shown by two characters. First, a Chinese man named Mr. Ho serves as the boss's right-hand man and interpreter. Ho is portrayed as an effeminate man who dresses flamboyantly, prances, minces, giggles flirtatiously, and coyly admires Tang's musculature. The most problematic aspect of this representation is that it equates his implied homosexuality with his duplicity and betrayal of his co-ethnics.[12] Second, at the climax of the film, Uncle Wang literally stabs two waiters in the back and reveals that he has been conspiring to sell the restaurant all along so that he can return home to his wife and children in Hong Kong. The treachery of Ho and Uncle Wang completely destabilizes the dichotomy of Chinese as good and Westerners as evil.

The third and final dichotomy that fails to hold up equates Asians with kung fu and karate and Europeans and Americans with boxing. Although the film begins by making this distinction clear, as discussed above, its conclusion muddies things considerably. After Tang defeats all of the local thugs in Rome, the boss imports three highly skilled martial artists to take care of him. The first is played by hapkido expert Whang Ing Sik, who inexplicably is portrayed as a karateka. The second, also a karate master, is played by Robert Wall, a white American billed as "World Professional Karate Champion 1970" in the credits. Whang and Wall are each determined to be the one to take on Tang Lung and are sparring against each other for the honor of fighting the man Ho calls "that Chinaman" when the boss returns with the third, and most fearsome, martial artist. Colt, played by the conspicuously white Chuck Norris, has flown in from the United States for the purpose of fighting Tang. When the boss grants him the honor, Whang slaps himself on the chest and demands, "Who can do karate better than Japanese?" The unstated comedy is that the Korean Whang is neither a karateka nor Japanese. Norris and Whang fight each other, with the American besting the supposed Japanese at karate. In the final analysis, the best karate master is not Asian at all, but a white American. The film thus refuses crude equations of race and martial artistry and reveals easy dichotomies to be unsustainable.

The climactic fight between Tang Lung and Colt in the Colosseum is arguably the most iconic scene in the history of martial arts films. It would be easy to see the clash of the Chinese Tang versus the American Colt, set in the two millennia-old masterpiece of Roman architecture in the cradle of Western civilization, as emblematizing East versus West in a battle of modern-day gladiators. This interpretation is bolstered by the fact that "Tang" can be a synonym for Chinese. Indeed, the huge success of *Way of the Dragon* among Chinese audiences in Hong Kong and throughout Asia owed in no small part to an interpretation of the film as a restoration of ethnic pride, a statement that China could stand up against any nation on earth. However, just as with *Fist of Fury*, an alternative reading reveals complexity rather than simplicity and hybridity rather than purity.

The film establishes a stark visual distinction between Tang and Colt, who prepare for combat by stripping to their waists and limbering up. Colt unveils his muscular upper body, thick rounded shoulders and biceps, and hair, lots of hair—on his shoulders, chest, stomach, arms, and back. In contrast, Tang reveals a smooth torso, not a hair in sight, and the famed Bruce Lee physique—lean and extraordinarily defined. Colt appears powerful, whereas Tang makes Michelangelo's statue of David look fat and out of shape. Once they begin sparring, Colt's physical advantage becomes clear. His superior size enables him to strike Tang before Tang can get within reach.

After being knocked down twice, Tang realizes the futility of his approach and makes a quick adaptation that signals his rejection of purity in favor of hybridity. When Tang rises, instead of assuming a kung fu stance, he begins to dance like a boxer. Colt throws a series of kicks and punches, but Tang bobs and weaves away. Bruce Lee was known to admire the boxer Muhammad Ali and avidly studied his movements on film. In this scene, his movements resemble the "float like a butterfly" strategy of The Greatest.[13]

As a further example of how cultures flow in unpredictable and intriguing ways, Amy Ongiri notes the immense popularity of kung fu movies in African American communities in the 1970s, due in no small part to their portrayal of "the body as a raw tool for the articulation of violent retribution against societal inequities and personal wrongs."[14] This phenomenon illustrates an extended circuit: Bruce Lee incorporated the movements of a black boxer to fight against the white Norris (who has, incidentally, absorbed the Japanese style of karate), and in turn, black audiences in the U.S. embraced kung fu cinema. The influence of Asian martial performances lasted far beyond the 1970s, extending, for example, to the hip-hop group Wu-Tang Clan.

Tang Lung's stylistic change to boxing marks the turning point of the battle in the Colosseum. From then on, Tang bobs and weaves, using speed to elude Colt's strikes and get inside the bigger man's reach. Tang destroys Colt's knees, leaving him immobile, but the valiant American refuses to give up and insists on fighting to the death like the gladiators of old. After Tang breaks Colt's neck, he gently lays down the body of the karate champion and sorrowfully covers him with his gi. This gesture signals Tang's respect for his opponent, whom he recognizes as a master of his own discipline. The combination of Tang's adaptation of boxing methods, last seen in the film used by the hapless thugs, and show of esteem for the karateka reveals Lee's ideology of synthesis and intermixture.

In the Hong Kong film over which he exercised near-total artistic control, Bruce Lee set up dichotomies of China versus Japan and East versus West only to subvert them in favor of combining martial arts forms and muddying distinctions between good and evil. Rather than valorizing the return to the homeland by diasporic sojourners—after all, Uncle Wang's perfidy is motivated by a desire to return home—*Way of the Dragon* highlights transnational migrations that may or may not return to the center. At the end of the film, Tang simply walks away. The cook muses to Chen, "In this world of guns and knives, wherever Tang Lung goes, he will always travel on his own." This open-ended finale stands in contrast to the fixed conclusions of *The Big Boss* and *Fist of Fury*, in which Lee's characters end up arrested or dead. As the credits roll, Tang strolls away, the camera showing only his back. Viewers don't know what will become of Tang, only that he will continue to "travel."

NOTES

1 Penny M. Von Eschen, "Globalizing Popular Culture in the 'American Century' and Beyond," *OAH Magazine of History*, July 2006, 56–63.

2 In this chapter, my references to Lee's "Hong Kong films" are aimed specifically at the three he made with Golden Harvest Studios after returning to Hong Kong as an adult, rather than the ones he acted in during his childhood.

3 Bruce Thomas, *Bruce Lee: Fighting Spirit* (Berkeley, CA: Blue Snake Books, 1994), 304.

4 Brian Kennedy and Elizabeth Guo, *Jingwu: The School That Transformed Kung Fu* (Berkeley, CA: Blue Snake Books, 2010).

5 Stephen Teo, *Hong Kong Cinema: The Extra Dimensions* (London: British Film Institute, 1997), 110–111.

6 Maxwell Pollard, "In Kato's Gung Fu Impact Is Instant," *Black Belt Magazine*, November 1967, 14–20.

7 Bruce Lee, *The Tao of Jeet Kune Do* (Burbank, CA: Ohara Publications, 1975), 12.

8 Information on Dan Inosanto is drawn from Perry William Kelly, *Dan Inosanto: The Man, the Teacher, the Artist* (Boulder, CO: Paladin Press, 2000).

9 Stephen Teo, *Chinese Martial Arts Cinema: The* Wuxia *Tradition* (Edinburgh: Edinburgh University Press, 2006), 78; John Little, *Words of the Dragon: Interviews, 1958–1973* (Boston: Charles Tuttle & Co., 1997), 19.

10 H. S. Chow, "Bruce's Fist Smashes $3.5M Mark," *China Mail*, April 5, 1972.

11 *China Mail*, January 25, 1973.

12 Interestingly, Wei Ping-Ao, the actor who plays Ho, is reprising his role as the traitorous translator in *Fist of Fury*.

13 Thomas, *Bruce Lee*, 96–97.

14 Amy Abugo Ongiri, "Bruce Lee in the Ghetto Connection: Kung Fu Theater and African Americans Reinventing Culture at the Margins," in *East Main Street: Asian American Popular Culture*, ed. Shilpa Davé, Leilani Nishime, and Tasha G. Oren (New York: NYU Press, 2005), 255–256.

2

"I'm Thankful for Manny"

Manny Pacquiao, Pugilistic Nationalism, and the Filipina/o Body

CONSTANCIO ARNALDO

The Filipino "Savior of Boxing": Manny "Pacman" Pacquiao

Manny "Pac-Man" Pacquiao is an eight-time world boxing champion from the Philippines and the twenty-first-century embodiment of the Philippine nation. Considered the "national fist"[1] of the Philippines and the "savior of boxing,"[2] Pacquiao has become the national hero for the "Filipino ringside community"[3] and a global celebrity for boxing fans. Pacquiao's image is highlighted by his undeniable success in the boxing ring and a carefully crafted media persona[4] that literally and digitally traverses national boundaries. He has graced the cover of *Time Magazine Asia* and in 2009 was named as one of *Time Magazine*'s "100 Most Influential People." Pacquiao's popularity has led to endorsements by Nike sportswear, Hewlett-Packard, Hennessey, Monster Energy, Wonderful Pistachio, and San Miguel Beer. Pacquiao's athletic success extends beyond the boxing ring: He is also a congressman for the Sarangani Province on the island of Mindanao and is lauded for his humanitarian efforts for the Philippine people.

While Pacquiao's performances as a global sporting icon permeate the mass-mediated global landscape, his iconicity manifests in local Filipina/o American cultural practices. In the first part of this chapter, I examine how Filipina/o Americans engage in diasporic practices through what I term "Pacquiao fight night spaces." These spaces allow Filipina/os to express a certain kind of belonging with the larger landscape of American social life imbued with Filipina/o *and* American experiences.

I then move beyond local renditions of Philippine national and ethnic fandom and investigates how Pacquiao's global reach extends beyond Filipinas/os. In doing so, I suggest that Pacquiao facilitates a particular kind of masculinity that is rooted in notions of assimilability, respectability, and religion that attempt to "racially displace"[5] Pacquiao as a post-racial hero. But beyond the mainstream constructions of his assimilable masculinity are interpretations that defy these dominant narratives. For one of my informants, Pacquiao has become a vehicle for speaking to alternative conceptions of Filipino masculinity. I analyze how Pacquiao's manhood is defined by, and negotiates with, race and gender through African American culture, machismo, and pre- and post-colonial renditions of religious masculinity that fall outside of the Catholic religion. In this way, I argue that, while there are possibilities in reimagining Pacquiao's masculinity, it inevitably falls short of its liberatory potential.

For some Filipina/o Americans, sports spectating is transformed into a desire for Pacquiao's Filipino body. This, in turn, creates co-ethnic bonds while also fostering and negotiating a diasporic collectivity. One of the ways this is carried out is through Pacquiao fight night spaces.[6] These fight night spaces primarily consist of Filipina/o and Filipina/o American families and friends who collectively cheer for Pacquiao by transforming their living rooms into localized versions of national and ethnic fandom. Indeed, this viewing practice was a popular activity among the majority of my informants. And while my informants were, for the most part, located in Southern California, large pockets of Filipinos in the Bay Area of California also partook in this popular national and ethnic pastime. I also witnessed this firsthand in Champaign, Illinois, where a Filipino family invited me to watch Pacquiao's fight against the New York fighter Chris Algieri. These fight gatherings are ritualized[7] hybrid spaces where Filipina/o Americans merge sporting practice with familiar notions of performing what it means to be Filipina/o *and* American. In other words, these spaces mark one's sense of *Filipinoness* in the United States—sustained by family formations in which social interactions among different family members take place and among the cultural artifacts that allow them to express their Filipina/o American identities. Throughout my fieldwork, informants shared how they would often start planning for Pacquiao's fights by inviting family members across a generational spectrum. During one fight night space I was invited to, I was introduced to aunts, uncles, cousins, grandparents, and grandchildren, all of whom were avid Pacquiao fans.

Thus, while space, Pacquiao's body, and families facilitate diasporic ties that enable Filipinas/os to come together, these spaces are also imbued with cultural repertoires, including language and food, that allow them to negotiate a distinct Filipina/o American place-making experience. Sounds of regional Filipino dialects are spoken, including Tagalog, Ilocano, Visayan, and a mix of Taglish.[8] For example, during Pacquiao's first fight against Timothy Bradley, I overheard Tagalog and Visayan spoken as the family provided commentary on the fight. At the end of the fight, it was announced that Bradley had defeated Pacquiao. This came as a surprise because throughout the fight, it was clear to us that Pacquiao handily defeated Bradley. One of the aunts spoke out loud, "Anong yang yare?" [What happened?] One of the nephews chimed in, "I didn't think it was a split decision. Terrible, bogus decision." Finally, taste and smells of certain Filipino food from various regions of the Philippines help to play a part in "facilitating a sense of shared collective identity."[9] In this space, these foods included a "fusion" dish one of the nephews called "Bicol pork sliders"; Tahong, a soup dish; and

Pinakbet, a vegetable-based dish with shrimp or other seafood that is cooked with shrimp paste. Yet there were also other foods including chips and green salsa and guacamole.

There is a recurring theme as to why Filipina/o respondents cheer for Pacquiao: "Because he's Filipino," declared one respondent, puzzled as to why I would ask such a banal question. Pacquiao's national origins and representativeness is understood to offer viewers unique versions and interpretations of being Filipino into their own lives. For them, seeing Pacquiao on television or watching videos of him on the Internet bring them closer to "home," even if it is an imagined home.[10] Therefore, these fight night spaces become moments of diasporic intimacy among hundreds, if not thousands, of Filipinos, and Pacquiao's ethnic and national body, behaviors, and culturally informed rituals breathe an air of familiarity to Filipina/o Americans, produced by an assemblage of media images that materialize on movie screens, televisions, and computers. Such images allow them to collapse distance, space, and time. Pacquiao, as the embodiment of the Philippines, is brought into the living rooms of diasporic Filipinas/os without their having to travel to the homeland. Thus, through the constant repertoire of media imagery, Filipinas/os interpret Pacquiao and creatively place a constellation of meanings that is reworked through their own practices of ascription and aspiration. In these meaning-making practices, Filipinas/os express a certain kind of belonging within the larger landscape of American social life. A recurring sense of feeling invisible to the mainstream permeates the discourses about why my respondents hold Pacquiao in such high esteem. Marie, a college-student and second-generation Filipina American, shared how when she went to Las Vegas, she saw a Nike-sponsored Pacquiao paraphernalia at a Foot Locker store. She was taken aback by its overt national symbolism. She recalls, "Non-Filipinos are seeing this and just the fact that it's catching their eye, like, "What is this?" To what country does that belong, those colors belong to? It's really increasing the awareness of Filipinos everywhere." Indeed, Filipinas/os are everywhere. But the global pervasiveness of Filipinas/os must be situated a laboring context, in the post-colonial moment in which the Philippine government and vestiges of empire continue to shape Filipina/o immigrant lives.[11] Filipinas/os, in other words, are a global labor force.

Witnessing Pacquiao's success enables them to embody and share in his own victories. Iris, a second-generation Filipina American college student, recalls that after Pacquiao wins a fight, she'll say, "Yeah we won the fight, 'Go Filipinos!' Or afterwards, I remember me and my cousins were talking, I remember our freshman and sophomore year we just felt like we were so cool, 'Nobody is going to mess with us now because they think we can fight.' [Laughs.] That kind of attitude." Rather than embodying a failed national masculinity, Iris sees Pacquiao, a winning fighter, as the embodiment of the Philippine nation.

Marketing Pacquiao's Assimilable Masculinity

Pacquiao's global appeal has facilitated an interest beyond the Filipina/o diasporic community. Indeed, throughout my fieldwork, non-Filipinos including black, white, Latina/o, and other Asian American communities shared
their deep admiration for the Filipino pugilist. How might we make sense of
this admiration? How do these communities consume his masculinity? Upon
closer examination, it is through a particular kind of masculinity that facilitates
this admiration. In other words, dominant mainstream media representations
produce Pacquiao's masculinity as an assimilable one. He is often celebrated for
being religious, humble, selfless, soft-spoken, a family man, and a good person,
while also performing in a sport that requires masculine attributes and behaviors such as toughness, aggression, and overt physicality. But these ideas of Pacquiao's assimilable masculinity are inextricably tied to immigrant narratives and
corporate logics. It follows that Pacquiao's success and viable commercialism
are evidence that as long as poor or marginalized groups dedicate and commit
themselves to work hard, they, too, can earn their way out of their low socioeconomic position. As the humanities scholar Kathleen Woodward posits, "The
rags-to-riches, ghetto-to-the-mainstream stories are part of boxing's imaginary,
and underpin identifications that are made with heroic public figures."[12] This
boxing imaginary parallels with Pacquiao's life story and is reproduced in the
media. However, such narratives absolve the structural and institutional barriers that have shaped marginalized groups' experiences and ignore how sporting
media conglomerates capitalize on these storylines.[13]

Additionally, while Pacquiao performs the hypermasculine practices expected
of a boxer, he is also considered respectable because he exhibits high moral values vis-à-vis his religious devotion to God and his sportsmanship in the ring.
Part of the narrative of heroic boxers involve what Woodward calls "moral trajectories,"[14] whereby the theater of prizefighting pits boxers against each other
as good versus evil. For example, in the buildup to his fight against the Mexican
fighter Antonio "El Tijuana" Margarito, Pacquiao was seen as the morally conscious boxer ("good") whereas Margarito was seen as the cheater ("evil"). This
happened in part because of Margarito's "moral" transgressions a year before
he fought Pacquiao. On January 24, 2009, Margarito was set to face off against
"Sugar" Shane Mosley. Before the fight, Margarito was caught wearing illegal
handwraps. Handwraps are a combination of gauze and adhesive tape wrapped
in between a boxer's fingers. They are the initial layer placed before putting on
boxing gloves. Applying liquid to the handwraps is prohibited because it hardens
them. Margarito's handwraps contained a hardened, plaster-like substance that
would have inflicted further damage to Mosley during the fight. After discovering this, officials from the California State Athletic Commission confiscated the

handwraps and ordered Margarito's trainer to re-wrap his hands. While Margarito was still allowed to fight Mosley—in a fight that he lost—he was subsequently suspended from boxing for a year because of the illegal handwraps.[15] Given this controversy, the stage was set for the narratives to unfold when Top Rank—Pacquiao and Margarito's promotion company—announced that both fighters had agreed to fight. Indeed, prior to the bout, narratives featuring both boxers emphasized Pacquiao's morality (religion, humanitarianism) and Margarito's illegal handwraps; these narratives were a point of emphasis in the weeks leading up to the fight.

Moral trajectories were also performed during the Pacquiao/Margarito bout. Throughout the fight, Pacquiao's speed was too much for his Mexican counterpart. Margarito could not handle Pacquiao's dizzying array of punches. In fact, Pacquiao was handily defeating Margarito and was moving in and out of reach of his heavier and taller opponent. As the fight wore on, Pacquiao constantly threw punches, repeatedly landing them on Margarito's right eye. It got the point where his eye socket swelled so badly that he could not see out of it. Instead of battering his opponent and targeting Margarito's eye, Pacquiao pulled his punches so as not to cause further, possibly permanent damage.[16] During the post-fight press conference, a media member asked Pacquiao about pulling his punches. Pacquiao explained, "I did not want to damage him permanently. That's not what boxing is about."[17] In this way, Pacquiao's performance in the ring, coupled with his response to the reporter, demonstrates a masculinity grounded in an ethics of care,[18] a kind, respectable, and thus acceptable masculinity grounded in morality, fair play, and sportsmanship.[19]

These performances in the ring notwithstanding, we must also situate Pacquiao's assimilable masculinity in relation to the black and white bodies where his assimilable masculinity is made legible. Pacquiao's poor and working-class background are neatly framed in relation to notions of respectability that often square with "respectable" white, working-class fighters. For example, Kelly "The Ghost" Pavlik and Ricky "Hitman" Hatton, who hail from the working classes of the United States and Great Britain, respectively, are considered "heroes" to their communities and nation.[20] According to James Rhodes, "'Respectability' connotes a form of 'moral authority,' representing a means through which groups and individuals distinguish themselves from "other" social and symbolic positions—not only between but also within groupings."[21] Pacquiao's status as a family man is often highlighted as evidence of such moral authority. The blogger Will Osgood suggests that,

> probably most importantly, he is a loyal family man. He and his wife, Maria Geraldine "Jinkee" Jamora, have four young children—two boys and two girls. He is the epitome of responsibility, after being raised in an environment that didn't exactly

support such a thing. Responsibility being the key word. At 33 years of age, he recognizes his responsibility to make the most of his life and live with a purpose. He uses boxing to help other people and not just to glorify himself.[22]

Here, middle-class family values merge with conventional notions of manhood as breadwinner and provider. Despite Pacquiao's working-class roots, he embodies what Osgood values: a benevolent masculinity[23] that is not only grounded in family responsibility but also engages in philanthropic practices. While Osgood celebrates Pacquiao's supposed "fidelity," one of my informants critiqued Pacquiao's infidelity. At one point, rumors circulated in the Philippines about Pacquiao cheating on Jinkee Jocelyn. A second-generation Filipina American followed these narratives and shared how she "[felt] bad for Jinkee and as a 'national hero' who says he has a responsibility towards fans, I think it's weird for him to be displaying his manhood by having *queridas* (mistresses) all over the place. It really shows how Filipino virility and masculinity is manifested by how many mistresses you have. It's condoned and practically encouraged."

At the same time, these narratives also work in relation to African American masculinity that consequently creates distance between racial groups. These examples are part of a "model minority" discourse that positions Asian Americans as the preferred minority in relation to African Americans and Latinas/os. While Pacquiao is not Asian American, he nonetheless embodies the model minority through "close-knit [normative] family and its values."[24] For example, in a veiled commentary on African American athletes, Daine Pavloski, a featured columnist writing about Pacquiao, opines that, "whether it's someone changing their name to something ludicrous, a whiny wide receiver doing sit-ups in his driveway, or another player getting into an altercation at a nightclub, professional athletes spend more time looking like idiots than anything else. Thankfully for the sports world—and the sanity of sports fans—there are guys like Manny Pacquiao."[25] In other words, Pacquiao is respectable because he is not what other professional athletes—specifically African American ones—are: petulant, self-absorbed, and inherently violent. This in turn adds to Pacquiao's popularity among the mainstream media because he is not *one of them*. Importantly, these two examples also highlight how white male sports writers construct these narratives.[26]

One of the key features to marketing Pacquiao is not only through his success as a world-class boxer but also through a marketing campaign that emphasizes his Catholic religion. Nike capitalizes on this by featuring advertisements that position Pacquiao's body through tropes of sacrifice, selflessness, and humility. These tropes appeal a global audience. Such religious symbolism invites consumers to identify with its overtly Christian meanings. This is particularly significant when placed within the context of the sociopolitical climate of the "war on terror" in which Arab, Muslim, and Sikh communities have been subjected to increased state surveillance in the aftermath of 9/11.[27] As a "safer" and less "threatening" masculinity, Pacquiao's Catholicism is celebrated to create a "particular definition of nation and of 'other'" to "legitimate certain national subjects over others, offer support for a state-led 'war on terror' and (re)affirm the (neo) imperial trajectories of the neo-liberal market."[28]

Images of Pacquiao as a devout Catholic practitioner show him consistently performing the familiar Catholic gesture of the sign of the cross and, without fail, articulating a sense of gratitude to God. Some of my respondents have placed him in deified realms: "Religious," "spiritual," and "humble" were adjectives consistently used to describe Pacquiao. And biblical references to David beating Goliath are woven into an unfolding narrative of Pacquiao defeating opponents who are bigger and stronger than he. Two second-generation Filipina Americans went so far as to say, "I'm thankful for Manny," referencing the Catholic tradition of "Thanks be to God" during Catholic mass. In fact, Nike, Pacquiao's sporting apparel sponsor, created a website that draws upon imagery equating his body to Jesus Christ, bringing Pacquiao's body into full-deified view.[29] In the ad, Pacquiao is kneeling down in the corner of a boxing ring, his head bowed with his back turned to the gaze of the viewer. His arms are spread out as if to emulate bearing the cross. He is in full boxing gear with his gloves, shorts, and boxing shoes. The ad appears with red lettering that reads "Give us this day," followed by the date in white lettering, "12–06–08," the date Pacquiao was scheduled to fight the then-perennial title contender, Mexican American Oscar De La Hoya, "The Golden Boy." In addition to these religious motifs ascribed to Pacquiao's masculinity, there are also U.S. popular cultural forms, particularly hip-hop culture, that inflect and shape Pacquiao's masculinity as a tough masculinity.

Over the last several years, Pacquiao's global exposure has exponentially increased as emerging flows of global technology—social media websites such as Facebook and Twitter and the easy availability of search engines—have accelerated new forms of mobility across the global landscape. These flows create new opportunities for the consumption and production of cultural forms and practices and consequently encourage and spur nationalist claims made by Filipina/o Americans. This, in turn, shapes the kinds of mediated interpretations and responses Filipina/o Americans have when making sense of Pacquiao's image.

Pacquiao's contemporary reach follows a historical arc that began in the late nineteenth and early twentieth centuries, which was set in motion by the onset of U.S. colonial rule. When the United States colonized the Philippines in 1898, part of the colonizing process involved the implementation of American-style government, education, and sport. Following a dogmatic belief in "manifest destiny" and ideologies of racial superiority over Filipinos,[30] U.S. colonial administrators worked with the Young Men's Christian Association

(YMCA) by institutionalizing sport. This collaboration was driven by the idea that sport would "civilize" the racially "inferior" Filipinos. Under the aegis of the U.S. education system (primarily through the category of "physical education"), sport and recreation was part and parcel of the U.S. educational colonial process. Through outdoor activities and the promotion of physicality embodied by white, muscular Christian men, it was believed that sport could transform the "effeminate," "inferior," and "savage" Filipino bodies into "good colonial subjects."[31] Such ideas about Filipino racial inferiority and white racial superiority were challenged in the early twentieth century by Filipinos who achieved success as pugilists in places like Australia and the United States.[32] In this way, Filipino boxers and spectators engaged with the processes of masculinity learned in the Philippines and the United States by transforming the boxing space to affirm their manliness in organized boxing events.[33] Linda España-Maram's groundbreaking study on working class Filipinos in Los Angeles's Little Manila from the 1920s through the 1940s, for example, demonstrates how Filipino working-class laborers attached meanings of masculinity to Filipino boxers to create a "cast of heroes" for themselves and their community. As she argues, "Athletes legitimized a space for self-definition by defying the dominant society's assumptions about race and ability."[34] Boxing in the United States has long been seen as a way for working-class youth to advance their socioeconomic status, in part because it rejected Victorian notions of manliness through alternative masculinities.[35] Such alternative masculinities particularly resonated with Filipino working-class laborers who worked in occupations considered "feminized," such as domestic work. Thus boxing served to validate their masculinity "as virile men."[36] More recently, professional boxers like Oscar De La Hoya, Amir Khan, and Barry McGuian have inspired other ethnic communities to claim fighters as one of their own.[37] In this way, ideas of the Filipino body became part of Filipino popular and cultural memory, not only historically but also in the contemporary moment. At the same time, iterations of race and gender emerge through Pacquiao's body, and residual effects of U.S. colonial discourses remain. Like Bruce Lee's body, as analyzed by Mimi Thi Nguyen, Pacquiao's body "is a built body, a carefully constructed instrument. His body is also a historical situation and valued commodity, a technologized collection of words, sounds and images that 'stands for' the person who is the star."[38] Following Nguyen's lead, I see Pacquiao's body as a transnational, digitized rendering of Filipino masculinity, whose physicality runs counter to dominant discourses of the infantilized, weak, effeminate Asian body. Boxing, long considered "the manly art,"[39] has relied on physical attributes in the ring such as strength, power, speed, and quickness. Pacquiao's boxing achievements challenge how these physical attributes are not fit for Asian bodies precisely because Asian male bodies have historically been constructed as antithetical to the premises of a sport that requires aggression, strength, speed, and power.[40]

Appropriating Political Blackness and the Possibility of Transcendence

In many ways, Pacquiao can also be read alongside what Michael Eric Dyson terms "The Pedagogy of Desire."[41] Writing about retired National Basketball Association (NBA) basketball player Michael Jordan, Dyson examines the figure of Jordan as a cultural icon against the historical, social, and cultural backdrop of twentieth-century American life. Dyson posits that Jordan's body works in contradictory ways. His athletic mastery reflects elements of African American cultural imagination. He was a symbol of "personal possibility, creativity, and desire," particularly for African American youth.[42] But Jordan is also a product, whose body is commodified, packaged, valued, and distributed through the culture of consumption. In this way, Jordan's athletic excellence and body work as a signifier that subsumes any critical discussions of race and racism, inevitably offering up "proof" that we live in a post-racial society.[43] Drawing parallels to Michael Jordan, Pacquiao, too, is a product of the cultural and market forces of the day. Like Jordan, Pacquiao is a global icon who enjoys a cult-like following from Filipinas/os and non-Filipinas/os throughout the world. And like Jordan, Pacquiao is configured as a post-racial "white hero," as his racial identity becomes palatable to a white public. In line with Dyson (2004), Andrews (2000), and Farred (2006), I see Pacquiao's commodified body as a symbol of possibility that concurrently works to de-politicize race. While Pacquiao is presented as a "post-racial" hero, the interviewees interpret his body in ways that betray this dominant narrative.

Thug Passion of the Christ

Through appropriating blackness via hip-hop culture, Manila Ryce,[44] a third-generation Filipino American artist and activist, used art as a creative outlet to convey the disruptive, transgressive, and revolutionary character of Pacquiao for Filipina/o American communities. During our interview, Manila Ryce shared that he has been doing art his whole life but that he started taking it more seriously in college. As our interview unfolded, he introduced me to a piece, entitled, *Thug Passion of the Christ* (fig. 2.1), created out of oil and laser on a lightly colored maple wood. The maple wood is shaped to resemble a "Weapons of Moroland" plaque from the island of Mindanao in the Philippines. On the top, middle portion of the shield appears the Philippine sun's rays extending upward and outward. Right below the sun, on the left and right margins, are leaves and stars. In between the leaves and stars are seven hands that meet in the middle; three appear on the left, and three appear on the right, while a "West Side" hand gesture is placed in between. In the middle of the shield features Manny "Pac-Man" Pacquiao's chiseled, naked upper body. He is wearing a bandana on his head with his arms placed behind his back, as if he is shackled. He is also wearing a cross around his neck nestled in between his chest muscles. His pose is similar to that of the late Tupac Shakur, an African American hip-hop artist who was shot in Las Vegas, Nevada, in 1996. Pacquiao has a number of tattoos marking his body, all of which resemble the famous ones tattooed on Shakur's body.[45] The lower left portion of the ribbon reads "*makibaka*" (Tagalog for "struggle") while the lower right side is inscribed with "freedom." Both the Tagalog and English words are written in babayin, a pre-colonial Philippine writing script.

Manila Ryce was inspired to create *Thug Passion* using "a combination of [Pacquiao's] emblems which is a take off the weapons of Moroland." He shares:

> With this image it's more modern-day, weapons of resistance and it's maybe more of what I wish Pacquiao was, rather than what he is because similarly Tupac was a figure like that. Where he was seen as an idol of the people who's larger-than-life, larger than what he actually was. But he was associated with this revolution and consciousness, and with Pacquiao, he's an inspiration, but he's an icon, and it kind of stops with that. He's not really an advocate for any specific direction or liberation, and so with this piece, I want to take the old weapons of Moroland and kind of update it and use a figure who is iconic that can kind of be the spokesperson for that.

Here, Tupac Shakur's political blackness is appropriated and transposed onto Pacquiao's body in order to reconcile the failure of Pacquiao's radical consciousness. The fact that "he's an inspiration, . . . and it kind of stops with that" emphasizes the limitations of Pacquiao's iconicity. This artwork also represents a kind of hypermasculine, Filipino nation inflected by and laden with the politics of blackness, consciousness, and revolution, all of which were cultivated throughout Shakur's life, perhaps a gesture to the Afro-Asia connection as documented by Vijay Prashad.[46]

Manila Ryce creates an image that is linked to popular culture representations of the late Tupac Shakur[47] while deploying Filipina/o inflected cultural cues. The babayin writing script, the Philippine sun, Pacquiao's body, and the "2pacquiao" appearing below are appropriated to make it uniquely Filipina/o. Yet the marking of Pacquiao's body vis-à-vis Tupac Shakur's tattoos, the placing of a bandana on Pacquiao's head, and the familiar pose and the gaze by Pacquiao reflect the same kind of imagery circulated about the slain rapper—an imagery that projects a tough, working-class, hypermasculine aesthetic. Thus, rather than catering to the dominant narrative of Pacquiao as a cultural icon neutralized by multiculturalist discourse and made possible by transnational corporations like Nike, Manila Ryce actively subverts that image by taking cues from Tupac Shakur's iconicity, whose music, style and performance of masculinity create alternative renderings of Pacquiao and the *possibility* of something more than just an icon.

Figure 2.1. *Thug Passion of the Christ*. Credit: Manila Ryce.

Moreover, the *Thug Passion* piece represents Pacquiao as embodying a powerful image of Filipino masculinity in ways that directly challenge the emasculated Asian male stereotype.[48] Manila Ryce's artwork is also paired with other images circulating on the Internet that also represent Pacquiao, and thus the Asian male body, in masculine ways. These images show Pacquiao performing a "most muscular pose," a bodybuilding pose that emphasizes the naked muscularity of the upper, front torso of a person's body. In one such popular image, Pacquiao appears half naked with abdominals flexed, his sinewy muscle fibers accentuating his upper body. Pacquiao's gaze is striking; he is staring at the camera with his head slightly tilted downward.[49] Pacquiao's muscular body from these still images comes to life in an HBO documentary special titled "Mayweather/Pacquiao: At Last."[50] The HBO documentary features Pacquiao and his opponent four weeks before their boxing match, mixing in storylines and videos of each boxer's training routine to capture viewers' interest. Pacquiao is shown working out, highlighting his training regimen—a mix of circuit training, boxing workouts, and sparring sessions. These moving images emphasize Pacquiao's muscular, lean, and dynamic body, focusing on his disciplined workout routines. Indeed, respondents have described Pacquiao's physicality as strong, powerful, and fast. Jenilyn, a second-generation Filipina American, describes Pacquiao as a powerful puncher with a left hook that consistently catches the attention of his opponents:

> [Pacquiao] has a strong left hook or something, not hook but left hand. There's power. Every boxer that they interviewed that fought against him, they always talk about the power of his punch. And Freddie Roach, his coach, seems to have a lot of faith in him. So I could see it, I could see it in some of his fights, his power punches, you see his opponents definitely go down.

Pacquiao's preparation through his vigorous training is culminated in his performance in the ring. And key to Pacquiao's status as a perennial pound-for-pound best fighter is his reputation for moving up in weight classes and defeating bigger and stronger fighters. In fact, Pacquiao is known to invite pain, encouraging his opponent to test his chin by allowing his opponent to hit him. Francisco, a second-generation Filipino American college student, is well aware of these attributes and Pacquiao's role as a showman, and he senses that Pacquiao knows full well that the cameras are following his every move:

> When the camera's on he's being distracted by the press, still being determined [by] what he's doing. Even during the fights he's smiling. I remember he was already high on the points, he's just taunting the guy, "C'mon let's fight, let's put on a good show." I remember one time he snapped his gloves together and smiled, and when [his opponent] hit him he would smile after he would get hit. He's a showman as a boxer, he wants to put on a good fight.

Here, Pacquiao's toughness is animated by his willingness to absorb punches, as if an aura of invincibility seemingly surrounds him in the ring. These observations also signal a larger discourse of reinventing Pacquiao's body as a strong, hard, powerful, courageous, Asian male athletic body. Pacquiao's body therefore represents the possibility of Filipino and Asian American masculinity and physicality by re-masculinizing him in ways that are aggressive and tough and thus challenges the centuries-old stereotypes of the Orientalist Asian male figure as soft, weak, and effeminate. For example, Manila Ryce states:

> I think with Filipina/o Americans, because in America the culture is more heterogeneous and Asian males are emasculated, as seen as emotionless robots who do good on their SATs and that's about it. And it's kind of similar to Jeremy Lin saying right now is that to see an Asian in sports who's actually doing well and doing better than the stereotypical over what people think is supposed to be what constitutes a good basketball player, what constitutes a good boxer, that they're actually breaking these barriers brick by brick, dismantling this idea that Asians are emasculated. I think mostly that's what it is for mostly Asian Americans to have a role model who isn't an accountant or a doctor or somebody like that. It's empowering in that sense.

Manila Ryce emphasizes dominant orientalist stereotypes of Asian bodies as rote and mindless while also pointing out how race and gender intersect to produce and imagine an emasculated Asian male body. He is critical of the pervasive stereotype of Asians as the "model minority," a discourse that frequently praises Asian Americans for their high-achieving success in education, business, science, and competitiveness in the global world.[51] In addition, Manila Ryce cites dominant representations of athletes along the black and white paradigm while simultaneously asserting, and therefore recuperating, failed Asian masculinity through sports.

The constitutive elements of hip-hop and its progressive strands enable Filipina/o Americans to adapt, create, and affirm a positive Filipina/o American identity through Pacquiao's body. But appropriating hip-hop images and aesthetics force us to question how it might fall short of its liberating potential. Issues of homophobia, gender tensions, and outright misogyny within hip-hop culture are enduring issues that must be critically assessed because[52] its aesthetics, while no doubt rooted in resistance strands,[53] are also complicit in its own set of gender and sexual hierarchies and exclusions.

To conclude, Manny "Pac-man" Pacquiao's global presence and transnational reach transcend his boxing exploits, especially for members of the Filipina/o diaspora. Indeed, the rituals, familiar sights, smells, and sounds of *Filipinoness* create diasporic bonds that are part and parcel of Pacquiao fight nights. His racialized masculinity—as a powerful, strong dynamic—and athletic body challenge historical and contemporary stereotypes of "race and ability,"[54] particularly as he works in relation to Asian, African American and white male athletic bodies. The recruitment of popular cultural forms like hip-hop further provide alternative imaginings and political possibilities that extend beyond the realm of Pacquiao's sanitized, corporate image. But his body also produces complicated meanings of identity, diasporic intimacy, national belonging, and the possibilities *and* contradictions that are mapped onto it. At the same time, such alternative possibilities also reinscribe social hierarchies that continue to affect certain members of the Filipina/o community.

Post-Script: The Fight of the Century

On May 2, 2015, in Las Vegas, Floyd "Money" Mayweather and Manny "Pac-Man" Pacquiao finally took center stage in what was billed as the "Fight of the Century." Indeed, Mayweather and Pacquiao are two of the most popular fighters in prizefighting. The fight was supposed to have happened six years ago, when both boxers were at the peak of their careers. Throughout my interviews and during my field observations, Mayweather's presence loomed large. His name would often come up during interviews without me prompting it, and I recall his name being brought up in informal conversations in public places. Sport media, fans, and boxing pundits clamored for the two "pound-for-pound" fighters to square off. Finally, after weeks of back-and-forth between the boxers' management teams and a fortuitous encounter during an NBA game in Miami where Mayweather and Pacquiao were both in attendance, the two boxers met in person to reiterate their desire to fight.[55] As soon as ESPN announced the fight, I booked my flight to conduct more fieldwork. Social media platforms like Twitter erupted with a #MayweatherPacquiao[56] hashtag campaign, and fight fans posted their thoughts about the upcoming bout. The global community of fans finally had a chance to witness this highly anticipated boxing match, even if both fighters were past their prime. Ticket prices for the fight averaged $1,500, yet only five hundred tickets were made available to the general public.[57] Actors, music moguls, and former and current athletes sat courtside to catch the fight, including among others, Mark Wahlberg, Robert De Niro, Denzel Washington, P. Diddy Combs, Nicki Minaj, Beyoncé, Jay Z, Mike Tyson, and Michael Strahan.[58] The *Washington Post* published a poll asking the public, "Who will win?" Out of the 6,763 responses, 34 percent of them believed that Pacquiao would win by knockout, and 26 percent voted that he would win by a judges' decision. Twenty-three percent believed Mayweather would win via a judges' decision, while only 12 percent believed he would win by knockout. Four percent believed the bout would result in a draw.[59] Global public interest reflected the demand that Mayweather and Pacquiao wielded. In fact, according to Dan Rafael of ESPN, the Nevada State Athletic Commission announced that "Mayweather-Pacquiao generated $72,198,500 from the sale of 16,219 tickets at the MGM Grand Garden Arena."[60] It was clear that, to watch the fight live, it meant you were well connected, well known, and wealthy. The mega event was rumored to generate close to $1 billion for the Las Vegas economy.[61] Whereas the fight night spaces generated a diasporic intimacy in the privacy of Filipina/o homes, Pacquiao's global persona enabled hundreds, if not thousands, of Filipinos from the diaspora to flock to Las Vegas to see this once-in-a-lifetime event. One wonders just how many could actually afford to watch the fight live. One Filipina American hotel vendor in her mid-forties was critical of how the MGM was preventing people like her from buying tickets. "You will see all of the royalty and the rich people at the fight. They are the ones who can afford to buy the tickets." There is something complex and contradictory about her sentiments. Watching this fight live—and, thus, engaging in a diasporic practice—comes at a cost. Here the bonds that facilitate Filipina/o American connections in fight night spaces (like the ones I discussed at the beginning of this chapter) are severed. She was prevented from participating in this practice.

Despite the buildup of the "Fight of the Century" and Pacquiao promising that he would take the fight to Mayweather, the match was a dud. Neither fighter provided much action, and Mayweather, known for his defensive prowess and unparalleled boxing technique, kept Pacquiao at bay by economically throwing jabs and landing cleaner and more decisive punches. In the end, Mayweather defeated Pacquiao by unanimous decision, leaving fans disappointed.[62] The mega event felt more like what anthropologist Anna Tsing terms an "economy of appearances" for Las Vegas: a way in which the convergence of (athletic) performance, drama, and the spectacularity of brown and black pugilists harmoniously worked in order to generate free-flowing capital in the local and global arena meant only for a select few.[63]

NOTES

1 See Poole (2010).
2 See Chua-Eoan and Tharor (2009).
3 Costello (2009).
4 Andrews (2000); Whannel (2002); and Carrington (2010).
5 Andrews (2000). South Asian American basketball communities engage in this practice as well. See Thangaraj (2015).
6 Guerra (2015).
7 Turner (1967).
8 Bonus (2000).
9 Thangaraj (2015), 83.
10 Anderson (1991).
11 Okamura (1998); Rodriguez (2010); and Fajardo (2011).
12 Woodward (2007), 118.
13 For an extended analysis of transnational media sport, see Joo (2012).
14 Joo (2012), 101.
15 Rafael (2012).
16 Floyd (2010).
17 Rafael (2010a).
18 See Shimizu (2012).
19 James (1984).
20 Rhodes (2011).
21 Rhodes (2011), 360.
22 Osgood (2012).
23 Thangaraj (2015).
24 Joo (2012).
25 Pavloski (2012).
26 See Trujillo (2000).
27 Silk (2012).
28 Silk (2012), 4.
29 *NikeTalk* (2008).
30 Kramer (2006).
31 Such concerns about moral fiber not only applied to colonized Filipino bodies in the Philippines but also applied to other non-white peoples in the Pacific. These concerns about colonial subjects, termed "hemispheric anxiety" by Micronesian studies scholar Vicente Diaz, circulated in and through the United States's new colonial possessions. See Diaz (2002).
32 Filipinos recognized that their own experiences of racial oppression were also part of a larger global phenomenon; boxing in particular inspired Filipinos to embed these racial griev- ances through the sporting body of Jack Johnson, the first African American heavyweight champion. In Reno, Nevada, on July 4, 1910, Johnson fought white American Jim Jeffries in the "Fight of the Century." See Runstedtler (2012).
33 España-Maram (2006); Runstedtler (2012).
34 España-Maram (2006), 92.

35 Riess (2007).

36 España-Maram (2006), 94.

37 Rodriguez (2002); Delgado (2005); and Burdsey (2007).

38 Ongiri (2005); Nguyen (2007).

39 Gorn (1986).

40 Burdsey (2007) 288.

41 Dyson (1993).

42 Dyson (1993).

43 See Andrews (2000); and Farred (2006).

44 Manila Ryce is my informant's artist name.

45 On Pacquiao's left chest muscle, the phrase "2PAC" is inscribed, with a side profile of Queen Nefertete, an Egyptian Queen, appearing with the phrase "2.DIE.4" below it. On Pacquiao's sternum, the number "50" sits on top of an AK-47 assault rifle. Tattooed in his lower abdominal area are the words, "THUG LIFE." He appears to be wearing shorts or sweats. Underneath his torso appears a star with the phrase, "2pacquiao" appearing below it. Framing Pacquiao's upper body are four downward-facing guns on each side. A ribbon lines the lower portion of the shield.

46 Prashad (2001).

47 See Powell (1996).

48 Eng (2001).

49 Boxing Scene (2011).

50 HBO Sports (2015).

51 See Bascara (2006).

52 Rose (2008); Hill and Ramsaran (2009).

53 Kelley (1996).

54 España-Maram (2006), 92.

55 Rafael (2015).

56 See Twitter hashtag #MayweatherPacquiao at https://twitter.com/search?q=%23Mayweather Pacquiao&src=typd (accessed June 3, 2015).

57 Sanneh (2015).

58 Remling (2015).

59 Washington Post (2015).

60 Rafael (2015b).

61 This was based on numerous informal conversations I had with a number of vendors who were selling fight gear.

62 Rafael (2015a).

63 Tsing (2005), 57.

REFERENCES

ABS-CBN News. 2009. "Pacquiao on TIME Magazine Cover." November 6. http://www.abs-cbn news.com/sports/11/06/09/pacquiao-time-magazine-cover, accessed April 2, 2010.

Anderson, Benedict. 1991. Imagined Communities: Reflections on the Origin and Spread of Nationalism. London: Verso.

Andrews, David. 2000. "Excavating Michael Jordan's Blackness." In Reading Sport: Critical Essays on Power and Representation, ed. Susan Birrell and Mary G. McDonald. Boston: Northeastern University Press.

Bonus, Rick. 2000. Locating Filipino Americans: Ethnicity and the Cultural Politics of Space. Asian American History and Culture. Philadelphia: Temple University Press.

Boxing Scene. 2011. "Photos: Manny Pacquiao Ripped, Training in Beast Mode." October 26. http://www.boxingscene.com/photos-manny-pacquiao-ripped-training-beast-mode--45376, accessed November 27, 2011.

Burdsey, Daniel. 2007. "Role with the Punches: The Construction and Representation of Amir Khan as a Role Model for Multiethnic Britain." *Sociological Review* 55, no. 3:611–631.

Carrington, Ben. 2010. *Race, Sport and Politics: The Sporting Black Diaspora.* Theory, Culture and Society. Los Angeles and Thousand Oaks, CA: Sage.

Chua-Eoan, Howard, and Ishaan Tharor. 2009. "The Meaning and Mythos of Manny Pacquiao." *Time Magazine*, November 16. http://www.time.com/time/magazine/article/0,9171,1935091,00 .html, accessed January 23, 2010.

Costello, Margaret Louise. 2009. "The Filipino Ringside Community: National Identity and the Heroic Myth of Manny Pacquiao." M.A., Georgetown University.

Delgado, Fernando. 2005. "Golden but Not Brown: Oscar De La Hoya and the Complications of Culture, Manhood, and Boxing." *International Journal of the History of Sport* 22, no. 2:196–211.

Diaz, Vicente M. 2002. "'Fight Boys till the Last': Football and the Remasculinization of Indige-neity in Guam." In *Pacific Diaspora: Island Peoples in the United States and the Pacific*, ed. Paul Spickard, Joanne Rondilla, and Deborah Hippolite Wright, 167–94. Honolulu : University of Hawaii Press.

Dyson, Michael Eric. 1993. "Be Like Mike? Michael Jordan and the Pedagogy of Desire." *Cultural Studies* 7, no. 1:64–72.

Eng, David L. 2001. *Racial Castration: Managing Masculinity in Asian America.* Durham, NC: Duke University Press.

España-Maram, Linda. 2006. *Creating Masculinity in Los Angeles's Little Manila: Working-Class Filipinos and Popular Culture, 1920s–1950s.* Popular Cultures, Everyday Lives. New York: Columbia University Press.

Fajardo, Kale Bantigue. 2011. *Filipino Crosscurrents: Oceanographies of Seafaring, Masculinities, and Globalization.* Minneapolis: University of Minnesota Press.

Farred, Grant. 2006. *Phantom Calls: Race and the Globalization of the NBA.* Chicago: Prickly Paradigm Press.

Floyd, Brian. 2010. "Pacquiao vs. Margarito Results: What's Next for Manny, the Filipino Phe-nom?" *SB Nation*, November 14. http://www.sbnation.com/2010/11/14/1812966/pacquiao-vs -margarito-results, accessed September 16, 2015.

Gorn, Elliott J. 1986. *The Manly Art: Bare-Knuckle Prize Fighting in America.* Ithaca, NY: Cornell University Press.

Guerra, Denise. 2015. "For Filipinos, Manny Pacquiao Remains a Symbol of Hope." National Public Radio, May 1. http://www.npr.org/2015/05/03/404027999/for-filipinos-manny -pacquiao-remains-a-symbol-of-hope, accessed June 2, 2015.

HBO Sports. 2015. "Mayweather/Pacquiao: At Last." HBO documentary special, April 18. http:// www.hbo.com/boxing/fights/2015/05-02-floyd-mayweather-vs-manny-pacquiao/video/ mayweather-pacquiao-at-last.html?autoplay=true, accessed September 16, 2015.

Hill, Simona, and Dave Ramsaran. 2009. *Hip Hop and Inequality: Searching for the "Real" Slim Shady.* Amherst, NY: Cambria Press.

James, C. L. R. 1984. *Beyond a Boundary.* New York: Pantheon Books. Originally published 1963.

Joo, Rachael Miyung. 2012. *Transnational Sport: Gender, Media, and Global Korea.* Durham, NC: Duke University Press.

Kelley, Robin. 1996. *Race Rebels: Culture, Politics, and the Black Working Class.* New York: Simon & Schuster.

Kramer, Paul A. 2006. *The Blood of Government: Race, Empire, the United States, and the Philippines.* Chapel Hill: University of North Carolina Press.

Nguyen, Mimi Thi. 2007. "Bruce Lee I Love You: Discourses of Race and Masculinity in the Queer Superstardom of JJ Chinois." In *Alien Encounters: Popular Culture in Asian America,* ed. Mimi Thi Nguyen and Thuy Linh Nguyen Tu, 271–304. Durham, NC: Duke University Press, 2007.

NikeTalk. 2008. "Give Us This Day . . . 12.06.2008." November 21. http://niketalk.com/t/129565/give-us-this-day-12-06-2008, accessed November 13, 2015.

Okamura, Jonathan Y. 1998. *Imagining the Filipino American Diaspora: Transnational Relations, Identities, and Communities.* Asian Americans. New York: Garland Publishing.

Ongiri, Amy Abugo. 2005. "Bruce Lee in the Ghetto Connection: Kung Fu Theatre and African Americans Reinventing Culture at the Margins." In *East Main Street: Asian American Popular Culture,* ed. Shilpa Davé, Leilani Nishime, and Tasha G. Oren, 249–261. New York: NYU Press.

Osgood, Will. 2012. "Manny Pacquiao: What Young Athletes and Boxers Can Learn from Pac-Man." *Bleacher Report,* December 7. http://bleacherreport.com/articles/1435505-manny-pacquiao-what-young-athletes-and-boxers-can-learn-from-pac-man, accessed January 8, 2013.

Pavloski, Daine. 2012. "Manny Pacquiao: The Definition of a Respectable Athlete in Today's Sports World." *Bleacher Report,* December 6. http://bleacherreport.com/articles/1435798-manny-pacquiao-is-definition-of-a-respectable-athlete-in-todays-sports-world, accessed March 3, 2013.

Poole, Gary Andrew. 2010. *PacMan: Behind the Scenes with Manny Pacquiao: The Greatest Pound-for-Pound Fighter in the World.* Cambridge, MA: Da Capo Press.

Powell, Kevin. 1996. "Tupac Shakur: 1971–1996." *Rolling Stone Magazine,* October 31. http://www.rollingstone.com/music/news/tupac-shakur-1971-1996-19961031, accessed February 5 2012.

Prashad, Vijay. 2001. *Everybody Was Kung Fu Fighting: Afro-Asian Connections and the Myth of Cultural Purity.* Boston: Beacon Press.

Rafael, Dan. 2010a. "Manny Pacquiao Unanimous Winner." November 13. http://espn.go.com/espn/print?id=5804295, accessed December 20, 2010.

———. 2010b. "Antonio Margarito to Have Surgery." ESPN, November 15. http://sports.espn.go.com/dallas/news/story?id=5805223, accessed September 16, 2015.

———. 2012. "Margarito, Trainer Banned in U.S." ESPN, May 19. http://sports.espn.go.com/sports/boxing/news/story?id=3897765, accessed July 9, 2013.

———. 2015a. "Floyd Mayweather Beats Manny Pacquiao in Unanimous Decision." ESPN, May 3. http://espn.go.com/boxing/story/_/id/12810858/floyd-mayweather-defeats-manny-pacquiao-unanimous-decision, accessed June 5, 2015.

———. 2015b. "Mayweather-Pacquiao Eclipses 4.4 Million PPV Buys, $72M Gate." ESPN, May 12. http://espn.go.com/boxing/story/_/id/12872711/floyd-mayweather-manny-pacquiao-fight-shatters-all-live-gate-record, accessed June 5, 2015.

Remling, Amanda. 2015. "Photos: Celebrities at the Mayweather vs. Pacquiao Fight; Lil Wayne, Christina Milian, Beyoncé and More." *International Business Times,* May 15. http://www.ibtimes.com/photos-celebrities-mayweather-vs-pacquiao-fight-lil-wayne-christina-milian-beyonce-1906374, accessed September 16, 2015.

Rhodes, James. 2011. "Fighting for 'Respectability': Media Representations of the White, 'Working-Class' Male Boxing 'Hero.'" *Journal of Sport and Social Issues* 35 (November 2011): 350–376. doi: 10.1177/0193723511426291.

Riess, Steven A. 2007. "Sport and the Redefinition of American Middle-Class Masculinity." *International Journal of the History of Sport* 8, no. 1:5–27.

Rodriguez, Gregory. 2002. "Boxing and Masculinity: The History and (Her)story of Oscar de la Hoya." In *Latino/a Popular Culture*, ed. Michelle Habell-Pallan and Mary Romero. New York: NYU Press.

Rodriguez, Robyn Magalit. 2010. *Migrants for Export: How the Philippine State Brokers Labor to the World*. Minneapolis: University of Minnesota Press.

Rose, Tricia. 2008. *The Hip Hop Wars: What We Talk about When We Talk about Hip Hop—and Why It Matters*. New York: Basic Civitas Books.

Runstedtler, Theresa. 2012. *Jack Johnson, Rebel Sojourner: Boxing in the Shadow of the Global Color Line*. American Crossroads, vol. 33. Berkeley: University of California Press.

Sanneh, Kelefa. 2015. "How Much Do Pacquiao-Mayweather Tickets Cost?" *New Yorker*, May 1. http://www.newyorker.com/news/sporting-scene/how-much-do-pacquiao-mayweather-tickets-cost, accessed May 28, 2015.

Shimizu, Celine Parreñas. 2012. *Straitjacket Sexualities: Unbinding Asian American Manhoods in the Movies*. Stanford: Stanford University Press.

Silk, Michael L. 2012. *The Cultural Politics of Post-9/11 American Sport: Power, Pedagogy and the Popular*. Routledge Research in Sport, Culture and Society. 1st ed., vol. 10. New York: Routledge.

Thangaraj, Stanley. 2015. *Desi Hoop Dreams: Pickup Basketball and the Making of Asian American Masculinity*. New York: NYU Press.

Trujillo, Nick. 2000. "Hegemonic Masculinity on the Mound." In *Reading Sport: Critical Essays on Power and Representation*, ed. Susan Birrell and Mary G. McDonald. Boston: Northeastern University Press.

Tsing, Anna Lowenhaupt. 2005. *Friction: An Ethnography of Global Connection*. Princeton, NJ: Princeton University Press.

Turner, Victor W. 1967. *The Forest of Symbols: Aspects of Ndembu Ritual*. Ithaca, NY: Cornell University Press.

Washington Post. 2015. "Mayweather vs. Pacquiao: Poll, Previews and Pay-per-View Info." May 1. http://www.washingtonpost.com/blogs/early-lead/wp/2015/04/30/mayweather-pacquiao-fight-latest-previews-and-pay-per-view-info, accessed June 5, 2015.

Whannel, Garry. 2002. *Media Sport Stars: Masculinities and Moralities*. London and New York: Routledge.

Woodward, Kath. 2007. *Boxing, Masculinity and Identity: The "I" of the Tiger*. Routledge Critical Studies in Sport. London and New York: Routledge.

3

A History of Race and He(te)rosexuality in the Movies

James Shigeta's Asian American Male Stardom

CELINE PARREÑAS SHIMIZU

Claims about an Asian American male malaise in Hollywood movies run too rampantly in U.S. media history.[1] In *The Slanted Screen* (Adachi 2007), the definitive documentary on images of Asian American men in the media, the film director Gene Cajayon remarks: "Mainstream America, for the most part, gets uncomfortable with seeing an Asian man portrayed in a sexual light." For the writer Ky Phong Paul Tran, Asian American men never kiss, or get, the girl. They have a "cross" to bear, which means that "throughout American pop culture . . . never being depicted . . . OR being depicted in the most humiliating and emasculating light possible. It means you can never be the lead but always the sidekick . . . never handsome or suave or a lady's man" (Tran 2012). Yet the career and stardom of the Japanese American actor James Shigeta presents a compelling counterexample in Hollywood history. In four Hollywood movies from the 1950s and 1960s, Shigeta held leading roles in which he kissed, sexed, and married both white and Asian women. Shigeta, a second-generation Japanese American born in 1933, became a romantic star despite limited opportunities facing other Asian American actors.

Stunning to discover in the Hollywood archive is not only Shigeta's romantic lead roles but how his performances in *Crimson Kimono* (Fuller 1959), *Walk Like a Dragon* (Clavell 1960), *Flower Drum Song* (Koster 1961), and *Bridge to the Sun* (Périer 1961) specifically confronted Asian and Asian American men's socially disprized status in romantic and sexual realms. Shigeta's characters, across different contexts, challenge the perception that his race and gender make him undesirable to women. He also accessed heterosexual desire typically associated with the heroic white male protagonist. Shigeta's leading ladies and love interests recognize his characters' racial difference, find his manhood desirable, and confront the consequences borne of acting on those desires.

Shigeta's achievement of what is a racial stardom disrupts the claim of Hollywood's cuckolding of Asian American males. His truly singular and unique performances reveal how the contemporary lament ignores a history rich with complex Asian American characters on screen. As such, accounting for Shigeta's work on screen asserts the importance of learning to read performances in the historical archive in order to understand our legacy and shape our hopes for Asian American masculinities on and off screen. His performances show an undoing of limited definitions of manhood that faced his characters, exploding the claims of sexual failure too frequently touted as male racial wounding in the twenty-first century. My historical and textual analysis of Shigeta's performances shows how the claim that Asian American males never get the girl justifies an upholding of macho definitions of manhood in popular culture today. Shigeta's stardom powerfully speaks otherwise, where his lead characters portray a variety of romantic leading men who exploit the emotional experience brought by on screen performance that establishes uniqueness, heroism, and worth. To acknowledge his legacy is to indict the attachment to male racial wounding and limited criteria of manhood.

In 1959, the Hawaii-born James Shigeta—who had graduated from New York University and performed in Las Vegas, Japan, and Australia—became a movie star when cast in the leading role of Samuel Fuller's noir feature film, *The Crimson Kimono*. As I analyze in *Straitjacket Sexualities* (Parreñas Shimizu 2012), Shigeta played the leading man, a detective who wins the girl that his partner, a white man, also desires. In the three films analyzed in this essay, Shigeta plays heterosexual cisgendered men who struggle for love—in romance, coupling, and marriage—across differing power relations. In *Walk like a Dragon*, he plays a Chinese indentured laborer who competes with a wealthy white man for the love of an enslaved Chinese woman during the Gold Rush era. In *Flower Drum Song*, a film based on the popular Rodgers and Hammerstein musical about getting married and belonging in the United States, Shigeta plays a young Chinese American college student who has to decide between Chinese American women who desire him. In *Bridge to the Sun*, he portrays a Japanese diplomat who marries a white woman during World War II. My close readings reveal how his characters show emotional vulnerability and courage in their struggle to become assured, certain, and ultimately self-confident subjects in the face of social disregard. In these films, his characters are bound by the racialization of his sex and gender, bonds he confronts so as to unbind his manhood.

Cool and Assured on Uncertain Terrain: An Asian American Heterosexual Heartthrob?

With his tall stature, deep round voice, handsome face, and strong carriage, James Shigeta was not the first Asian American man to achieve stardom in U.S. industry cinema. He was predated by Sessue Hayakawa in the 1910s and 1920s and Philip Ahn in the 1940s. While they each fulfilled exceptions to white hegemonic standards of male beauty, they met normative cisgendered desirability on screen. Yet only in the 1950s and 1960s did Asian Americans appear in the U.S. media as potentially assimilable subjects. In the movies, this occurred in storylines involving heterosexual marriage. According to Robert G. Lee in *Orientals* (1999), the ability to marry represented integration for racial minorities, showing the rest of the world that the United States was a country where Asian Americans can participate in institutions of citizenship. The historian Scott Kurashige further illuminates that when "American leaders called on their citizenry to accept Japan as a special ally and to embrace things Japanese" (Kurashige 2008, 187) they also solidified a narrative of U.S. triumph over racism in the Cold War period. The most profound demonstration of this revisionist idea, however, was the companion argument that internment was a beneficial and "benevolent" policy for Japanese Americans (Kurashige 2008, 187). In effect, the attempt to forge relations with Japan required the suppression of very recent Japanese American history and grievances. Moreover, the notion of Asian Americans as a docile and silent minority directly contrasted with the emerging "militancy" of African Americans and other sexual minorities at the dawn of the Civil Rights era. Popular articles did not shy away from such comparisons, suggesting the "successful transformation of the Oriental from the exotic to the acceptable as a narrative of Americanization . . . through which America's anxieties about communism, [black] race-mixing, and [gay] transgressive sexuality might be contained and eventually tamed" (Lee 1999, 146). So the heterosexual marriages of Asian American men and Asian American women to whites supposedly showed racial tolerance and acceptance while also working to suppress the demands of sexual minorities.

Lee and Kurashige, however, do not bring the same level of critical attention to gender and patriarchy in their discussions of Asian women who marry white men. In their studies of *Sayonara* (Logan 1957), a Marlon Brando film featuring interracial marriages, and *Flower Drum Song*, Lee asserts that the Asian American woman is disciplined into "domesticity and a stalwart of restored postwar patriarchy" (Lee 1999, 162). Similarly, in Kurashige's analysis, feminization and emasculation are simply undesirable. He uses the limited framework of what I call "straitjacketed sexualities" (Parreñas Shimizu 2012) when asserting that in *Sayonara* "an emasculated Japanese nation serves as the feminine partner of white America . . . [while the] depiction of white men marrying Japanese women parallels the paternalistic relationship between America and Japan" (Kurashige 2008, 201–202). In this way, the contemporary complaint about Asian American masculinity as undesirably effeminate is perpetuated by scholars as well. Indeed, Kurashige argues, "If hypermasculinity was a defining trait of the Yellow Peril, feminization was just as critical to white America's embrace of the model minority" (Kurashige 2008, 202). In such an evaluation, the assessment of feminization and emasculation subscribes to limited criteria for viable manhood. Shigeta's performances and roles, however, offer a more nuanced picture of gender roles for racialized men than Lee's and Kurashige's remarks might suggest.

Shigeta's work in the cinema provides us the time and space to fall in love with a character that is at first disprized in his purported lack of desirability, until we really see and spend time with him as he wrestles with those very issues. Through Shigeta's use of the cinematic experience to engage issues of race, gender, and sexuality, his particularity in occupying these identities emerges and then seduces viewers, thereby dispelling the notions of heroic manhood as phallic and white and Asian American manhood as feminine and lacking. Instead, we see the strength of male vulnerability rather than macho invincibility and the exposure of his want and desire as a man, rather than inscrutability and impenetrability.

Walk like a Dragon: Flight from the Gendered Roles of the Frontier

Shigeta appears as the tall, handsome, and serious Cheng Lu in James Clavell's *Walk like a Dragon* (1959), a film set in Gold Rush–era California, a time and place that the historian Susan Lee Johnson describes as the "tremendous contest about maleness and femaleness, about color and culture, and about wealth and power" (Johnson 2000, 51). *Walk like a Dragon* depicts a love triangle between Lincoln "Linc" Bartlett (Jack Lord), a white male cowboy conflicted about race and gender discrimination; Cheng Lu, also known as Jack, a proud and poor Chinese immigrant man; and Kim (Nobu McCarthy), a Chinese woman trafficked among an emigrant population in the new western frontier of the United States. While the *Variety* Staff (1959) review of the film about the "interracial love triangle" is largely dismissive, my reading emphasizes the significant engagement of racial inequality in relations of intimacy at the frontier. In the duel between these men, for example, we see white and Asian counterparts in meeting heterosexual and cisgendered norms for men: tall, dashing, handsome, and serious. The confrontation between the two men looks unequal in primarily racial terms. In this way, it directly confronts racial inequality in terms of competing manhoods.

Jack and Linc encounter a typically beautiful young Chinese woman named Kim as she enters an auction site where we learn that "girls are sold into brothels." The other white men literally salivate over her; against Linc's handsome face and tall elegant stature, they look wild, dirty, lascivious, and lustful. Linc, recently returned from the Civil War, buys her so that he can set her free. Named after Abraham Lincoln, he represents the fight against slavery. He thus embodies freedom, which he takes for granted. It is a freedom that Jack does not possess but clearly understands. Jack explains that, even though the girl is free, she is now Linc's responsibility and has nowhere to go in an economy where women are trafficked. With the understanding that his male status can afford her protection, Jack then offers to buy Kim, at the same time requesting a loan for the purchase. Linc is disgusted. He tears up Kim's bill of sale, saying, "We don't buy and sell people here, Jack. Not anymore! I just got through fighting a war for the slaves." Here, the white man's purchase of the woman gives her freedom in a way that the Asian man's cannot, as legitimized by the anti-slavery narrative.

According to the social world of the film where the expression of desire by the Asian man is immoral and his lack of money shameful, Jack is unworthy of Kim, despite his sensitivity to and compassion for her. For Kim, to acknowledge his heterosexual desire is not feasible, considering that he has no currency as a man, in terms that race determines: sexual, moral, or financial. Indeed, Jack's offer to buy Kim from Linc is not without sexual innuendo, which is deemed inappropriate. That is, his expression of desire is one that asserts his subjectivity and is thus excessive. In his kind voice and in his compassionate look, we see Jack attempt a connection with Kim—a husbandly proposal—that Linc sees as rapacious and lewd. But Jack aspires to a normative and respectable masculine position in relation to her. And within the constraints of their roles—and their negotiations with their lack of mobility and freedom—they express awareness of each other's shared position as Chinese Americans denied access to the dominant gender roles that form the basis of romantic heterosexual relationships.

In the world depicted in the film, where white manhood means owning women and dominating non-racial others, Jack Lu mimics the model of white manhood and desires a woman as an assertion of his heterosexuality and in turn, a validation of his own racialized manhood. Among other Chinese, he asks why they must act deferentially toward whites and declares his intent to buy Kim back: "I want that woman." He also links his desire with a promise: "I swear by my ancestors I will walk tall like a dragon in Jericho." This statement underlines that it is only in America that his place as a man is denigrated and it is also the place where he intends to claim an American manhood. He invokes his ancestors to access an otherwise unattainable manhood in the frontier. But to "walk like a dragon" is to claim his manhood by possessing a woman. This is a patriarchal aspiration that remains enthralled to dominant masculinity and that marks women as property; it validates male power through the possession of females as the solution to male racial disempowerment.

Jack imagines his inclusion in the frontier's heterosexual matrix from which Chinese men are excluded because they are feminized. For Jack, this is not the natural order of things, although whites persistently relegated him to this role. In *White Weddings: Romancing Heterosexuality in Popular Culture*, Chrys Ingraham (2008) identifies the concept of the "heterosexual imaginary" as that which allows us to imagine the possibilities of participating in romance. She clarifies that "'imaginary' here does not mean 'false' or 'pretend' but, rather, an illusory relationship between an individual and their social world" (Ingraham 2008, 26). I am interested in this formulation because in *Walk Like a Dragon* Jack's heterosexual imaginary is expressed in his swagger, as a form of racial style, or what bell hooks calls "cool" in her study of black male style as resistance to their racialization (hooks 2004). Similarly for Jack, his bodily comportment defies his assigned role, and his walk negotiates his constraints on the very streets of Jericho where encounters with white others occur. And unlike Kim, he imagines a world where they can come together in a romantic coupling. Jack at first competes with Linc in these terms—he wants to buy her and maintain her as property just as Linc initially did. I will show how Jack ultimately figures out a different way out of patriarchy to reach Kim.

As Linc and Kim come together toward marriage, Jack fears for her and the limits she faces as an Asian woman in America even within marriage. When he asks her not to go with Linc, she responds, "You are not my master, I cannot take orders from you." In this exchange, she registers her own racial and gendered bind. We see a kind of regret in Kim's face; she looks at him desperately as if trying to express the impossibility of their coupling as a choice for her. They both express awareness of racism as a unifying force in preventing the possibility of their pairing. She recognizes that he is bound to his racial and gendered lot and is unable to occupy the position of gendered mastery, and she sees in this an opening of new possibilities. Similarly, he comes to see her racialized lot, recognizing that his own racial empowerment cannot require her disempowerment.

With these new realizations, Jack no longer competes with Linc in white male terms of romance premised on heterosexual property and heteronormative gender roles when he no longer wants to buy Kim. He asks her to choose freely—so as to become free in making her own choice between him and Linc. Jack wants recognition from a free woman of what their coupling can accomplish. When Kim chooses to go with him, it becomes a new formulation of race and gender that won't participate in the white male traffic in women or Asian male patriarchy that mimics it. When he offers the racial stakes of her choosing him instead, she considers going with Jack as a way to reimagine gender relations. Here, she and Jack transform to imagine access to a heterosexuality that is now actually possible for them as racialized subjects. Through each other, they have a way out of their disprized status. In this way, the film follows the two characters' transformations into their Asian American gendered identities, where love is negotiated within their social context. They pursue love made possible within the social order. At the same time, she makes this choice by recognizing the impossibility of her interracial coupling with Linc.

The film concludes with the Asian American romantic leads' larger transformation. James Shigeta's character Jack wants recognition from a free woman of what their coupling can accomplish—access to same-ethnicity romantic coupling previously denied them. Kim chooses to go with him in a new formulation of race (they access heterosexuality) and gender (she becomes the sexual model minority gone awry, and he refuses to buy her and participate in the white male traffic in women) as they imagine the possibilities of their new coupling. Kim now sees Jack as someone with whom she shares racial alliance in remaking gender from their positions of marginalization. Jack Lu recognizes the significance of the choice, promising, "I swear by my ancestors, I will make you happy." The last line of this phrase replaces his previous declaration of "walk like a dragon"—meaning to claim mastery over women. Instead, he transforms his goal to be one in which he hopes for heterosexual romance. The western ultimately privileges the Asian American couple and validates love, romance, and marriage as a way to reimagine and live their social classifications. It is through marriage that Kim and Jack work their way out of Asian American female domesticity and Asian American male worthlessness. They flee the frontier, and both of their prescribed roles there, to go elsewhere, allowing the viewer to re-imagine gender relations in their future.

Flower Drum Song: Asian American Male Power over Asian American Women

The musical *Flower Drum Song* presented Asian Americans singing and dancing in a musical about their immigration and citizenship through marriage, what Christina Klein (2003) argues is part of the harmonic construction of Asian American relations in the Cold War era. At the center of this story is James Shigeta's character Wang Ta, whom the story follows in 1950s San Francisco Chinatown as he attempts to choose which of two women to marry: Mei Li (a newly immigrated picture bride) or Linda Low (a Chinese American night club singer). Later, a third option arises: Helen Chao (a Chinese American friend). The *New York Times*'s review of the film classifies the characters as caricatures, or mere rehearsals of ethnic stereotyping: "quaint," "old-world," and "clowns" (Crowther 1961b). As scholars like Anne Anlin Cheng have shown us, the stereotypes here are ripe for much richer evaluation. Building upon Cheng's analysis of the women in the movie as a choice between Asian, American, and Asian American subjectivity, I show how the primacy of Ta's wielding male power in marriage and love reveals the dependent subjectivity of women.

The historian Xiaojian Zhao (2002) focuses on the historical era that contextualizes *Flower Drum Song*. She argues that this period was a watershed because it created a community among Chinese Americans. Zhao argues that, although family was the foundational relation for thousands of years, it did not come to dominate Chinese American life until the post–World War II era, with the passage of laws including the 1945 War Brides Act and the Chinese Alien Wives of American Citizens Act in 1946, which corrected the gender imbalance among Chinese Americans in the United States. The migration of many Chinese women in the United States also galvanized political organizing, congressional lobbying, and legal activism for family unification, which then led to a strong ethnic identity. Moreover, for Zhao, "the cultural struggle" of the community exceeded binaristic formulations of "Chinese versus American, traditional versus modern, or rural versus urban" (Zhao 2002, 150). Rather, these Chinese American men and women accounted for the multi-faceted dynamics in forging their "own" modernity as young Americans and children of immigrants (Zhao 2002, 151). Indeed, the film portrays couplings that reflect the increasing heterogeneity of racialized heterosexual formations, especially in terms of the various modern masculinities and femininities represented for Asian Americans.

In this context, we see James Shigeta's Wang Ta representing the Chinese American son of Chinese immigrant parents. Essentially, he serves as the center of the family narrative. From the beginning Wang Ta resists his father's suggestions of arranged marriage, saying that, in America, we marry for love. Indeed, the ritual of marriage transformed with immigration, as Chinese Americans encounter the western notion of love as an emotional force. This is especially important against a definition of love within eastern tradition as pragmatism. Anne Anlin Cheng studies the choices Ta makes between the women as national choices, with each woman representing the American, the Asian American, and the Asian. I read the differences between these women within the dynamics of gender and sexuality, specifically the derivative status of women to men in patriarchy, even if we seem to witness a wide range of subjectivity in female power and vulnerability.

At first, we see Ta flirt with Linda Low, who represents emotional and sexual love. She drives him wild with desire. After arranging a date, Low launches into the classic song, "I Enjoy Being a Girl," illustrating her passion for female desirability. She sings, "I am strictly a female female / And I hope that my future will be / In the home of a brave and free male / Who enjoys being a guy having a girl like me," as she gazes at herself in the mirror with the look of someone aware of her objectification as a site for harvesting her own agency. To be looked upon by Ta as desirable confirms not only her own capital but the power of his gaze upon her as a force she can wield. Wang Ta's conferral of the look, however, is conflicted. The film presents her as ultimately incompatible to him, for his sexual and emotional love may be insufficient in the face of a manipulative woman. Her femininity is aggressive, and his masculinity is more timid. This is not necessarily the manhood to which he aspires. But he still has other options.

Mei Li's shy demeanor is directly contrasted with Linda Low's overt sexuality. As opposed to physical desire, Wang Ta's interest in her is "polite and anthropological." When he encounters Mei Li, their conversation flows with the tension of romantic misrecognition. She knows he is her intended husband, while he is completely unaware of the match. He shows genuine interest as an American who interrogates a newly arrived foreigner: "How long have you been here? . . . Tell me, Ms. Li, what do you intend to do here in San Francisco?" The response is that of a good woman, rather than the free-wheeling Linda Low who seemingly enjoys toying with men as a form of female power: "I intend to get married." As

Figure 3.1. Shigeta as Wang Ta.

a woman in this 1960 film, she indeed has a clear goal. Here, Mei Li represents the most traditional option in terms of gendered and sexualized normativity. She portrays the devoted gender and sex to his patriarchal position.

In the third female possibility, when looking through the lens of Helen Chao's unrequited affection, we can see Ta's privileged and even roguish position. In the case of Helen, her approaches are met with indifference. When she delivers his graduation robes, which she sewed for him as a labor of love, she enters his bedroom as he emerges from the bathroom. He wears no more than his undershirt tucked into his pants. She is disconcerted at seeing him so closely and somewhat exposed in the confined privacy of his room. Although they are in the intimate space of the bedroom, his interaction and interest in her are neither physical (as with Linda Low) nor intellectual (as with Mei Li). While he may seem oblivious, he actually toys with her. Her presence in his room does not affect him, even as his presence shatters her composure. It is cruel on his part, however. He goes about his business of getting ready and dressed, as if flaunting his power over her. He invites her to come to the graduation party in a casual fashion, but to her it is a pregnant, and long-awaited, invitation. "Do you want me to?" she asks with hope. His response is yes, "You are part of the family." It is not commensurate with her own feelings. It hurts her. In an illustration of her unrequited love, she is disappointed and looks down sadly while he checks himself out in the mirror. His cool is callous. She inspires no emotional or libidinal love in him and possesses no pragmatic family value. She brings no family or ancestral line. As such, she remains an outsider, in gendered and sexualized terms, to the traditional formation of marriage. As she stands so vulnerably in his bedroom, she is neither a respectable woman like Mei Li nor a woman in possession of gendered and sexualized power like Linda Low. Helen is clearly the least possible option for him. He offers her no recognition. And in the book upon which the film is based, she actually commits suicide.

At this juncture, we see the different female faces that respond to Ta. To Linda Low, he is childlike and sweet; to Mei Li, he is interested and kind; and to Helen, he is oblivious and gorgeous. Each projection of masculinity here condenses to form an idealized Asian American cisgendered heterosexual, heroic, and patriarchal manhood. Shigeta's character achieves the status of heartthrob in the gazes of these women, which includes his role as a brute who disregards women who care for him. Here, his racial cool functions as disregard for certain women. In this film, Ta occupies the position of power in that his gaze and desire confers social legitimacy for women. For those who hold value, such as Linda Low with her sexual expertise, or Mei Li with her fulfillment of traditional womanhood supported by family and ancestral tradition, it can be a dynamic contest. But for Helen, who really is alone without father or country (unlike Mei Li), and whose working class renders her plain in dress and lacking in wiles (unlike Linda Low), the relation can be a form of subordination and marginality.

Indeed, as Christina Klein (2003) argues, the film ends with a harmonious image in two very different heteronormal formations for Asian American men and women, when Wang Ta marries Mei Li and Sammy (the smooth-talking nightclub owner) marries Linda. Wang Ta and Mei Li—as we can see in their names—prioritize a Chinese American marriage that carries traditions and ethnic belonging, making sense of both cultures in one family. Another couple, Linda and Sammy, forge ahead by making up their own rules in their marriage; he does not have to come home every night, and she might or might not go out with him, but each knows the arrangement. The Asian American men and women choose mates to contour their own manhoods and womanhoods in relation to community, to reflect a changing society in which couples move out of ethnic enclaves into a more vastly located Chinese America. I argue, expanding from Zhao (2002), that this movement also sees heterosexualities that are much more heterogeneous in both conventional and unconventional pairings. Most significant, though, Helen is sacrificed for the pleasure of Wang Ta, who ultimately occupies a position of privilege that can punish less socially equal subjects.

The film depicts exactly what Asian American men supposedly do not have: the access to patriarchy in "getting the girl" and even relinquishing other women. Here, patriarchal male success and male gendered power is not problematized but actually celebrated, even if others suffer along the way. In the next film, however, marriage fails, and in the process, an Asian American man in the movies becomes inscrutable, showing us that marriage or getting the girl is not quite the romantic solution to Asian American male sexual problems in the movies.

Bridge to the Sun: The Failure of Marriage and the Opacity of the Other

Based on the autobiography of Gwen Terasaki (1957), *Bridge to the Sun* tells the story of an interracial couple during a time of war—where the man and woman represent warring nations, in a metaphor for the marriage itself. Told from Terasaki's perspective, the Japanese man seems even more inscrutable to the viewer. In James Shigeta's last film as a romantic lead, we see a study of marriage and the strength it requires to maintain an intimate interracial relationship. This period in the film was a time that rendered Japanese as the enemy in popular culture, which the film attempts to revisit twenty years later, albeit wistfully. For the Japanese man and the white American woman, their love is a site of emotional and psychic violence from without and within. Here, not only does the foreign Asian man marry the white American woman, but the marriage encounters disparaging classifications, and these perceptions permeate the very fabric of the relationship.

Gwen (Caroll Baker), a fresh-faced young blonde with small facial features and large eyes, meets a Japanese ambassador, Hidenari Terasaki, or "Terry," played by James Shigeta. They fall in love and marry, despite protests from both of their communities. The *New York Times*'s review of the film by Bosley Crowther belittles Shigeta's romantic leading role. Crowther places Shigeta's performance between poles of "genial dignity" and "crisp oriental formality"—refusing his work as romantic hero. In the review, Shigeta is inscrutable as a mere "romantic symbol than a troubled human being" (Crowther 1961a). When Gwen and Terry meet in an art gallery, we detect the sexual tension between them. It is notable that the mystery of the other's different background certainly shapes their mesmerized looks at each other. Instead of looking at the art, they look at each other's faces intently; they seem to be actively trying to make sense of their attraction across their racial difference, which they confront immediately.

On their first date, Gwen reveals that she had lied to her chaperone aunt about seeing him that night. The way he manages this revelation indicates a great deal about his self-confidence; he looks at her directly and asks why she could not tell the truth about seeing him. He remains friendly and gently prods her with, "Perhaps I know why." His direct approach seems to calm her pouting voice and defiant stance: "Look, Terry, it is true I was afraid what they'd say if told them we had a date. [It's] just the way we were raised. The awful thing is even I was ashamed—I'm not anymore, cross my heart." In this, they actually discuss the racial dynamics between them. In his confidence, as an assertion of his self-worth, she realizes his expectations from her, not only of recognition but dignity.

He enables her to acknowledge her own racism. In these striking conversations about race and romance, they make a pact to align themselves in acknowledging race as a social problem that also fuels their romantic interest in each other. I must note that while their racial backgrounds do not compose a typical romance, their pairing meets cisnormative gendered coupling: She is little, petulant, and wild while he is tall, calm, and confident.

Others outside their marriage definitely feel entitled to police it. As an ambassador, Terry must get approval from his embassy regarding their marriage. When she breaks up with him, as the embassy suggests, her aunt unleashes this sweetly voiced reproach: "I must say he was a lovely man for an Oriental. When I think of all these clean nice men." Gwen becomes furious at her aunt's racial characterizations of white men as clean and thus of Terry as dirty. Despite state and family interventions, however, they continue with their marriage. However, it is when they go to Japan that they ultimately unravel as a couple because of his troubles with gender and her troubles with race. The site of their unraveling thus occurs in a more intolerant East. There, she becomes more and more frustrated with the gendered order. She defies the boundaries that separate men's conversations from women's and angers Terry. For him, her act insults a guest and dishonors him as her husband. Terry asserts his privilege as a man, which is not hers. She screams about treating women like human beings and being "sick of a place where you cannot show human emotions!" But when he leaves to go to the geisha house where the men will continue their conversation, he ends up punching his friend for dismissing his marriage. He tells her, "I was cruel and stupid. I do not want Japanese wife, I want you." This is his first spoken indication of his doubts about their interracial relationship.

As the war continues, the couple must physically separate, so she and the children retreat to the countryside for safety. She experiences increasing exhaustion, hunger, and loneliness. She asks him, begs him, to "love me, please." Unlike Gwen, who remains fervent in her devotion to marriage, and even sexually hungry for him, Terry refuses to respond. In revealing the waning of his passion, he watches her walk away. Throughout, he struggles in his effort to get her to return to the United States instead of staying in Japan. His dispassion is unmatched. She "can't think of going back without [him]." It turns out that he has been hiding a terminal illness from her. She discovers this only because she catches him visiting his parents' graves, which she understands is a Japanese cultural ritual that indicates he is going to die. He attempts to send her away because he does not want her to see him die. In the end of the film, he remains confused about his role as a husband. Ultimately, the film presents him as increasingly opaque and hard to know. The marriage fails for cultural reasons—he closes off even as she opens up. In this film, his cool at first functions as enticing and transformative, then becomes impossible to penetrate. It is a film and novel that ultimately privileges her transparency and his opacity.

For the male racial other to get the girl is thus a very rich and complicated terrain of storytelling in U.S. popular culture, one that goes beyond the patriarchal victory and male ownership of women that simplistic celebratory claims make. Just because such pairings occur does not mean it is a romantic or ideal story, especially where the male racial other is not American and national difference fails their love. The space of interracial marriage continues to be a site of contention in which public disregard can permeate intimacy so incessantly as to determine the relationship. Yet Shigeta's dignified countenance and proud face provides a contrast to Asian American male anxiety amplified in the claims of never getting the girl. He not only got the girl but continued to puzzle over the more important questions about how to be a worthwhile partner to her in their new formulation of interracial heterosexuality and intimacy.

James Shigeta's Legacy

For a short window of time, 1959–1961, James Shigeta occupied a powerful role as a subject of love and object of desire in Hollywood films. His characters are central and important, indeed, but they also show us a manhood we can learn from: how to love, how to defy interpellation, how to create one's own mirror, how to reappropriate others' misnamings, and how to move beyond and even laugh at them. In his films, James Shigeta's performances of an Asian and Asian American manhood reveal inner complexity and critique of the outside world. In *Walk like a Dragon*, he is a devoted lover who claims social stature to be deserving of his wife. Together, they will reform their racialized genders and sexualities. In *Flower Drum Song*, he is both an agent of gendered discipline and gendered partnership. In *Bridge to the Sun*, he demonstrates the power of love and the inability to keep a marriage alive. A variety of manhoods become available to Asian American men through James Shigeta's performances. In each, we detect the investment in the self as worthy rather than anxious. This self-love demands regard, recognition, and dignity in the form of love and respect for self and from others.

In Shigeta's roles, he confronts the criterion of failing normative manhood—that he is not a white male hero—and by arresting its limits, he finds manhood beyond the disprized, deficient, and weak. His screen presence—the very visibility of his racial difference and its legibility as a desiring and desirable subject to mainstream audiences—also allows Asian American men to explore their way out of anxiety and question the privileging of marriage and even traditional heroism if it means the relegation of women to subordination by gender. This Shigeta is ultimately swoon-worthy, for when arresting racial, gendered, and sexual wounding, he ascends by exploring the dimensions of male failure within existing constructs of race and heterosexuality. The work of James Shigeta is important today because it is not about getting the girl but about confronting the challenge of loving oneself and others in the face of racism that not only hates racial others but encourages hate of the self as a racial other. The eighty-five-year old James Shigeta passed away on July 29, 2014. He retains the last laugh. You may see him as an octogenarian debonair lover to a much younger white woman in Quentin Lee's film *The People I've Slept With* (2009). In this film, he leaves us images of him dancing with his lover around a California swimming pool and even counseling his daughter on owning her own sexuality.

James Shigeta's smoldering gaze emanates desire and the desirability of a man deserving not only of social value but of intimate regard. In his confident demeanor, assuredness, and self-possession in the face of racialization, a stardom critical of established ideas of race, gender, and sexuality, as well as heroism, emerges. It is through the experience of his wrestling with the improbability of his viability that viewers also come to love him as his partners do. Thus the racial stardom Shigeta achieves is in his occupation of romantic roles in American cinema and his performances that present a more expansive view of Asian American masculinity and stardom.

Shigeta's achievement of what is a racial stardom disrupts the claim of Hollywood's cuckolding of Asian American males. His truly singular and unique performances reveal how the contemporary lament ignores a history rich with complex Asian American characters on screen. As such, accounting for Shigeta's work on screen asserts the importance of learning to read performances in the historical archive in order to understand our legacy and shape our hopes for Asian American masculinities on and off screen. His performances show an undoing of limited definitions of manhood that faced his characters, exploding the claims of sexual failure too frequently touted as male racial wounding in the twenty-first century. My historical and textual analysis of Shigeta's performances shows how the claim that Asian American males never get the girl justifies an upholding of macho definitions of manhood in popular culture today. Shigeta's stardom powerfully speaks otherwise, in which his lead characters portray a variety of romantic leading men who exploit the emotional experience brought by on screen performance that establishes uniqueness, heroism, and worth. To acknowledge his legacy is to indict the attachment to male racial wounding and limited criteria of manhood.

NOTE

1 This essay is dedicated to my beloved son Lakas Parreñas Shimizu, who suddenly and unexpectedly died on Christmas Day, 2013. In his eight short years of life, he showed me what was possible in this changing world: His movie-star smile and his friendly confidence opened many hearts.

Thank you to the editors Shilpa Davé, Leilani Nishime, and Tasha Oren for their careful reading and astute suggestions. I am especially grateful to Shilpa Davé for her clarity and guidance. I completed this work while in residence at the United States Studies Centre at the University of Sydney in Australia and presented this work as my farewell lecture as professor of Asian American Studies at the University of California at Santa Barbara.

REFERENCES

Adachi, Jeff, dir. 2006. *The Slanted Screen*. Documentary. San Francisco: AAMM Productions.

Cheng, Anne Anlin. 2001. *The Melancholy of Race: Psychoanalysis, Assimilation and Hidden Grief*. New York: Oxford University Press.

Clavell, James, dir. 1959. *Walk like a Dragon*. Hollywood, CA: Paramount Pictures.

Crowther, Bosley. 1961a. "Movie Review: *Bridge to the Sun* (1961)." *New York Times*, October 18. http://www.nytimes.com/movie/review?res=9D07E2DC133BE13ABC4052DFB667838A679 EDE, accessed October 19, 2015

———. 1961b. "Movie Review: *Flower Drum Song* (1961)." *New York Times*, November 10. http://www.nytimes.com/movie/review?res=9C0CEFDD143CEE32A25753C1A9679D946091D6CF, accessed October 19, 2015.

Fuller, Samuel, dir. 1959. *Crimson Kimono*. Culver City, CA: Columbia Pictures.

hooks, bell. 2003. *We Real Cool: Black Men and Masculinity*. New York: Routledge.

Ingraham, Chrys. 2008. *White Weddings: Romancing Heterosexuality in Popular Culture*. New York: Routledge.

Johnson, Susan Lee. 2000. *Roaring Camp: The Social World of the California Gold Rush*. New York: Norton.

Klein, Christina. 2003. *Cold War Orientalism*. Berkeley: University of California Press, 2003.

Koster, Henry, dir. 1961. *Flower Drum Song*. Universal City, CA: Universal Studios.

Kurashige, Scott. 2008. *The Shifting Grounds of Race*. Princeton, NJ: Princeton University Press.

Lee, C. Y. 1957. *The Flower Drum Song*. New York: Farrar, Straus & Cudahy.

Lee, Quentin, dir. 2009. *The People I've Slept With*. Los Angeles: Margin Films; Cupertino, CA: 408 Films.

Lee, Robert G. 1999. *Orientals*. Philadelphia: Temple University Press.

Logan, Joshua, dir. 1957. *Sayonara*. Burbank, CA: Warner Brothers.

Parreñas, Rhacel. 2011. *Illicit Flirtations: Labor, Migration and Sex Trafficking in Tokyo*. Stanford, CA: Stanford University Press.

Parreñas Shimizu, Celine. 2012. *Straitjacket Sexualities: Unbinding Asian American Manhoods in the Movies*. Stanford, CA: Stanford University Press.

Périer, Etienne, dir. 1961. *Bridge to the Sun*. Beverly Hills, CA: MGM.

Terasaki, Gwen. 1957. *Bridge to the Sun*. Chapel Hill: University of North Carolina Press.

Tran, Ky Phong Paul. 2012. "Why Jeremy Lin Matters." *New America Media*, February 15. http://newamericamedia.org/2012/02/why-jeremy-lin-matters-asian-male-image-in-the-media.php, accessed June 18, 2014.

Variety Staff. 1959. Review: "Walk like a Dragon." December 31. http://variety.com/1959/film/reviews/walk-like-a-dragon-1200419518, accessed October 19, 2015.

Zhao, Xiaojian. 2002. *Remaking Chinese America: Immigration, Family, and Community, 1940–1965*. New Brunswick, NJ: Rutgers University Press.

4

Model Maternity

Amy Chua and Asian American Motherhood

JULIA H. LEE

On January 8, 2011, the *Wall Street Journal* published an article titled "Why Chinese Mothers Are Superior," catapulting its author, Amy Chua, to national celebrity and triggering an onslaught of commentary regarding the benefits of "Chinese"-style parenting over its "Western" counterpart.[1] The debate—much of which was fueled by outrage over some of the more sensationalistic aspects of Chua's parenting style—only gained momentum when *Battle Hymn of the Tiger Mother*—the memoir from which the article had been excerpted—was published a few weeks later. Chua's subsequent publicity tour saw her alternate between pushing back against her critics (she defiantly noted in her *Today* show interview that "I know that a lot of Asian parents are secretly shocked and horrified by many aspects of Western parenting") and attempting to tamp down the vitriol leveled against her.[2] Her efforts in the latter case amounted to insisting that the memoir was not a "how-to" manual but, rather, a satirical self-portrait of her own failures as a parent, a claim that seems to be undermined by the memoir's opening lines: "A lot of people wonder how Chinese parents raise such stereotypically successful kids. They wonder what these parents do to produce so many math whizzes and music prodigies. . . . Well, I can tell them, because I've done it."[3]

Chua's wavering between defiance and defensiveness in the wake of her book's publication echoes the widely divergent responses that her memoir provoked.[4] Some readers focused on Chua's mothering techniques, praising her or castigating her for her mothering style. Ayelet Waldman, in her January 16, 2011, *Wall Street Journal* article on the memoir, professed feelings of "gratitude" and "awe" for Chua's insistence upon high standards, even as she opined (using her own daughter as an example) that many children would not respond to—let alone thrive under—the harsh discipline the book describes.[5] In the January 20, 2012, issue of the *New York Times*, reviewer Janet Maslin dismissed the book as "diabolically well-packaged" and "a slickly well-shaped story" in which Chua, "driven, snobbish and hellbent on raising certifiably Grade A children," "never fails to make herself its center of attention."[6] Asian American bloggers and writers like Jen Wang and Jeffrey Yang defended Chua on her mothering tactics; Wang expressed a wish that her own mother had been as demanding during her childhood, while Yang argued that the *Wall Street Journal*'s excerpt distorted the intention and arc of the memoir itself (making Chua in the process, much less likable).[7] Other readers and critics have been much more interested in assessing the ethnonationalism underlying Chua's assumption that the Chinese are "superior" to Westerners in terms of parenting. Wesley Yang, in a profanity-laced essay for *New York Magazine*, rejected the "Asian values" and model minority expectations that *Battle Hymn* seems to trumpet and that white Americans seem to love.[8] Commentators on the *Wall Street Journal* website vociferously debated the respective strengths and weaknesses of China and the United States in terms of each nation's respective geopolitical influence, economic policies, educational systems, and treatment of women and children. Based on the volume and intensity of these various reactions, it is no wonder that a reviewer for the *New York Review of Books* queried: "Why has the book excited such extreme reactions"?[9]

This article attempts to answer that question by examining how Chua constructs Chinese American racial identity in what Jodi Melamed has called the age of "neoliberal multiculturalism."[10] I am particularly struck by the way that Chua and her interlocutors make Chinese American motherhood a crucial site where issues of race, gender, and class intersect with U.S. ideals regarding family and citizenship as well as its imperialist histories and practices, especially in relation to China and Asia. As Grace Wang has astutely noted, *Battle Hymn* stands at the crossroad of a "waning U.S. hegemony, growing Chinese dominance, and proper forms of parenting in an era of global competition."[11] I argue that the controversy around Chua and *Battle Hymn* can be productively analyzed by situating it "domestically" (i.e., within the nation's cultural discourses on immigration and kinship) and "globally" (i.e., as a product of U.S. imperialism and Asian American transnationalism). Amy Kaplan's argument that "notions of the domestic and the foreign mutually constitute one another" is particularly important in thinking about the Chinese, who for the last century have been viewed as a threat to U.S. global supremacy both militarily and economically and as unassimilable internal aliens who threaten the nation's sovereignty.[12] Jodi Kim approaches the question of Asian American identity formation in a similar manner, arguing that the encounters of U.S. empire in the Cold War period "constitute[d] . . . the conditions of possibility for the post–World War II formation of Asian America" within the United States.[13] Thus Chinese American representations of themselves as Americans are "informed and deformed" (to borrow Kaplan's phrase) by the racial and gendered histories of political exclusion as well as by American anxieties regarding China as a rising superpower.[14] *Battle Hymn* makes clear how Chinese American identity is constituted and remade by the interplay between the domestic and the foreign, the national and international, the immigrant and the imperial.

Battle Hymn, however, is far from the first text to link issues of Chinese American identity and national belonging to motherhood. From Maxine Hong

Kingston, to Amy Tan, to Margaret Cho, motherhood has been a rich topos for the exploration of Asian American identity in national and international contexts. In fact, in the early twenty-first century, narratives of Asian American motherhood have proliferated in popular culture and literature to the point where it has become a highly recognizable—we might even go so far as to say, foundational—component to the articulation of the Asian American experience. This essay begins with a brief history of Asian American motherhood, a history marked by a variety of erasures and impossibilities, before moving on to consider *Battle Hymn*'s place in that history and how it continues the erasure of Asian American motherhood, even as it seems to trumpet it. Chua's construction of Chinese American motherhood excludes and attempts to render invisible any version of this identity that does not fit into its highly hierarchical and market-driven construction of that position. The irony here is that the mothers that Chua most readily identifies as outsiders to her tiger motherhood are the Asian nationals she encounters, whom she describes as ineluctably foreign and vaguely suspicious. Chua's motherhood, in other words, is haunted by those who are outside of the privileges of class, culture, and citizenship that she wields. Chua's enjoyment of her privilege and her insistence that her daughters embody that privilege is haunted by those Chinese and Asian subjects consigned to the edges of the U.S. polity or who do not have access to the kind of cultural and financial capital that she—as a law professor at Yale—can access. Her acceptance into the United States is purchased only by their rigorous exclusion.

Mother Knows Best

To talk of Chua erasing Chinese American motherhood might seem strange, given the fact that she hammers home repeatedly throughout her memoir how intensively she took up the mantle of "Chinese" motherhood once her daughters were born. The equation of Chinese mothers and "tiger mothers" in the public's mind is perhaps now and forever firmly implanted; however, in all the fuss over Chua's memoir, no mention has been made of the fact that *Battle Hymn* is not alone in exploring the agonistic relationship between mothers and daughters, a fact that Chua herself notes in her work. This is a history that was produced by the Yellow Peril discourse and is consequently deeply informed by the various political and social exclusions that Asians, especially the Chinese, have faced in the United States. The fact that "Chinese mothers" have become the symbol of contemporary successful, disciplined motherhood counters a national history that has until recently rendered full Asian American inclusion impossible.

The history of anti-Chinese racism and exclusion is well known at this point, and many critics have productively brought to light and discussed how federal exclusion and anti-miscegenation laws racialized and gendered the Chinese in America.[15] The question of how this history has affected cultural discourse of Chinese American motherhood has not been explored as thoroughly. For much of the twentieth century, immigration laws and legislative prohibitions have played decisive roles in the representation of Asian American women. The Page Act of 1875 exemplifies how the nation constructed Chinese femininity in these years. As Robert Lee writes, the Page Act "ostensibly prohibited 'Chinese, Japanese, and Mongolian women' from being brought to or entering the United States to 'engage in immoral or licentious activities.'"[16] The law "legitimized the criminalization of the Chinese, falsely averring that every Chinese woman was seeking admission on false pretenses and that each was a potential prostitute until proven otherwise."[17] The association between the Chinese and sexual immorality—and Chinese women and prostitution, in particular—served as one of the many justifications for the passage of the Chinese Exclusion Act in 1882.[18] While the Page Act reflected the nation's perception that Chinese women were morally unfit to be included in the nation, the Chinese Exclusion Act actually made it difficult for the concept of the Chinese mother to exist in the United States at all. The Exclusion Act made it extremely difficult for Chinese or other Asian women to migrate to the United States and illegal to gain U.S. citizenship. The act ensured that the ratio of Chinese men to women in the United States would remain heavily lopsided well into the twentieth century; various prohibitions against miscegenation and land ownership kept the U.S.-born Chinese population from growing.[19]

The impossibility of establishing Chinese American families affected men and women quite differently. While Chinese men during the Exclusion era were able to create contingent networks of "paper fathers" and "paper sons," these arrangements left women out of reconstituted kinship networks. The formation of paper families created legal and social bonds between men; they were families that did not require the presence of mothers to exist or flourish. Thus, unlike black mothers, who have been vilified for the emasculation of African American men and pathologized as monstrous mothers, Asian American mothers have been characterized by their absence for the first half of the twentieth century. As Christina Marie Tourino notes, "contemporary ethnic women's fiction is marked not so much by a saturation of maternity a . . . but by its disruption or absence."[20]

The historical erasure of Asian American motherhood makes what followed in the late twentieth-century all the more striking. The last thirty years have witnessed a cultural shift from an impossible Asian American mother to Asian American mothers dominating narratives of Asian American experience and identity. The popularity of this relatively new narrative is due to a number of factors: the loosening of immigration laws that enabled Asian women to migrate to the United States with fewer restrictions than before; the second-wave feminist movements of the 1970s; the increasing visibility of Asian Americans in social, political, and cultural realms; and the continuing popularity of the immigrant autobiography as a genre of literature. Maxine Hong Kingston's 1975 critically acclaimed memoir *The Woman Warrior* and Amy Tan's 1989 blockbuster novel *The Joy Luck Club* introduced a wide swath of the American reading public to Chinese American mothers who insult, chastise, frighten, and intimidate their daughters.[21] *The Woman Warrior* and *The Joy Luck Club* are perhaps the best-known literary examples of Asian American maternity, but narratives in which a conflicted matrilineal relationship plays a prominent—if not central—role abound: Theresa Hak Kyung Cha's *Dictée* (1982), Lan Samantha Chang's *Inheritance* (2004), Jung Chang's *Wild Swans* (1991), Margaret Cho's film *I'm the One That I Want* (2000), Nora Okja Keller's *Comfort Woman* (1998), Ronyoung Kim's *Clay Walls* (1987), Joy Kogawa's *Obasan* (1981), Fae Ng's *Bone* (1993), Lisa See's *On Gold Mountain* (1995), Cathy Song's *Picture Bride* (1982), Alice Wu's film *Saving Face* (2004), Hisaye Yamamoto's short story "Seventeen Syllables" (1994), and Wakako Yamauchi's collection of works, "Songs My Mother Taught Me" (1994). More recently, a cluster of memoirs and essay collections have more humorously explored this emerging stereotype of the difficult Asian American mother: Annie Choi's *Happy Birthday or Whatever: Track Suits, Kimchee, and Other Family Disasters* (2007), Teresa and Serena Wu's *My Mom Is a Fob: Earnest Advice in Broken English from Your Asian American Mom* (2011), and Elaine Lui's *Listen to the Squawking Chicken: When Mother Knows Best, What's a Daughter to Do?* (2013).

Of these, Margaret Cho's impersonation of her own mother Young-Hie Cho in *I'm the One That I Want*, a film of Cho's stand-up performance at the Warfield Theater in San Francisco, is perhaps the best-known. The differences between this stand-up routine and the companion book that bears the same title[22] exemplifies how familiar Americans have become with the image of the Asian American mother and the centrality of Asian American maternity in the public perception and performance of Asian American identity. Cho's mother is clearly the centerpiece of her stand-up routine; the moments in which Cho impersonates her are the most anticipated and garner the most applause and laughter from her audience. Cho's memoir, however, paints a different picture. In it, she describes the difficulties she had with *both* her parents. Her father periodically abandoned the family without explanation, and her mother's method of coping with the domestic uncertainty was to crash diet and ignore Margaret. Cho says both of her parents told her they hated her because she was a failure academically, and both relentlessly criticized her about her weight, particularly during the stressful time when she was filming her television show, "All American Girl." In the film version of *I'm the One That I Want*, however, Cho almost never mentions her father. During the stand-up routine, Cho's father is only brought up at those moments when Cho is impersonating her mother; more important, throughout her entire career, Cho has never done an impersonation of her father.

Yet it is important to note that we aren't really seeing Mrs. Cho on stage: we are seeing Margaret's representation of her. Mrs. Cho is always mediated through

Margaret so that she herself is both hypervisible (the most famous and beloved part of Cho's stand-up) and also completely non-existent (most of Cho's audience wouldn't recognize Mrs. Cho if they saw her on the street). Cho's stand-up indicates the extent to which the public representation of Asian American subjectivity depends upon the presence and absence of an Asian American mother; Asian American motherhood simultaneously defines Asian American experience and yet is rendered completely invisible by it.

Ugly Asians

The tension between hypervisibility and invisibility that is present in *I'm the One That I Want* and that characterizes the history of Asian American motherhood reaches its apotheosis in *Battle Hymn of the Tiger Mother*. How exactly does *Battle Hymn* construct and represent Asian American motherhood?

The first chapter of the memoir seems to offer a capacious answer. On the second page, Chua announces that she uses the terms "Chinese mother" and "Western mother" "loosely." She "knows some Korean, Indian, Jamaican, Irish, and Ghanaian parents who qualify" as Chinese mothers; she also knows "some mothers of Chinese heritage, almost always born in the West, who are *not* Chinese mothers, by choice or otherwise" (4). Her prime example of how *anyone* can be a Chinese mother is the "working-class father" of a pointedly unnamed "supersuccessful white guy from South Dakota" whom we've seen on television (she is referencing Tom Brokaw). According to Chua, Brokaw's father was "definitely . . . a Chinese mother" (4). Chua's insistence on an anti-essential and anti-ethnocentric understanding of Chinese motherhood repeats itself at the book's end, when she makes the humorous claim that "politically correct Western social norms . . . are obviously stupid. And not even rooted historically. What are the origins of the Playdate anyway? Do you think our Founding Fathers had Sleepovers? I actually think America's Founding Fathers had Chinese values" (228). In two swift moves, Chua seems to co-opt two iconic symbols of American democracy and polity—the founders of the Republic and the evening newscaster who with the Voice of God reads the news to the nation every evening—into Chinese culture and Chinese motherhood.

In contrast, we can view Chua's unmooring of the term "Chinese"—from China, its current inhabitants, and those of Chinese descent—as an anti-essentializing move. However, the disavowals of essentialist notions of race based on biology that bookend *Battle Hymn* are completely contradicted by everything that appears in between these two moments. Indeed, two paragraphs after her anecdote about how even a "working-class" "white guy" can be a Chinese mother, Chua insists that there is a "marked and quantifiable difference" between "Chinese and Westerners when it comes to parenting" (5). In talking about the traditions and culturally accepted socially practices, Chua complains that as "the eldest daughter of Chinese immigrants, I don't have time to impro-vise or make up my own rules. I have a family name to uphold, aging parents to make proud. I like clear goals, and clear ways of measuring success" (26). These "clear goals" and "clear ways" inform the generational model that Chua presents for understanding ethnic and racial identity, one that is clearly based on the notion that culture and character are passed down from father to son, mother to daughter, over time and biologically. And this essentialism is not limited to being Chinese. Chua expresses relief when her mother-in-law expresses dismay at the selection of cheeses that Chua has picked out for a party; her mother-in-law's adherence to certain kinds of archaic, class-anxious niceties meant that "good taste ran in my daughters' genes" (99). Chua's vociferous and seemingly provocative championing of the "Chinese values" that inform Chinese mother-hood, then, is merely another way of re-inscribing the nation's racialized and racist notions of "blood."

More important, the Tom Brokaw and Founding Fathers anecdotes re-inforce gendered and racialized hierarchies of power, in which the West can lay imperialistic claim to Chinese values, but not the other way around. Brokaw can claim Chinese motherhood for his family, or Chua can insist that George Washington was really a Chinese mother, but this relationship between China and the West is, as always, highly asymmetrical; she cannot, for example, claim to be a Founding Father any more than one of her daughters can claim to be a "supersuccessful white guy" who appears on television. Rather than descry-ing this power asymmetry, however, Chua trumpets, because in it she can lay the foundation for her own inclusion at the expense of other Chinese. In her discussion of classical music—in which she explains why she prefers Western musical instruments (such as the violin and piano) to something like those of the gamelan, the Javanese musical instrument ensemble that has fascinated some Western composers—Chua opines that

> personally, I think [Claude] Debussy was just going through a phase, fetishizing the exotic. The same thing happened to Debussy's fellow Frenchmen Henry Rous-seau and Paul Gauguin. . . . A particularly disgusting variation of this phenom-enon can be found in modern-day California: men with Yellow Fever, who date only Asian women—sometimes dozens in a row—*no matter how ugly or which kind of Asian.* For the record, Jed did not date any Asian women before me. (41; emphasis mine)

I want to take some time with this passage, as I believe that it is crucial to unpacking how Chua constructs racial identity. Chua's critique of Debussy's ori-entalism is based on her assumption that he found the gamelan "exotic" and "foreign." And yet her very attitude toward the gamelan seems strikingly simi-lar to the one she attributes to Debussy. Chua dislikes the gamelan and other non-Western instrument ensembles because she finds their music to be "simple, unstructured, and repetitive" (41). Chua goes on to justify her preference by insisting that the difference between a gamelan instrumentation and the violin is "the difference between a bamboo hut, which has its charms, and the Palace of Versailles" (41). Setting aside the ridiculousness of the comparison, we are confronted not with an Asian American critic and the Orientalizing object of her critique but rather *two* approaches to the same Orientalist discourse. If we think of Orientalism as a system of knowledge for "making statements about [the Orient], authorizing view of it, describing it, by teaching it, settling it, ruling over it"[23] that enables the West to always retains a "positional superiority,"[24] then what we have here is Chua further cementing the power of Orientalism by dismissing those who (like Debussy, Rousseau, and Gauguin) are not attentive to the "correct" way to produce it. In other words, while it seems that Chua is critiquing the Orientalism of Debussy and his like-minded cohort, what she is actually doing is offering a competing and much more appealing version of it to her readers. The Orientalism embraced by Debussy and his ilk is based on a passing phase and is the spring of "disgusting" modern attitudes toward Asian women; the China that Chua offers is the opposite of that "simple, structured, and repetitive" Orient of previous generations. Chua figures China as a product that only the most discerning consumer would covet because her China only covets Western things to begin with.

It is not particularly surprising then that in this passage Chua moves so effortlessly from a critique of Asian "things" (instruments, huts) to Asian "women," as this is the very nature of imperialist discourse. In this passage, we catch a glimpse of what drives Chinese American maternity in *Battle Hymn of the Tiger Mother*: to build Chinese American motherhood on the exclusion of non-conforming/non-marketable Asian women, here described as "ugly," ethnically non-specific, and indistinguishable from each other. Chua dismisses these women for their lack of physical beauty and their inability to marry the right kind of man; rejection of them occurs at the same moment that she hastily insists that her husband never dated an Asian woman before he met her.

Two other passages give us a sense of the kind of exclusionary logics that motivate "Chinese mothers":

Of course, I also wanted Sophia to benefit from the best aspects of American society. I did not want her to end up like one of those *weird Asian automatons who feel so much pressure from their parents* that they kill themselves after coming in second on the national civil service exam. (8; emphasis mine)

In the waiting area, we saw Asian parents everywhere, pacing back and forth, *grim-faced* and *single-minded*. They seem so *unsubtle*, I thought to myself, *can they possibly love music*? Then it hit me that almost all the other parents were *foreigners* or *immigrants* and that music was a ticket for them, and I thought, I'm not like them. I don't have what it takes. (141–142; all emphasis mine)

Chua's Chinese motherhood is predicated on the exclusion of the "weird Asian automatons," the "grim-faced," "single-minded" Asian parents who are "so unsubtle" and clearly have no real love of classical music, and the dozens of "ugly," non-ethnically specific "Asian women" who have no choice but to date white men.

These are the figures that haunt Chua's Chinese American motherhood, that are called up uneasily and are rigorously—but never completely—dismissed. Chua is acutely aware of the presence of these Asian women and mothers, just as she is acutely aware of the fact that her narrative of Asian American mother-hood does not stand alone. Chua notes that there are a lot of "new books out there portraying Asian mothers as scheming, callous, overdriven people indifferent to their kids' true interest" (62). While it is unclear what texts exactly she is referencing, she does explicitly name three of the best-known examples of what she calls "epic" stories "about mother-daughter relationships spanning several generations" (30). These are Kingston's *The Woman Warrior*, Tan's *The Joy Luck Club*, and Chang's *Wild Swans*.[25] But the lineage that Chua constructs between herself and these predecessors is not premised on shared histories of exclusion, abuse, and miscommunication; rather, the way she understands these books is that they "all beat me to it" (33):

> At first, I was bitter and resentful, but then I got over it and came up with a new idea. Combining my law degree with my own family's background, I would write about law and ethnicity in the developing world. Ethnicity was my favorite thing to talk about anyway. Law and development, which very few people were studying at the time, would be my specialty. (33)

Chua's choice of career then is based on a resentment toward those Chinese American women who "beat her" toward sharing her story. Chua's statement suggests that there is a finite number of stories regarding Chinese American motherhood to be told and that these women beat her to "it." But the "it" that Kingston, Tan, and Chang have arrived at before Chua seems to consist of more than critical applause or popular adulation; "it" is the ability to define for an American reading audience what Asian American subjectivity is. This highly competitive, zero-sum conception of understanding racial identity constructs it as an object with market value; Kingston, Tan, and Chang have essentially put a product out before Chua can, necessitating her search for another "new idea" to present and market. This is a first glimpse into Chua's sense of Asian American identity: that is based on excluding others who might identify the same way because there is a limited audience for these stories. If racial identity is cultural capital, then these other Chinese American writers represent potential competition in the market for her own product: her Chinese American story. This market approach is affirmed by Chua's admission that she only went to law school "because I didn't want to go to medical school" and that once in law school she realized that she "didn't care about the rights of criminals the way others did. . . . I wasn't naturally skeptical and questioning. I just wanted to write down everything the professor said and memorize it" (31). The logic at work in Chua's decision to become a lawyer is the same logic that structures her understanding of identity, race, gender, class affiliation, musical instrument preferences, and the like. For Chua, these markers of selfhood are never socially produced, nor do they have material consequences on an individual or the people around her. Instead, what drives Chua's notion of identity is the market: It is up to "Chinese mothers" to teach their children what is valuable and to trade upon that value to the fullest extent possible.

This is the great irony of *Battle Hymn*, that for all of its proclamations about the "Chinese" versus "Western" way of approaching children, the text betrays a profound discomfort with a racial identity that is not built upon market principles. Sophia, Chua's older and more obedient daughter, triggers Chua's anxieties on the subject with a simple declaration:

> "Mommy—I'm not Chinese."
>
> "Yes, you are."
>
> "No, Mommy—you're the only one who thinks so. No one in China thinks I'm Chinese. No one in America thinks I'm Chinese."
>
> This bothered me intensely, but all I said was, "Well, they're all wrong. You *are* Chinese." (56–57)

Strikingly, this incident, which annoys and bothers Chua, is not explored in any further detail. Indeed, the text seems to move abruptly, without a passage break or explanation, to descriptions of Chua's preparation for Sofia's first big musical recital. Chua summarizes her preparations for the party: how she blew up the article in a local paper about Sophia's musical ability and had it framed; how she "invited more than a hundred people to the concert and planned a huge after-party; and finally, how she "bought Sofia her first full-length gown and new shoes" (57). Chua's perturbation at Sophia's forthright declaration, based on what she has experienced for herself and the pronouncements of others around, manifests itself in her immediate grounding of Sophia's Chinese-ness in material terms. Later in the book, Chua describes another party that she organizes in honor of another Sophia piano recital, and the litany of excess repeats almost exactly the previous description but increases the financial stakes: Sophia's dress is purchased from Barney's, the reception is held at the St. Regis Hotel, and Chua methodically lists all of the menu items she ordered (138).

The point I am trying to make here isn't that those Chinese and American individuals are right or wrong to call Sophia "not Chinese" but that Chua cannot understand identity in any way other than as a commodity that has a market value. Implicitly, she counters the charge that Sophia is not "really" Chinese by essentially going on an orgy of excessive acquisition, as if to *prove* to others as well as herself that her daughter is Chinese. Chua's obsessive repetition of these kinds of material details less than one hundred pages apart fits in David Harvey's explanation that neoliberalism delivers a "world of pseudo-satisfactions that [are] superficially exciting but [are] hollow at [their] core."[26] Chinese identity is about transactions, spectacles of consumerism; it's about buying a daughter a new dress at Barney's (presumably because David's Bridal is too déclassé) and making sure that hundreds of people are stuffed with raw oyster and Peking duck for the event.

Chua's construction of Asian American identity as based on its exchange value is inextricable from her narrative of motherhood. *Battle Hymn* espouses a decidedly neoliberal approach to Chinese American motherhood, transforming race into a commodity that can be coveted and offspring into assets that reveal a parent's economic, intellectual, and cultural worth. Chua's representation of how her own identity is wrapped up in her daughters' mastery of certain skills emblematizes David Eng's argument that "the possession of a child . . . has today become the sign of guarantee not only for family but also for full and robust citizenship—for being a fully realized political, economic, and social subject in American life."[27]

Conclusion

What does it mean to read Asian American texts in the age of late capital, in which neoliberalism seems to permeate every aspect of human life and Asian American authors seem as likely to embrace and financially exploit stereotypes about racial difference as to critique them? It is my contention that Chua's autobiography of Chinese American motherhood represents a shift in the popular construction of Asian American identity, from one that valorizes resistance and is glossolalic/elliptical in its articulation to one that founds itself on neoliberal notions of value/exchange and is profoundly and proudly monolithic in its construction of racial difference.

In this regard, *Battle Hymn of the Tiger Mother* calls into question many of the reading practices that undergird Asian American cultural critique. It behooves us to remember that Chua's memoir is both a textual object (something to be read and interpreted) as well as an expression of an agency that trades upon racial and gender codes/discourses as much as it is captive to them. Reading *Battle Hymn* means recognizing that Asian American racial formation is both imposed upon a racialized population and embraced and revised by Asian

Americans themselves for ends that may not be particularly liberalizing, radical, or politically complicated. *Battle Hymn of the Tiger Mother* is a text that attempts to control and appropriate narratives of racialized motherhood at the same time that it is simultaneously re-inscribed within racial and gender discourses that exceed and overwhelm it. Chua's memoir reminds us that Asian American racial formations are the product of a particular dialectic between what erin Khuê Ninh has called "the externally imposed 'assignation' of model minority status" and "the internally driven 'assertion' of that identification."[28] Chua uses Chinese American motherhood to transform race and offspring into commodities and assets that reveal a parent's economic, cultural, and political value to the state. Far from alienating American ideals, these Chinese American mothers produce productive, consumer subjects who can be easily disciplined by the state and its educational institutions. What Chua makes crystal clear is the fact that Asian American cultural producers are as implicated in the commodification of Asian American identity and cultural practices as any "mainstream" entity. Reading *Battle Hymn of the Tiger Mother* means recognizing that Asian American racial formation is both imposed upon a racialized population and embraced and revised by Asian Americans themselves.

NOTES

1　Amy Chua, "Why Chinese Mothers Are Superior," *Wall Street Journal*, January 8, 2011, http://online.wsj.com/news/articles/SB10001424052748704111504576059713528698754#articleTabs%3Dcomments.

2　*Today Show*, "Battle Hymn Tiger Mother," interview with Amy Chua, NBC, video on YouTube, Jan 4, 2012, http://www.youtube.com/watch?v=0PIhIDMFkWY.

3　Amy Chua, *Battle Hymn of the Tiger Mother* (New York: Penguin Press, 2011), 3. All further references to this book will be cited parenthetically in the text.

4　*Battle Hymn* was listed on *New York Times* bestseller list for eleven weeks. The *Hollywood Reporter* stated on January 26, 2011, that the producers of the film version of *The Joy Luck Club* were interested in acquiring the film rights.

5　Ayelet Waldman, "In Defense of the Guilty, Ambivalent, Preoccupied Western Mom," *Wall Street Journal*, January 16, 2011, http://www.wsj.com/articles/SB10001424052748703333504576080422577800488.

6　Janet Maslin, "But Will It All Make 'Tiger Mom' Happy?" *New York Times*, January 19, 2011, http://www.nytimes.com/2011/01/20/books/20book.html.

7　Jen Wang, "Battle Hymn of the Tiger Mother: You Hated the Excerpt, Now Read the Book," *Disgrasian* (blog), January 14, 2011, http://disgrasian.com/2011/01/battle-hymn-of-the-tiger-mother-you-hated-the-excerpt-now-read-the-book; Jeffrey Wang, "Mother, Superior?" *SF Gate*, January 13, 2001, http://www.sfgate.com/entertainment/article/Mother-superior-2383957.php.

8　Wesley Yang, "Paper Tigers," *New York Magazine*, May 8, 2011, http://nymag.com/news/features/asian-americans-2011-5.

9　Diane Johnson, "Finish That Homework!" *New York Review of Books*, August 18, 2011, http://www.nybooks.com/articles/archives/2011/aug/18/finish-that-homework-tiger-mother/?pagination=false.

10 Jodi Melamed, *Represent and Destroy: Rationalizing Violence in the New Racial Capitalism* (Minneapolis: University of Minnesota Press, 2011), 1.

11 Grace Wang, "On Tiger Mothers and Music Moms," *Amerasia Journal* 37, no. 2 (2011): 130.

12 Amy Kaplan, *The Anarchy of Empire in the Making of U.S. Culture* (Cambridge, MA: Harvard University Press, 2002), 4.

13 Jodi Kim, *Ends of Empire: Asian American Critique and the Cold War* (Minneapolis: University of Minnesota Press, 2010), 6.

14 Kaplan, *The Anarchy of Empire*, 16.

15 To name just a few examples, see Sau-ling C. Wong and Jeffrey J. Santa Ana, "Gender and Sexuality in Asian American Literature," *Signs* 25, no. 1 (1999): 171–226; Robert Lee, *Orientals: Asian American in Popular Culture* (Philadelphia: Temple University Press, 1999); Mary Ting Yi Lui, *The Chinatown Trunk Mystery: Murder, Miscegenation and other Dangerous Encounters in Turn-of-the-Century New York City* (Princeton, NJ: Princeton University Press, 2005); Jinqi Ling, "Identity Crisis and Gender Politics: Reappropriating Asian American Masculinity," in *An Interethnic Companion to Asian American Literature*, ed. King-Kok Cheung (Cambridge: Cambridge University Press, 1997), 312–337.

16 Lee, *Orientals*, 89.

17 Yufing Cho, "Yellow Slavery, Narratives of Rescue, and Sui Sin Far/Edith Maude Eaton's 'Lin John,'" *Journal of Asian American Studies* 12, no. 1 (2009): 39.

18 The supposed sexual immorality of Chinese women was inextricably linked to the space of Chinatown itself, which was imagined as a den of vice, where white women fell into the clutches of "white slavery" and where the sanctity of Christian marriage was under threat by deviant Chinese men and "fallen" Chinese women. Literary works such as Frank Norris's short story "The Third Circle" reinforced the pervasive notion that Chinatown was a threat to innocent American women. See Frank Norris, "The Third Circle," in *The Third Circle*, introduction by Will Irwin (New York: John Lane, 1909).

19 According to Iris Chang, in 1880, the male-to-female ratio in the Chinese community in America was approximately twenty to one: 100,686 men to 4,779 women. By 1920, the overall Chinese population had shrunk owing to the exclusion laws, as well as to deaths and departures, but Chinese men still outnumbered Chinese women by about seven to one. Iris Chang, *The Chinese in America: A Narrative History* (New York: Penguin, 2003), 173.

20 Christina Tourino, "Ethnic Reproduction and the Amniotic Deep: Joy Kogawa's *Obasan*," *Frontiers: A Journal of Women Studies* 24, no. 1 (2003): 135.

21 Maxine Hong Kingston, *The Woman Warrior* (New York: Random House, 1975); Amy Tan, *The Joy Luck Club* (New York: Putnam's, 1989).

22 Margaret Cho, *I'm the One That I Want* (New York: Ballantine, 2001).

23 Edward Said, *Orientalism* (New York: Vintage, 1979), 3.

24 Ibid., 7.

25 Jung Chang, *Wild Swans: Three Daughters of China* (New York: Simon & Schuster).

26 David Harvey, *A Brief History of Neoliberalism* (New York: Oxford University Press, 2006), 170.

27 David Eng, "Transnational Adoption and Queer Diasporas," *Social Text* 21, no. 3 (2003): 7–8.

28 erin Khuê Ninh, *Ingratitude: The Debt-Bound Daughter in Asian American Literature* (New York: NYU Press, 2011), 10.

5

YouTube Made the TV Star

KevJumba's Star Appearance on The Amazing Race 17

VINCENT PHAM AND KENT A. ONO

Growing up in Houston, Texas, and participating in the mundane activities of a college prep teenager, Kevin Wu created an online persona and YouTube channel, "Kevjumba." Drawn to YouTube because of its surfeit of dance videos, Wu first posted his own dance video on February 6, 2007, but garnered few "views." On a whim, and inspired by mainstream comedians, he then uploaded a comedic video and was eventually featured on YouTube's homepage, vaulting him into Internet stardom. Over the course of eight years, Wu became an influential YouTube star, a pioneer of Asian American Web 2.0 culture, and a producer of one of the most popular YouTube channels, with 2.99 million subscribers and approximately 357 million views of his channel (as of June 11, 2015).

KevJumba's fan following and subsequent mainstream popularity provided Kevin Wu with opportunities offline, gaining attention from both brand marketers and networks—traditional media outlets.[1] iStardom, Inc., identified Kev-Jumba as a 2008 top-ten Web entertainer, ranking him no. 9.[2] Daisy Whitney, TelevisionWeek's new media reporter and host of "New Media Minute," explains why such organizations might be interested in the highly visible Wu: "Brand marketers, production companies, and traditional media should pay attention to who's hot online and find creative ways to partner with them."[3] In the same year that iStardom identified KevJumba's brand potential, HBOLab, an online subsidiary of Home Box Office studios, launched a scripted webseries titled, *Hooking Up*, featuring YouTube stars Lonelygirl15, sxePhil, and KevJumba.[4] While the series title refers to the informal romantic relations between younger people, it also refers to the possibility that YouTube stardom may create opportunities outside it. The move from YouTube to more mainstream media contexts is part of vertical integration, but like all media productions there is risk, success is not assured, and stardom in one medium does not guarantee equivalent stardom in another.

While the Internet presence of Asian Americans is substantial, in mainstream and offline media spaces Asian American representation is either sparse or degrading, or both, reproducing problematic racial caricatures, stereotypes, and discourses of mockery.[5] By examining Asian American online media superstardom, we explore the central question that has to be asked about Asian American media representation and new media: Has the overall condition and situation for Asian Americans changed as a result of the prevalence of new media? In order to investigate this question, we focus on YouTube superstar (and, in Internet-time and parlance, "legend") KevJumba and his foray into reality television, in which he and his fellow superstar father appeared on *The Amazing Race 17* (hereafter, *TAR17*). Scholars have focused on crossover media—the transition of figures from the Internet into older forms of media—but they have not studied the effects of *multimedia migration*—the migration of Internet stars across various media platforms who use their Internet celebrity to inhabit other genres and media platforms, such as television, but also then return to and maintain their Internet stardom.[6] By studying Kevin Wu's migration from YouTube to *TAR17* and back to YouTube, we emphasize the interanimation, interdependence, and integration of media culture and institutions and the interplay between representation and self-representation.

Specifically, we consider Wu's migrations to and from YouTube, cable network's online spaces, and broadcast television, specifically focusing on KevJumba and his father's appearance on *TAR17*. Instead of focusing solely on Wu's crossover, we are also interested in how he negotiates the way his character is portrayed on *TAR17* in relation to his own, self-produced Internet persona, KevJumba. By illustrating Kevin Wu's success as a media convergent figure, ultimately we suggest that Asian American media convergence risks falling into traditional model minority exceptionalist representations with the resulting effect of diminishing the mainstream media's overall impact on Asian American representation but also allows for continued Asian American self-representation on the Internet on their own terms.

Media Convergence and Its Asian American Condition

The specific advent of YouTube has altered communities. While YouTube's early success involved the illegal exhibition of copyrighted material, the crux of YouTube's current success arguably revolves around the technical ease of accessing material and the possibility of profit by producing and uploading videos. YouTube is a video-archiving and -streaming application that affords relatively easy access for viewers, consumers, and producers. As a technology, it allows for the easy upload of videos to the Internet, without the costly purchase or rental of servers and without having to build a website. As a streaming medium, people can easily view videos without having to download large files. As a result, YouTube has become the primary Internet repository of uploaded video content.[7] Importantly, viewers can communicate with other viewers via comment streams, even with the content creator. Thus communities build up around media content, whereas traditional and older media technologies such as television and cinema (as discrete media) lack the ease and back-and-forth of this Internet community-building function.

Because of the lack of cost and the ease of uploading and viewing diverse content (both licit and illicit), and because of its diverse and global reach, YouTube has also been a fan favorite for (among other groups) Asian Americans. Asian Americans have used new media spaces to form identities and representations in mainstream media for some time; thus, perhaps it is not coincidental that Asian American media stardom is prevalent on YouTube, a pattern that has not gone unnoticed by the popular press.[8] In a 2007 *AsianWeek* article, Arabella Santiago states that "building community, making a living and showcasing talent are just some of the things the land of YouTube has to offer," providing examples of Christine Gambito, Ryan Higa, David Choi, and Kevin Wu as pioneers of this trend, all who have garnered a large base of subscribed viewers to their YouTube channels.[9] In a July 29, 2011, *New York Times* article, journalist Austin Considine highlights the prevalence of Asian American YouTube stars, noting the comparative lack of equivalent Hollywood roles.[10] Yet the popular press tends to overlook the attempts, successes, and failures of stars who have crossed from YouTube to the mainstream and YouTube's interconnectedness with the mainstream, which has become a significant dimension of contemporary Asian American media representational culture.[11]

Partly owing to their successes on YouTube and the larger Web 2.0 environment, web stars have attempted to migrate into more traditional media environments, away from the Internet.[12] A profoundly important dimension of crossing over has to do with stars' ability to maintain the integrity of their performance and identity, which sometimes means a struggle to control the process of the crossover, negotiations over contracts, and the relationship between the way an online persona circulates in relation to the way the persona circulates in more mainstream and traditional venues.[13]

One example of such success, both in forming previously unseen identities and crossing over to the mainstream, is Tila Tequila, the *MySpace* personality turned reality television star. Lisa Nakamura's study of Tila Tequila's popularity as the "first Internet star" illustrates the perils and possibilities of Web 2.0. Nakamura points to Tila Tequila's celebrity persona as a "bisexual Asian woman fleeing religious repression, poverty, and urban violence" and her constant referencing of her *MySpace* fans and popularity as an example of a simultaneously "user-generated" and "self-made" creative subject.[14] However, Tila Tequila's celebrity is attributed to a "diasporic and polysexual" racialized subjectivity that she has created. That is, her subjectivity led to popularity, which was then converted into and sold as hypersexual subjectivity, subsequently appearing on mainstream reality television. Tila Tequila is an example of online success leading to broadcast television success, only to have the newfound success supplant and ultimately redefine her stardom, instead of merely supplementing and sustaining her online stardom. Once her mainstream popularity faded, however, she ultimately disappeared from media culture.

Even if Internet celebrities do move into mainstream media, which sometimes results in failure, this has not stopped stars from making an attempt, hoping their audiences will follow them from medium to medium. Henry Jenkins defines media convergence as a cultural shift that "involves both a change in the way media is produced and a change in the way media is consumed."[15] While media convergence also refers to audience consumptive habits, we are primarily concerned with other aspects of convergence, particularly with the content produced and shared across multiple media.[16] Indeed, media industries recognize this and seek to facilitate "the flow of content across multiple media platforms, the cooperation between multiple media industries, and the migratory behavior of media audiences who will go almost anywhere in search of the kinds of entertainment experiences they want."[17] This action by consumers, who are "encouraged to seek out new info and make connections among dispersed media content," and the communities and relationships shaped by this active audience agency are expedited by a Web 2.0 context and technologies in which social, participatory, and user-generated media dominate and blur media boundaries.[18] Thus, if audiences want to find out more about their favorite celebrities or watch them perform, there appears to be little to stop them.

Given the ease of migration across media platforms and on- and offline contexts, it is no wonder that once celebrities have crossed over from YouTube into mainstream and traditional media, they may maintain their successful online star persona. The use of online platforms (and their low barrier to entry) can be seen as a transitional step to ultimate mainstream popularity and celebrity. Similar to "return migration," eventually media "migrants" may go back to YouTube with newfound knowledge learned and experiences gained from mainstream performances.[19] Indeed, if we now live in a media-convergent world, the question "Who drives convergence and cooperation between media industries?" is less important than "What might this media migration look like for an Internet star?" and "What does this afford those who crisscross back and forth among multiple media platforms?" While Jenkins argues that "everyone will survive if everyone works together," will we all survive (or thrive) equally?[20]

To explore these questions, we compare the representation of TeamJumba on *TAR17* to KevJumba's summary and commentary of his progress on his YouTube channel. First, we describe the format and the structure of the television show before describing the representation of Kevin Wu on the series. Then we study KevJumba's "recap" videos on his YouTube channel about his presence on *TAR17*. In our analysis, we suggest that, while mainstream media frame the persona of KevJumba in one fashion on television, KevJumba re-narrates his actions on TV using his YouTube channel and, hence, retains and contributes to the construction of his own persona as he crosses over to the mainstream and back.

Enter TeamJumba!

In a September 7, 2010, post, KevJumba announced that the rumors were true that he and his dad, PapaJumba (real name Michael), were to appear on the seventeenth season of *The Amazing Race*. Thus KevJumba was to join a line of other Asian Americans in reality television.[21] *The Amazing Race*, a well-known and highly rated reality television show, requires contestants to accomplish tasks that lead them on a quest around the world. In teams of two, contestants apply to be on the show, completing a thirteen-page application that asks them to characterize themselves and their teammates and their attitudes toward traveling, in addition to asking them to provide other personal information. Previous Asian American teams featured the brothers Erwin and Godwin Cho, the married couple Joe and Heidi Wang, the siblings Tamara and Victor Jih, and father and daughter Ron and Christina Hsu. For TeamJumba, the introduction of an Asian American father/son duo that also creates online media content for millions of viewers is a novel story plugged into a reality television formula.

Each episode of *TAR17* follows a formulaic structure. First, each episode is organized around one stage in the race. To reach the end of the stage, teams must complete a series of tasks, except for "roadblocks," which one member must complete without the assistance of the other team member. Second, the episode tracks the progress of the teams, using the leading team to describe the roadblocks and tasks as they encounter them and the lagging teams to demonstrate the difficulty of the tasks. Thus the trials and tribulations of each team, their interpersonal relationships, and their successful and (in)efficient completion of the tasks create the sense of drama and suspense within the show. Finally, the first team to complete the stage sometimes wins an extra prize (such as a trip or vacation) and is allowed to begin the next stage first. The second team to arrive is then the second team to begin the next stage, and so on. The last team, however, is often (although not always) eliminated from the race.

Given the structure of the episodes and nature of the show, the majority of the time is spent moving from one task to another, giving the show a feel of urgency. Importantly, the screen time is divided up among the initial eleven teams from the outset to the three in the final stage. Since each episode is approximately forty-three minutes long (without advertisements), this limits the amount of continuous screen time for each team. Teams are often shown in short segments, approximately five to ten seconds long, as they rush from one point to another in an attempt to complete the stage quickly. However, teams that struggle and succeed often have more screen time. In either case, the theme of the "race" and episode structure affects the amount of total screen time for each contestant.

The reality show formula often constructs Asian Americans in narrow ways. Grace Wang investigates race and representation in reality television programs such as *Top Chef* and *Project Runway*.[22] Conceiving of the concept "technical robot" as a kind of typecast character that exists within the reality TV genre—unfeeling, technical, and machine-line—she argues that Asian American performance is held to a technocratic standard of evaluation. She finds that a meritocratic standard of evaluating Asians and Asian Americans within the reality TV setting is employed, and the racial approach taken aims for race neutrality, even as it functions to racialize narratives of Asian American performance. To some extent, TeamJumba is held to such a requirement.

The structure of the show, the fragmented way it features characters, and assumptions regarding reality television shows influence viewers' perceptions of the show and its characters. Rachel Dubrofsky argues that reality television shows and their structure are dependent on and circulate a "rhetoric of realism," producing a narrative form and discursive content that, together, promote the idea that these are "real" people doing "real" things.[23] Thus *TAR17* constructs participants as everyday people who apply to be on the show and are selected for audiences' viewing pleasure. However, Dubrofsky argues that we should understand that the characters on reality television are not "real" people per se as much as they are discursive constructions narrated, in part, by a television host and framed by selected footage and sound bites. Since the structure of *TAR17* favors interpersonal conflicts and the difficulty or ease in completing tasks, utterances of frustration and joy during the show are condensed into five-to-ten-second shots that eventually add up to roughly three to five minutes of screen time per episode. These fragments, as constructed by *TAR17*, shape viewer understandings of each team, including Kevin and Michael Wu, and help frame audiences' judgments about the relationship of, in their case, a second-generation Asian American son and his first-generation Asian American father.

For audiences unfamiliar with Internet star "KevJumba," the story of the father-son team of Michael and Kevin Wu is a common and familiar narrative of intergenerational and intercultural clash. In Episode 1, Michael and Kevin are described as a father-and-son team who are "Internet sensations from Sugarland, Texas." In their introduction, Kevin utilizes the narrative to explain the uniqueness of their team, mistakenly stating that "what's funny about us is that he's an immigrant and I'm this first-generation Asian American, and we sort of have [these] conflicting cultures, and when people see it on camera, it's funny." Kevin Wu's mistaken generational categorization frames him as "American" against his father as "foreign." Thus, the narrative of cultural and generational clash is how the *TAR17* audiences and those unfamiliar to KevJumba come to view him.

Yet the show's construction of Kevin and Michael Wu differs from their Internet YouTube construction as KevJumba and PapaJumba. Thus the mainstream audiences (and those who do not migrate over to watch KevJumba on his YouTube channel) might understand Kevin as an overly competitive and sometimes disrespectful son who often uses a condescending tone and has a know-it-all attitude toward his father, vocally expressing a lack of confidence in his father's abilities. Even while his father struggles at particular roadblocks, Kevin's words of encouragement can also be understood to be disingenuous. This is evident throughout the season but particularly in episode 7, in which Kevin and Michael are ultimately eliminated.

Episode 7's coverage of Kevin and Michael is extensive and concentrated, given that they suffered a series of missteps eventually leading to their elimination. The majority of TeamJumba's screen time focuses on Michael's struggles and Kevin's exasperations. In one moment of foreshadowing, Michael advises Kevin to "read every clue carefully." Quickly solving the mysteries and looking like the inevitable winners of the stage, they encounter difficulty as the final task, which is to complete three rounds of the Russian game of *gorodki*. Michael takes a roadblock challenge, requiring him to toss a bat at a stick arrangement. While the first to arrive at this task, Kevin and his father are the second from last to complete it. Unable to help, Kevin is relegated to watching and speaking to his father, who struggles to complete the task. At one point, Michael chuckles uncomfortably, only to have Kevin respond curtly, "I don't think this is funny," to which Michael replies, "I don't think this is funny either," attempting to assuage him. Kevin mutters to the camera, "We're gonna get last because of this," as he walks away with his hands on his hips. Michael manages to complete the task after an hour. They pay the taxi and proceed to the end of the stage, only to find that they have broken two rules (utilizing the taxi as both a guide and for transportation). As they await their penalty, Kevin looks over the clue and then buries his face into the sheet as he lets out an "Oh." Michael asks, "What does it say?" and reads out loud, "You must walk to your next destination." Kevin says, "I didn't even see that." With a slight chuckle, his dad replies, "You didn't read it," alluding to his earlier advice to "read every clue carefully." As a result of the penalties associated with this mistake, they come in last place and thus are eliminated from the show.[24] As they check in, Michael comments, "We done our best. If we're last, we're last," only to have Phil Keogan (the host) reply with, "Your son, on the other hand, doesn't look too happy" (see fig. 5.1). This representation and construction of Kevin as a disrespectful son, having little faith or confidence in his father's abilities, and stubborn in his belief that he knows what is best for the team, is what drives their narrative arc within the show while inverting the stereotypical trope of an overbearing Asian father. Rather, Michael is seen as a laid-back and enthusiastic father who chooses to participate with his son in order to strengthen and forge a better relationship.

Even though the story about Kevin and Michael Wu is primarily one of intergenerational and intercultural negotiation, the show also relies on the model minority myth as a backdrop and implicitly constructs the Asian Americans on the show as hyperintelligent. In episode 3, Kevin states a main concern that "physically, it's hard for us to match up with these other teams who are in their

The Amazing Race 17 - A Disappointed Kevin

CBS · 56,862 videos

Subscribe 510,639

23,948

112 11

Figure 5.1. Screenshot of Kevin Wu after finishing last place. Titled and uploaded by CBS.

20s or 30s. . . . We just have to play smart . . . experience these different countries." For them, the competition requires a strategy of deploying intellect to compensate for their physical disadvantage. In the following episode, while the teams are waiting at the airport for a flight they are all scheduled to take, Kevin and Michael reschedule to an earlier flight in order to arrive at the destination earlier. The other Asian American participant is part of the team of doctors who also find an earlier flight via an Internet cafe. While discussing which teams made it on the earlier flight, Katie and Rachel, the team of white female volleyball teammates, know Michael and Kevin as "the Asians." They are seen as exceptional (being the oldest and youngest participants on *TAR17*) and as relying on composite intellect as opposed to physical prowess.

While *TAR* depends on, and profits from, a notion of "real people" doing "real" tasks that lead to their "true" selves being revealed on television, Internet personas in the genre of videoblogging also purport to be "real." After each *TAR17* episode, Kevin Wu posted a video on his KevJumba YouTube channel to speak to his 2.6 million subscribers. Thus, there are competing and complimentary realisms—one circulating within mainstream media and another circulated by Kevin Wu on his YouTube channel.

The Amazing Race on KevJumba

Since the attention span of a YouTube viewer might be relatively short, each of the *TAR17* recap videos that KevJumba uploaded to this YouTube channel after each episode of *TAR17* ranged between four and five minutes in length. Each video summarizes the main events of the *TAR17* episode, with the TeamJumba segments re-edited into one continuous viewing experience that focuses only on TeamJumba. The amount and type of narration per episode varies. The shortest narration occurs in the video titled, "We're Not Ghana [*sic*] Make It," which replays the story of Michael's difficulties on the show in its entirety. In this recap, there is no narration except for in the final twenty seconds of the video, when Kevin thanks his dad for "being awesome." For the most part, the narration is peppered throughout the recap videos and uses an informal conversational tone that circulates a different discursive construction of Kevin Wu on *TAR17*.

In a conversational tone, KevJumba's recounts his actions on *TAR17* and challenges the show's construction of him. He employs three types of commentary that we characterize as justifications, recognitions, and remixes. For instance, he justifies (but does not take blame for) the decisions he and his father made on the show, especially questionable decisions or ones that might lead to viewers reacting. For example, while the rules of the "Russian Mystery" episode required them to ask locals for help, they were penalized when they asked their taxi driver. In the video, Kevin sarcastically states, "Apparently taxi drivers aren't locals, we had no idea." In talking about the second penalty, which they incurred when they used the taxi for transportation, KevJumba states, "We didn't know that the previous rules . . . about walking applied to this part as well." He concludes by adding, "A few other teams made the same mistake," thus contextualizing his understanding and suggesting that mistakes were not uncommon.

While justifications explain decisions, recognitions are self-reflexive, acknowledging the seemingly questionable decisions or brash actions done on the show. For example, KevJumba explicitly mentions his mistakes. In the task categorized as "classic music or classic cinema," he confidently thought his experience with YouTube videos would make the task easy to accomplish. Upon discovering that it required him to sort through rolls of film, he quickly follows by saying, "I was wrong," using straightforward remarks to justify his actions but then realizing that rationalizing preventable errors is ridiculous. For example, when they are trekking through snowy Sweden, Kevin wears ankle socks. The viewer might wonder, "Why in the world would he wear ankle socks?" to which KevJumba replies, "Ankle socks are cool, that's why I wore them. Yeah. You're right. I probably should have worn thicker socks." The realization of his error in wearing ankle socks in Sweden establishes a connection between his audience and him, expressing his self-reflective realization. This shows viewers that KevJumba, while occasionally arrogant and overconfident, is still "one of us," able to make faults and mistakes and laugh about it.

While justifications and recognitions rely on verbal narration to reshape audience understanding of Kevin and Michael Wu's involvement with *TAR17*, remixes manipulate and reshape our understanding of KevJumba and his involvement with *TAR17* by using audio and image manipulation. Wu re-edits original *TAR* footage, using repetition and slow motion and providing a different soundtrack to imagine it as a comedic effect. By deploying the humor that has helped make him an Internet sensation, KevJumba uses remixing to alter our engagement with the mainstream footage. Remixing only occurs in the "I fell in love with a Russian babushka" video recap. In it, an older Russian woman with a headscarf tied under her chin gives him a kiss on the cheek—the clue to the next task. KevJumba intersperses *TAR17* footage with footage of him saying, "After I made love to the Russian babushka . . ." He then puts his head down as the video cuts over to remixed footage of Kevin being kissed, while the "babushka" says, "I love you." The *TAR17* footage shows Kevin rubbing the side of his cheek in slow motion while Marvin Gaye's "Let's Get It On" plays in the background. Neither fully a justification nor a self-reflective admission of error, this remix transforms *TAR17* footage into a KevJumba YouTube artifact. Thus he manipulates, remixes, and reframes mainstream *TAR17* footage from his appearance on the show into a video that he uploads onto his YouTube channel for his subscribers, using his mainstream appearance on *TAR17* and bringing it into his Internet star context.

KevJumba: The Convergent and Spreadable Star

The migration from Internet sites to mainstream ones has been fraught with perilous possibilities. In previous work, we explored the negotiation between mainstream and independent as Asian American media producers crossed over independent to the mainstream contexts.[25] Currently, YouTube and other social media make it possible to migrate to and from non-mainstream (i.e., Internet) to mainstream contexts. Other YouTube stars have also followed the path (or blazed in parallel) with KevJumba. Michelle Phan has parlayed her makeup tutorials into her own cosmetics line with L'Oreal and a 2014 Diet Dr. Pepper Super Bowl advertisement. The Fung Brothers' comedy sketches—food tributes to Asian American culture, with nearly one million subscribers (as of June 11, 2015)—have led to the launching of a food and travel show, *What the Fung?!* broadcast in May 2015 on the FYI network.[26] Distribution, content creation, and audience reach that in the past were only possible within the mainstream are now readily available for aspiring YouTube stars to use for YouTube communities and to break into the mainstream.

YouTube, thus, helps flatten power relations, which requires an implicit and explicit understanding of both mainstream and new media content production. Producers of *TAR17* likely assumed KevJumba's stardom would help draw Internet viewers to television by KevJumba's mere appearance on the reality show. Producers bypassed the regular application process in order to get him on the show, and he was younger than the standard minimum age of twenty-one. KevJumba explained how he and his father came to be on the show, stating briefly, "We were asked to be on the show, and we didn't know how to respond." While *TAR17* gained access to KevJumba, KevJumba also gained access to mainstream audiences and other benefits associated with the mainstream. Neither the mainstream broadcast television nor the Internet star became solely exploited; rather, the mutual use of each media for the sake of its own stars and platforms became the practice, an example of media convergence and spreadable media.[27]

Considering that YouTube videoblogging and reality television thrive on the perception that their characters are "real," the migration to *TAR17* was not considerably difficult, yet the representational stakes differed. Kevin Wu had a "*TAR17* persona," just like he has a "YouTube persona." The difference is that *TAR17* had the ability and right to construct Kevin Wu and his father discursively. In contrast, Kevin Wu controls the production of his Internet stardom. He actively integrates footage from *TAR17* into his YouTube videos (see fig. 5.2). His YouTube commentary provides a competing reality that also makes adjustments to his own Internet persona as it manipulates the image of him appearing on mainstream television. While *TAR17* portrays Wu as an overconfident, sometimes seemingly disrespectful college student, on YouTube he appears as a thoughtful and considerate son who is cognizant of, and able to make fun of, his own flaws.

Thus, KevJumba's presence on *TAR17* is a unique case of media convergence, one in which a YouTube star's migration to broadcast television and back to his YouTube channel seems to have benefited both parties. Kevin Wu's appearance on the seventeenth season of *The Amazing Race* increased his Internet audience and brought his KevJumba Internet celebrity status into a traditional offline and formulaic reality show format. In bringing KevJumba into *TAR17*, the reality show relied on narrative constructions of intergenerational and intercultural negotiation and model minorities that is so much a part of historical-mainstream representations often associated with the use, exploitation, and ultimate discarding of marginal stars for profit.

However, because of his ability to self-represent himself on his own channel, KevJumba was able to dictate the terms of that representation by reconfiguring and reshaping his representation on TV for his YouTube audience. His repeated migration to and from reality television and his YouTube channel elucidates the

Figure 5.2. Screenshot of KevJumba YouTube channel playlist of TAR17 clips.

dangers and difficulty of mainstream media representation as it attempts to fit him into well-worn tropes. More important, the crisscrossing between TV and YouTube provides multiple points of engagement for both KevJumba's YouTube fans and the *TAR17* audience, allowing for his self-representation to permeate in ways that protects his YouTube stardom through his creative remixing. While he appeared on *TAR17*, KevJumba retained his Internet stardom, possibly added mainstream audiences to his already robust Internet audience, and gained useful experience working on a mainstream television network production.

After *TAR17*, Kevin Wu continued producing videos for his KevJumba YouTube channel and joined the newly formed YouTube network YOMYOMF (You Offend Me, You Offend My Family), which was initiated by *Fast and Furious* film director Justin Lin in June 2012.[28] In July 2014, he posted a video blog called "Growing Up," directly addressing his audience about how he has grown up with his audience over the last seven years and thanking them for this "relationship," even as he distances himself from YouTube by making sometimes unpopular choices (like growing a mullet hairstyle) and, more important, by pursuing other creative projects. Since *TAR17*, Wu has written, produced, and acted in two independent features, *Hang Loose* (2012), co-starring Dante Basco, and *Man Up* (2015), co-starring Justin Chon, and he has experimented with alternative modes of video distribution while he takes a hiatus from YouTube.

At the end of this process of negotiating the spur-of-the-moment interanimation of traditional offline media with online content epitomized by his involvement with *TAR17*, it was simply Kevin Wu making videos and hanging out with his father. It is in this hanging out—this collaborative and humorous YouTube father/son duo migration to mainstream media—that we can see Kevin and Michael Wu's impact. TeamJumba is a rare representation of an actual son and father on television. While it is subject to the formula of father/son intergenerational, intercultural negotiation and model minority discourses, it disrupts them through KevJumba's YouTube videos and elimination on the *TAR17*. Ultimately, it domesticates television not by reproducing norms, per se, but by figuring Asian American men, their bonding, and their relationship not only on a reality television show but also in the reality of a self-produced and self-represented YouTube channel.

NOTES

1 We refer to KevJumba as Kevin Wu's online persona. While KevJumba implies Kevin Wu, it also functions as a brand cultivated for consumption.

2 *Business Wire*, "2008 Web Celebrity Rankings Announced by iStardom," January 7, 2009, http://www.businesswire.com/news/home/20090107005444/en/2008-Web-Celebrity-Rankings-Announced-iStardom, accessed June 11, 2015.

3 Ibid.

4 Lindsay Stidham, "'Hooking Up'—Did HBOLab's Web Celeb Experiment Work?" *Tubefilter*, November 7, 2008, http://www.tubefilter.com/2008/11/07/hooking-up-did-hbolabs-web-celeb-experiment-work, accessed June 11, 2015.

5 Kent A. Ono and Vincent Pham, *Asian Americans and the Media* (Malden, MA: Polity, 2009); Vincent N. Pham and Kent A. Ono, "'Artful Bigotry and Kitsch': A Study of Stereotype, Mimicry, and Satire in Asian American T-Shirt Rhetoric," in *Representations: Doing Asian American Rhetoric.*, ed. LuMing Mao and Morris Young, 175–197 (Logan: Utah State University Press, 2008).

6 Lisa Nakamura, "Cyberrace," *PMLA* 123, no. 5 (2008): 1673–1682; Ono and Pham, *Asian Americans and the Media.*

7 Jean Burgess and Joshua Green, *YouTube: Online Video and Participatory Culture* (Malden, MA: Polity, 2009). Burgess and Green argue that mainstream media characterized YouTube as a "lawless repository for a flood of amateur content or as a big player in the new economy" (15).

8 Ono and Pham, *Asian Americans and the Media.*

9 Arabella Santiago, "YouTube, Land of the Brave Asian American," *AsianWeek: The Voice of Asian America*, December 26, 2007, http://www.asianweek.com/2007/12/26/youtube-land-of-the-brave-asian-american, accessed June 11, 2015.

10 Austin Considine, "For Asian-American Stars, Many Web Fans," *New York Times*, July 29, 2011, http://www.nytimes.com/2011/07/31/fashion/for-asian-stars-many-web-fans.html, accessed June 11, 2015.

11 Stidham, "Hooking Up." HBOLab experimented with cross-pollinating audiences by backing a scripted webseries (*Hooking Up*) with resources from a major production company, collaborating with YouTube stars but operating in the margins of HBO.

12 Mario Dumual, "Fil-Am YouTube Star Is New DOT Ambassador," *The Pinoy*, January 24, 2008, http://thepinoy.net/?p=1081, accessed November 4, 2015. Christine Gambito, "About," *HappySlip*, June 11, 2015, https://www.youtube.com/user/HappySlip/about, accessed June 11, 2015. Christine Gambito, also known as HappySlip, was appointed ambassador for Philippine tourism by the Department of Tourism in 2008. Before YouTube, She was also a Screen Actors Guild–American Federation of Television and Radio Artists (SAG-AFTRA) actress landing parts in television commercials and movies.

13 Arjun Appadurai, "Disjuncture and Difference in the Global Cultural Economy," *Public Culture* 2, no. 2 (1990): 1–24. Appadurai describes mediascapes not only as the technological capability to produce and disseminate information and images of the world but also, importantly, as the distribution of this capability (9). That is, who are the people, and what

companies have the ability to create the media images around us and distribute that image? And, more important, what interest might they have?

14 Nakamura, "Cyberrace," 1680.

15 Henry Jenkins, *Convergence Culture: Where Old and New Media Collide* (New York: NYU Press, 2006), 16.

16 Amanda D. Lotz, *The Television Will Be Revolutionized* (New York: NYU Press, 2007); Lauren Rabinovitz, "Sitcoms and Single Moms: Representations of Feminism on American TV," *Cinema Journal* 29, no. 1 (1989): 3–19. Rabinovitz's study explores the interrelationship of media consumption experience, particularly on how "the televisual framework" of sitcoms activates other text (16). Lotz's work tracks the technological influences on the creation, distribution, consumption, and control of content.

17 Jenkins, *Convergence Culture*, 2.

18 Ibid., 3. "Web 2.0" refers to the current context of user-generated, collaborative, and social action nature of the Internet. There, however, have always been niche audiences that openly and freely criss-crossed media spheres, like fan communities who participate and have participated in vernacular and mainstream communities. For instance, see the following works on participatory culture: Henry Jenkins, *Textual Poachers: Television Fans and Participatory Culture*, 2nd ed. (New York: Routledge, 2012); and Constance Penley, "Feminism, Psychoanalysis, and the Study of Popular Culture," in *Cultural Studies*, ed. Lawrence Grossberg, Cary Nelson, and Paula A. Treichler, 479–500 (New York: Routledge, 1992).

19 Wei Li and Lucia Lo, "New Geographies of Migration? A Canada-U.S. Comparison of Highly Skilled Chinese and Indian Migration," *Journal of Asian American Studies* 15, no. 1 (2012): 1–34; Lisong Liu, "Return Migration and Selective Citizenship: A Study of Returning Chinese Professional Migrants from the United States," *Journal of Asian American Studies* 15, no. 1 (2012): 35–68. Interestingly, migration across platforms and on- and offline spaces metaphorically parallels certain parts of Asian American migration history, like Asian American workers and immigrants who may have families that have or who may have themselves crossed oceans and borders to (for instance) escape persecution or to pursue the "American dream." See Li and Lo, "New Geographies of Migration?" and Liu, "Return Migration and Selective Citizenship," for more information about reverse migration and its effects on emerging economies, nationality, and citizenship.

20 Jenkins, *Convergence Culture*, 10.

21 Yul Kwon is the most notable reality TV star, winning the competitive *Survivor: Cook Islands* reality show in 2006.

22 Grace Wang, "A Shot at Half-Exposure: Asian Americans in Reality TV Shows," *Television and New Media* 11, no. 5 (2010): 404–427.

23 Rachel Dubrofsky, "*The Bachelor*: Whiteness in the Harem." *Critical Studies in Media Communication* 23, no. 1 (2006): 41.

24 After a team is eliminated, they are moved to an "Elimination Station" with other eliminated teams. They continue on with the race, and their activities are recorded and aired in webisodes.

25 Ono and Pham, *Asian Americans and the Media*. Margaret Cho's foray into the mainstream resulted in a canceled television show as mainstream networks attempted to contain Cho's edgy humor in a sitcom. Justin Lin's transition to mainstream was more covert, inserting Asian Americanist themes in mainstream movies while advocating for the consideration of Asian American actors in prominent roles.

26 Traci G. Lee, "The Fung Brothers Make the Leap from Online to On-Air," *NBC News*, May 13, 2015, http://www.nbcnews.com/news/asian-america/fung-brothers-leap-youtube-stardom-network-fame-n357016, accessed June 11, 2015.

27 Henry Jenkins, Sam Ford, and Joshua Green, *Spreadable Media: Creating Value and Meaning in a Networked Culture* (New York: NYU Press, 2013). In considering KevJumba as spreadable, we recognize that Wu, as KevJumba, is both circulating his own image and *TAR17*'s content (and representation) of him through a variety of media platforms and cultural reproductions.

28 The YOMYOMF network was part of larger push by Google to create multichannel networks on YouTube in 2012.

6

David Choe's "KOREANS GONE BAD"

The LA Riots, Comparative Racialization, and Branding a Politics of Deviance

WENDY SUNG

I saw my childhood in flames, it was all burning to the ground . . . I was watching the laws and rules of society crumble. . . . We looted all the stores that said black owned to equalize the odds, we were the only Koreans that looted during the riots, it's why I still get called a nigger by my own people.
—David Choe (2010)[1]

Ignited by the "not guilty" verdict for the four police officers who brutally beat the Black motorist Rodney King, the 1992 Los Angeles riots were a six-day period of chaotic violence and outrage, as well as a deadly spectacle that unfolded live on the nation's television screens. Broadcast around the globe, the riots resulted in fifty-four deaths, thousands of injuries, over one billion dollars worth of property damage, and was America's first "multicultural" riot, with Black, Latino, white, and Asian residents shown in conflict. Despite the uprising's multiracial composition, the popular imaginary ushered in a so-called race war, pitting Korean American shopkeepers against African American looters and rioters, and shifted the registers of the racial imaginary of the United States. On the surface, the violence seemed to stem from the acquittal handed down by twelve jurors—ten white, one Latino, and one Asian—in spite of the video evidence testifying to use of excessive force during the Rodney King beating. But the underlying structural causes were far more complex than a convenient narrative of a race war; a police force that routinely exerted violence against communities of color, corporate disinvestment in South Los Angeles, and a long history of structural, racial, and class inequity were the more difficult to explain factors that ultimately led to the nation's worst riot.

It was during this conflict that a sixteen-year-old Korean American and Koreatown native named David Choe cruised in a stolen delivery truck, traversing the streets of South Los Angeles. Shortly after, he wrote an account of his experience of the six days of chaos as a school assignment. His report was suffused with powerful moments that index the complicated nexus of race, gender, class, and identity within multicultural Los Angeles: the dissonance of the "hell on earth" in South Los Angeles compared to the line of police patrolling the

89

pristine and silent border of Beverly Hills; seeing Eazy-E pumping a shotgun from a white convertible and feeling "overjoyed and in disbelief to see him living out his lyrics like that"; his hurt when shunned by his Black childhood friend who pretended to not recognize him while looting a Gap store. But Choe's artwork and narrative complexity represent something beyond a captivating first-hand account of the Los Angeles riots. This story would serve as the opening statement to Choe's self-titled book of selected artwork, published nearly twenty years later, testifying to the formative place of the riots to Choe as an artist but also to the reiterative quality of memory itself.

This essay looks to Choe's work as a window into the operations of racialization, memory, and masculinity in Los Angeles' contemporary Asian American street art culture. By examining Choe's self-titled book and his "dirty style" of artistic practice, I interrogate how his work registers, remediates, and revises the memory of the riots, intervening into dominant portrayals of the conflict from both mainstream and Asian American media, and makes visible how racial violence and cross-racial affinities continue to haunt everyday life. While an exhaustive look at Choe's collected art book of over three hundred pages is impossible, my intention is to bring to light the main themes of his work and demonstrate how these articulations draw out the tensions and imaginaries of Los Angeles' multiculturalism and racial formation on a national stage. By teasing out Choe's negotiations with Blackness as well as the highly gendered dynamics of his work, Choe forces us to see the multiple registers of Asian American masculinity legible in a matrix of racial relationality, representing in Cathy J. Cohen's words "a politics of deviancy."[2] In this examination, I push against the historiographic narrative of the riots within Asian American studies and ultimately posit that Choe represents an alternate imagining of what I call the "sa-i-gu subject," a powerful post-riot figure created out of Asian American responses to the conflict and grounded in a public image of suffering. In the end, Choe's work indexes how the memory of the riots are shaped, revised, and imagined alongside the multiplicities of racialization.

David Choe's self-titled art book is a selection of Choe's graffiti, commissioned art for street-wear companies, and photographs taken by and of the artist, alongside scrawled annotations on his personal history, musings, and process. Despite being published in 2010, two years shy of the twentieth anniversary of the riots, Choe opens with the aforementioned personal account of the riots and visually cites its formative place through thematic reference throughout the compilation. In fact, the book's first visual and narrative vignette consists of a photograph of a blurry sixteen-year-old Choe during the riots, yelling at the camera in front of the fiery remnants of a storefront ablaze. The short story that Choe wrote as an English assignment that details Choe's experience of the riots, his rage, and the family's business burning down runs down the opposite page, the typed story superimposed upon sketched figures in poses of suffering and rage. Choe writes

Figure 6.1. A photograph of a blurry sixteen-year old
Choe during the riots, yelling at the camera in front
of the fiery remnants of a storefront ablaze. From
David Choe, *David Choe*. San Francisco: Chronicle
Books, 2010.

that he used to "prophesize about a day when the minorities and the have nots
would rise up and take over." The riots then, provided the reason and the excuse,
and for Choe, he "felt as if [he] had finally come home."

"Getting crazy looks because of their slanted eyes," Choe and his friends tra-
versed the streets of South Los Angeles, embodying a sense of teenage defiance
and nihilism. Early into the story, Choe declares the "race war" over, replaced
by rampant chaos, but he, his brother, and his friend Fred threw huge rocks
and boulders at "the white people in their fancy cars" as the Black and Mexican
neighborhoods burned. As the riots escalated, so did Choe's awareness of the
racial divisions guiding the conflict. Both in the story in the book *David Choe*
and in the documentary film *Dirty Hands: The Art and Crimes of David Choe*,[3]
the most poignant moment of Choe's story comes when the riots' politics of
racialization become crystallized in a personal encounter:

And there were a few crazy and hurtful things that I saw. One, we drive down Mel-
rose and a few stores are getting looted and I see this Black kid that I grew up with

and he was a childhood friend. And he's looting with all of his Black friends. And I'm like, "Sean what's up?!" And all his friends are watching him look at me, and so it's like he couldn't say hi to a Korean person, so he just ignored me. And I was like, whoa, that let me know *how real all this shit was.* There was fire everywhere, and dust and everything just smells different. How do you just wake up tomorrow and it's all good? And it's not. We find out the next day that our parents' business burned down.[4]

Tellingly, it is this disavowal of recognition, of failed interpellation, that concretized the riots and his reality—it is this moment when he realizes just "how real all this shit was." In this way, Choe's proximity and relationship to Blackness is both pivotal and ambivalent. His identification with Eazy-E and the painful yet eye-opening failure of his Black childhood friend to acknowledge him exists within the same narrative of looting Black-owned stores to "even the odds." Taken alongside the stunning quote that begins this essay, we can see that Choe ascribes to narratives that construct Korean-ness and Blackness as diametrically opposed and at the same time demonstrates the inaccuracies of these assumptions.

This complexity and ambivalence stand as a stark contrast to the dominant portrayals of the riots within mainstream news media. Drawing from footage of Korean American men shopkeepers with guns defending their storefronts from Black looters during the six days of rioting, mainstream news-cycle broadcasting not only disappeared Latino and white participation but also crafted a hypervisible and lasting narrative of Korean-Black racial conflict that persists in the public imaginary. A number of factors have been proposed for the simmering tensions: linguistic barriers that made it easy for misunderstandings between Korean merchants and Black customers, as well as resentment from those who believed that Koreans funneled money out of Black communities without any regard for their customers, operated in tense tandem. While I do not dismiss the real racial antipathy as well as the oft-overlooked instances of empathy that do exist within these realms of interaction, the tension and violence seen during the post-verdict riots necessitate considerations of much larger contextual factors such as declining wages, rising economic inequality, and increasing racial inequity—or, as Rhonda M. Williams puts it, the machinations of ruthless capitalist accumulation.[5] Scholars like Mike Davis have pointed out that the riots are more accurately described as a "bread riot" in its initial stages—a rush for the resources that have been decimated by the cutting of manufacturing jobs in the region and the economic policies of the Reagan-Bush era that have benefited the wealthy. The culmination of these complex structural and economic factors ultimately found a flashpoint within the interpersonal resentments and interactions between communities, specifically between merchants and customers. Therefore, the looting of Korean stores was part of a complicated and frustrated

Figure 6.2. Photo of a Korean shopkeeper behind the register with his pit bull and a TEC-9.

response to the long-dwindling prospects of the underserved in South Los Angeles and not necessarily the vitriolic race war many media outlets touted.

Clearly, Choe is highly cognizant of these narratives. Offering a rebuttal to the dominant media construction of the riots' Black-Korean conflict with a photo of a Korean shopkeeper behind the register with his pit bull and a TEC-9, he offers this caption:

> Perpetrating [*sic*] the stereotype, my cousin Tommy is a Korean liquor store owner. Unlike the movies and songs, the blacks who frequent Tommy's Shop have no desire to see his store burn down or see him dead. In fact they love him and the brindled pitbull "TAI" which he got off a crackhead in the parking lot for a pack of smokes. He knows his regulars by name and knows what brand of cigs they all smoke. Tai keeps a fierce one eye on the register and another one on would be shoplifters. Pay for the Funyons or get splashed with the tech.

Refuting the media's race-war narrative with the story of Tommy's relationship to his customers, Choe nonetheless makes it clear that "getting splashed with the tech" is an option. Doing so nevertheless crafts Korean American masculinity in relation to guns and demonstrates that Choe registers a deeply unsettled relationship, both asserting and denying the riots' media conventions within one photo and its caption. In fact, on the very next page, a smirking Choe stands in a Wal-Mart between a recoiling white man and giggling Black woman, pointing two handguns, with price tags dangling down, at the camera. As a winking embrace of the news coverage that showed Koreans with guns guarding their shops without regard for human life, Choe is positioned literally between proxy figures of Reginald Denny and Latasha Harlins.[6] Alongside Choe's personal recount of the riots, I contend that these images are visual re-enactments and rebuttals to mainstream riots coverage, which concentrated on the "Black-Korean conflict," and stand as examples that directly reference the riots and their mediation to reveal Choe's negotiations with the way that history functions and how meanings have been placed onto certain bodies.

While mainstream media depictions focused on the ostensible Black-Korean conflict, the film *Sa-I-Gu: From Korean Women's Perspective* (1993)[7] was made as a counterpoint. The directors Dai Sil Kim-Gibson, Christine Choy, and Elaine Kim's film was a corrective impulse, a fact that is most obviously manifest through the politics of naming. As an alternative to the "uprising" within the Black imagination or the "civil unrest" in the minds of white residents, the film's title, which literally means 4–29 in Korean—the dates the riots began— has become the Los Angeles Korean community's de facto name for events that transpired in late April of 1992. Portraying a mother who lost her only son, immigrants who lost their livelihood, the film unveiled their profound grief and mourning—mourning not solely focused on loved ones and property but also on their aspirations and belief in the American Dream as they sought to parse the meanings behind the conflict. If, as Min Song points out, mainstream news images made Koreans "the most prominent (if blurry) symbols of an alien invasion tolerated by too-liberal immigration laws and a too-hasty retreat from the policies of assimilation,"[8] the film provided a forum where no other forum existed and provided an important and necessary corrective to these two tenets. Its images played a crucial part in reclaiming agency within the Korean American community, one that crafted Korean women shop owners as the prominent voices of the conflict.

Now canonized within Asian American studies, the term "sa-i-gu" has become the moniker and textual representative of the Korean American perspective of the riots. Though this is an understandable tendency, given the limited possibilities for alternative voices, the film unwittingly produced its own constrictive binds of representation. While the documentary *Sa-I-Gu* cannot and should not be saddled with sole representational responsibility since it sought to provide a reprieve from the onslaught of news images, it nevertheless functioned to create what I call the "sa-i-gu subject." Inspired by Herman Gray's civil rights subject,[9] the dominance of this figure in the post-riot Asian American imaginary created a presiding way of thinking of the conflict that focused on suffering rather than on the complexity of disenfranchisement and empowerment and was heavily contingent on a racial politic of respectability and white sympathy as paramount. In the end, the film unwittingly constructed a powerful post-riot figure that became synonymous with the conflict: suffering, hardworking, Korean immigrant women merchants who, despite disillusionment, still looked to the state for protection and justice through claims of citizenship.

Just as civil rights memory work within popular culture re-scripted the movement into one of black suffering rather than empowerment, the sa-i-gu subject utilized normative conscriptions of citizenship and instantiated the formation of a Korean post-riot identity based on victimhood, loss, and the mourning of capital and imaginary dreams.[10] Significantly, this emphasis caused "suffering [to resonate] in politically useful but inherently limiting ways."[11] These limitations inflect the ways of conceptualizing identity itself, and a return to the quote that opens this essay, "We were the only Koreans that looted during the riots, it's why I still get called a nigger by my own people," is simultaneously a testament of anti-Black racism and an indication that the prescriptive notions of imagined Korean-ness and Blackness are rigid and distinct. Seeking a way out of these binds, whether knowingly or unknowingly, David Choe's vision of the riots presents an alternative riot subject whose strategies for resistance are less legible precisely because they work against essentialist conceptions of Korean-ness and the sa-i-gu subject by celebrating his own tenet of a politics of deviancy.

Indeed, articulated through a series of contradictory and complex gestures, Choe's process of identification and disavowal highlights negotiations within racial hierarchies and the process of racial construction through relationality. This theme appears again in Choe's collection of artwork in a scrawled meditation of how Jews and Koreans are "basically the same people" because they both "had a monopoly on liquor stores in South Central and both were so untrusting of dark-skinned people that we incited riots (the Jews in the '60s and the gooks in the '90s)." In this instance, Choe mobilizes a model minority construct for a commonality between Korean-ness and Jewishness and places the blame on anti-Black racism for both the Watts riots of 1965 and the Los Angeles riots of 1992.

As the comparative ethnic studies scholar Leslie Bow has noted, anti-Blackness has long dominated the conditions of entry: The immigrant will to incorporation "manifests in the learned racism against African Americans, the performance of which is not primarily addressed to its abject object but to power."[12] In other words, part of the assimilative process is an incorporation of racism against the reviled Other, one determined by the lack of privilege and power. Positioning Koreans and Jews as equivalents based on the logic of anti-Blackness, Choe struggles to uncover and make sense of the relationality of racial formation, class, and oppression, despite misreading the structures that continually place people of color against one another. The sociologist Claire Jean Kim's theory of racial triangulation details the way that Asian Americans have often been caught in a rhetorical middle within America's dominant racial hierarchy, seen as simultaneously worthwhile and industrious as well as inassimilable, perpetually foreign, and unsuitable for the melting pot of America.[13] Applied to

Figure 6.3. An intricate pen drawing of a Hasidic Jew, bent over, his peyos clutched by a young African American girl who uses them for double Dutch with three other Black girls, complicating Choe's anti-Black explanation.

Choe's seemingly contradictory statements, racial triangulation makes visible the multiple and intersecting constellations of racial meanings that inform our racial categories.

Although Choe's claims about Jewish-Korean commonality hint at climbing the assimilative ladder toward the privileges of whiteness, the accompanying image depicts something quite different. An intricate pen drawing of a Hasidic Jew, bent over, his peyos clutched by a young African American girl who uses them for double Dutch with three other Black girls, complicates Choe's anti-Black explanation. The peyos, markers of ethnic and racial difference, are cast as a visual crux: The visual impact of the sketch depends on their exaggerated length and appearance, a literal excess and manifestation of ethnic Otherness. But pivotally, the peyos are so excessively long that these African American girls utilize them as jump ropes. Rather than a condemnation of ethnic difference, instead the peyos function as a tool for cross-racial interaction, marking a transition from a physical manifestation of foreign-ness and apprehension to playfulness and joy.

Within this example, Choe articulates two modes of assimilation: His written assessment crafts a narrative that abides by dominant media constructions of racial antipathy and the vertical assimilative mode that require jockeying for the privileges of whiteness through anti-Black racism. The other assimilative mode implies a horizontal affinity that, in the words of Vijay Prashad,

[does] not strive to be accepted by the terms set by white supremacy. . . . Instead, they seek recognition, solidarity, and safety in embracing others also oppressed by white supremacy in something of a horizontal assimilation. Consider the rebel Africans, who fled the slave plantations and took refuge among the Amerindians to create communities such as the Seminoles'; the South Asian workers who jumped ship in eighteenth-century Salem, Massachusetts, to enter the black community; Frederick Douglass's defense of Chinese "coolie" laborers in the nineteenth century; the interactions of the Black Panther Party with the Red Guard and the Brown Berets in the mid-twentieth century; and finally the multiethnic working-class gathering in the new century.[14]

Taking into consideration Choe's narrative of the riots—his embrace of Eazy-E and his inner alliances with other people of color "who would rise up and take over"—his horizontal mode of assimilation is evident. But in distinction to the straightforward examples of Prashad's account, the artist pushes against the legible notions of political affinity and anti-racist opposition described by registering, at times, a deep ambivalence with Blackness.

A proclivity of comparative ethnic studies literature is to dwell on often-invisible yet valiant political alliances of people of color, centering on historical analyses of empathy while minimizing the concrete eruptions of racial antipathy. While affinity remains crucially important, this body of work has to reckon with the historical circumstances that have proven that racial antipathy, ambivalence, and strife can often live as bedfellows to such cross-racial potentials. In a way, this teleological view of solidarity and tendency toward similarity can serve to fetishize it and produce knowledges that obfuscate difference as well as antipathy and conflict. Indeed, as Maria Cotera notes, paraphrasing Gloria Anzaldúa, this type of "convergent thinking is a tendency of Western thinking to use 'rationality to move toward a single goal'" and is a Eurocentric discourse that can again homogenize racial difference.[15] Thus, this tenet of comparative ethnic studies has moved simultaneously toward and away from a demystifying model of comparison.

Most obviously, the riot stands as one of the most recent examples of the racial complexity that begs a comparativist practice, an instance that cannot collapse difference into a totalizing narrative of solidarity. Choe's ambivalence toward Blackness and Latino-ness[16] is not a normative politically mobilized position of affinity, nor is it an easily designated narrative of oppositional resistance. To fully understand the ideological work he enacts, I contend that Choe's body of work breaks the periodizing and moralizing constraints of the post-riot subject that was constructed in the wake of the conflict and illustrates that the afterlife of the riots continues, in a multitude of places and ways.

Moreover, Choe's riot references indicate a clear self-identification with the event. Insomuch as his paradoxical assertions are significant precisely because they complicate the canonized narratives of the riots, they also provide him with a formative and controversial personal narrative. In truth, Choe's association with the violent and highly racialized conflict equips him with a type of cultural capital and legitimacy within the street-art circuit, which he has monetized greatly. More than merely contributing to the public discourse on the riots, Choe utilizes the event to underpin much of his public narrative and image, and as well as his artistic brand, which he labels "KOREANS GONE BAD."

In Sarah Banet-Weiser's *Authentic*™,[17] the author traces the contradictory notions within street art's anti-brand-driven culture. Though an anti-establishment critique of state and corporate power is a strong thematic current in the genre, many prominent street artists paradoxically monetize their personas and brand identities as an integral part of their artistic praxis and commercial success. For Choe, part of selling his work is his persona and associating his personal narrative to sites of criminality, pornography, the spectacle of violence, and the riots themselves, enacting a public type of legitimizing performance to buttress his marginal status, one innately tied to the expectations of graffiti and street art.

Increasingly visible to the mainstream art world, street art is a distinct and recently popular subgenre of public artwork with strong ties to hip-hop and graffiti histories and subcultures. Some historians have tied its origins back to radicalized youth of the 1960s and 1970s civil rights and cultural nationalists movements, with the Chicana/o scholar Guisela Latorre noting that the visual expressions, traditions, and sociopolitical context of Chicano muralism and graffiti dovetail in a historically significant and poignant way.[18] But often practitioners from all different racial and socioeconomic backgrounds share a political interest in the reclamation of public space—a reclamation most eagerly taken up in urban, marginalized communities of color.[19] As the noted hip-hop historian Jeff Chang, channeling Greg Tate, notes, graffiti can be seen as a "reverse colonization," marks to testify to one's presence in a society that incessantly tries to erase poor people and people of color.[20] Therefore, we can find new avenues of investigation within street art that announce hidden articulations of experience that are often overlooked.

As important to note, however, is how graffiti and their attendant offshoots of visual expression have diversified from their beginnings just as widely as the genre's wide-ranging spectrum of reception. The street-art poster boy, and Choe's contemporary, Shepard Fairey designed the renowned Barack Obama "HOPE" poster utilized by Obama's 2008 campaign, which was afterward acquired by the Smithsonian, and Choe's portrait of then-senator Barack Obama was used for a grassroots campaign and later displayed in the White House. This recent acclaim is in stark contrast to the swift criminalization of graffiti in the 1970s and 1980s as part of New York's "revitalization" project, which specifically targeted poor and working-class communities of color. From vandalism charges, jail time for tagging, and even death-by-cop to exorbitant purchase prices and Banksy's art-world darling status, street art has the distinction of being one of the few genres of art to occupy the simultaneous spaces of criminalization and exaltation, illegality and respectability. Bound up in these stark ambivalences is the inference that specificity, history, and, importantly, which bodies perform this genre matter. Bodies matter not only in critical reception but also in the real-life consequences for those who are lauded and revered and those who are incarcerated and the object of state-sanctioned violence. In this way, it is clear that the story of street art is simultaneously a story of race, racial difference, and relationality, one that is also innately and powerfully tied to notions of the street, illegality, and authenticity.

While many prominent graffiti artists have found popular acclaim through an intricate negotiation among mainstream venues, street visibility, and the associated prominence of their graffiti crews, Choe forged an atypical path: shuttling between solitary art practice on the streets and Los Angeles' *Giant Robot* magazine, a bi-monthly magazine dedicated exclusively to Asian and Asian American popular culture. Choe became the most visible member of a cadre of artists to come out of *Giant Robot*. His early partnership with the zine would make for a mutually beneficial relationship, catapulting both to the forefront of commercial Asian American art culture. Hence, Choe's work is not only formatively influenced by his racialization and the riots, but his publicity and celebrity persona, too, are indebted to such strategically essentialized and racially specific platforms.

Writing on the commercial branding of the genre, Banet-Wiser argues that the current formulation of street art negotiates an uneasy relationship between commerce and creativity, in which the celebrity of particular street artists play heavily into the visibility of the artwork. Looking to the genre's best-known artists, Banksy and Shepard Fairey, she observes that they often publicly tout illicit and illegal activity to imbue their work with an aura of authenticity and deflect criticism of commercialism. While remaining skeptical of the idea of authenticity, Banet-Weiser nonetheless identifies how authenticity is commodified within the genre by artists engaging in illicit activity to accumulate street credibility. In this, David Choe is not an outlier but does in fact represent an interesting case in which his utility of these associations collides with the differential politics of racialization.

In *David Choe*, the opening title page is a photograph of baby David Choe, dressed in a checkered bow tie and vest. Outstretched parental-like disembodied hands adjust his bowtie while another hand pats his head soothingly. A bold sharpie tag above the cherubic image reads, "KOREANS GONE BAD," juxtaposing the image of the innocent and well-behaved Choe with an inner, unseen deviance that foreshadows what is to come. In doing so, the book crafts a narrative of spoilt innocence at birth and alerts readers at the onset that the tale of model minority success is not to be found in the following pages. The documentary film centered on Choe's work and life also buttresses this "KOREANS GONE BAD" trope. Not only does the detailed discussion of Choe's artistic practice serve as a para-text to his art, but so does the very title of the documentary, *Dirty Hands: The Art and Crimes of David Choe*, framing his criminality and his art as one and the same. Quite obviously, *Dirty Hands* is a double entendre meant to signal the dirtiness of making art as well as the criminality of Choe's past and present.

This type of criminality and deviance acts in part as a commodity spectacle, legitimizing his street art performance and marking the axes of difference within graffiti culture itself. The contexts of graffiti and street art cannot be divorced from certain conceptions of masculinity. The sociologist Nancy MacDonald examines the link between two, asserting that graffiti writing is a type of homosocial enactment in which masculinity gains meaning through construction and display.[21] It could be said then that Choe performs these expectations of a particular racialized masculinity. In essence, he performs an assimilation gone awry—he refuses to assimilate to white bourgeois heteronormative ideals or to the respectability politics often mobilized by communities of color for political, social, and economic upward mobility. Moreover, Choe simultaneously rejects the social worth imbued in the politics of racial affinity, exemplified by Prashad's examples. Instead, Choe embraces deviancy and criminality, perhaps aping the warped and criminalized media depictions of Blackness and Latinoness as well as adhering to the expectations of the street. What becomes clear in this relationship are the performative qualities of masculinity as well as its relationality and social construction.

Cohen's "Deviance as Resistance" advocates looking to those individuals whose lives are outside the realm of respectability and normativity, those thought to be "morally wanting by both dominant society and other indigenous group members" and who are "indicative of the intersection of marked identities and regulatory processes, relative powerlessness and limited and contradictory agency."[22] What we know of Choe detailed in the documentary—his destructive looting, his parents' business burning down, his resentments, and as well as his varying time of incarceration within the United States and in Japan for fraud and assaulting a police officer, respectively—all are constituents of Cohen's definition of deviance. And, indeed, by embodying an alternative to the sa-i-gu subject, Choe rejects respectability and the expectation that "conformity will confer full citizenship" and informs a re-imagining of the afterlife of the riots, one that demands critique in spite of and, perhaps, precisely because of its denigrated social value.

While much is in line with Cohen's tenets of deviancy, it is clear that Choe does not adhere fully to her assessments; he is a well-known artist with an international following and undoubtedly financially solvent. And as fascinating as

Choe's reimagining of the riots is, it is nonetheless contextually framed by his other work—much of it exhibiting a type of overt, brutal misogyny unparalleled in other noted street art. Making kaleidoscopic mosaics out of female genitalia, reveling in his self-proclaimed "perversion" and obsession with pornography and adult film stars, Choe's racial and gendered identity is clearly at play. One could surmise that his overblown misogyny has been formulated by the dual formations of patriarchy and the persistent characterization of Asian men as emasculated and asexual, a response that I refuse to uncritically support. In fact, Cohen's reconsideration of deviance, inspired by queer of color and Black feminist critique, does not mean an "unexamined position of support for every counter normative and seemingly self-destructive behavior" but instead will lead us to an "engagement with the normative assumptions that structure Black politics and the lives of Black people, interrogating whole rule-breaking will be labeled deviant, altering significantly their political, social, and economic standing."[23] Thus Cohen's conclusion is circumscribed and contradicted by the intersecting and intertwined histories and ideologies located in Choe's work, that of an event, a genre of art, an identity, and a media construction.

With this in mind, I take a more speculative, rather than conclusive, stance and posit that this might enable us to see his artwork as having the potential to create certain, if not unproblematic, counterframeworks that might take the shape of a radical politics of deviance, in spite of its blatant misogyny and many faults. In doing so, I still refuse to embrace this particular variant of deviancy, branded by Choe as "KOREANS GONE BAD." However, his commodified deviancy ushers in constellations of questioning and obfuscation that query Asian American respectability politics, intersectional analyses, and the limits of representation in a neoliberal world. As an alternative imagining of the postriot subject, his contradictions and commodification of narratives of race, racism, and violence constitute Choe as a complex figure imbricated by media and memory, one whose memory remediates and brings current the shifting registers of racialization to the fore of his work.

As a historical and mediated flashpoint, the 1992 riots caused paradigmatic shifts in the entwined discourses surrounding race, multiculturalism, nation, and citizenship. The riots and their status in the public imaginary as the nation's first "multicultural" riot, one that involved Black, Latino, Asian, and white participants, shifted the language of race in dominant discourse from a Black-white paradigm to a multiracial complexity previously unseen. At a twentieth-anniversary conference and commemoration of the riots in Koreatown, which I attended, the subject of Asian American—specifically, Korean American—suffering was consistently emphasized. In some cases, anti-Blackness was the response; another response was to dwell in the space of Asian suffering. While these inclinations are understandable, by drawing attention to the sa-i-gu subject and Choe's revision of the riots, it is evident that the extrasystemic politics of the riots and of multiculturalism, as well as racial violence's specter, still live on in the everyday lives of those left in its wake. During the events, the riots themselves became a historical citation for the present: participants alluded to similar contexts of high-unemployment rates, structural inequity, and parallels between Rodney King and Trayvon Martin, illustrating how the memory of the riots does so much more than refer to an event; it points to how the past remains in the present.

What is more, as Michael Omi and Howard Winant remind us, the processes by which racial categories are created, inhabited, transformed, and destroyed are located within a matrix of race's relationality.[24] Therefore, the riots, which brought Asians' hypervisibility into the national imaginary, have profound effects on all racial meanings and the very category of race itself. It is with this attendant reminder that Choe's work resonates. Proliferating perhaps even more widening questions than answers, what Choe's artwork and remediation of the riots offer us is a window into the negotiations of Los Angeles' multiracial space, to reckon with ambivalences, ambiguities, and contradictions, highlighting how art, media, masculinity, commerce, and race work in concert, enabling us to imagine a different, if deviant, way of being.

NOTES

1 David Choe, *David Choe* (San Francisco: Chronicle Books, 2010). Unattributed quotations in this essay come from Choe's art book.

2 Cathy J. Cohen, "Deviance as Resistance: A New Research Agenda for the Study of Black Politics," *Du Bois Review* 1, no. 1 (2004): 27.

3 Since *David Choe* centers primarily on personal anecdotes and stories, a consideration of both the film and art book is necessary for an in-depth understanding of the artist's thematic work and artistic practices.

4 Harry Kim, dir., *Dirty Hands: The Art and Crimes of David Choe* (DVD; Dirty Hands Film, 2008). Emphasis mine.

5 Rhonda M. Williams, "Accumulation as Evisceration: Urban Rebellion and New Growth Dynamics," in *Reading Rodney King, Reading Urban Uprising*, ed. Robert Gooding-Williams (London: Routledge, 1993), 93.

6 Denny and Harlins figured prominently in the riots coverage, though the latter's death was utilized as an explanation for the simmering tensions between Korean and Black communities.

7 Dai Sil Kim-Gibson, Christine Choy, and Elaine Kim, dirs., *Sa-I-Gu: From Korean Women's Perspective* (DVD; Center for Asian American Media, 1993).

8 Min Song, *Strange Future: Pessimism and the 1992 Los Angeles Riots* (Durham, NC: Duke University Press, 2005), 135.

9 Gray's civil rights subject was a cultural figure that embodied middle-class citizenry, "complex codes of behavior and propriety that make it an exemplar of citizenship and responsibility," and mobilized a public image of a Black non-violent, suffering, victim of white violence to marshal moral outrage and make claims to equal citizenship. See Herman Gray, "Remembering Civil Rights: Television, Memory, and the 1960s," in *The Revolution Wasn't Televised: Television and Social Conflict*, ed. Lynn Spigel and Michael Curtin (New York: Routledge, 1997), 349–358.

10 Far from disavowing the suffering and loss of Koreans and Korean Americans during the riots, I believe it imperative to investigate alternative memories and imaginings of the riots to get at the multitudes of experience that exists.

11 Martin Berger, *Seeing through Race: A Reinterpretation of Civil Rights Photography* (Berkeley: University of California Press, 2011), xii.

12 Leslie Bow, *Partly Colored: Asian Americans and Racial Anomaly in the Segregated South* (New York: NYU Press, 2010), 10.

13 Claire Jean Kim, "The Racial Triangulation of Asian Americans," *Politics and Society* 29 (March 1997): 110–112.

14 Vijay Prashad, "Introduction," in *AfroAsian Encounters: Culture, History, Politics*, ed. Heike Raphael-Hernandez and Shannon Steen (New York: NYU Press, 2006), x.

15 María Eugenia Cotera, *Native Speakers: Ella Deloria, Zora Neale Hurston, Jovita González, and the Poetics of Culture* (Austin: University of Texas Press, 2008), 9.

16 Latinos appear throughout Choe's book. Opposite the picture of Tommy is a photo montage that reflects the racial heterogeneity outside the Black-Korean narrative: a shot of four young Latino men being forced to sit on the curb as policeman surveil one of their friends, two elderly white women walking hand in hand. While this racial heterogeneity deserves critical attention, my analysis is focused on the popular imaginary and how the Black-Korean conflict was mediated.

17 Sarah Banet-Weiser, *Authentic™: The Politics of Ambivalence in a Brand Culture* (New York: NYU Press, 2012).

18 Guisela Latorre, *Walls of Empowerment: Chicana/o Indigenist Murals of California*, 1st ed. (Austin: University of Texas Press, 2008), 101.

19 Banet-Weiser, *Authentic™*, 103.

20 Jeff Chang, *Can't Stop Won't Stop: A History of the Hip-Hop Generation* (New York: Picador, 2005), 74.

21 Nancy MacDonald, *The Graffiti Subculture: Youth, Masculinity and Identity in London and New York* (London: Palgrave Macmillan, 2003), 97.

22 Cohen, "Deviance as Resistance," 29.

23 Ibid., 42.

24 Michael Omi and Howard Winant, *Racial Formation in the United States: From the 1960s to the 1990s* (London: Routledge, 1994), 55.

PART II

Making Community

From the Mekong to the Merrimack and Back

The Transnational Terrains of Cambodian American Rap

CATHY J. SCHLUND-VIALS

While doing chores in the kitchen, [my mom] would randomly speak of how we had to leave our Cambodian home and run to Thailand because the Khmer Rouge were invading our province. Bong Thoeun would also tell me . . . how beautiful and vast our farmland was. . . . Hearing these stories makes me wonder how I would be living "if the war had never happened." I figure my Khmer speaking ability would be near perfect and I would probably spend most of my time chilling on my farm drinking palm wine and smoking home grown tobacco. Maybe by 18 or 20 I would have moved to the city of Phnom Penh to pursue my art and music career and become the Cambodian Jay Z or Nas. Hahaaa! Who really knows?
—Sambath "Sam" Hy, Cambodian American rapper, February 4, 2011[1]

Rap's global industry-orchestrated (but not industry-oriented) presence illustrates the power of the language of rap and the salience of stories of oppression and creative resistance its music and lyrics tell.
—Tricia Rose, *Black Noise*.[2]

If central to contemporary hip-hop is an identifiable space (i.e., an urban setting) as expressed via overt declarations of place (e.g., NWA's "Straight Outta Compton"), then Lowell, Massachusetts, makes "demographic sense" as a setting for Cambodian American rap. Roughly twenty-five miles northwest of Boston, where U.S. Highway 3 intersects with Interstate 495, Lowell sits at the tri-water juncture of the Merrimack River, the Concord River, and Pawtucket Falls. The Northeastern city is home to the second-largest Cambodian American population in the United States. Long Beach, California, houses the nation's largest Khmer population at nearly fifty thousand, while nearby Lynn, Massachusetts, ranks a close third.[3] Drawn like their West Coast counterparts to the United States by the 1980s Refugee Act and promises of post-conflict asylum, Cambodian Lowellians, who number an estimated twenty-five thousand to thirty thousand, have left an indelible mark on the mill city's landscape. Commercially and culturally, these impacts are evident in the preponderance of traditional Khmer restaurants, Khmer American–owned businesses, and Cambodian

American enclaves in Lowell's Acre and Lower Highlands neighborhoods.[4] Such locales serve as chief settings for traditional ceremonies, Theravada Buddhist observances, Angkor Dance Troupe performances, and Cambodian New Year celebrations. Last, but certainly not least, these Khmerican collisions are arguably most visible in the annual Lowell Southeast Asian Water Festival, a late-summer celebration that brings tens of thousands to the city's Heritage State Park and Esplanade and Sampas Pavilion.

To be sure, Lowell's present-day status as a Southeast Asian hub would certainly surprise its nineteenth-century founders, who originally envisioned a utopic "Manchester in America."[5] While at one point a leading manufacturing city, Lowell, like other U.S. commercial municipalities, endured the long-lasting economic impacts of the Great Depression, post–World War II suburbanization, and mid-century deindustrialization. For instance, by the mid-1940s, 40 percent of Lowell's denizens were on relief, though World War II temporarily revitalized the city's textile economy as factory workers furiously labored to meet wartime parachute demand.[6] Even with this change in the city's economic fortunes, white ethnic Lowellians—à la their compatriots in Buffalo, New York; Pittsburgh, Pennsylvania; Detroit, Michigan; Youngstown, Ohio; and Gary, Indiana—abandoned their city dwellings during the 1950s postwar boom, moving to nearby Chelmsford, Tewksbury, and Dracut. By 1960, the so-known City of Spindles suffered a 10 percent population loss through "white flight," a demographic trend that would continue in the next three decades.[7]

As long-term residents moved to surrounding suburbs in-state, companies moved to locations out-of-state: to rural communities, small towns, and cities in the American south. Active mills seemingly transformed into abandoned buildings overnight, and by the mid-1970s, without a solid manufacturing base, the unemployment rate crept to 13 percent.[8] The mill city's economic landscape shifted yet again in 1976, when Wang Laboratories set up headquarters in the former textile capital.[9] Wang Laboratories was a fiscal harbinger of the so-called 1980s Massachusetts Miracle, wherein state unemployment fell from 12 percent to 3 percent despite nationwide stagflation, inflation, and recession. At one point in the late 1980s, Wang Laboratories boasted $3 billion revenues and had 33,000 employees.[10] Nevertheless, Lowell's domestic fortunes further declined during the Clinton administration as global outsourcing became not so much the exception but rather the rule for U.S. businesses. Wang Laboratories filed for bankruptcy in 1992, closed its proverbial factory doors in 1997, and was bought by Getronics (a Dutch company) in 1999.[11]

Set adjacent the mass movement of bodies, manufacturing, and capital out of state *and* out of country, Lowell's diverse present-day population testifies to demographic growth in the face of omnipresent deindustrialization. While the city's white population decreased by 18.5 percent between 1980 and 2010, so-termed minority populations (inclusive of African Americans, Latinos, and Asian

Americans) grew from 4.1 percent to 31.4 percent, indicative of a 400 percent total increase.[12] Whereas African American and Latino populations increased by 367 percent and 321 percent, respectively, the greatest upsurge involved Asian Americans, whose numbers grew by 2,876 percent.[13] Of that number, the majority of Asian Lowellians are Cambodian Americans, who constitute 10.3 percent of the city's present-day population. This diverse story of population growth undeniably reflects shifts in immigration policy, such as the 1965 Immigration and Nationality Act. It is equally connected to the "ends" of the Vietnam War (post–April 30, 1975) and, as will later be discussed, the contemporaneous rise of the authoritarian Khmer Rouge (1975–1979), which was responsible for the deaths of an estimated 1.7 million Cambodians.[14]

These demographic shifts—particularly those involving Cambodian refugees and Cambodian Americans—are germane to this chapter's overall focus, which considers the transnational, domestic, and political registers of Khmer American rap.[15] Set against histories of war-driven dislocation and forced relocation, Cambodian American rap determinedly recollects, through lyrics and samples, the aforementioned Cambodian genocide and its refugee aftermath. As important, the current state of Lowell's Cambodian American affairs—marked by low-skilled employment and delimited by recent state-authorized deportation—are explored in critical rhymes about everyday life, racism, xenophobia, and the ongoing War on Terror. This intersection of art and politics, guided by the realities of deindustrialization and the logics of migration, is provocatively emblematized by Cambodian Lowellian rapper Sambath "Sam" Hy, whose personal journey from "the Mekong to the Merrimack" provides this chapter's title and foregrounds its examinations of Khmerican hip-hop's transnational terrains.

Toward a Cambodian American "VOA"

In the opening epigraph, Hy nostalgically meditates on how "he would be living" if "'the war had never happened'" while articulating a desire to be a "Cambodian Jay Z or Nas." When asked to expand, the Cambodian American hip hopper responds:

> Coming from Cambodia I feel a natural need to represent my country and to tell my personal story about where I come from. But "my whole music" is not only that. I also write about many other subjects that I faced in my life, such as Cambodian American life in the USA, growing up bilingual, racial discrimination, racial profiling, identity crisis, gangsta peers, deportation, immigration, being a teenage parent and the struggles, poverty, welfare, revelations of your homeland, dropping out of school, cold cash jobs, theft, politics, haters, lovers, resident aliens, green card holders, arts . . . the list goes on and on. . . . I am a poet. I rap about everything in my life as I know it.[16]

Figure 7.1. Hy at Western Avenue Studies in Lowell, Massachusetts; the studio served as his workshop in 2014. Photograph by Felix Khut.

Like many 1.5-generation Cambodian Americans, Hy originally hails not from Cambodia but instead from a refugee camp. Born on June 3, 1977, on the border of Thailand and Cambodia in Khao-I-Dong Holding Center, Hy and his family were initially relocated to a small rural town: Spring Valley, Illinois. While in Illinois, his family worked on their sponsor's farm. Almost five years later, in 1984, Hy and his family moved to Seattle, Washington. After a three-year stint in Seattle, Hy—then ten years old—and his family permanently relocated to Lowell, Massachusetts, on October 31, 1987. Remembering his first impression of Lowell, the Khmerican rapper notes, "I saw all the mills, old bridges, and old brick walls. . . . It made me just want to move back to Spring Valley. Little did I know this amazing city would make me realize and appreciate the Cambodian within me."[17]

A true hip-hop poet, Hy's insistence that he "rap[s] about everything in his life" overlaps with what Public Enemy's Chuck D famous characterization of rap as the "Black CNN." Central to Chuck D's conceptualization is a reading of hip hop as hard-hitting street reportage, in which stories detail acts of systemic racism (for instance, police brutality, economic discrimination, and disproportionate imprisonment) and practices of African American life (such as playing "the dozens"). Similarly, Hy's artistic desire to represent his country of origin and "Cambodian life in the USA," inclusive of "revelations of [the] homeland," "resident aliens," and "green card holders," resembles a "Cambodian American VOA" (Voice of America). As the leading diasporic news outlet for Cambodians outside Cambodia, VOA's mass media reach is replicated in the international purview and transnational emphases at the forefront of Khmer American rap.[18]

This hip-hop-oriented "Cambodian American VOA" testifies to a traumatic Cambodian history (expressly war and genocide) while providing multifaceted accounts of Cambodian American experiences. Contemporary Khmerican hip-hop is, as Hy's allusion to a "Cambodian Jay Z or Nas" suggests, necessarily informed by both the mass circulation of hip-hop production and the minority position of Cambodian Americans in the United States. Recalling that he was most influenced by Wu-Tang Clan and P.M. Dawn, Hy admits, "As a child, I always wondered why Cambodians were not on TV or seen on cassette tape covers. I always wondered why I was different and frequently asked myself, while trying to sleep, why am I who I am."[19] This struggle over self-identification reveals dominant senses of race in the United States, indicative of both overt xenophobia and anti-Asian racialization.

As Hy confesses, "The biggest issue I have with living as Cambodian American in the U.S.A. is *identity* [emphasis in original]. I was brought to this country when I was one and a half years old." He continues:

> I always thought of myself as American, but my exterior shows that I am Cambodian or for people that don't know . . . I am some kind of Asian or brown foreigner. This bothered me greatly when I was growing up. . . . Kids told me to go back to where I came from. Teenage Caucasian guys would hurl 7-Eleven ice slushies at me while they sped off in their Iroc-Z, shouting, "You gook!" . . . I was a very quiet and bothered child. Why do I have to be this four syllable word: Cam-Bo-Di-An? I used to cry myself to sleep wishing I would wake up as a different nationality— something more common, please!!![20]

As "some kind of Asian or brown foreigner," Hy's "biggest issue" speaks to a sense that terms such as "Cambodian American" and "Asian American" are, as Mimi Thi Nguyen and Thuy Linh Nguyen Tu summarize, "intrinsically relational" and indicative of dominant U.S. readings of race (as black/white, domestic and foreign) and characterizations of Asian America (as primarily comprised of East Asian Americans).[21] Indeed, even though Hy "always thought of [himself] as American," his racial identity ("exterior") is read as foreign, a point made painfully clear by the remembrance of racial slurs and memories of his peers telling him "to go back to where [he] came from." Moreover, as a "Cam-Bo-Di-An," his ethnicity is not as "common," prompting a childhood desire to "wake up as a different nationality." In sum, Hy's exterior/interior conflicts bring together competing notions of affective citizenship (as American vs. Cambodian) alongside political belonging (e.g., a more "common" nationality).

Alternatively, Hy's observation of Cambodian invisibility via systemic racism, reflected in the overt use of racial slurs and declarations to "go back to where he came from," becomes even more significant when set within the context of a larger popular cultural imaginary. As Nguyen and Tu further contend, while mainstream representations of Asian Americans "are always framed and conditioned by historical, cultural, and political forces, even (and especially) when they appear to be at odds with them," the question remains as to how "Asian Americans 'get to' participate in it and how might their participation shape its contours."[22] In this instance, Hy's "Cambodian-ness" is hypervisible *and* illegible. Even so, it is through hip-hop that Hy "gets to" participate in American popular culture. Hy's introduction to hip-hop—which involved a "live urban performance"—accentuates a transformative interracial cultural encounter. Noting that his "first observation of hip-hop" was through break dancing, Hy explains, "I thought it was the coolest thing. I remember seeing these African American males dancing on flat cardboard boxes on the corner down the street from my apartment in Seattle. . . . It was so powerful and magical. I can still remember the bass pounding through my chest. That moment will always make sense."[23]

On the one hand, as a displaced Cambodian American subject, Hy's transnational, interracial characterization of his work through popular culture recalls what Tricia Rose asserts in the opening epigraph as hip-hop's global reach. Such international connections and inclusive relations, as Rose evocatively argues, are attributable to hip-hop's ability to accommodate oppressive histories through tactical acts of "creative resistance." On the other hand, Sam Hy's mention of "immigration," "racial profiling," and "deportation" as key creative themes in his work operates as a compelling shorthand for the Cambodian American experience. These key words—along with mentions of culture and politics—acknowledge politicized movements from Southeast Asia to the United States. Such foci also highlight a vexed trajectory from the United States back to Cambodia. Most recently, as Cambodian Americans are exiled "back home" (as will be subsequently analyzed), these mobilizations lay bare the racialized and racist politics of a post-9/11 War on Terror present.

Such back-and-forth "refugee movements" are apparent in "The Full View," a solo track Hy released on YouTube in 2006. Focused on the rapper's "coming of age" in the United States, "The Full View" interrogates Cambodian American masculinity via violence, precariousness, and uncertainty. At its artistic forefront, "The Full View" represents a multi-sited journey from Cambodia's "killing fields" to Lowell's deindustrialized neighborhoods. As Hy lyricizes:

Seeing tragedies and gunshots surrounding my vicinities / it's hard to find peace in a world that's befriending me, ending me like a diseased piece of poetry, bending my knees as I bleed folding me / I need angels close to me God to be holding me, those that oppose me be out like ghost be . . . / ghosts and demons try to hold me down / but Cambodian child inside still cries that sound / . . . still cries the sounds / There's something missing in America, / The way we live / something missing in America / how much I have to give?[24]

Maintaining that "there's something missing in America," Hy emphasizes a sense of precarity and non-belonging, grounded in "tragedies and gunshots" in the neighborhood ("my vicinities") and involving inner hauntings ("ghosts and demons"). While "The Full View" commences with refugee-oriented despair, it nevertheless insists that art is key to individual and communal liberation, made clear by Hy's concluding lyrics, which stress that in "telling truth," he is "teaching roots to the youth to promote my group."[25]

As Hy's artistic trajectory and "The Full View" underscores, Cambodian American rap remains rooted in transnational histories of state-authorized conflict that, as the next section makes clear, reflect the legacies of the Khmer Rouge period. It is likewise fixed to stories of displacement from Southeast Asia and connected to narratives of relocation to the United States. Lowell's Cambodian American rap scene—via Hy's work—reveals what Lisa Lowe evocatively argues is central to Asian American cultural production: a tireless reckoning with the past that carries a simultaneous critique of the present.[26] Shifting from politicized senses of space to the racialized politics of place, Hy's work as a member of Lowell-based rap trio Seasia (Soul Elements of Asia) further clarifies this relationship between genocidal history, intergenerational memory, and Cambodian American belonging. These historical frames and cultural analyses undergird this chapter's concluding argument, which returns to the relationship between critique and Cambodian American cultural production. As I have previously argued, what distinguishes Cambodian American cultural production is its intimate connection to war, genocide, and juridical activism; such connections, which build on Lowe's observation of critical cultural remembrances, make identifiable a distinct Cambodian Americanist critique.[27]

Droppin' Khmerican Science: The Killing Fields and Beyond

The main reason why I am interested in the Killing Fields is due to the fact that when I was young I always wondered why I was living in America and not surrounded by more people like me. . . . I can't say I know everything there is to know about the Killing Fields. My main focus in my war-related music is to describe how Cambodians were affected by the war and how I am personally affected. My music is about the lives of people, not just the war itself. The songs that I have were inspired by talking to survivors and hearing their stories.[28]

—Sambath "Sam" Hy

During the Vietnam War, between 1969 and 1973, the Nixon administration launched an illegal bombing campaign of the Cambodian countryside per a disastrous policy to "contain" the threat of North Vietnamese troops along the Cambodian/Vietnam border. The United States simultaneously supported the vehemently right-wing General Lon Nol's regime, which waged a bloody civil war with the communist Khmer Rouge. Lon Nol's rule came to an end on April 17, 1975, when Khmer Rouge troops overtook the nation's capital (Phnom Penh) and renamed the country "Democratic Kampuchea." For Cambodians exhausted from in-state violence, the Khmer Rouge promised an end to war and a peaceful, collective redistribution of resources. Despite such promises, the Khmer Rouge enacted a series of catastrophic policies intended to turn the country back to "year zero." Focused on eliminating Western influence from all facets of Khmer life, the Khmer Rouge emptied Cambodia's cities and forced Cambodians into agricultural camps. The regime also engaged in the strategic killing of "enemies of the people."

Such a categorization was distressingly "inclusive," encompassing doctors, lawyers, teachers, judges, Vietnamese Cambodians (Khmer Khrom), Muslim Cambodians (the Cham), fellow leftists, and anyone else who fell outside the regime's increasingly authoritarian parameters. Over the course of the next three years, eight months, and twenty days (1975–1979), almost two million Cambodians perished as a result of starvation, execution, disease, and forced labor.[29] On January 7, 1979, an invading Vietnamese army "liberated" Cambodia's capital, signaling the end to the Khmer Rouge era (though members of the regime still remain in Cambodia and hold varying positions of power).[30] Survivors of the regime, who faced famine, no infrastructure, and political uncertainty, struggled in the months that followed: An estimated 510,000 Cambodians fled to neighboring Thailand, while another 100,000 sought refuge in Vietnam.[31] Between 1980 and 1985, almost 150,000 Cambodians came to the United States.[32] To date, more than 280,000 individuals of Khmer descent live in the United States.[33]

This story of war, genocide, and relocation coheres with Sambath Hy's confessional artistic engagement with the "Killing Fields" era, fixed to the childhood question as to "why I was living in America and not surrounded by more people like me." As the above passage indicates, Hy's cultural initiation into that history—Roland Joffé's Academy Award–winning film, *The Killing Fields*—highlights the extent to which Cambodian American selfhood (within the dominant imagination) begins and ends with the Khmer Rouge period. Such bodies are highly visible Cambodian human rights subjects yet simultaneously invisible within a domestic imaginary as Cambodian *American* subjects. As Hy admits, "The era of the Killing Fields are part of my history that I have to explain. It's how I live knowing the fact we come from such a tragic history. There's no escaping it." This "fact," a starting point for Hy's own identity exploration and hip-hop examination, is paradoxically remembered and forgotten. While the genocide as "remembered event" remains at the forefront of the current UN/Khmer Rouge Tribunal (aka the "Extraordinary Chambers in the Courts of Cambodia"), only three Khmer Rouge officials—Kaing Guek Eav, Nuon Chea, and Khieu Samphan—have been successfully tried and convicted for war crimes.[34]

Whereas this wartime history and genocidal past are responsible for bringing Cambodians to the United States, the present-day Khmerican experience is increasingly shaped by a series of post-9/11 deportations. According to a recent *Boston Globe Magazine* article, almost six hundred Cambodian Americans, "virtually all of them male and a majority convicted criminals, have been shipped to Asia's most traumatized nation since 2002, when Cambodia signed a repatriation agreement with the United States."[35] An estimated 1,600 Cambodians have been slated for deportation. Between 2001 and 2010, deportations averaged forty-one per year; this number almost doubled in 2011 and 2012. As Olesia Plokhii and Tom Mashburg elaborate,

> Brought here as victims of the Vietnam War and the Killing Fields of the Khmer Rouge, most were dropped into ghettos in Lowell, Lynn, and Long Beach, California, and left to overcome cultural and language barriers with little support from the government that took them in. While illiterate adults fell into low-pay work, their children stumbled through crowded public schools or took to the streets in violent gangs. Many of those eventually deported had become hardened felons, but others were exiled for first-time misdemeanors like shoplifting or check fraud. A major reason for their expulsion is that they never obtained citizenship, an option open to them was war refugees.[36]

These domestic realities are referenced in Hy's assertion that both the Killing Fields era and his present-day experiences as a Khmerican male inform his hip-hop oeuvre. For 1.5-generation Cambodian Lowellians like Hy who faced "crowded public schools" and "violent gangs," hip-hop offers an alternative possibility for belonging and personhood. As Hy remembers, "I was drawn to hip hop because . . . these MC's are truly masters of the ceremony. I had always been a quiet kid in school, never really raised my hand much in class. I also had dreams of being the articulate and talkative one. Today I feel rap gave me that opportunity."[37] Such opportunities are fixed to hip-hop as a diverse form, wherein Hy was admittedly "moved by how powerful controversial rap can be with tracks like '911's a Joke' [Public Enemy] or how stylish and funky it can be with tracks like 'Cool Like That'[Digable Planets] or even funny like the tracks 'Ya Mama' [WUF Ticket] and 'The Pee Wee Rap' [D. Harris & J. Phillips]."[38]

As a flexible mode of politicized cultural expression, hip-hop has, as Oliver Wang observes, not surprisingly "been a dominant cultural and musical force for Asian American youth" since the 1990s.[39] Even so, Asian American rappers (most famously, MC Jin) continue to face what Wang argues is an "authenticity crisis" vis-à-vis dominant U.S. racial logics, wherein "black masculinity is associated with stereotypes of hypermasculinity and sexuality, physical aggression, and the underclasses." Such stereotypes "stand in almost diametric opposition to so-called model minority stereotypes of Asian masculinity: effete or asexual, passive, and middle class."[40] Nevertheless, as the contemporary experiences of Cambodian Americans make clear, this model minoritization blatantly dis-remembers the extent to which Khmerican rap is informed by transnational histories of oppression, domestic racialization, and economic disenfranchisement. Situated adjacent a tumultuous political and economic imaginary, Cambodian American rap becomes a significant site upon which to lay bare a still-to-be-reconciled genocidal past, multiple refugee movements (from Cambodia to the United States), and the current Khmerican deportation crisis. To be sure, the experiences of 1.5-generation Cambodian Americans, born "over there" but raised "over here," instantiates a concomitant evaluation regarding the role of cultural space in the making of local, national, and transnational notions of place.

This Janus-faced reading of Cambodian American hip-hop—which situates a violent past alongside a still-contested present—is reflected by Hy, whose conflict-oriented work as a solo artist and with Seasia is consistently concerned with how he and other Cambodians were—and remain—"affected by the war" and the Killing Fields era. In this regard, Hy's hip-hop project coheres with the work of other Cambodian American rappers like the Khmer K.I.D. (from Los Angeles) and AZI Fellas (a Philadelphia-based crew), who strategically use hip-hop as a way to negotiate what compatriot emcee praCh reminds us are "stories told from our parents to us / about the killing fields not long ago."[41] Khmerican hip-hop militates against dominant U.S. ethnoracial logics through lyrics focused on social justice, deportation, and violence specific to Cambodian American communities. In turn, these productions becomes spaces for Cambodian American "creative resistance." Such cultural production accesses the resistive roots of hip-hop, which, from the outset, was guided by a late-1960s cultural politics of self-determination, communal expression, and social justice. Moreover, the use of traditional Khmer music as a guiding principle and musical backdrop memorializes those lost during the Killing Fields era and monumentalizes the resilience of survivors and contemporary Khmericans. As a "Cambodian American VOA," then, Khmer American rap engages genocide remembrance while concomitantly commenting on racialized practices that continue to circumscribe

1.5-generation Cambodian Americans in the United States. These acts of "creative resistance" are evident in Hy's work with the aforementioned, now-defunct R&B/hip-hop crew, Seasia.

From the Merrimack to the Mekong: Seasia's Transnational Hip-Hop Project

In an August 23, 2002, *New York Times* piece titled, "The Sound of Home: An 8,690-Mile Echo," travel writer Sara Rimer opens with a description of Lowell's previously mentioned Southeast Asian Water Festival, which is "modeled on the water festivals that have been held in Cambodia for hundreds of years." A transnational endeavor, the festival features Southeast Asian monks, "colorful dragon boats," and "performances of traditional music and dance alternating with young Cambodian women doing their best to emulate Whitney Houston . . . and Celine Dion."[42] Such "east/west" collisions are evident in commodities sold by local vendors, which include American products (such as inflatable Spider-Man dolls), Laotian cuisine, Vietnamese textiles, and Khmer crafts. Boat teams bear names such as "Angkorian Warriors" and "Lao-Bodian"; traditional Khmer poetry occurs alongside master pin peat performances; and there is even a competition for the best "papaya salad."[43] Such diasporic registers reflect the original vision behind the celebration. Indeed, while serving as the head of the Cambodian Mutual Assistance Association (CMAA), festival founder Samkhann Khoeun was "fascinated by the Merrimack" because it reminded the Khmer refugee of "the Mekong River. The Merrimack was a source of life—to power the mills. The Mekong is likewise: for growing rice, fishing, farming, transport of goods."[44]

Indubitably, Lowell's Southeast Asian Water Festival celebrates contemporary Khmer American culture *and* commemorates traditional Khmer modes via performance, vision, and venue. Given that an estimated 90 percent of traditional Khmer court musicians and dancers were executed during the Democratic Kampuchean era, the hyper-visible presence of such cultural modes on the main stage underscores a revitalization concomitant to the festival's Southeast Asian roots. Moreover, for 1.5-generation Cambodian Americans (like Hy) who "came of age" not in Cambodia but in the United States, the focus on mainstream American popular culture (e.g., Whitney Houston) underscores a cultural affiliation with the country of settlement. In its vision to collapse the geographic spaces between the Mekong and the Merrimack, the Southeast Asian Water Festival engenders an analogous transnational movement of bodies and ideas across borders that intersects with the rise of Cambodian American hip-hop as a distinct cultural mode.

It was at the 2002 Southeast Asian Water Festival that the Lowell-based hip-hop crew Seasia performed in front of an excited crowd of primarily Cambodian

American youth. Dressed in "baggy jeans, football jerseys and sneakers," Seasia's members—Tony Auyeth Roun (24), Hy (25), and Felix Sros Khut (24)—took the festival main stage. According to Rimer,

> The band, a highlight of the festival, had been delayed, partly because two members had been stuck in traffic and then had to walk a half mile because they didn't want to shell out $5 for a parking fee. (Popular they may be. Rich they are not. The group received $500 for its appearance at the festival. They are not about to give up their day jobs.)

Over the course of a fifteen-minute performance, Seasia's largely teenaged audience enthusiastically cheered, applauding band shout-outs about "Khmer pride" and "Asian pride." In her reportage about the festival and Seasia, Rimer focuses her journalistic attention on "long journeys," which encompasses the circuitous migration of Cambodian refugees to the United States. Apropos Lowell's status as a Southeast Asian/American mecca and the hometown of the famed wandering writer Jack Kerouac, these artistic travels—as Rimer highlights—are transnational *and* intergenerational, involving artistic dialogues between first and 1.5-generation Cambodian Americans. To that end, the travel reporter writes, Seasia's "journey . . . has been more than just the physical distance of the 8,690

Figure 7.2. Seasia is interviewed on Channel 3 News (in Phnom Phen) after performance with master Khmer artists. Hy is the third figure from stage right. (2001).

miles from Cambodia to Lowell. They spent their early years in Lowell in a poor neighborhood—"We called it the Khmer ghetto," Mr. Khut said—and sharing the streets with local gang members. The three friends resisted joining gangs, not, however, without something of a struggle to find their own identity."[45]

This "identity struggle" hearkens back to Hy's previous motivation to know "who he is," yet it also reflects Seasia's community roots. Since their first encounter as sophomores at Lowell High School, Roun, Khut, and Hy maintained a close friendship as members of the "GAP [Good Asian People] Posse," which was "not a gang but more of a unity of good friendship between mainly Khmer guys." Notwithstanding a close high school friendship, the three Khmericans "went on to do different things" after graduation. As Hy recalls, in the mid-1990s, "Tony [Roun] started working with CMAA, Felix [Khut] went on to study marine biology at UMass. I was working third shift at a New Balance shoe factory trying to support my newborn son and my girlfriend at the time."[46] Interested in reuniting the "GAP Posse" in order to form a band, Roun convinced Khut to "try out singing"; he also invited Hy to visit CMAA, where he showed him a "compilation CD album that they had put together with other local Khmer artist." As Hy recalls,

> I was amazed by the CD and the cool cover pictures. I totally wanted to be involved in some way. . . . I told them I would like to be part of Seasia but I can't sing! I tried a few times at recording sessions but I couldn't hold a key even it if had a 'key chain.' . . . It was very frustrating. I then thought . . . I can do narrations and intros! Like soft R&B rap! . . . So I wrote a short rap verse for a track called "Make up Your Mind" (1999). I rapped that verse with another high school friend who only did that one track then quit the group. . . . I discovered my role. . . . I went on to not only write my rap verses but also wrote a lot of the song lyrics for Seasia.[47]

Officially formed in 1995, Seasia quickly collaborated with Cambodian Living Arts co-founder Arn Chorn Pond, a founding member of the Cambodian Masters Performers Project (CMPP). Pond encouraged the trio to compose a song for an upcoming play starring Yolanda King (Martin Luther King's daughter) titled "Children of War." Seated at Pond's kitchen table, Roun and Hy wrote "Children of Tomorrow," which eventually received a positive reception when the play eventually premiered. Crediting Pond as his personal mentor, Hy notes, "He was the one man that was so instrumental to the success of Seasia. He single-handedly catapulted us to heights we never thought possible. I mean, being able to perform at dozens of prestigious schools, teaching people about where we are from, and about our musical crusade."[48]

Known locally as the "Flute Player," Pond was both the subject of a 2003 documentary (produced by Boston-based Over the Moon Productions) and a key figure in the revitalization of traditional Khmer Arts on the East Coast. As Rimer notes, Pond, who during the Killing Fields era "was forced to play for his captors at a death camp," was "determined to bring back the traditional music that was outlawed when Pol Pot's Khmer Rouge regime took over the country . . . and began to wipe out the educated classes, including musicians." Guided by the desire to rediscover and reclaim surviving Cambodian master musicians, Pond was committed to linking master practitioners with 1.5-generation Cambodian American artists such as Hy, Roun, and Khut, who were for the most part illiterate in Khmer but fluent in English. As Khut noted, "Arn showed us you can't turn your back on your own culture," a sense confirmed by fellow Seasia member Hy, who likewise credits Pond with teaching him about "his country."[49]

It was through this collaboration with Cambodian Living Arts that Seasia released *From the Killing Fields to Strawberry Fields* (2002), which featured R&B, rap, and traditional Khmer backbeats. The production of this CD coincided with Hy's first trip to Cambodia in 2001, where he returned as a self-described "Cambodian American pop star." As Seasia toured in Cambodian cities such as Phnom Penh and visited Siem Reap's Angkor Wat, Hy stresses that

> [I] learned so much. I saw all the struggles facing master artists and poverty-stricken Cambodians. I got to record with Cambodian master instrumentalists in the studio . . . so absolutely inspiring. I got to walk barefoot on sandstone and see the story of Angkor Wat and see the smiling faces of the Bayon, awe!!! I got to see firsthand the difference between Cambodian and Cambodian American life, what a revelation. I got to smell the dirty smoke from the trashland village and also breathe the fresh warm area from the ocean in Kampong Som village. I also got to see how native Cambodians look at us and assume we are from Thailand because of our look. . . . I am grateful for all my experiences, I learn as I go. Being in Cambodia was like filling a missing piece of my jigsaw puzzle of life, and of course that missing piece was in the shape of Cambodia.[50]

Set against a dizzying backdrop of grand Cambodian religious sites (such as Angkor Wat) and impoverished Khmer villages, Hy's description evocatively vacillates between a celebration of Khmer personhood and a contemplation of the realities of contemporary Cambodian life that refracts the paradoxical registers of transnational Khmer American selfhood. Correspondingly at stake in Hy's "return" is a "jigsaw puzzle" metaphor that potently encapsulates particular differences "between Cambodian and Cambodian American life" that nevertheless converge in Hy's hip-hop sensibility.

Embedded in pluralistic traditions and reflective of histories of relocation, then, contemporary Cambodian American hip-hop is, as Hy's work with Pond and other master musicians suggests, incontrovertibly multidisciplinary and transnational. Such engagements and movements engender an understanding of relocation through the valorization of the homeland and the reclamation of lost histories.[51] As apparent in Hy's contemporary consideration of Cambodia and Cambodian America, these multivalent hip-hop stories are fluidly and simultaneously situated in U.S. and Khmer contexts. Armed with Khmer beats and English-language raps, informed by experiences in the United States and Cambodia, Hy creates intergenerational stories of survival alongside the fabric of contemporary Cambodian America. These transnational terrains, born out of Khmer Rouge authoritarianism, circumscribed by contemporary U.S. racial logics, and critically concerned with the global flow of bodies and capital across borders, render visible the degree to which Khmerican rappers like Hy defiantly refuse to occupy the proverbial and political margins.

NOTES

1 I conducted an email interview with Sambath "Sam" Hy, receiving a response from Hy on February 4, 2011. The term "Bong" means "older brother."

2 Tricia Rose, *Black Noise: Rap Music and Black Culture in Contemporary America* (Middletown, CT: Wesleyan University Press, 1994), 19.

3 From the U.S. 2010 Census. See "City of Lowell, MA Census 2010," *Zip-Codes.com*, n.d., http://www.zip-codes.com/city/MA-LOWELL-2010-census.asp, accessed 30 October 2015.

4 City of Lowell, Division of Planning and Development, "City of Lowell: Race and Ethnicity Trends," in "City of Lowell Master Plan" (Lowell, MA: Division of Planning and Development).

5 National Park Service, "Lowell National Historical Park, Massachusetts," n.d., http://www.nps.gov/lowe/index.htm, accessed 2 January 2013.

6 Interestingly, Lowell's economic downturn actually predated the Great Depression. With decreased demands for textiles, the city began its downturn in 1926. See Paul Marion, "Timeline of Lowell History," *Yankee Magazine*, November 2009, http://www.yankeemagazine.com/article/features/lowell-timeline, accessed 30 October 2015.

7 "1960 Census of Population and Housing—Census Tracts: Lowell, Massachusetts," *Census of Population and Housing: Final Report PHC*, vol. 60, no. 84 (Washington, DC: U.S. Government Printing Office, 1960).

8 This figure—13 percent—represents the highest of any Massachusetts city and corresponds to the lowest population count at 92,000. See Rebecca Gross, "Building on the Past: The Creative Rebirth of Lowell, Massachusetts," *NEA Arts Magazine*, no. 1 (2012), http://www.nea.gov/about/nearts/storyNew.php?id=02_building&issue=2012_v1, accessed 12 January 2013.

9 Ibid.

10 City of Lowell, Division of Planning and Development, "City of Lowell: Race and Ethnicity Trends."

11 See Bart Ziegler, "Once-Booming Wang Laboratories Failed to Heed the Changing Market," *Seattle Times*, August 23, 1992, http://community.seattletimes.nwsource.com/archive/?date=19920823&slug=1508984, accessed 12 January 2013.

12 City of Lowell, Division of Planning and Development, "City of Lowell: Race and Ethnicity Trends."

13 Ibid.

14 The 1965 Immigration and Nationality Act (also known as the Hart-Cellar Act) removed nation-state quotas from immigration policy. The act divided immigrants into hemispheric groups: 120,000 immigrants from the "Western Hemisphere" were granted access; 170,000

immigrants from the "Eastern Hemisphere" were allowed entry. For Southeast Asians, the 1975 Indochinese Act and the 1980 Refugee Act enabled migration en masse from nations affected by the Vietnam War (including Laos, Cambodia, Vietnam, and Thailand).

15 The four elements of hip-hop include deejaying, emceeing (rap), break dancing, and graffiti.

16 Hy, interview.

17 Ibid. Hy attended seven schools before he reached sixth grade.

18 This reading of a Cambodian American "VOA" is one that encapsulates the work of other Khmer American rappers, namely Prach Ly, who hails from Long Beach, California. See Cathy J. Schlund-Vials, *War, Genocide, and Justice: Cambodian American Memory Work* (Minneapolis: University of Minnesota Press, 2012).

19 Hy, interview. Hy's influences and tastes in music are quite eclectic. According to Hy, he was drawn to "Run DMC, Fat Boys, Zapp, LL Coll J, Beastie Boys, Lords of the Underground, Pharcyde, Biz Markie, Das Effex, Black Sheep, Fresh Prince, Kriss Kross, Naughty by Nature, Marky Mark, C&C Music Factory, Snow, Rob Base, Salt n Peppa, Young Black Teenagers, TLC, Tribe Called Quest, Jedi Mind Trikcs, Common, Mos Def, Jay Electronica" and the "list goes on."

20 Ibid.

21 See Mimi Thi Nguyen and Thuy Linh Nguyen Tu, "Introduction," in *Alien Encounters: Popular Culture in Asian America*, ed. Mimi Thi Nguyen and Thuy Linh Nguyen Tu (Durham, NC: Duke University Press, 2007).

22 Ibid., 11, 7.

23 Hy, interview.

24 Lyrics provided by Sambath Hy via an email correspondence on December 13, 2013.

25 Ibid.

26 See Lisa Lowe, *Immigrant Acts: On Asian American Cultural Politics* (Durham, NC: Duke University Press, 1996).

27 See Schlund-Vials, *War, Genocide, and Justice.*

28 Hy, interview.

29 The "Killing Fields" is a term coined by the Cambodian survivor, journalist, and activist Dith Pran in a January 20, 1980, *New York Times* magazine article written by Sydney Schanberg titled, "The Death and Life of Dith Pran." In Cambodia, this era is known as "Pol Pot time."

30 Prime Minister Hun Sen, Cambodia's head of state since the 1980s, was a low-ranking Khmer Rouge soldier.

31 Walter Leitner International Human Rights Clinic, "Removing Refugees: U.S. Deportation Policy and the Cambodian-American Community" (New York: Leitner Center for International Law and Justice, 2010), available through the Southeast Asian Resource Center, www.searac.org/sites/default/files/2010%20Cambodia%20Report_FINAL.pdf, accessed June 12, 2010.

32 Ibid.

33 Ibid.

34 Kaing Guek Eav, aka "Comrade Duch," was the head warden for the notorious Tuol Sleng Prison (S-21). An estimated twelve thousand to fourteen thousand Cambodians were detained at S-21; less than two hundred survived. Nuon Chea was known as "Brother Number Two," and Khieu Samphan was a former Khmer Rouge prime minister. Chea and Samphan are presently facing charges of genocide. For more about the state of memory and justice vis-à-vis the tribunal, see Schlund-Vials, *War, Genocide, and Justice.*

35 See Olesia Plokhii and Tom Mashberg, "One-Way Trip to an Unknown Land," *Boston Globe Magazine* (January 27, 2013), 27.

36 Ibid.

37 Hy, interview.
38 Ibid.
39 See Oliver Wang, "Rapping and Repping Asian: Race, Authenticity, and the Asian American MC," in Nguyen and Tu, *Alien Encounters*, 61.
40 Ibid., 41.
41 praCh [Prach Ly], "Stories," in *Dalama: The Lost Chapter* (audio recording; Long Beach, CA: Mujestic Records, 2002).
42 Sara Rimer, "Journeys; the Sound of Home: An 8,690-Mile Echo," *New York Times*, August 23, 2002.
43 See "Lowell Southeast Asian Water Festival: Preserving Culture through Community Building and Performance," n.d., http://www.lowellwaterfestival.com, accessed January 20, 2013.
44 Ibid.
45 Quoted in Rimer, "Journeys."
46 Hy, interview.
47 Ibid.
48 Ibid.
49 See Rimer, "Journeys."
50 Hy, interview.
51 I appreciate Shilpa Davé's critical suggestion re the valorization and reclamation of the country of origin.

8

"You'll Learn Much about Pakistanis from Listening to Radio"

Pakistani Radio Programming in Houston, Texas

AHMED AFZAL

I had been in Houston for less than a week when I realized the difficulty in finding interlocutors for my research—Pakistani immigrants and Pakistani Americans. Like many new immigrants in Houston, Pakistanis also reside throughout Greater Houston. Even in the sections of southwest Houston along Hillcroft Avenue, Harwin Drive, and Bissonnet Street, where Pakistani businesses and residential enclaves predominate, Pakistanis are a part of an ethnically diverse landscape that also includes, among others, Bangladeshi, Chinese, Ecuadorian, Indian, Japanese, Korean, Mexican, Nigerian, Palestinian, and Vietnamese business enterprises and residential communities. During this initial period of research, I could not discern a recognizable South Asian ethnic center that would not only anchor my research but also provide me with a sense of ethnic rootedness and belonging in an as yet unfamiliar city.

On one of my first exploratory visits into southwest Houston, wondering how, in a city like this, I would ever find Pakistani interlocutors, I got into a cab to continue my tour of multi-ethnic Houston. The cab driver was Wasim, a middle-aged Pakistani man. As I learned during the cab ride, Wasim had re-located with his family from New York City to Houston a few years ago. "I wanted to be closer to my brother who lives here," he told me. "Besides, it's tough to raise a family in New York—life is so fast there. Houston is better that way."

As we continued our conversation, Wasim asked me: "So, what brings you to Houston?"

"My research is on Pakistanis in Houston; you know, their cultural life here," I told him, trying to explain my research.

"You must listen to the radio then," he said as he turned up the volume of the car radio. A Pakistani folk song permeated the cab. A male radio programmer, speaking in Urdu, introduced the next song. Wasim continued: "There are so many Pakistani radio programs on 1150 AM—it is basically a Pakistani radio station. I always listen to it whenever I am driving—the programs are on all the time. You'll learn much about Pakistanis from listening to radio."

Wandering around in a taxicab, looking for interlocutors for my research, I was thus first introduced to Pakistani radio programs in Houston. Importantly, Wasim had not taken me to a spatially bound ethnic enclave or neighborhood or pointed me to the institutional space of a mosque or a Pakistani or South Asian community-based organization. Instead, Wasim had directed me to look for the Pakistani community through its participation in commercial radio. What is significant in Wasim's observation is the connection he makes between radio and the production of Pakistani "culture" and community in Houston. Indeed, radio is a ubiquitous presence in Pakistani public life in Houston. For the Pakistani community that is dispersed throughout the Greater Houston metropolitan area, radio is a site of connectivity and convergence that transcends boundaries of class, gender, generation, and geography. In 2001, there were fifteen Pakistani radio programs on the air—a high number even for a city with one of the largest Pakistani immigrant populations of any city in the United States. These Houston-based Pakistani radio programs provide reports on culture and politics in Houston, South Asia, the Muslim world, and beyond, from a Pakistani Muslim American perspective. These programs also provide entertainment by playing Indian and Pakistani songs and music, information about local South Asian businesses and services, and a calendar of local cultural events. Finally, these programs are a vital forum for advertising South Asian ethnic businesses based in Houston.

In spite of the apparent ubiquity of radio in the Pakistani ethnoreligious environment in Houston, non-English language radio programming in the United States presents an under-studied aspect of transnational cultural flows that has been largely ignored in recent ethnographic studies of new immigrant communities. Recent literature has focused on the role of feature films and television programs produced in the homeland in representing the relation between the diaspora and the homeland to people in both sites.[1] Where the social importance of radio has been documented, as in Erik Barnouw's classic study of broadcasting in the United States,[2] scant attention is paid to the role of Latinos, African Americans, and Asian Americans in the enterprise.[3] Only a few ethnographic studies examine the relationship between non-English language radio programming and practices of cultural production in new immigrant communities in the United States.[4]

This essay brings radio to the forefront of a cultural analysis of new immigrant formations in the United States in the early twenty-first century. Analytical consideration of Pakistani programs in Houston shows the tremendous endurance and relevance of radio, a technology over a century old, in the life of new immigrant communities in the United States. Indeed, non-English language Pakistani radio in Houston has been central in negotiations of transnational and cultural belonging. Historicizing Pakistani radio production in Houston over four decades (from the 1970s to the present) illuminates the role radio has played, and continues to play, in shaping the immigrant experience and reconfiguring contours of transnational community and identity within the Houston-based Pakistani population.

I examine two distinct periods in the short history of Pakistani radio programming in Houston to demonstrate the centrality of radio in reconfigurations of transnational community and identity. The first period, from the 1970s until the early 1990s, marks the beginning of Pakistani radio on the non-profit Pacifica radio station. *Khekashan Ke Sitare* ("A Galaxy of Stars") was one of the only Pakistani radio programs during this time. The program attempted to bring together the numerically small and upwardly mobile middle-class grouping of Indian and Pakistani professionals—most of whom were employed in hospitals, aerospace industry, oil exploration, and construction—and students at local colleges and universities in Houston. Program segments included live poetry recitals and dramatic skits and replays of Urdu- and Hindi-language songs. Through these segments, the program attempted to mediate the differences of national origin and religion among the South Asian nationality groups and create a shared South Asian diasporic aesthetic, identity, and community.

The second period pertains to Pakistani radio programming in Houston since the late 1990s. Pakistani radio programming in Houston had grown to over fifteen radio programs. Unlike the invocation of nostalgia for the homeland and the construction of a shared South Asian diasporic aesthetic, identity, and community that had characterized the first period of Pakistani programming, contemporary Pakistani programming is a site for accentuating cultural, religious, and national differences between the Houston-based South Asian communities. Moreover, unlike the non-profit orientation of the first radio programming period in the 1970s and the 1980s, contemporary programs air on commercial networks and are guided by commerce and financial imperatives and intertwine with the local South Asian ethnic economies. Specifically, most of these radio programmers are entrepreneurs who use the radio program as an affordable outlet for advertising their businesses while also acquiring visibility and status in the local Pakistani ethnoreligious environment. The competition for "advertising dollars" has contributed to instances of infighting and conflict between radio programmers that often spill over into on-air broadcasts. The analysis in this essay demonstrates how radio reconfigures not only the terms of cultural and transnational belonging but also, and equally, the intersection of commerce-based imperatives with mass media in such reconfigurations.

Given the paucity of listener-based reception studies of contemporary non-English language programming and new immigrant communities in the United States, it is difficult to generalize Pakistani radio listening patterns in Houston. My ethnographic research on radio audiences, including questions about radio in the over 200 oral life histories I collected during the period of the research, complicates conventional understandings that indicate listenership primarily among newly arrived immigrants and the first generation and decreasing levels among the second and the third generations.[5] On the contrary, several Pakistani radio programs are hosted by second generation students, professionals and entrepreneurs. It is also reasonable to assume that Pakistani radio programs reach a considerable percentage of the Pakistani community in Houston. In the vast majority of the structured oral life histories that I collected as well as conversations with hundreds of interlocutors throughout the period of my research, radio reoccurred as a topic of discussion, suggesting the significance of Pakistani radio within the larger Pakistani community in Houston.

An ethnographic study of Pakistani radio also participates in an intellectual project that attempts to bridge the research and examine the intersections of Asian American and Muslim American fields of study. Pakistani immigrants are well situated within genealogies of post-1965 Asian American labor flows. Moreover, shared South Asian colonial, post-colonial, and transnational histories, ethno-linguistic affiliations, and experiences foreground community formations and alliance building, as well as historically contingent tensions between different South Asian nationality groups that encompass Bangladesh, Bhutan, India, the Maldives, Nepal, Pakistan, and Sri Lanka.

At the same time, the racialization of Pakistanis as Muslim in U.S. racial formations has shaped the imagination of Pakistani immigrants in the post-9/11 epoch, demonstrating historical continuities in categorizations of Muslims. In *Terrifying Muslims*, the anthropologist Junaid Rana astutely argues that, in the 1980s–2000s, U.S. foreign policy constructed terrorism as an enemy of the state and as a legitimate site of state violence and biopolitics.[6] Equally, it marked and produced certain nationality groups, such as Pakistani immigrants, as a terror threat and as a racial category that is policed by the state. Moreover, this category is central in anti-immigrant ideologies, practices, and narratives that construct illegality and criminality. This register of subjectification characterizes Pakistani Americans uniquely in the United States in ways that are otherwise elided in categorizations of Pakistanis as South Asians or Asian Americans. It is this intersection of Asian American and Muslim American genealogies, then, that instructively informs a discussion of radio and community formation in this essay.

Nostalgia and the Making of a South Asian Diasporic Aesthetic and Community: The Beginnings of Pakistani Radio in Houston in the 1970s

Pakistanis are relatively new entrants to the ethnic landscape in Houston, arriving in large numbers only in the 1970s.[7] The first Pakistani radio program, *Khekashan Ke Sitare*, began broadcasting in Houston in 1978, co-hosted by S. M. Saleem and his wife, Suriya. After an extremely popular twelve-year run, the program went off the air when Saleem passed away. The program was off the air for a year when Saleem's friend, also a regular volunteer on *Khekashan Ke*

Sitare, convinced Suriya to re-commence broadcasts. A dramatically re-vamped program began broadcasting in 1990 and has since been on the air.

I first met Suriya and Azhar, the current co-hosts of *Khekashan Ke Sitare*, at the radio station from where the program is broadcast. The managerial offices and the recording studios for the private radio station are located in a high-rise that also includes the offices of law and accounting firms, insurance companies, and travel agencies, among other service-sector companies. The ambiance may at first underwhelm a visitor. The recording studio is devoid of any personal or cultural artifacts, or larger-than-life celebrity photographs, or pictorial documentation of the radio station and programs. In the seemingly nondescript space of the radio studio, it is the soundscapes that transform space into a transnational Pakistani place. The voice of the co-hosts speaking in Urdu, the informality of conversations between listeners and the radio hosts during call-in segments, and the replay of Pakistani and Indian film songs transform aurality into what the anthropologist Laura Kunreuther has termed "a sign of emotional directness, authenticity and immediacy."[8]

It is difficult to describe the camaraderie between the two co-hosts as they engage in effortless banter, on issues both extraordinary and banal, with each finishing the other's sentence and moving from one topic to the next, and back to the first—all within a few minutes. It is equally difficult to define the genre of the radio program given its focus on everyday Pakistani life in Houston, which includes the hosts' visits to a Pakistani restaurant or attendance at Pakistani cultural events, as well as discussions on the U.S.-led "war on terrorism." The program is unscripted and invokes nostalgia and "deeply personal and vivid memories"[9] of living room conversations between two old friends in Pakistan. The conversations have an air of indeterminacy, taking form through spontaneous interactions with listeners.[10] Often known to either or both of the co-hosts, listeners may call in to request a specific Pakistani song, or enter into the ongoing conversation between the hosts, or request information about a Pakistani event, business, or service that has been advertised during the broadcast. As the anthropologists Lucas Bessire and Daniel Fisher suggest, such voice-centered mediation endows the space of the radio studio with cultural meanings, interpellates "listeners as members of audiences, collectives, and publics,"[11] and shapes affective experiences. The airplay of an occasional song—often a classical or well-known contemporary Urdu song produced and recorded in Pakistan—combines with the informality, immediacy, and intimacy of the program to create nostalgia for the homeland and invoke culturally specific modes of listening, conversation, and sociality.

Khekashan Ke Sitare, as part of the first period of Pakistani programming in Houston, illustrates an important diasporic space that mediated differences of religion and national origin among Pakistani and Indian listeners. Invoking nostalgia through the airplay of Indian and Pakistani music and songs and the production of dramatic skits found on radio in India and Pakistan, the program attempted to represent a culturally conceived diasporic aesthetic and community, inclusive of all South Asian nationality groups who either spoke or understood Urdu. In an interview published in 1983 in the oldest South Asian newspaper in Houston, the *Indo-American News*, Saleem explained the mission of the program by emphasizing that the audience for his program included both Pakistanis and Indians in Houston. According to Saleem:

> The radio program is for people who want to remember their culture and language. There is not much of a difference in the Indian and Pakistani culture. People on both sides listen to the same music and songs. It is for people who want to keep in touch with their roots and understand their origin better.

The program's mission, production, and reception were intertwined, which made it an important site for South Asian diasporic community-building. Pakistani and Indian middle-class professionals were not just listeners but in fact assumed ownership of the program by making financial contributions, volunteering at the studio, acting in the dramatic segments, and providing source material for the program. Reminiscing fondly about these collaborations, Suriya recalled to me that

> there were very few [South Asians] at the time, but they all enjoyed helping out with the program. They would cooperate fully with us. . . . If they were visiting Pakistan or India, they would bring back audiocassettes of songs and Urdu plays. We had contacts at Radio Pakistan in Pakistan so we would get scripts of plays from them and then dramatize them on our radio program here. We also had a *Khekashan* Drama Unit made up of volunteers who were professionals in their fields.

Suriya and Saleem's emphasis on community-based programming and in engaging their listeners in the production process was responded to in kind by full participation of the South Asian community. Saleem and Suriya nurtured their relationship with their listeners by excluding on-air discussions of potentially divisive and contentious issues, especially those pertaining to South Asian politics and religion.[12] Suriya emphasized to me that

> we wouldn't do anything that would upset someone's religious sentiments. . . . See, one of the things that we have tried to ensure over the years is to stay clear of politics, particularly the politics of the India-Pakistan or the Bangladesh-Pakistan relationships. We have several Hindu, Sikh, and Muslim listeners from India and Bangladesh, and we would never hurt their religious or political sentiments.

Democratizing the Airwaves: Pakistani Radio in Houston since the 1990s

Khekashan Ke Sitare, in its twenty-third year of broadcast when I carried out my field research in Houston during the years 2001–2002, had become part of a widely diversified Pakistani media landscape that included over fifteen regularly scheduled Pakistani radio programs, several newspapers in English and Urdu languages, Indian radio programs, South Asian DVD and video stores, and multiplex cinemas that screened first-run Hindi-language feature films several times daily. The broadcast of Pakistan- and India-based satellite and cable television networks in Houston provides one more piece of a media assemblage through which Indian and Pakistani music and popular culture circulates globally and reaches diasporic audiences.

Certainly, not all Pakistani Muslims in Houston listen to these radio programs, and some listeners try to distance themselves from these broadcasts because of the eruption of on-air conflicts between radio hosts. Shahzad, a host of a Pakistani radio program, describes a love-hate relationship that most Pakistani listeners have had with radio since 2001:

> People *do* listen to the radio. . . . Although it is kind of funny because the average Pakistani in Houston does not want to ever admit that he listens to the Pakistani radio programs. When you talk to most people, they always say: "We don't listen to the radio." Then five minutes later they will tell you, "Oh, this host said this on the radio and that fellow said that . . ." Yes, some people in North Houston do not have as much exposure because some of the stations do not reach that far.

Shahzad's description of a vexed audience demonstrates a significantly different relationship with listeners than that described by Suriya in terms of a close-knit, well-known, and supportive audience. Some understanding of these differences is a function of increased numbers of radio programs. Pakistani radio programs air throughout Greater Houston on three different AM radio stations. Five programs air for several hours during weekday evenings. The remaining programs air on Saturdays and Sundays from 9:00 AM until 10:00 PM.

Digital technologies and new web-based social media sites such as YouTube, Twitter, and Facebook are further transforming Pakistani radio, deterritorializing the reach of radio and its availability in multiple geographical contexts that extend far beyond Houston. Theorizing about such ongoing transformations in the reception of radio, the scholar Susan Douglas suggests that they reflect "a dialectical relationship between oligopoly control of radio programming and technology on the one hand and technological insurgencies defying this control on the other."[13]

Contemporary Pakistani radio programming also complicates the pervasive conception of non-English language radio programming solely through the lens of community-based radio stations centered on cultural activism and production.[14] Instead, contemporary Pakistani radio may well be characterized as a business venture. While Saleem and Suriya had drawn on their vast experience at Radio Pakistan to create *Khekashan Ke Sitare*, a professional background in media broadcasting and/or academic education and training in media studies or communication is not a prerequisite for entry into the commercial Pakistani radio market in Houston today. The changing financial imperatives have contributed to a reconfiguration of the capital required for entry and success in the Houston's Pakistani radio market. The ease of entry coupled with the low labor and resource cost for running a radio program, and a rich available repertoire of South Asian songs and music, make it a highly attractive avenue for entrepreneurs and professionals who are looking to market their businesses or services to a targeted South Asian Muslim consumer base. At a bare minimum, a good supply of CDs of Indian and Pakistani and Indian songs alone, interspersed with commercials read aloud by the radio host/programmer to advertise businesses, suffice to defray the cost of broadcasts.

Despite low entry costs, there is intense competition for sponsorship from South Asian businesses in Houston. This competition has sometimes contributed to rather volatile airings of personal conflicts and grievances between radio programmers, examples of which I discuss in the next section. The public airing of grievances has played a major role in the denigration of radio by some segments in the South Asian communities in Houston. Several of my interlocutors—also listeners of the Pakistani radio programs—narrated accounts of personal conflicts and infighting between Pakistani radio hosts/programmers. A few interlocutors distanced themselves entirely from Pakistani radio, and some even tried to steer me away from researching radio based on their perception that these on-air broadcasts of personal fights represented the Pakistani community in a negative light. An upper-middle-class Pakistani female interlocutor, for example, whom I had met several months into my research on Pakistani radio, expressed embarrassment and dismay. "Oh, I wish I had met you earlier. I would have pointed you to another direction—we are doing so many *good* things in Houston," she stated.

Grievances, Sponsorship Imperatives, and Recuperation of Muslim Masculinity

In the 2000s, Pakistani radio emerged as a volatile site for the airing of personal conflicts and grievances between radio hosts. In one instance, a Pakistani radio host used his radio show to make allegedly inflammatory statements about specific religious leaders and minority Muslim sectarian communities in Houston. Nabeel, a co-host of a Pakistani music and variety radio show, had worked as the liaison between the radio hosts and the radio station management during the time of conflict between the radio programmers, representing different Muslim sectarian communities. When I asked Nabeel about the reasons for these conflicts, he responded, "It is ego problems mainly. Everyone thinks that they are the leader of the community. They think that because they are doing radio that they are leaders. They think that they are celebrities."

Personal conflicts and "ego problems," as Nabeel aptly put it, are intertwined with the desire to make money through private sponsorship by primarily Muslim and South Asian businesses, organizations, and services. In a formal interview, Shahzad discussed in animated detail the infighting that has characterized some of the programming in Houston:

> I think a lot of it has to do with the advertising money. Most of the squabbles that I have seen have to do with the competition over the advertising dollar. It is still going on . . . the infighting . . . slander . . . personal attacks . . . name-calling. . . . Yes, there has been a lot of that. . . . The community is much divided, and whoever likes can verbally attack another. That is why no one respects Pakistani radio programs today. It is very much seen negatively in the community.

It is in large part because of the infighting and the "negative" perception of some shows within the Pakistani population that Nabeel added a tagline to his radio program—*Radio Naya Andaz: Pollution-Free Radio*. When I asked Nabeel to say more about this, he explained at length:

> People are more cautious about what they say on the air. But still some radio hosts will bring up religious issues or controversial issues so that their ratings go up. They thrive on the word-of-mouth publicity through controversies. . . . Radio programs are meant to strictly provide information and entertainment and unite the community and not divide it. We have been doing our show for the past six years and never once had a problem. We support charitable events and speak about charitable and civic causes, but we do not bring up religious or political issues on the air. That's why we added "Pollution Free Radio" as our tag line—to differentiate ourselves from other radio programs.

Motivated by the competition for advertising dollars and listenership positions provides viable explanation for the eruptions of personal controversy on Pakistani radio. These conflicts also illustrate the discursive deployment of radio for articulating Islamic sectarian differences, notably between Shia and Sunni Muslim communities in Houston. Conflicts between Pakistani and Indian radio programmers further complicate the scenario and demonstrate a mapping of historically situated colonial and post-colonial differences between Indians and Pakistanis onto the space of radio in Houston. For example, as Nabeel recalled to me:

A couple of years ago, a radio program supported a live show with [Indian film superstar] Aamir Khan, and then a [local Pakistani] newspaper reported that the show's contributions were going towards supporting the Indian army in Kashmir. . . . It became a big issue. It caused conflict between the Indian and Pakistani communities here. The conflict was not just about radio. It was about telling people not to shop in Indian grocery stores and restaurants.

As a result, several Pakistani radio hosts/programmers advocated a boycott of local Indian businesses in Houston. The boycott extended to watching Indian films, a hugely popular leisure activity among middle-class Pakistanis in Houston. Several Pakistani radio programs stopped playing Indian film music and songs—something that persisted through the 2000s. Instead, Pakistani radio programs began to vigorously promote Pakistani popular and film music and soundtracks.

The proposed boycott drew on long-distance nationalism but was only somewhat successful in part because of the engagement of Pakistani entrepreneurs and businesses in Indian media and popular culture. Most South Asian DVD and video sale and rental stores, and the two multiplex cinemas that feature new Indian films several times daily, are owned and managed by Pakistani families and entrepreneurs. Thus the protests demonstrated a precarious negotiation between affirming transnational belonging to Pakistan and Islam, on the one hand, and exigencies of the neoliberal market economy, on the other. These negotiations were embodied by the pronouncements made by a Pakistani radio host who also owned one of the multiplex cinemas. As tensions escalated, he went on air with the following plea:

> Music is a part of life. Music is the common ground between Indians and Pakistanis and all South Asians. Whenever there is tension in our [home] countries, I think it is our duty to encourage and arrange programs that promote harmony and friendship between our communities. For businessmen, religion is business. We are here for economic reasons. We did not come here to fight. It is our moral duty to stick together and promote each other's businesses and promote harmony.

By 2001, even though the boycott had been only a partial success, it transformed Pakistani radio from a medium for developing a shared, united diasporic South Asian community in the 1970s and the 1980s into one that emphasized "difference" and separation on the basis of religion and national origin. The fact that South Asian communities in Houston include members of the Pakistani Hindu communities as well as Indian Muslim communities was obscured in such hegemonic constructions of India as a Hindu nation and Pakistan as a Muslim nation.

I suggest that the competition for sponsorship and listeners and assertions of long-distance nationalism provide only partial explanations for on-air conflicts between radio programmers, however. Rather, the racism experienced by Muslim men in mainstream U.S. society also finds expression and an outlet in the uncensored and volatile grievances that are aired on radio. The airing of personal grievances represents another facet of the spirited and emotional on-air discussions of the situation of Muslims following 9/11. In the weeks after 9/11, Pakistani radio in Houston emerged as an important forum for discussing issues such as hate crimes directed at Muslims and properties associated with Muslim Americans, Muslim self-presentations in the mainstream public spheres, and the U.S. led "war on terrorism." For example, community leaders appeared on radio to offer support to victims of hate crimes and to address concerns over government surveillance in localities in southwest Houston such as Hillcroft Avenue and Bissonnet Street, where Pakistani businesses and mosques predominate.

Listeners called in with a broad range of questions, transforming radio into a vital resource during a period of crisis. During the weeks following 9/11, listeners called in with some version of the following questions: Do Pakistanis on student visas have to report to immigration agencies? Would the government deport Pakistanis who had overstayed their tourist or work visa? Can they be fired from their jobs because they are from Pakistan? Will federal agents be visiting businesses? What should one do if they are approached by federal agents? These and other similar questions indexed the fears, anxieties, and vulnerabilities within the larger Pakistani ethnoreligious environment in Houston and also pointed to an absence of transparency and clarity in government intentions and programs following 9/11. That radio provided a community resource points to the significance and the uses of this media for the Pakistani population in Houston during periods of crisis.

Radio programs also engaged with issues of public, self-presentation of Muslims, and the tense negotiations between assertions of a Muslim identity and effacement of difference. As reports of the harassment of Muslim women wearing the hijab (head scarf) circulated among Muslim communities in Houston, some community leaders encouraged women who wore the hijab to go out in groups rather than alone. The suggestion provoked heated debate and controversy on one of the Pakistani radio programs in Houston. During an on-air panel discussion, one community leader suggested that women consider not wearing the hijab until things had calmed down. "Should we stop practicing our religion and abandon our religious practices just to be safe?" responded a Pakistani American man involved in a community-based organization, exasperated and angry, as he reacted to the suggestion.

Radio also provided an outlet and a voice for critiquing the U.S.-led "war on terrorism" and the subsequent U.S. occupation of Iraq, military engagements in Afghanistan, and drone strikes in Pakistan. The drone strikes, for example, raised questions about the U.S. led "war on terrorism," on the one hand, and the sovereignty of the Pakistani nation-state, on the other. These engagements blurred distinctions between radio production and reception, as discourses became shaped by the on-air interactions among listeners, radio hosts, and invited panelists.

The perceived U.S. governmental involvement in the Palestine-Israel conflict and U.S. economic engagements in Saudi Arabia, the Gulf States, the Middle East, and South Asia were also the subject of discussion on Pakistani radio, indicating a critical engagement with a broad range of geopolitical situations. Community leaders appeared on radio and voiced support for the United States but also offered a critique, citing the failure of U.S. support for Pakistan following the end of the Soviet occupation of Afghanistan in the 1980s. Such concerns draw attention to the complicity of the United States and the CIA with what the scholar Jasbir Puar refers to as a "buildup of Pakistan's terrorist industrial complex: military dictators, opium markets, terrorist training centers set up to fight the Soviets."[15]

During an on-air discussion, a Pakistani community leader and activist grew increasingly passionate as he stated that,

> after the Afghanistan and Soviet Union war, Pakistan ended up with 2.5 million Afghan refugees. We never had a Kalashnikov culture in our country [Pakistan]. We never had a drug problem in our country. We never had a high crime rate in our country. We never had such a high rate of terrorism in our country. Why did we end up having all? Because after the Afghanistan–Soviet Union war, nobody thought about Pakistan. The U.S. packed their bags and went home and started imposing sanctions. So the American-Pakistani relationship is a classic story of a one-sided friendship in which Pakistan has always stood up for its friends but nobody has ever stood up for Pakistan.

As gleaned from these post-9/11 uses of the airwaves, Pakistani radio in Houston is a valuable communicative practice that is vitally important during periods of crisis. Racialized Muslim subjectification is produced in not only race regimes and labor flows but equally in Islamophobia in the late twentieth century. Examined through the lens of this racialized construction of the Muslim, the on-air mediations of personal grievances and conflicts, reflections on the post-9/11 situation of Muslims, and participation in radio in general suggest a desire to claim a freedom of speech denied in the mainstream, and as the scholar Susan Douglas puts it, "a yearning for some form of public discourse, [and] for a place where less slick and less mainstream opinions could be articulated."[16] In the process of creating these alternative public spheres, "the profoundly embodied nature of listening and sounding makes radio deeply entangled with the inner lives and political agency of its users."[17] Like on-air discussions of 9/11, personal grievances and conflicts also serve to recuperate a Muslim masculinity that is rendered deviant and a terror threat and an agency that is constrained in the United States.

Conclusion

Pakistani radio programming provides an important case study for examining the changing contours of identity and community within the Pakistani population in Houston. Pakistani radio programming first emerged in the 1970s on a non-profit station in Houston. Through its programming, the first Pakistani radio program emphasized cultural convergences between South Asian nationality communities, notably Indians and Pakistanis. Structured around aurality, the first radio program drew on culturally familiar genres of radio broadcasting and enabled the construction of associative memories, nostalgia, and imagination among listeners.

By the 1990s, the rapid increase in the Pakistani immigrant population in Houston contributed to an increase in the number of programs to fifteen regularly scheduled programs. Pakistani radio in Houston was also transformed from a community-centered initiative into a business enterprise. Pakistani radio programmers created radio programs as vehicles to market their business and services. As business ventures, these radio programs depend on sponsorship from other businesses, and the intense competition for sponsorship has led to the airing of grievances between radio hosts. Rather than place these conflicts solely within the domain of financial imperatives or long-distance nationalism, I suggest that these arguments also represent the desire for voice and agency and mark a discursive response to the experience of Muslim marginality, alienation, and racism in mainstream U.S. society especially following 9/11.

Radio, an understudied facet of transnationality, represents an important and mass-mediated site through which identities and communities are generated and a sense of cultural and transnational belonging is produced among new immigrant communities in the early twenty-first century United States. Moreover, attention to Pakistani radio also provides an important context for examining the intersections between Muslim American and Asian American studies.

NOTES

1 See Purnima Mankekar, *Screening Culture, Viewing Politics: An Ethnography of Television, Womanhood and Nation in Post-colonial India* (Durham, NC: Duke University Press, 1999).

2 See Erik Barnouw, *The Golden Web: A History of Broadcasting in the United States* (New York: Oxford University Press, 1968).

3 Most of the available ethnographic analyses of contemporary radio focus on radio production and reception in the non-West and only cursorily examine non-English-language media produced by new immigrant communities in the United States. Available ethnographic studies of radio cover a wide range of field sites and thematic concerns. See, e.g.,

Mike Cormack, "Minority Languages, Nationalism and Broadcasting: The British and Irish Examples," *Nations and Nationalism* 6, no. 3 (2000): 383–398; Max Easterman, "One-Legged Media, Lame Democracy: Experiences from Albania and Bosnia," *International Journal of Cultural Studies* 3, no. 2 (2000): 240–246; Yesudhasan Thomas Jayaprakash, "Remote Audiences beyond 2000: Radio, Everyday Life and Development in South India," in "Radiocracy," special issue, *International Journal of Cultural Studies* 3, no. 2 (2000): 227–239; Danny Kaplan, "The Songs of the Siren: Engineering National Time on Israeli Radio," *Cultural Anthropology* 24, no. 2 (2009): 313–345; Laura Kunreuther, "Technologies of the Voice: FM Radio, Telephone, and the Nepali Diaspora in Kathmandu," in "Culture at Large: Forum with George Lipsitz," special issue, *Cultural Anthropology* 21, no. 3 (2006): 323–353; L. Mtimde, "Radio Broadcasting in South Africa: An Overview," *International Journal of Cultural Studies* 3, no. 2 (2000): 173–179; Debra Spitulnik, "Mobile Machines and Fluid Audiences: Rethinking Reception through Zambian Radio Culture," in *Media Worlds: Anthropology on a New Terrain*, ed. Faye D. Ginsburg, Lila Abu-Lughod, and Brian Larkin, 337–365 (Berkeley: University of California Press, 2002).

4 The literature on South Asian Americans and Muslim Americans has focused primarily on the circulation of Indian cinema in the United States. See, e.g., Gayatri Gopinath, *Impossible Desires: Queer Diasporas and South Asian Public Cultures* (Durham, NC: Duke University Press, 2005); Purnima Mankekar, "Brides Who Travel: Gender, Transnationalism, and Nationalism in Hindi Film," *Positions* 7, no. 3 (1999): 731–762; Shalini Shankar, *Desi Land: Teen Culture, Class, and Success in Silicon Valley* (Durham, NC: Duke University Press, 2008).

   Other analyses have focused on the use of *bhangra*, Bollywood film music, and hip-hop in the production of Indian American youth cultures in London and New York. See, e.g., Sunaina Maira, *Desis in the House: Indian Youth Cultures in New York City* (Philadelphia: Temple University Press, 2000). In the case of Muslim Americans, ethnographic research has documented Iranian American television and radio production in Los Angeles. See Hamid Naficy, *The Making of Exile Cultures: Iranian Television in Los Angeles* (Minnesota: University of Minneapolis Press, 1993).

5 See, e.g., Donald Browne, "Speaking in Our Own Tongues: Linguistic Minority Radio in the United States," in *Radio Cultures: The South Medium in American Life*, ed. Michael Keith, 23–46 (New York: Peter Lang, 2008).

6 See Junaid Rana, *Terrifying Muslims: Race and Labor in the South Asian Diaspora* (Durham, NC: Duke University Press, 2011).

7 My archival research and interviews with Pakistani men and women revealed numerous reasons immigrants chose Houston. First, the thriving oil- and gas-based economy and the presence of one of the largest medical complexes in the United States made, and continue to make, Houston ideally suited for Pakistani students and professionals specializing in engineering, medicine, and administration. Second, the mild weather, reminiscent of the tropical climate of Pakistani cities like Karachi—the city of origin for an overwhelming majority of Pakistani immigrants—makes Houston and not New York City or Chicago the preferred U.S. city in which to settle. Third, several Pakistani immigrants also mentioned the affordable cost of living and higher education in Houston, compared to other American cities in the Northeast and the West Coast, as a major reason they chose to reside in Houston.

8 Kunreuther, "Technologies of the Voice," 324.

9 Susan J. Douglas, *Listening In: Radio and the American Imagination* (Minneapolis: University of Minnesota Press, 2004), 8.

10 Ian Hutchby, "Frame Attunement and Footing in the Organization of Talk Radio Openings," *Journal of Sociolinguistics* 3, no. 1 (1999): 41–64.

11 Lucas Bessire and Daniel Fisher, eds., *Radio Fields: Anthropology and Wireless Sound in the 21st Century* (New York: NYU Press, 2012), 21.

12 The years preceding and following the formation of Pakistan witnessed the forced migration of millions of South Asians and a violent transition into the post-colonial epoch. Hindu-Muslim riots, lootings, and rape precipitated the migration of Hindus and Sikhs from Pakistan and Muslims from India. In the contemporary moment, the ongoing dispute over the territory of Kashmir, which both India and Pakistan claim as part of their nation-states, further sustains government-sponsored militaristic action, diplomatic impasse, and distrust on both sides of the India-Pakistan border.

13 Douglas, *Listening In*, 16.

14 See, e.g., Melinda Hinkson, "The Cultural Politics of Radio: Two Views from the Warlpiri Public Sphere," in Bessire and Fisher, *Radio Fields*, 142–159.

15 Jasbir Puar, *Terrorist Assemblages: Homonationalism in Queer Times* (Durham, NC: Duke University Press, 2007), 72.

16 Douglas, *Listening In*, 19.

17 Bessire and Fisher, *Radio Fields*, 4.

9

Online Asian American Popular Culture, Digitization, and Museums

KONRAD NG

The opening decades of the twenty-first century have seen what can be called the "increasing digitalization" of culture, an expanding set of medium and tools for popular and national meaning making.[1] With the widening use of social media and networking services such as Facebook (established 2004), YouTube (established 2005), Twitter (established 2006), and more, along with increasingly complex mobile, visual, and dimensional technologies, the nature of our cultural industries and relationships have become ever more dynamic, volatile, and potent—a point made by Henry Jenkins in his early work on "convergence culture" and the digital age's increased interactivity and repositioning of cultural producers, consumers, and industries.[2] As I have argued elsewhere, digital life has become a compelling thread of the Asian American experience in ways that reconsider the role and pedagogy of traditional sources for popular and national narratives about agency.[3] From the activist blogging of Angry Asian Man[4] to the hashtag Twitter activism of #NotYourAsianSidekick[5] and #CancelColbert,[6] from YouTube celebrities and entrepreneurialism[7] to the peak of professional basketball player Jeremy Lin's #Linsanity, Asian American culture has become a vibrant online popular culture with social consequence and creative possibility. Asian America is the most wired and engaged online community in the United States,[8] and Asian Americans form a core constituency of America's "creative class" of professionals in the arts, sciences, and fields of technology, education, entertainment, and design.[9] In sum, digital Asian America has become a cultural laboratory for popular meaning production and consumption; digital platforms have become the place to fashion a cultural economy with in-the-world, offline impact and activity.

It may be tempting to view Asian American online life through a neoliberal lens, as evidence of some post-racial, multicultural Internet in democratic society. In other words, some might suggest that Asian Americans are the model minority of the Web. However, I contend something more dynamic is happening. Studies of race and the Internet reveal how the relationship between digital technologies, online life, and race is complex and unique. Lisa Nakamura argues for recognizing the digital formation of racial identity and the role of technology in framing racial identities and experiences. The digital representation and expression of racial identities shape the public understanding of race. People of color often view new media as a space of opportunity for cultural and political engagement, allowing for an envisioning of shared racial experiences and self-representations that serve as argumentative examples of a more congruent representation of lived experience.[10] Wendy Hui Kyong Chun develops the premise of digital racial formation by outlining a consideration of race *as* technology, to shift "from the what of race to the how of race, from knowing race to doing race by emphasizing the similarities between race and technology."[11] Digital racial formation can reframe biopolitical takes on race—what race is and is not and the focus on race as physical and biological differences and authentic performances of racial identity—to ethic ones, how race may be the starting point for studying relations between subject positions: "What relations does race set up?"[12] This view on digital racial formation opens the opportunity for a coalitional and self-reflective political engagement. In sum, the concept of "digitalization" for people of color—communities who have been underrepresented or misrepresented in mainstream institutions and industries of culture—means wider opportunities for creative and critical expressions, new ways to manifest community and identity, and the chance to imaginatively engage with race in alternate spaces of meaning. The Asian American thread in digital popular culture inflects digitalization discourses and the politics of race. What does this moment mean for traditional sources for national meaning making such as museums? How can museums both narrate the nation and imagined communities when the online popular discourse of race has reached beyond the anachronistic sounding catchphrase "2.0"?

Overall, the question of race has been vexing in the larger discourses that explore the intersection of technology and society—what has come to be known as the "digital humanities"—and the intersection of computational and technological theories and applications with the teaching and study of the humanities. For the most part, the digital humanities have focused on the technological augmentation, supplementation, and organization of large sets of material—as opposed to seeing technology as an opportunity to deepen social critique. As Tara McPherson asks, "Why Are the Digital Humanities So White?"[13] The sense that there is more to the digital than being a technological asset to existing cultural material, that the digital is a popular medium in which critical concepts such as race may achieve a dynamic sense of agency, has been a core belief in my professional life—as a museum curator of film and video, an international film festival programmer, a professor of creative media, and presidential campaign volunteer to my current position as director of the only Asian American national museum center—the Smithsonian Institution's Asian Pacific American Center. Each position has been an opportunity to connect critical race theory and Asian American studies with curatorial practice at the national level; to show that the

Asian American experience as expressed through creative media—like art, cinema, and design—yields unique insights into the politics of race and nation; to show how creative media can affect the cultural economy of the nation and what counts as being "American." Throughout this journey, my activism, research, teaching, and curatorial and political work have been guided by a belief that genres of popular culture are tied to our understanding of race, that through popular culture, we can arrive at a more nuanced and more complex understanding of Asian American cultural identity and, in so doing, assume a more empowered self-understanding of being Asian American. This understanding was deepened during my outreach work for the first presidential campaign of my brother-in-law, Barack Obama. I focused on outreach and engagement to Asian Americans, Pacific Islanders, and Native Hawaiians. While citizenship is often practiced through the exercise of rights and responsibilities, it was clear to me that what compels citizenship is our cultural experience of it—if we are reflected in the institutions and canons of national culture.

That the office of president could be, and eventually was, filled by a person of color animated an unprecedented range of cultural production. As Jeff Chang argued in 2004, the Obama election conjured a long simmering post-multiracial artistic swell of citizenship.[14] For some Asian Americans, Obama was the first "Asian American" president, eliciting a range of creative Asian American digital practices that invested in his agency and candidacy a re-understanding and rallying cry for Asian American collective identity; in this instance, an Afro-Asian digital formation became possible, thus introducing a novel understanding of race.[15] Digital popular culture is transforming the institutions and canons of national culture, including museums. The belief that museums remain sacred spaces for knowledge, high culture, heritage, and privilege is softening. Museums have entered an existential phase, reconciling their material, collections-based galleries with the fluidity of digital ubiquity. This opportunity to rethink the concept and purpose of a museum is happening where I currently work: the Smithsonian Institution, the museum system charged with being the steward of the national patrimony.

Established by Congress in 1846 for the "increase and diffusion of knowledge," the Smithsonian has grown into a network of nineteen museums, nine research centers, and a zoological park housing a collection of over 137 million objects, artworks, and specimens. Since its founding, the Smithsonian has been a place of education, exhibition, research, and preservation, a cultural broker in the representation of the American experience and the understanding of the world from the American perspective. Like the bulk of digital humanities work, digitization at the Smithsonian has primarily been about metrics, digitizing collections, and broadening public access to collections.[16] For me, the Smithsonian has provided an opportunity to use the vitality of Asian American online popular culture to rethink the concept of digitization and the way museums can have meaningful conversations about race. From a scholar-activist perspective, the question was to view the Smithsonian as a theory of power.

Museums continue to serve as a key broker in the politics of recognition, and during an age of digital racial formation, digitization can be a critical enterprise rather than serve only as a digital affirmation of collections being the primary source for museum knowledge; museums can create and curate galleries of digital cultural significance. In my capacity as director of the Smithsonian Institution's Asian Pacific American Center, I have, with my colleagues, been able to explore and experiment with how the popular digital meaning making of Asian America is the meaning making of national identity. This means that our curatorial work has often used digital exhibitions and initiatives to render the Asian American experience in *unfamiliar* ways. That is, we believe that museum work is more than objects and exhibitions. We believe that there is more to museum digitization than the "big data" digitization. We believe in thinking that the vibrancy of Asian American digital culture is not an example of Asian Americans being the model minority of the web. Finally, we believe that there is more than one way of being Asian American, that a richer understanding of Asian American cultural identity is found in its intersection with other discourses of meaning making. Like Chun's suggestion of considering race *as* technology, the center's work treats race as a question of ethics, about the relations that race sets up. To render Asian Americans in unfamiliar terms means exploring how the formation of national culture is revealed in the treatment of being Asian American; the Asian American experience is not simply an idealized or reviled part of the American experience—forever foreign or model minority—but a site for new identities and cultural currency. To this end, I want to share three online initiatives undertaken by the Smithsonian's Asian Pacific American Center to suggest a different understanding of museum digitization and race: the online comic book version of the exhibition *I Want the Wide American Earth: An Asian Pacific American Story*; the online exhibition of Korean taco food trucks featured in the *Smithsonian Asian-Latino Project*; and initiatives hosted during Asian Pacific American Heritage Month on Wikipedia, Flickr, and Instagram.

Online Comic

I Want the Wide American Earth: An Asian Pacific American Story is a traveling exhibition consisting of thirty freestanding banners with text, photographs, art, and graphics about the American experience from a pan-Asian American perspective. The title was taken from a poem by the Filipino American activist and poet Carlos Bulosan that argued for the recognition of Asian Americans as being a core part of the American experience. Our approach to the exhibition was to balance the presentation of Asian Americans as being notable for their contributions to America with the processes of racialization that have categorized Asian Americans as distinct from the meaning of "American."

Each banner outlines events, figures, and cultural influences significant to the understanding of being Asian in the United States, how the conceptualizations of "Asia," "Asians," and "citizen" have advanced American interests at home and abroad. *I Want the Wide American Earth* also depicts Asian Americans as active participants within iconic American narratives such as athletics, infrastructure, civil rights, politics, popular culture, the military, and more, and it also presents Asian American identity in uncommon narrative forms, such as mixed-race communities, as refugees, and as part of LGBT, African American, Latino, and Native narratives. The exhibition opened in May 2013 during Asian Pacific American Heritage Month at the Smithsonian's National Museum of American History and was on display until August 2013 before traveling to museums, libraries, and cultural organizations across the country. In order to amplify the impact of the *I Want the Wide American Earth* exhibition beyond its physical form, we developed a comic book version for online circulation. The goal was to recast the meaning of "exhibition" such that it re-appropriated an American popular culture canon—the comic book—onto a medium that resonated with Asian America—the Internet—to re-present Asian American history and culture.

The *I Want the Wide American Earth* comic was developed in partnership with the Secret Identities collective,[17] a group of Asian American creative talent in the comics industry who saw parallels between the tropes of Asian American experiences and the popular culture of America's comic book superheroes and the lack of Asian Americans characters as American superheroes. Rather than visualize fiction, the Secret Identities collective visualized historical fact by transforming key banners from the exhibition into comics that were distributed online without cost. The Secret Identities collective used the arc of the exhibition to envision key threads of the Asian American experience, from the Chinese laborers recruited to build the Transcontinental Railway to the Japanese American internment and military service during World War II, and from Wong Kim Ark and Bhagat Singh Thind, who shaped how America defined citizenship legally, to the death of Vincent Chin and the subsequent pan–Asian American political mobilization. The key image of the comic book and exhibition was an animated version of an archival photo of Japanese Americans interned at Tule Lake Internment Camp in California. Tule Lake was one of the more notorious Japanese American internment camps, known for harshly interning Japanese Americans whose "loyalty" to the United States was in question in spite of their citizenship. The objective was to circulate challenging depictions of Asian American characters and events—as protagonists and as catalysts in the American narrative—in the realm of online popular culture to make "unfamiliar" the

Figure 9.1. APAC Comic.

understanding of Asian American experience and what digitization can mean in a museum context. While online comics emphasized visual culture and interactions in an alternative narrative form of Asian American history, food became an opportunity to discuss the impact and intersection of immigration and popular culture in conjunction with Asian and Latino communities.

Online Exhibition

In 2013, the Asian Pacific American Center collaborated with the Smithsonian Latino Center to launch the *Smithsonian Asian-Latino Project* to explore the cultural, historical, and artistic intersections between Asian and Latino communities in the United States. The aim of the project was to present a more sophisticated understanding of the American experience at the Smithsonian, where museum collections have been organized and valued in silo-like frameworks. Both Smithsonian centers were motivated by the desire to complicate and enrich U.S. Census projections stating that Asian American and Latino communities are America's fastest growing communities, as well as the debates around immigration and American identity.[18] The project offered an alternate understanding of America's Asian and Latino experiences, how they intersect historically, politically, artistically, and in popular culture. Rather than assume that the racial formation of Asian Americans and Latinos emerge in isolation from each other, we presented an intersectional understanding of cultural identity. The *Smithsonian Asian-Latino Project* consisted of a series of initiatives—a public program with chefs discussing Asian-Latino culinary histories, a pop-up art gallery that projected artistic interpretations of Asian-Latino life and history in public spaces, and an online exhibition built around the emergence of the Korean taco.

The project was an intentional and experimental shift to valuing vernacular, consumptive objects of popular culture instead of sanctified collections to expand the scope of experiences appropriate for understanding race and American identity. The digital show focused on food trucks across the United States that served Korean tacos to provide a cultural geography of where Asian and Latino cultures have intersected through food. Our premise was that the Korean taco was a portal for community histories and cultural innovation. The center solicited photographs and personal essays from food truck proprietors to present their interpretation of Asian-Latino life through their food and lived experience. The curatorial vision was to weave agency and history into an online visual display of Asian-Latino foodways to suggest how the Korean taco could be more than a cultural fad; the food re-imagines the representation of the national patrimony from the perspective of minority communities.

Indeed, the focus on food reflects the argument by Robert Ji-Song Ku, Martin F. Manalansan IV and Anita Mannur recognizing the alimentary dimensions to the Asian American experience: Asian America as the "cross-articulation of ethnic, racial, class, and gender concerns with the transnational and global circulation of peoples, technologies, and ideas through food, cooking, and eating."[19] As a digital initiative, the Korean taco exhibition provided an alternate interpretation of digitization and museums. While the majority of museums treat digitization as an augment to museum collections, an online exhibition suggests how digital life may be constitutive to the Asian American experience. In her study of food trucks and Asian-Latino food, Lok Siu offers this observation: The popularity of food trucks and their success is rooted in the "intensive connectivity" enabled by social media and mobile technologies. Siu's claim means that digitization is a tool of promotion as well as a platform that builds the cultural capital of its phenomena; people consume the Korean taco and frequent food trucks, in part, because of the cultural capital each holds online.[20] To present the Korean taco as an online exhibition speaks to the dimensionality of digitization and its connection to Asian-Latino communities. The importance of highlighting online presence was the next focus of the center's initiatives for the commemoration of heritage.

Enriching Online Content

From Lunar New Year to Asian Pacific American Heritage Month (May), the American calendar year is peppered with popular and national commemorations of Asian American history, art, and culture. For the most part, the recognition of culturally significant events by museums is formulaic, accomplished by offering cultural performances, food, craft making and other applied arts, and a brief homage to an event's cultural significance.

While the commemoration of heritage is a core part of cultural identity, the goal of the Smithsonian Asian Pacific American Center has been to use digital popular culture to cultivate a more critical dynamic. Our curatorial notion of digitizing commemorations is informed by the idea that active knowledge about Asian Americans is derived from online sources—as opposed to the knowledge gained from the collections in museums and the cultural performances they offer—and how Asian Americans see platforms of online popular culture as legitimate sources for the Asian American experience. In practice, this means crowdsourcing material or using popularly created digital forms of communication such as Internet memes to circulate a wider range of attitudes toward Asian American identity. To recognize Lunar New Year, the Smithsonian Asian Pacific American Center produced a series of Internet memes to mark the occasions. For the 2014 and 2015 Lunar New Years, we produced a series of Internet memes that were visually irreverent or literal and used each meme to mark lesser-known experiences and practices of being Asian in America. The idea was to circulate alternate renderings of Asian American life across the Internet. By presenting facts such as the connection between the Dalai Lama's exile and his celebration of Losar, the Tibetan New Year, in America and the history of Chinese New Year in Butte, Montana, as an allegory for the Chinese American experience, our Lunar New Year Internet memes mixed online popular cultures with national culture.

For the 2014 Asian Pacific American Heritage Month, the Smithsonian Asian Pacific American Center chose May 10, 2014, to launch two online initiatives to enrich Asian American content circulating across online platforms of popular culture—Wikipedia, Flickr, and Instagram. The hashtags #WikiAPA and #LifeAPA used the 145th anniversary of the completion of the Transcontinental Railway to produce content for online consumption. The Transcontinental Railway was an unprecedented national project that relied heavily on Chinese labor, but those laborers were excluded from the iconic visual documentation of that history—the picture of the Golden Spike ceremony at Promontory, Utah, taken on May 10, 1869. Our objective was to respond to this exclusion using two crowdsourced digitization initiatives to populate the online world with Asian American representations of life on that day, thereby envisioning an Asian American counternarrative to an iconic American story. Over two thousand

Figure 9.2. Smithsonian Lunar New Year Internet meme in Butte, Montana.

videos and photos were submitted to #LifeAPA, and the project became the center's largest online exhibition of Asian American life as lived throughout the world. The exhibition stood as an online experiment in envisioning the Asian America experience as a living, vast, and complex identity that exceeds the scope of a physical museum collection

#WikiAPA involved staging edit-a-thons across the country to create or edit entries relating to Asian America and Asian Americans on the popular free and volunteer managed online encyclopedia Wikipedia. The center called for volunteers to join organized sessions to review a list of key articles and topics. The organization of the edit-a-thons was managed entirely online via the Center's #WikiAPA Meetup Page and covered logistics regarding the time/date of each meetup as well as a list of priorities. Each session began with an orientation to Wikipedia and the role of edit-a-thons in improving online content. #LifeAPA was a similar initiative that used social media image hosting websites, Flickr and Instagram, to circulate and post images and short videos about Asian American contemporary life taken on May 10, 2014. In the months leading up to the date, the center solicited contributions and contributors by invitation and open call. The curatorial vision was to solicit interpretations of Asian American life within a variety of frameworks—local and global, national and transnational, diaspora, refugees and more—to provide an expansive notion of the Asian experience as it has intersected with America. Uploads of the more than two thousand images and videos from over five hundred contributors were tagged with the hashtag #LifeAPA and were accompanied by titles, captions, location, the local time when the photo was taken, and other information deemed notable by the contributor. The Center opened the exhibition on July 4, 2014, to coincide with Independence Day, framing the project—like America—as an experiment in cultural democracy and suggesting Asian American digital life as a legitimate expression of patriotism.

Both #WikiAPA and #LifeAPA presented treatments of Asian American history, art, and culture as digital experiences and the digitization of museums as an opportunity for empowerment.

Conclusion

In my museum work, digitization is not entirely about bringing the content of a museum—a collection—to the online world; it is also a way to make the dynamic force of critique that is available in the online world the focus of museum content. Digital augments such as improving collections management and metadata, amplifying public engagement, and/or incorporating the latest technological inventions do not fully realize how museums can adapt in ways that embrace the symbolic economy of online popular culture as being part of the national patrimony. Museums can use online popular culture to empower minority communities in ways that circumvent the barriers that have prevented the acquisition of meaningful objects about their experience. For the Smithsonian Asian Pacific American Center, an office that traces its founding to the long history of Asian American cultural activism and advocacy, digitization is an activity of cultural production in the representation of the Asian American experience. The center has become a culture laboratory that recognizes how museums can use online popular culture to do more than simply collect objects. The center's version of a digital museum is a continuing movement, a platform of constant experimentation, in which Asian Americans can incubate cultural capital that expands the sources for understanding race and America.

The Smithsonian Asian Pacific American Center suggests an alternate possibility for museum digitization. When Smithsonian Secretary Wayne Clough—the chief administrator of the Smithsonian from 2008 to 2014—wrote that the Smithsonian had the "best of both worlds" through matching its collections and digital capabilities, he noted that the prioritization of digitization efforts to broaden access to museum collections would be especially timely since the attendance of minority communities to museums had been in decline.[21] My belief is that something else may work. Museums can become relevant to racial minorities, not through increasing access to collections, but through using the digital to speak about race in the ways that people of color use the digital to create meaning. If this is the case, then the digitalization efforts by the Smithsonian Asian

Pacific American Center and the study of Asian American popular culture as a driver of digitization are as important to democracy as the digitization of objects in a museum collection.

NOTES

1 My gratitude to Shilpa Davé, Tasha Oren, and Leilani Nishime for their encouragement, guidance, and valuable feedback for this piece.

2 Henry Jenkins, *Convergence Culture: Where Old and New Media Collide* (New York: NYU Press, 2006), 2.

3 Konrad Ng, "Hacking a Museum: Asian American Digital Life as Archive," in *Identity Palimpsests*, ed. Dominique Daniel and Amalia Skarlatou, 261–276 (Sacramento, CA: Litwin Books, 2014).

4 Konrad Ng, "Angry Asian Man," in *Asian American Society: An Encyclopedia*, ed. Mary Yu Danico, 41–42 (Thousand Oaks, CA: Sage Publications, 2014).

5 See Suey Park, "The Viral Success of #NotYourAsianSidekick Wasn't about Me, but All of Us," *xojane*, January 21, 2014, http://www.xojane.com/issues/suey-park-notyourasiansidekick, accessed November 29, 2014.

6 For a range of perspectives on #CancelColbert, see Suey Park and Eunsong Kim, "We Want to #CancelColbert," *Time*, March 28, 2014, http://time.com/42174/we-want-to-cancelcolbert, accessed November 29, 2014; Julia Carrie Wong, "Who's Afraid of Suey Park?" *Nation*, March 31, 2014, http://www.thenation.com/blog/179084/whos-afraid-suey-park, accessed November 29, 2014; and Jeff Yang, "Stephen Colbert, Racism and the Weaponized Hashtag," *Wall Street Journal*, March 29, 2014, http://blogs.wsj.com/speakeasy/2014/03/29/stephen-colbert-racism-and-the-weaponized-hashtag, accessed November, 29, 2014.

7 Austin Considine, "For Asian-American Stars, Many Web Fans," *New York Times*, July 29, 2011, http://www.nytimes.com/2011/07/31/fashion/for-asian-stars-many-web-fans.html, accessed July 29, 2011; Hayley Tsukayama, "In Online Video, Minorities Find an Audience," *Washington Post*, April 20, 2012, http://www.washingtonpost.com/business/economy/in-online-video-minorities-find-an-audience/2012/04/20/gIQAdhliWT_story.html, accessed April 20, 2012; and Hayley Tsukayama, "YouTube Channel YOMYOMF Launches, Focus on Asian-American Pop Culture," *Washington Post*, June 15, 2012, http://www.washingtonpost.com/business/technology/youtube-channel-yomyomf-launches-focus-on-asian-american-pop-culture/2012/06/15/gJQAhEbKfV_story.html, accessed June 15, 2012.

8 Lee Rainie, "Asian-Americans and Technology," *Pew Research Internet Project*, January 6, 2011, http://www.pewinternet.org/2011/01/06/asian-americans-and-technology, accessed January 6, 2011.

9 Richard Florida, "Race, Gender, and the Creative Class," *Atlantic*, June 27 2012, http://www.theatlanticcities.com/jobs-and-economy/2012/06/race-gender-and-creative-class/2225, accessed June 27, 2012.

10 Key studies include Lisa Nakamura, *Digitizing Race: Visual Culture of the Internet* (Minneapolis: University of Minnesota Press, 2008); Lisa Nakamura and Peter Chow-White, eds., *Race after the Internet* (New York: Routledge, 2012); and Kent Ono and Vincent Pham, *Asian Americans and the Media* (Malden, MA: Polity Press, 2009).

11 Wendy Hui Kyong Chun, "Race and/as Technology, or How to Do Things to Race," in Nakamura and Chow-White, *Race after the Internet*, 38.

12 Chun, "Race and/as Technology," 56–57.

13 Tara McPherson, "Why Are the Digital Humanities So White? Or, Thinking the Histories of Race and Computation," in *Debates in the Digital Humanities*, ed. Matthew K. Gold

(Minneapolis: University of Minnesota Press, 2012), http://dhdebates.gc.cuny.edu/debates/text/29, accessed November 29, 2014.

14 Jeff Chang, *Who We Be: The Colorization of America* (New York: St. Martin's Press, 2014).

15 Konrad Ng, "Beyond the Candidate: Obama, YouTube, and (My) Asian-ness," in *The Obama Effect: Multidisciplinary Renderings of the 2008 Campaign*, ed. Heather Harris, Kimberly Moffitt, and Catherine Squires, 89–100 (Albany: SUNY Press 2010).

16 Smithsonian Institution, *Creating a Digital Smithsonian: Digitization Strategic Plan, FY2010–2015* (Washington, DC: Smithsonian Institution, 2010).

17 The Secret Identities collective was formed by Jeff Yang, Parry Shen, Keith Chow, Jerry May, and Jef Castro and produced its first graphic novel featuring Asian American superheroes in 2009; see *Secret Identities: The Asian American Superheroes Anthology*, http://www.secretidentities.org, accessed October 7, 2015.

18 U.S. Census Bureau, "Asians Fastest-Growing Race or Ethnicity Group in 2012," release no. CB13–112, June 13, 2013, http://www.census.gov/newsroom/press-releases/2013/cb13-112.html, accessed October 7, 2015.

19 Robert Ji-Song Ku, Martin F. Manalansan IV, and Anita Mannur, eds., *Eating Asian America: A Food Studies Reader* (New York: NYU Press, 2013), 5.

20 Lok Siu, "Twenty-First-Century Food Trucks: Mobility, Social Media, and Urban Hipness," in Ku, Manalansan, and Mannur, *Eating Asian America*, 231–244.

21 Wayne Clough, *Best of Both Worlds: Museums, Libraries, and Archives in a Digital Age* (Washington, DC: Smithsonian Institution, 2013), 10.

10

Asian American Food Blogging as Racial Branding

Rewriting the Search for Authenticity

LORI KIDO LOPEZ

Asian Americans have become enormously successful and visible within every aspect of the online foodosphere—sharing daily reviews of their favorite restaurants, running hundreds of blogs that focus on cooking and dining, and posting mouth-watering photographs of every bite. *Hyphen Magazine* found that 15 percent of reviewers on Yelp (an online business rating review company) are Asian American, prompting the question, "What is it about the chance to review the newest Mission Street food cart or that downtown Italian-Haitian-Inuit fusion restaurant that brings out our inner Anthony Bourdain?"[1] Similarly, an Asian American food blogger called kevinEats penned an entire blog entry with the title "Why Are There So Many Asian Food Bloggers?"[2] in which he attempts to explain the reasons behind the unusual abundance of Asian Americans in the world of food blogging. While kevinEats conjectures that the answer has to do with the cultural significance of food and a propensity for conspicuous consumption, among other factors, I do not purport to have any explanation for this trend. Nevertheless, these blogs are deserving of analysis for what they convey about Asian American identities, communities, and foodscapes. Within these descriptions of meals, stories about eating, and details of recipes, Asian Americans are clearly using food to explore the rich contours of cultural expression within Asian America.

Food blogs provide a fertile ground for exploring transnational identity formations, as many of the writers who focus on Asian food have complex relationships to their countries of ancestry and the places they call home. As Nancy Pollock argues in her discussion of the mobile communities of Pacific peoples, "Tracing transnational influences through foodscapes enables us to highlight the cultural continuities and innovations, choices that communities make to enhance their identity."[3] Researchers have long theorized the connection between food cultures and identity, but these blogs provide a unique space for exposing the changing shape of these relationships as they are lived out in daily activities and interactions. Unlike pricey cookbooks, Food Network television shows, glossy food magazines, and other more traditional food media, blogs give their readers a peek into the everyday culinary adventures of Asian

American food lovers. Bloggers tell their own stories using the format of regularly updated posts that are readily accessible to their online communities—a format that is both intimate and personal yet carefully constructed for a public and even global readership.

In particular, the global identities embodied within Asian American food blogs provide a space for examining and untangling discourses of authenticity and their relationship to hierarchies of cultural value. For Asian American bloggers who blog about Asian food, a key "selling point" of their blogs—meaning a draw for readership, but also the potential to monetize their labor—is that the blogger's racial or ethnic heritage is invoked in order to frame his or her take on this kind of food as *authentic*. This is a cuisine they grew up with, or have experienced among natives, or have been taught to cook by immigrant family members, or otherwise understand with a high degree of authority. While these invocations of authenticity reflect hegemonic assumptions about cultural value, the blogs themselves simultaneously work to challenge and disrupt such notions. In this chapter, I perform a textual analysis of Asian American food blogs in order to illustrate the way that national identity, ethnic identity, and discourses of authenticity are contradictorily invoked and destabilized in the blogosphere using the logic of racial branding. In examining explicit and implicit invocations of authenticity as part of the work of creating a marketable brand, I argue that Asian American food blogging may seem like an act of individual expression, but these bodies of writing cannot be disentangled from the economic forces and cultural hierarchies that contribute to our understanding of the value of race as a brand.

Although the different genres of food blogs each offer interesting sites for investigation, for this study I focus on individually authored blogs that primarily share recipes. Given my interest in identity, branding, and authenticity, the creation and sharing of recipes provides a more fruitful site than foodies who report on their restaurant dining experiences. I specifically focus on the contents of twenty Asian American[4] food blogs that have been active for at least two years, providing me access to hundreds of entries to read and assess.[5] This sampling of blogs was selected because they represent a wide range of identities within the Asian American community—writers of different ethnicities, living in geographically dispersed areas, with different kinds of stories to tell. Despite their differences, they share a few traits in common that make them particularly useful for this study. The primary function of each blog is to share recipes, but most blog posts contain introductions that explain the food or tell a story about the food. It is these details, stories, explanations, and commentary that I explore in my analysis. Together they can be read for the way in which they mirror the shifting relationships that Asian Americans have to their own food cultures, to the way that they are perceived by others, and to their own sociohistorical positioning. Although I argue that authenticity clearly provides a kind currency for these blogs that relies on racial branding, a nuanced reading of their actual content reveals food blogs as a site for both invoking and dismantling the stability of such a concept as meaningful for Asian Americans in relation to their culinary identities.

Asian American Food Cultures

We can begin investigating Asian American food blogs by considering broadly the social role that they play and what function they serve to their writers and readers. Most bloggers explicitly state their motivations for creating and maintaining their recipe blog on their "About" page or within the text of their daily entries. These generally include a desire to create a collection of recipes for posterity, to document their process of learning about food, or to simply record their regular food activities. Such motivations are likely supplemented by the same reasons that people blog about any topic—to document their lives in a broadcast medium, to experience the intellectual pleasure or emotional catharsis of sharing their opinions with others, and to participate in a community of like-minded individuals.[6] In addition, each of the blogs included in this study has reached a level of popularity in reader hits (a kind of visibility that begets increased visibility through the algorithms used to discover the blogs on Google)[7] that contributes to yet another motivation for blogging—to gain a large readership and its associated benefits. These benefits can be intangible, such as feeling that one has successfully shared his or her creation with a wide audience, or tangible, such as being asked to author a cookbook or take photographs for a food event because of the blog's success.

Regardless of what purpose bloggers intend for their blogs to play, it is important to consider the way in which Asian American food blogs fit into the larger food landscape of the Internet. In particular, we must acknowledge the way that Asian American food blogs can be taken up by readers as "culinary tourism," which Lucy Long theorizes as the kind of encounter in which people intentionally explore culinary systems that are not their own.[8] Although culinary tourism is a common practice for "foodies" and other cosmopolitans, the specific histories of Asians in the United States do bring up some troubling questions for such practices. Asian Americans and other racial minorities have a particular relationship to the act of sharing food with the public. For many white Americans, eating at restaurants has served as an opportunity for acknowledging the existence of Asian immigrant families and for interacting with them. Although Asian Americans represent only around 5 percent of the entire U.S. population,[9] Americans in every city engage with Asian America through dining at Chinese restaurants, Thai restaurants, sushi bars, or any number of other readily available Asian eating establishments.[10] These encounters notably do not provide a neutral meeting ground; rather, Asian Americans are in the position of serving and providing a satisfying experience for the patron or the consumer, who is in the position of evaluation and compensation. Further, Asian eating establishments in the United States have a long history of deliberately catering to non-Asian customers. By altering their menus, décor, and service, they often seek to provide an experience that is suitably exotic and yet still comfortably palatable for Americans who may not have previously had meaningful interactions with Asian culture.[11]

This history of culinary tourism is an indelible element of Asian American cooking blogs. As Mark Padoongpatt argues in his analysis of Thai cuisine communities in Los Angeles, "It is imperative to continue to investigate the intersection of food and race, because race has been and continues to be the operative category for ethnic groups in U.S. society, whether we wish it to be or not."[12] Given the potential audience for food blogs that includes Americans who consistently view Asian food as "exotic" and "other," these collections of food writing must be read as contributing to a larger discourse on Asian cuisine, cultures, and social positioning. Even if the concept of "Asian cuisine" does not exist in reality, given the extreme diversity of food cultures within the broader region of Asia, food blogs work to continually reinscribe connections between geography and eating practices that preserve the illusion that such a term has meaning. Thus, although individual food blogs may focus very specifically on a single ethnicity, or even a single regional cuisine, it is still important to connect these disparate blogs together under the category of Asian American food blogs. Even if the bloggers themselves are not attempting to speak to a larger Asian American experience, the politicized collective identity of Asian America demands that we read such individual experiences as connected to one another in both their histories and their treatment by their audiences. If these blogs use food as a way of reflecting the position of Asians within our global society, I argue that their insistence on being viewed as authentic offers a starting point for understanding the way that national, cultural, and social identities are constructed and intertwined through this form of food writing.

Constructing Authenticity

Within the Asian American food blogs sampled for this study, the concept of authenticity stands out as a common topic of discussion. Recipes are first and foremost positioned as authentic through the framing of the blog and its author. Their "About" pages often explicitly characterize the blog's recipes as authentic, as in Bee Yinn Low's description that her blog *Rasa Malaysia* "offers easy, authentic, and tested recipes that work, plus mouthwatering and gorgeous food photography. [*Rasa Malaysia*] is about preserving authentic Asian cooking, narrated through easy-to-read articles."[13] Makiko Itoh's "About" page, on her blog, *Just Hungry*, states, "My recipes are authentically Japanese enough to satisfy my harshest critic—me!"[14] The authors of *The Ravenous Couple* state in their own introduction that "our mission is to show you how authentic Vietnamese food is simple, fresh, and delicious,"[15] emphasizing an educational goal that begins with the showcasing of authentic cuisine. The word itself is generously applied to a wide variety of food descriptions—a search for the word "authentic" among the recipes on *Beyond Kimchi* reveals 160 entries, with most simply tacked on to the beginning of a dish's name, such as "authentic bibimbap" or "authentic Korean beef." The blogs also repeatedly discuss the concept of authenticity within their posts, offering thoughts on what makes food authentic, the challenges of authenticity, and the efficacy of using authenticity as a metric for evaluating Asian or Asian American food. Through these, we can begin to see a preoccupation within Asian American blogs on the topic of authenticity, both in evoking an aura of authenticity about their own work and in actively shaping our understanding of what that term means.

Authenticity must be understood as a subjective quality that is socially constructed and relational, rather than an inherent quality of food, people, spaces, or media. As Arjun Appadurai argues, the idea that a culinary system can be authentic is inherently suspect, given that it is not clear whose authoritative voice stands to provide the source of authenticity. Moreover, the quality of authenticity is only given to cuisines that have undergone change, making it nearly impossible to characterize what is authentic in the face of shifting cultural tastes and traditions.[16] Despite this slipperiness, the term remains clearly imbued with social value, particularly for food blogs—here, bloggers are seen to encourage the belief that a more authentic blog is inherently more trustworthy and authoritative. This relationship of trust and loyalty seems tantamount to the success of blogs, whose currency often rests solely on page views and a blogger's ability to convince readers to return day after day.

Josee Johnston and Shyon Baumann[17] further explicate some of the different ways that authenticity has been constructed within the gourmet food world. They map out five qualities that are generally ascribed to what we would consider authentic food: simplicity, personal connection, geographic specificity, history/tradition, and ethnic connection. Johnston and Baumann's elaboration of these traits, determined through discourse analysis of their interviews with foodies, provides a helpful starting place for pinpointing the nuances of the concept, which can otherwise remain opaque. Although their work does not specifically mention the discourse of food bloggers, their findings become directly applicable when looking at the way that these qualities are deliberately made visible within this sample of Asian American food blogs. Here I demonstrate the fulfillment of these categories to show, not just that Asian American blogs are clearly upholding and reinforcing discourses of authenticity, but to consider the specific ways that discussions of food authenticity become connected to hierarchies of value that benefit Asian American bloggers.

The first two categories of simplicity and personal connection are inherent qualities of the genre of the food blog itself—writers of blogs tell their own personal stories that provide the connection between the cook and the food, and they tell stories about foods that they have created themselves. Given that most bloggers are home cooks, their writing is suffused with sincerity and handmade qualities that speak to the demands for authenticity through simplicity. We can see each of these traits in the writing on *Indian Simmer*, where Prerna Singh introduces each recipe with sentimental musing about the dish's relationship to her childhood, her experiences as a new mother, her relationship to her in-laws, or other aspects of her everyday life. Her description of shrimp with tandoori masala provides a strong example:

> The recipe I'm sharing today is very simple, quick, and soars with the taste of my mother in law's tandoori masala. This was our go-to summer recipe that paired amazingly well with a bottle of chilled beer. The photos might tell you so, mostly because Abhishek took them back in summer (yes I was nursing them in my computer all these months). We've cooked it while camping, served while entertaining friends at home and whipped in minutes for the butterfly's lunchbox.[18]

In this brief description of the dish we can see how a personal narrative can be deployed to give specificity while also shoring up the dish's utility—it originated from an elder family member, but it can be seamlessly deployed into the varied schedules of contemporary wives and mothers. Even in such a brief description, readers can get a sense for who she is as a person and how her life is intertwined with her cooking. This writing style is pervasive even among the bloggers who have become professional chefs or who sell their food, as they are still in the business of exposing stories behind their food and elucidating how their food is made, offering an authentic personal connection that would be missing in a corporate environment or the world of mass-produced food.

While this kind of authenticity seems inherent within the form of a personal food blog, we can see the other traits of authenticity that are tethered to Asian American sensibilities—geographic specificity, history/tradition, and ethnic connection—also carefully constructed through the narrative database that constitutes each blog. Within descriptions of a recipe the blogger often points out that it is authentic to a specific region or ethnic group. For instance, in the Filipino blog *Burnt Lumpia*, Marvin Gapultos proudly elaborates upon the culinary regions from which his dishes originate:

> Hailing from the Ilocos region of the Northern Philippines (Ilocos son, what?!!), Papaitan is usually comprised of the organ meats found within a goat such as its stomach and intestines, as well as its bitter bile. . . . Us crazy Ilocanos, we'll eat

anything. . . . But what's with the Filipino (or more specifically, Ilocano) love of bitter flavors?[19]

His discussion of the goat stew papaitan and other bitter regional dishes are laced with boastful swagger about the type of food that is unique to the Ilocos region and those who are capable of enjoying it. Makiko Itoh of the Japanese blog *Just Hungry* takes a different tack, using her regionally specific knowledge as a potential explanation for dishes that might fail to live up to the expectations of true locals. She asserts the most authority on dishes that reflect the Kanto region that encompasses Tokyo, such as her classic Kanto-style sukiyaki, "the quintessential Japanese beef hot pot." When presenting dishes from other regions, such as Osaka-style okonomiyaki, she is careful to state, "This is a fairly authentic recipe I think, or as authentic as a Tokyo born-and-bred girl can get."[20] Both of these kinds of claims to geographic specificity are shored up through personal narratives told about the specific area in which they grew up, having relatives from that area, or from frequently visiting or returning to that area. Food bloggers frequently pair their recipes with stories about a grandmother who made them the dish as a child or about helping their mother in the kitchen as she explained the origins of the dish. As Jun Belen states in the introduction to *junblog: Stories from My Filipino Kitchen*, "I learned how to cook through long-distance phone conversations with my mom, the lady who taught me the love of food and cooking. . . . My questions were endless. Sometimes silly. 'Taste it and you'll learn,' she taught me."[21] These narratives work to uphold the authenticity of the blogger through their close connection to the place and people who originated the dish, as well as through a connection to history and tradition. Authentic food is often characterized by being made in the same way it has always been made, in the place where it is from. By emphasizing stories about the generational longevity and unwavering history of a dish, bloggers reinforce the notion that these qualities are more valued than a brand-new flavor or the cooking of someone who does not understand or connect to a dish's history.

Johnston and Baumann's final element of authenticity is that it is made by "ethnic" people—a concept that is difficult to define and yet arguably present in these blogs. The quality of being "ethnic" often refers (somewhat problematically) to those who are not white or who are not assimilated into mainstream white culture in the United States. Thus many in Johnston and Baumann's study would define a restaurant as authentic when there were many non-white, non-assimilated "ethnic" people eating there or working there. This quality of being associated with a strong ethnic identity has already been gestured to in stories about connecting to a country or culture of origin and emphasizing the importance of family and family history in telling food stories. But another important element of tracing the ethnic identities of Asian American food bloggers is the literal movement of peoples between the United States and Asia and the transnational food identities that such flows create. Asian Americans embody this category of authenticity through movements that include the more permanent relocations associated with migration and the temporary sojourns associated with transnational travel. Within blogged recipes and their accompanying stories we read about residing in a number of different countries, traveling for work and for pleasure, participating in tourist excursions and homecomings, and otherwise finding ways to physically navigate the borders between the different cultural identities that constitute Asian America. Leela Punyaratabandhu of the blog *SheSimmers* shares traditional recipes and stories from her childhood in Thailand from her current home in Chicago,[22] while others disclose their transnational boundary crossing through tracking their travels across the Pacific. Marc Matsumoto of the blog *No Recipes*, who also goes by the title "The Wandering Cook," documents his favorite eating spots in places like Tokyo, Hong Kong, and Seoul.[23] Here we see how Asian American food bloggers benefit from the mobilities and transnational connections that often characterize Asian American experiences and narratives.

Beyond these implicit appeals to authenticity, many bloggers also directly discuss their own thoughts on the way that authenticity reflects hierarchies of cultural power. Through perceived threats to culinary authenticity, food bloggers are able to express the way that Asian American cultures are so frequently mishandled and misunderstood. On Bee Yin Low's *Rasa Malaysia*, she writes:

> No offense to the authors but your *fill-in-the-blank*-inspired creations are nothing but shallow, soulless, pieces of goo to my native Asian palate. If you intend to make a Vietnamese dish, please create it according to the native way rather than just casually throwing in a few Vietnamese herbs or a few dashes of fish sauce. Would you call an all-American burger "Thai-inspired Burger" by substituting the typical lettuce leaves for say, mint leaves?[24]

She is clearly insulted by the idea that a dish could be labeled Vietnamese when it is not made "according to the native way" or is made in a way that tastes bad to a "native Asian" person. This definition of authenticity emphasizes the role of the authenticator in being able to deem a dish authentic or not. When bloggers take on the role of the authenticator, they render their own opinion more legitimate than any other, privileging their own standards for authenticity and renouncing alternatives.

Racial Branding

In affirming these different tenets of authenticity, these Asian American food bloggers are doing more than simply increasing the value of their food blogs.

Such discourses serve as a form of racial branding—a process in which racial identities are carefully managed and packaged for consumption while simultaneously reifying and essentializing racial difference. Although it is rare to see discussions of financial incentives or economic motivations for blogging within the blogs themselves, it is undeniable that food blogging has led to many full-time careers. For entrepreneurial and popular Asian American food bloggers, we can see a number of success stories from individuals who started their blog as a humble platform for sharing recipes and ended up becoming food professionals. Out of the twenty blogs sampled, nine were connected to financial ventures—including writing cookbooks, becoming food journalists or food photographers, starring on cooking shows, and even manning a food truck. Being able to transition from unpaid blogger to food professional, or just being able to monetize a blog in any way, is an accomplishment that demands a powerful act of branding. That is, bloggers must be able to prove that their voices are unique and distinct and that their perspectives command loyal audiences. We can clearly see the logic of branding in play as many bloggers position themselves for financial profit through their blogging labor and steady readership. Given that a blog is a vehicle for a single personality and set of skills and knowledge, bloggers must be adept in shaping their brands so audiences will continue to support them, even when it costs money to do so.[25]

This logic of branding is also present in the work of bloggers who do not monetize their labor, as means for maintaining interest on the part of readers. If there is no semblance of coherency to the topics a blog addresses, or if there is no attempt to create and maintain a distinctive perspective, then readers are unlikely to return. To cultivate and retain interest in their brand, bloggers must carefully delineate their projects and their expertise using the tenets of promotional culture. Although this kind of labor might appear disconnected from the idea of financially profiting off of a blog, they are in fact intimately connected, as branding can never be seen as an exclusively financial process. In selecting a title for a blog, narrowing its specific focus, and creating a reliable location for procuring a specific set of information, bloggers are clearly deploying the logic of branding in order to gain and maintain readers—as well the many social, emotional, and intellectual benefits that accrue from doing so.

Importantly, for Asian American food bloggers, this desire for the maintenance of a marketable brand becomes a racialized project. As Viet Nguyen has argued, the panethnic entrepreneur has much to gain in capitalizing on the symbolic capital of race.[26] For Asian American fiction writers, this has often meant benefiting from the celebration of stories of struggle and resistance. For Asian American food writers, there is another realm of symbolic capital to be gained through the deployment of race—being recognized as experts on the topic of Asian cooking. Those panethnic entrepreneurs who write about food benefit from making race visible through descriptions of their racial/ethnic background, pictures of themselves, and stories of their Asian families, histories, and experiences. This serves a dual function of calling for identification and solidarity for readers of similar ethnic or racial backgrounds while also offering an extension of food tourism for non-Asian readers.

Although it may seem cynical to argue that bloggers participate in racial branding in order to establish their authority as Asian American food experts, this viewpoint importantly disavows a more essentialist view of Asian American food blogs. That is, the argument that racial branding is an act of labor that strives to create a uniquely Asian American perspective reminds us that Asian identities do not automatically translate to Asian expertise or authenticity. Rather, authenticity is a social construction that is always tenuous and under attack, always necessitating work to maintain a claim on it.

Conclusion: Destabilizing Authenticity through Hybridity

Thus far, I have argued that Asian American food blogs work to uphold notions of authenticity as a means of capitalizing on racialized branding. However, the ways in which this presumed ethnic authenticity is expressed within the blogs can itself be full of contradictions. Thus, while relying upon the authority of ethnic identity, Asian American food blogs can also be seen to disrupt a stable notion of authenticity. This is most evident in the instances where bloggers struggle with the concept of authenticity, openly admitting that it is a challenge to pinpoint its meaning. Leela Punyaratabandhu of *SheSimmers* writes on her blog about Thai food that, "when it comes to cuisine, 'authenticity' is to me a word that is—at a risk of sounding intoxicated—both loaded with meaning and meaningless at the same time, depending on how you look at it." She then lays out three different possibilities for defining authentic Thai food: the royal cuisine that aristocratic households traditionally prepared, dishes from searchable written records, or any Thai food that cannot be labeled "fusion." For each of these potential arguments, she systematically provides counterexamples to reveal the narrowness or arrogance of such claims to authenticity. As she argues,

> Food is not a static thing. It evolves much like language and everything else. Years ago, we didn't cook with carrots, because we didn't have carrots. Now that we have and want to use carrots in some dishes, we're committing the crime of fusion? Which period of history represents Thai cuisine at its peak and most authentic, then? At which point did Thai cuisine start to allegedly decline? And exactly what do we have right now?[27]

In this exploration we can see that discussions of authenticity are not always taken up as a way of affirming their value; on the contrary, many bloggers simultaneously participate in deconstructing the notion of authenticity through embracing the impossibility of defining its borders or requirements. Andrea Nguyen's Viet World Kitchen pointedly addresses the topic in an entry titled, "What is Authentic Asian Food?," confessing that wondering about authenticity keeps her up at night. She ultimately decides that the concept centers on a sense of typical food preparations, as well as relationships between people and food that are crafted from a true, honest position. But it is not easy for her to settle upon this definition, and she also ends the entry by asking her readers for their input because it is such a difficult concept.[28]

The deconstruction of authenticity also occurs implicitly through the recipes and writing of individual posts, in which bloggers inescapably participate in blending traditions from many cultures and celebrate the overlapping of cuisines as they move through different geographical spaces. Although bloggers may outwardly claim to be authentically representative of Japanese cuisine, Thai cuisine, or Vietnamese cuisine—and in doing so, reify the notion of Asian authenticity through its connection to their heritage and experiences—it is difficult to find a blog that exclusively focuses on just one cuisine or even one continent. Rather, food bloggers clearly delight in creating and consuming a diversity of dishes that trace their own unique journeys, both geographically and culturally, as they blend traditions from any number of cultures. For instance, in her blog Kimchi Mom, Amy Kim includes recipes for bibimbap burgers and ramen-grilled cheese; Diana Kuan, from Appetite for China, writes in detail about her favorite Thai pork salad larb, and Soma from eCurry describes naan pizza with balsamic roasted figs and goat cheese. Such posts evidence a playful blending of ethnic traditions and the wholesale embracing of food cultures outside their own. Some include posts about the cultural or historical reasons for how specific foods made their way across the Pacific, as in Marc Matsumoto writing in No Recipes about the difference between Japanese ham-ba-gu versus ham-ba-gah. But bloggers also simply write about their own favorite dishes that have nothing to do with their ethnic heritage because the reality is that there is no identity and no food culture that remains unchanged by contact with others.

These deviations from the so-called authentic dishes that characterize a blog's brand likely do nothing to damage the perceived authenticity of the overall blog; of course readers understand the prevalence (and enjoyment) of cross-cultural mixing in every aspect of life. But if authenticity of food knowledge is shored up through affirming a connection to one's specific ethnic identity, heritage, and experiences, as we have seen illustrated thus far, then the inclusion of these foods outside the specific ethnicity delineated as authentic only serve to remind us how unwieldy and fraught the concept of authenticity can be. Indeed, any connection between authenticity and identity becomes disrupted through engagements with hybridity. This proves important because one's identity may be connected to a specific food culture, but this connection is just as unstable as any aspect of our identities, which are always moving and shifting to reveal different articulations in different circumstances.

The political work of destabilizing an essential notion of identity through engagements with fusion cultures and cuisines must be tempered by Anita Mannur's concern that the framing of fusion cuisine has often served to uphold social inequalities, particularly in the case of Asian Americans.[29] Her fears about fusion cuisine falling prey to the "economy of desirability" are certainly relevant in the context of this discussion of how bloggers deliberately craft a brand that they believe will resonate with readers, and even more so with those who have begun to enter into mainstream professional food industries such as cookbook authoring. Nevertheless, there remain significant differences between the corporate food world that produces fusion cuisine for restaurants and programming on the Food Network and the possibilities offered by individual bloggers striving to gain audiences through self-branding. Alongside the attempts by bloggers to rely upon racial formations as a form of authenticity, food bloggers also call upon their authentic experiences as complex, imperfect, multifaceted human beings to set their blog apart and connect with readers. Individual bloggers have the space to express their own sensibilities about what constitutes fusion food, how it is understood, and how any particular dish might be enjoyed by their own friends and family. Although I have demonstrated the ways that these blogs are inherently subject to larger discourses surrounding race, culinary tourism, and the logic of branding, they also reflect the individual experiences of each blogger. It is through these individual responses to larger economic forces and the effort of laboring to represent their own specific experiences, tastes, and practices that we can more accurately see through these blogs that Asian America is in a constant state of cultural flux. Through the distinct voices of each writer, Asian American food blogs participate in opening up possibilities for challenging traditional discourses of authenticity and their connection to the process of racial branding—and in helping to redefine the shape of Asian American identities, cultures, and practices in doing so.

NOTES

1 Victoria Yue, "Do Asian Americans Yelp Like Crazy?" *Hyphen: Asian America Unabridged*, March 31, 2011, http://hyphenmagazine.com/blog/2011/3/31/do-asian-americans-yelp-crazy.

2 *kevinEats.com*, "Why Are There So Many Asian Food Bloggers?" January 11, 2010, http://www.kevineats.com/2010/01/why-are-there-so-many-asian-food.htm.

3 Nancy Pollock, "Food and Transnationalism: Reassertions of Pacific Identity," in *Migration and Transnationalism: Pacific Perspectives*, ed. Helen Lee and Steve Tupai Francis, 103–114 (Canberra: ANU E Press, 2009), 105.

4 Determining what counted as "Asian American" was a difficult undertaking for this study, given that I was simultaneously interested in the category of "Asian America" and the existence of transnational food cultures and identities. Each blog author identifies him or herself

within the blog as both Asian and American (although in many cases the phrase "Asian American" is never used). Yet some are mixed-race Asian and non-Asian, and some authors do not currently reside in the United States.

5 Blogs included for study include *Appetite for China* (appetiteforchina.com), *@Køkken* (www.atkokken.com), *Beyond Kimchee* (www.beyondkimchee.com), *Burnt Lumpia* (burntlumpiablog.com), *eCurry* (www.ecurry.com/blog), *Indian Simmer* (www .indiansimmer.com), *junblog* (blog.junbelen.com), *Just Hungry* (www.justhungry.com), *Just One Cookbook* (www.justonecookbook.com), *Kimchi Mom* (www.kimchimom.com), *Korean Bapsang* (www.koreanbapsang.com), *No Recipes* (norecipes.com), *NoobCook* (www .noobcook.com), *Rasa Malaysia* (rasamalaysia.com), *Red Cook* (redcook.net), *SheSimmers* (shesimmers.com), *Steamy Kitchen* (steamykitchen.com), *The Ravenous Couple* (www .theravenouscouple.com), *Viet World Kitchen* (www.vietworldkitchen.com), and *White on Rice Couple* (whiteonricecouple.com).

6 Bonnie A. Nardi, Diane J. Schiano, Michelle Gumbrecht, and Luke Swartz, "Why We Blog," *Communications of the ACM* 47, no. 12 (2004): 41–46.

7 By this I simply mean that I discovered the blogs for this study by using search terms such as "Asian American food blog" and "Filipino food blog." The top hits for these searches were obviously only the most popular sites.

8 Lucy M. Long, "Culinary Tourism: A Folkloristic Perspective on Eating and Otherness," in *Culinary Tourism*, ed. Lucy M. Long, 20–50 (Lexington: University of Kentucky Press, 2004).

9 Karen R. Humes, Nicholas Jones, and Roberto R. Ramirez, "Overview of Race and Hispanic Origin: 2010" (Washington, DC: U.S. Census Bureau, March 2011), http://www.census.gov/ prod/cen2010/briefs/c2010br-02.pdf.

10 Alan Warde, "Eating Globally: Cultural Flows and the Spread of Ethnic Restaurants," in *The Ends of Globalization: Bringing Society Back In*, ed. Don Kalb, Marco van der Land, Richard Staring, Bart van Steenbergen, and Nico Wilterdink, 299–316 (Lanham, MD: Rowman & Littlefield, 2000); Jennifer 8 Lee, *The Fortune Cookie Chronicles: Adventures in the World of Chinese Food* (New York: Hachette, 2009).

11 Shun Lu and Gary Alan Fine, "The Presentation of Ethnic Authenticity: Chinese Food as a Social Accomplishment," *Sociological Quarterly* 36, no. 3 (1995): 535–553.

12 Mark Padoongpatt, "Too Hot to Handle: Food, Empire, and Race in Thai Los Angeles," *Radical History Review*, no. 110 (2011): 83–108, quote at 85.

13 Bee Yinn Low, "About," *Rasa Malaysia*, http://rasamalaysia.com/about-rasa-malaysia, accessed January 24, 2010.

14 Makiko Itoh, "About," *Just Hungry*, n.d., http://justhungry.com/about, accessed January 13, 2014.

15 Hong Pham and Kim Pham, "About," *The Ravenous Couple*, n.d., http://www.theravenous couple.com/about, accessed June 5, 2015.

16 Arjun Appadurai, "On Culinary Authenticity," *Anthropology Today* 2, no. 4 (1986): 24–25.

17 Josee Johnston and Shyon Baumann, *Foodies: Democracy and Distinction in the Gourmet Foodscape* (New York: Routledge, 2009).

18 Prerna Singh, "Shrimp Sizzler with Tandoori Masala," *Indian Simmer*, December 6, 2013, http://www.indiansimmer.com/2013/12/shrimp-sizzler-with-tandoori-masala.html, accessed October 8, 2015.

19 Marvin Gapultos, "Papaitan: Offal and Bile Soup," *Burnt Lumpia: Finding Identity Through Food*, October 25, 2011, http://burntlumpiablog.com/2011/10/papaitan-offal-bile-soup.html, accessed October 8, 2015.

20 Makiko Itoh, "Classic Sukiyaki, the Quintessential Japanese Beef Hot Pot" (http://www .justhungry.com/classic-sukiyaki-quintessential-japanese-beef-hot-pot) and "Okonomiyaki,

Osaka Style" (http://justhungry.com/okonomiyaki-osaka-style), *Just Hungry*, http://just hungry.com, accessed October 8, 2015.

21 Jun Belen, "About," *junblog: Stories from my Filipino Kitchen*, http://blog.junbelen.com/about, accessed January 12, 2014.

22 Leela Punyaratabandhu, *SheSimmers: Thai Home Cooking*, http://shesimmers.com, accessed June 24, 2010.

23 Marc Matsumoto, *No Recipes: Make Good Food Better*, http://norecipes.com, accessed March 5, 2012.

24 Bee Yinn Low, "In Search of Authenticity," *Rasa Malaysia*, October 10, 2006, http://rasa malaysia.com/in-search-of-authenticity, accessed October 8, 2015.

25 Although there are plenty of Asian American food blogs that do not invoke authenticity and do not benefit from the practices of branding, their tiny readership and relative invisibility within the blogosphere make them difficult to track down for this study.

26 Viet Nguyen, *Race and Resistance: Literature and Politics in Asian America* (Oxford: Oxford University Press, 2002).

27 Leela Punyaratabandhu, "What Is Authentic 'Thai' Cuisine?" *SheSimmers: Thai Home Cooking*, September 18, 2012, http://shesimmers.com/2012/09/what-is-authentic-thai-cuisine-3.html, accessed October 8, 2015.

28 Andrea Nguyen, "What Is Authentic Asian Food?" *Viet World Kitchen*, April 10, 2008, http://vietworldkitchen.typepad.com/blog/2008/04/what-is-authent.html, accessed October 8, 2015.

29 Anita Mannur, "Model Minorities Can Cook: Fusion Cuisine in Asian America," in *East Main Street: Asian American Popular Culture*, by Shilpa Davé, Leilani Nishime, and Tasha G. Oren, 72–94 (New York: NYU Press, 2005).

11

Picturing the Past

Drawing Together Vietnamese American Transnational History

TIMOTHY K. AUGUST

"Individuals choose sides, families don't."
—GB Tran

Vietnamerica, published in 2010, chronicles GB Tran's attempt to draw together scattered societal fragments to create a Vietnamese American transnational history.[1] In *Vietnamerica*, Tran uses the graphic narrative form to create a unique visual plane that leverages sensory experiences so actors can traverse multiple times and places in a single scene. These sensory experiences provide glimpses of historical, if not political, reconciliation for the older characters in the story while bringing Tran closer to a coherent historical narrative for himself, despite not being able to experience the same sensory journeys directly. My analysis of this work proposes (1) that Tran uses a flattening of time and a multiplicity of perspectives to link the oft-neglected continuities between Vietnamese and Vietnamese American experiences, (2) that *Vietnamerica* presents what I call the "visible social body" to reflect upon the totality of the refugee population and the nameless others who did not survive the passage, and (3) that Tran's reflexive description of the process involved in compiling this narrative works to hail multigenerational readers. Together these narrative techniques reanimate sensual loss and gesture toward a uniquely somatic brand of "Vietnameseness" that can travel across the globe.

Vietnamerica follows Tran's search for his past following the death of his grandparents. Born and raised in the United States, Tran was previously uninterested in learning about his family's history, and his parents would rarely bring up older traumatic events, preferring instead to focus on the future. However, when Tran finds an inscription in a book about the war in Vietnam that reads "A Man without History Is a Tree without Roots," he "returns" to Vietnam to pay his respects to his departed elders. During this trip he learns about his paternal grandfather's decision to join the anti-colonial movement, his trials, and ultimate disillusionment with the cause, as well as his grandmother's long romantic affair with a French colonial officer. Tran also unravels the story of his mother's internal Vietnamese migration from the North to the South, as well as his father's previous marriage to a French woman. The narrative both starts and climaxes with the family fleeing Vietnam during the fall of Saigon, which is presented as a fraught jumble of bodies, cityscapes, and rumors. The three branches of this interwoven story are told in a non-chronological order, stringing the reader along, as information is uncovered in fits and starts, mirroring the learning process that required Tran to take multiple trips to Vietnam while writing the book. The vast research that Tran conducted in the seven years needed to complete this project is evident in the numerous well-developed characters throughout the story. Members of his family are often provided with unique color schemes and graphic compositions to create distinct perspectives, with the history taking the shape of a collective effort.

A recent *Los Angeles Times* review of the memoir criticized Tran for leaving the book "open-ended" and his experience "in the background."[2] Considering that the graphic narrative follows Tran's journey and, in the process, visually plots Tran's own body circulating through a myriad of spaces, it is curious that he could be accused of leaving his own experience in the background, for his icon is physically present in a majority of the panels, his voice pieces together the scenes, and the presence of his forceful visual style maneuvers the reader through a rush of people, sounds, memories, and places. I propose instead that Tran's presence is carefully refracted through the memories and experiences of others to make clear the situated relationships of post-war Vietnamese bodies and their environments—an approach that eschews anchoring the narrative around an intimate narrator who seeks to draw the reader into a singular identificatory relationship. This obstructed view of Tran, while lamented in the *Los Angeles Times* review, is an important rhetorical strategy that diverts the story away from becoming the tale of an easily consumable exceptional individual in favor of presenting a more complex, textured, and difficult Vietnamese social experience.

The dizzying array of characters circulating throughout the book and the lack of narrative closure leads the literary critic Jade Hidle to conclude that, for Tran, the "family is not separable from the self," and she interprets Tran's disorienting rhetorical techniques as an attempt to transfer to the reader the sense of those who are "perpetually negotiating our [Vietnamese] identity."[3] I would add to this conclusion that Tran's deeply historical investigation of his family unit tracks the interconnected nature of Vietnam's colonial, wartime, diasporic, and socialist eras. The tumultuous recent history of Vietnam and its diaspora has had a totalizing effect, where no family was untouched by events of dislocation and movement. While certainly over the last sixty years there were stark differences among class, gender, and religious positions, the commonalities found in Vietnamese experience are what Tran chooses to display in the book. By carefully unfolding and visually plotting the *social* experiences involved in his family's genesis, "his" story becomes a cultural touchstone for any number of other Vietnamese families. Precisely because the narrative is so materially situated within the rhythms, textures, smells, and landscapes of the places he visits, this story is less a symbolic treatise about the perpetual negotiation of identity than it is grounded as a particularly Vietnamese journey.

Representational Agency and the Transnational Graphic Narrative

Between 1975 and 2000 more than five hundred thousand Vietnamese refugees and asylum seekers entered the United States, and now the number of Vietnamese Americans has grown to over 1.7 million; this forms the fifth-biggest Asian American group and represents the largest conglomerate of people in the Vietnamese diaspora.[4] Despite this large physical presence, their image in the American popular media remains limited, often read interchangeably with older Chinese and Japanese American populations, or if their particularity is recognized they often must bear the weight of an unpopular war. In the broader American imagination Vietnam remains a syndrome, a military embarrassment, rather than a diverse and complex nation with a history of its own, and Vietnamese Americans have been dogged by the image of being unwelcomed former combatants. The first generation of Vietnamese Americans had to quickly develop narratives to explain their existence in various small towns, as the refugee relocation policy scattered small pockets of Vietnamese Americans across the United States, for a collective bodily presence was considered to be potentially upsetting to existing American communities. As the Vietnamese Americans eventually settled and grew more prosperous, they were able to tell new stories of capitalist success and cultural integration, contending that Vietnamese Americans had truly "arrived" and could finally throw off the image of tired huddled masses. However, social advancement did not come as easily as they had hoped as racially charged suspicions began to read these new Americans as fortune hunters, as opposed to former allies.[5]

Tran belongs to a group of 1.5- and second-generation Vietnamese American authors whose work reanimates family histories that were once thought to have been left behind in Vietnam.[6] These authors sit at the crossroads of an important juncture in Vietnamese history, as their multiple linguistic ties and the reintroduction of American diplomatic relations with Vietnam can allow them to engage with a transnational sense of Vietnamese identity. The digital age has increased access to a multitude of Vietnamese authors, media, and products. As well, it is now possible for Vietnamese American authors to visit people and physical landscapes that previously could only be experienced through the wistful secondhand recollections of their parents. Writing primarily in the English language has garnered these writers a larger readership on the world stage than their overseas counterparts who are writing, for the most part, in Vietnamese. They also benefit from working during a historical conjuncture in which there is a well-established canon of Asian American literature, academic programs and departments devoted to Asian American Studies, and a global audience interested in tales of diasporic experience. However, with this privilege also comes the responsibility to generate artistic forms that challenge the accepted modes of consuming Vietnamese literature while mapping the complex cultural flows that characterize the worldwide Vietnamese population.

I use the term "graphic narrative" to describe *Vietnamerica* instead of the more commonplace "graphic novel" as Tran is invested in the non-fictive mode to combat the diminishing historical memory of succeeding diasporic generations.[7] Leveraging the comic strip's unique formal (and informal) narrative opportunities, Tran constructs a multigenerational record that redresses historical absences produced by the traumatic passage out of Vietnam. While reflexively framing the narrative around his search for his family's own history, he tells the story through the voices of others whose tales are presented as representative of all of those left behind during the period. He creates what I am calling the "visible social body," in which multiple subjects move around a singular panel, and these assortments of bodies become the dominant compositional element in the frames as they bend, twist, and bleed into the landscape of both Vietnam and the United States. The human form, then, becomes the vehicle for transnational representation, visually arguing that the people constitute the history of these countries.

This form of social visibility is literalized in a haunting image (fig. 11.1) consisting of bodies straining to get out of the cavernous outline of Vietnam during the refugee period. The graphic weight of the panel focuses the gaze upon Southeast Asia, while a dark fiery horizon characterizes the foreboding, unknowable, global north. The gloomy dull grays of Laos, Thailand, and Cambodia suggest that little hope is to be found in other lands, and hence the majority of the bodies cram themselves into the bottom of the frame desperately reaching into the crisp light blues of the ocean—a liquid respite that would carry them off the page into the unknown. This technique of graphic bleeding, where the landscape spills over the page, illuminates the uncertainty that these bodies faced—fleeing the difficult past and dangerous present, desperately straining toward an uncertain future. Furthermore, the tiny undersized boats that could transport them away are literally overwhelmed by the size of this social body, alluding to older images of the Vietnamese refugee period, when an unthinkable number of people were crammed into these tight spaces and figures teemed across the decks of the boats. Finally, while the faces are drawn rather crudely, the lines of distress and horror are clearly visible, a diversity of hairstyles apparent, and small identifiable ornaments like glasses produce particularity before the bodies blend into a mass of humanity as the reader's eye travels northward. The lack of a caption or text box leaves an eerie silence and functions as a pause in the narrative in which the reader is left alone to contemplate the desperate physicality presented by the overall scene.

Tran complicates conventional readings of Vietnamese bodies and the Vietnamese American experience by diffusing the narrative focus, which also serves

Figure 11.1. An image of bodies straining to get out
of the cavernous outline of Vietnam during the
refugee period.

to subvert easy identificatory impulses. Open-endedness is achieved by radi-
cally mixing perspectives from panel to panel so that the reader cannot achieve
sequential closure without a concerted effort and is constantly reminded of the
personal and artistic mediation required to access this doggedly social story.
Identified as a common practice in Elaine Kim's inaugurating 1982 study *Asian
American Literature: An Introduction to Writing and Their Social Contexts*,[8]
the writing of Asian American literature has often required the artist to situate and explain his or her "invisible" community. This pressure can be seen to
limit the literary interventions that an Asian American author can make, as creative expression must be balanced with a pedagogical address and the burden of
speaking for his or her community. However, recent studies have investigated
the power of turning toward avant-garde art, suggesting that formal innovations
can posit the sociopolitical bind that Asian American authors face as an essential
component of the art object itself.[9] The graphic narrative, I contend, is particularly well equipped to work through this tension, as the drawings can satisfy the
demand for social representation and realism by placing the narrative in spaces
layered thickly with visual and sensory details that provide material context,
while the multipanel form frees the graphic artist to explore imaginative and psychological depth through the manipulation of color, framing, and panel order.

Tran takes advantage of the genre's expressive dexterity in a section relating his father's three years of torture and imprisonment in Vietnam. When describing the gritty experience of jail time, Tran uses a limited dark color scheme, detailed lines, and jarring sonic cues to express the sensory deprivation experienced during the time of confinement. While brooding in the jail cell, Tran's father reminisces upon the pleasant, carefree days of his adolescence, which is presented by Tran through a four-color palate found in traditional comic books—visually interjecting these lighter, innocent times into this gloomy section. This part of the story is related through a visual and narrative match, with the lighter scenes having greater iconic abstraction—for instance, the characters' eyes are plainly drawn to consist of two dark dots, while streets are lined with simply sketched boxed houses—producing an impression of unreality as his father strains to remember this past time from the confines of his cell. Being able to intersperse elements of both realism and abstraction within the same section allows Tran to display the material context that developed his father's psychological profile, in particular his emotional hardening, by contrasting Tran's father's captivity with the everyday life that circulates in the world around him. Furthermore, that his father can only relate dim sketchy outlines of the past calls into question the veracity of any singular history, implicitly illustrating why Tran cannot rely on any one perspective when trying to reconstruct his family's experience. Yet this section expresses this array of complex sentiments without alienating readers, as Tran's experimental moments fall well within the limits of an audiences' visual literacy. Formally, then, this part of the story is difficult without being taxing, and the multiple perspectives offered by this interplay enrich the pleasures of looking while providing emotional depth to this social history.

Sense Experience, Food, and the Visible Social Body

The physicality in *Vietnamerica* reverses the enduring image of the depredated Vietnamese body, an undifferentiated mass hardened through the refugee experience. The bodies in this context retain their multiplicity, distinction, and liveliness through Tran's use of synesthesia and subjective expressionistic techniques. Throughout the text food is an important tool that Tran relies on to visually animate the bodies within their social contexts, with sensory experiences providing the roadmap that he follows while reconstructing the social lives of those that constitute his past. Food contacts revive the tastes, noises, and smells across different Vietnamese locations and times—physical borders he then re-presents when constructing his own history.

Tran's mother relates her version of the family history at the beginning of each chapter, with Tran spotlighting her body in a dark square frame. All of these episodes start with her preparing food, and in figure 11.2 a sonic cue is also inserted to help activate the scene. Ripping a leafy vegetable registers the

Figure 11.2. Tran's mother relates her version of the family history.

sound and gesture involved in the telling of history and serves as a trigger that allows Tran and his mother to enter into their shared past. However, as the frame is dominated by the blackness surrounding his mother, the off-center window suggests, again, that this is only a slice of history. The imbalance in the graphic design suggests that what is not known, what lies beyond the reach of this story, is composed of much more than his mother could hope to communicate alone. Instead, cutting her body, in this case focusing on Tran's mother's face and hands, highlights how the gestures, rhythms, and aural cues of cooking and other bodily practices pass down cultural information through generations via a collective everyday effort, eschewing an individualized wholly conscious recollection. This fragmentary approach highlights the collaborative efforts required to interpret the symbolic information carried through each body, a task that both Tran and the reader must navigate. Drawing deep thick "gutters" (the technical term for space between each frame) emphasizes the gaps in recollection, and the radical changes in viewer perspective challenges the linearity of memory. Indeed, with this non-linear narrative that oscillates between the past and present, the characters in the story are constantly in action, discussing among themselves in order to pull together a "complete" frame of events. Following Tran's journey, then, readers are encouraged to become part of the experience of recollection, as they

Figure 11.3. The contrast between a clean atemporal ordering of events and the messiness of lived experience is evident in this two-page spread.

are presented with a hermeneutic demand to piece the story's formal elements together, as they negotiate Tran's abrupt changes in panel sizes, color schemes, and locations.

The amount of time held between each frame in a graphic narrative is uncertain, and the past, present, and future are simultaneously perceptible as the reader visually negotiates the panels laid out on one page. This flattening of time allows for the contemplation of different eras and multiple social orders all in the same instant. The contrast between a clean atemporal ordering of events and the messiness of lived experience is evident in the two-page spread of figure 11.3. The upper half of the left-hand page is dominated by an orderly family tree that neatly delineates his family relations. The bottom half of the same frame consists of a mealtime scenario in which each family member sits around a table, smiling, with their own plate of food, arranged spatially so that they are all separate and locatable. Each body is allowed to fully luxuriate and gesticulate in the setting, a frozen tableau of the distinct roots that constitute this healthy flourishing family. Whereas the interactions are clear, conversations are absent, as Tran uses a text box to elucidate the scene. While there is food no one is eating, and hence sensorial inputs do not complicate this clean, third-person representation of family life and intergenerational renewal. This static full-page tableau provides a remarkably different view of family life than the many small boxes that populate the right-hand page, which are presented as temporally continuous and active. In particular, in the small panel on the top left-hand corner of the second page, the family's bodies are, again, on display, but in this iteration of the mealtime setting bodies are crammed together, engulfing each other with overlapping conversations. In this setting the previous page's placid family picture springs to life with this abrupt change in perspective, in which conversation bubbles fill up the four sides of the frame. This very social scene provides a counterpoint to the dystopic vision of mass hysteria in figure 11.1, with the bodies clawing around and over each other to flee Vietnam. Instead, here the reader can explore the close quarters where bodies live, eat, and interact in everyday life. Indeed, as the conversations run into each other it is unclear where one body begins and another one ends as the entirety of the environment is made up of interpersonal flows.

Culinary cues are again at the fore on the right-hand page, as in the top three panels Tran's icon is actively ingesting food. In these scenes the culinary encounter is not presented as an innate or natural performance organically drawn out from his Vietnamese heritage; rather, his culinary experience requires mediation, as his Vietnamese family must constantly instruct him on how to interact with various unnamed substances. Whereas the first panel surrounds Tran in a sea of declarations, in the second panel the perspective changes, with the directives from unknown family members coming "off-screen" and immersing him in an environmental soundscape of voices that are intimate yet not fully recognizable to the reader. The third panel consists of a comedic representation of the battle going on in his digestive tract, where the incorporation of this Vietnamese edible is portrayed as a raucous party and battleground, as the food is causing a great commotion in his stomach. In this frame Tran humorously translates the previous panel's instructions of "Try this, it's a delicacy" to "Your tender American stomach doesn't stand a chance," identifying this gastronomic performance as a moment when the psychic distance he feels from family members who reside in Vietnam becomes physically manifest. Transnational digestion, then, is not a smooth process of ethnic consumption or assimilation for Tran, which runs counter to the idea of "eating the other," marketed toward culinary tourists in search of an easy transcultural fix. Instead, the culinary encounter is something to be reckoned with and marks his body's difference from those who stayed in Vietnam, in the process illustrating how this common transnational culinary history contains material cleavages. Food provides the rhythm, rituals, and tastes of places that become the basis for social memory, but Tran is cognizant that they require a difficult translation and access to this history is not assured. While food is often posited as a means to suture perceived ethnic incommensurability, in Tran's book edibles mark difference and require a difficult arbitration if they are going to be digested by him and/or a North American audience.

The interplay between Vietnamese and Vietnamese Americans is a productive tension throughout the book, where, despite the neatly ordered family tree,

living through colonialism, wartime, refugee status, communism, and capitalism has produced a multitude of generational, gendered, and class positions
that complicate even the small family unit. This uneven transnational cultural
development makes it difficult to represent the plurality of subject positions
under one narrative or formal style. Keeping his icon in the background of many
scenes is one technique that Tran uses to allow other subjectivities the room to
circulate and take turns at the forefront of a frame. This technique is evident
in the middle panel of the second page, which presents Tran staggering after a
culinary encounter—a tiny figure left behind by the movement and sounds of
the other more prominent bodies in the scene, who are more comfortable and
composed in this environment. Because the other bodies visually surround Tran
and converge into a "v" form, the graphic balance produced by the figural positions illuminate the relational qualities of the scene. In a panel like this, Tran
layers the space so that everyone inhabits a specific place, allowing their body
positions to express their connection to the setting, and instead of facing the
impossible task of recreating everyone's "voice," Tran provides these bodies with
a situated presence.

Rereading Vietnamese Americans in Popular Culture

Traditionally, the comic book has trafficked in stereotypes to quickly reach and
consolidate a paying audience. Yet as audiences become increasingly literate in
the language of the comic book, the quick connection between the reader and
text also presents the possibility of rapidly recoding unsavory representations by
literally reframing the body to produce different and more particularized ico-
nography.[10] As Vietnamese bodies, gestures, and practices are produced in a dialectical relationship with their space, *Vietnamerica* provides a staggering range
of what Vietnamese people are, and can be, by routing them through multiple
environmental contexts. No longer resigned to playing waiters, delivery men, or
tiger women—the roles often accorded to Asian Americans in popular films and
television shows—these bodies become agential figures that sculpt their own
spaces. In contrast to other visual media, like the theater or film, the numbers of
spaces a graphic narrative can reference are more numerous and can be larger
in scale, as the medium is not subject to the economic pressures of costly set
designs. For instance, Tran's chaotic scenes of motorbikes, towering buildings,
and aerial shots of large masses of people are easily achieved, helping to capture the sublime effect produced by physical environments. With a wide array of
physical options available to Tran, the narrative weight of the graphic text does
not always need to be carried by the actors and figures themselves, and therefore
visual displays of the bodies can be strategically deployed to capture the intrica-
cies of their *social* presence.

Strategically differentiating their subjectivity is of particular importance to the Vietnamese American community. In addition to being read as refugees from an unpopular war, Vietnamese Americans inherited the position of being Americans of color. These categorical markers, which have been assigned to them from their first days on U.S. soil, have brought an increased surveillance of their bodies and social practices, yet this gaze has not always brought about an increased interest or awareness of cultural particularity. This sanctioned ignorance is evident in incidents like the 1989 Cleveland School massacre in Stockton, California, where Patrick Purdy opened fire on both Vietnamese and Cambodian American children in an elementary school. The skin color of these fallen children signified an ambiguous sense of the American enemy for Parsons, and the horrific outcome speaks to the material consequences of an absence of cultural literacy and recognition of Vietnamese Americans as American subjects. Yet even when they are recognized, their position as visible minorities often brings unwanted attention, as in 1981 when the Ku Klux Klan in Texas burned boats in an attempt to chase away Vietnamese American fishermen—leading klansman and Vietnam war veteran Louis Beam to declare that he did not have to travel to Vietnam to help rid the country of communists. As the scholar Isabelle Thuy Pelaud relates, in both of these cases there was an alarming lack of differentiation between the history and bodies of Northern and Southern Vietnamese people and between those who are Cambodian or Vietnamese.[11] I would add, when examined in concert, these two incidents illustrate why there is a pressing need for popular American narratives to include Vietnamese American history and experiences while registering the specificity of Vietnamese American bodily signifying practices.

Whenever Vietnamese American authors engage a popular readership, then, they face the added burden of reorienting assumptions about the Vietnamese American experience in order to combat this structural violence. Indeed, there is a pressing need for their artistic creations to exceed a niche audience, and this ethical imperative demands they use artistic forms capable of reaching a broad range of readers. The graphic narrative is a popular form, accessible and affordable to many across the socioeconomic spectrum. That said, the popularity of ethnospecific graphic narratives should not be overstated, as many ethnic American publications are the product of alternative or underground presses that exist through the efforts of, and for, a niche market.[12] This business model may be changing as *Vietnamerica*'s publisher, Villard (an imprint of Random House), has produced a stunning full-color hardcover book, clearly banking on Tran's work reaching beyond a limited audience. The success of Gene Luen Yang's 2006 young-adult graphic novel *American Born Chinese* has changed the publishing landscape, providing precedent for Asian American graphic narratives to be distributed and promoted widely.[13] Tran's book has received critical acclaim with *Time Magazine* dubbing it one of the top ten graphic memoirs of all time. It has been translated into both French and Spanish and has been reviewed in such publications as the *Wall Street Journal*, *Miami Herald*, and the *Toronto Star*—in sum suggesting that the book holds the promise of reaching a broader and more diverse readership than many of its other niche-oriented counterparts.[14]

The graphic form's pedagogical value has been noticed by educators as well, with *American Born Chinese* being integrated into high school syllabi across the country. In the book, to detail the pressures of racial assimilation, Yang creates a character, Chin-Kee, who is a disturbing composite of mass media Orientalist stereotypes that the protagonist, Jin Wang, repeatedly tries to disassociate himself from. This extreme exaggeration of stereotypical "Oriental" bodily features and actions makes painfully clear how uncomfortable and prevalent these images are for many Asian Americans—presenting the racist tropes in such a way that their obsceneness should be evident to even the least color-conscious of readers. The book's introduction into the common curriculum suggests that this educational strategy has been effective, and the graphic form's rhetorical power is being recognized as an effective technology that can produce culturally literate readers from a young age.

Tran's aesthetic intervention follows the lead of Yang's book, relying on exaggerated physical movements to educate the reader. While conversations in the book tend to be simple and ordinary in narrative content, in every panel bodies react through amplified, easily identifiable expressions. In the background of many scenes anonymous people are gesticulating wildly, clearly expressing varying amounts of joy, sadness, frustration, and/or mirth. Rather than relying on quiet tableaus that focus the reader's eye on the main speakers, Tran uses a plethora of relentlessly active figures to populate the scenes. While the members of Tran's immediate family are the most developed characters in the book, this technique illustrates how they live within a world of movement and action, along with others who are busy with their own lives and are markedly uninterested in Tran's family's interactions. By not allowing his family to dominate the frames with their own self-interests, Tran makes the reader aware that they are but one example of the many families and actors who inhabit each chronotope. Tran's book ultimately reads differently than Yang's, then, by committing to more consistently realistic visual depictions of the book's subjects—intervening in accepted modes of reading Asian American bodies by presenting a diverse array of Asian and Asian American subjects instead of addressing pervasive historical stereotypes.

Rather than read Tran's embrace of this popular visual form solely as an attempt to reach a wide non-Vietnamese audience, I would like to suggest that the text is also well positioned to draw in a multigenerational Vietnamese readership. Younger Vietnamese Americans interested in discovering their own history are guided through the *process* of unearthing roots via Tran's iconic textual surrogate. Because of the narrative's diffused graphic focus, it is not the textual surrogate itself that seeks replication but, rather, the journey that Tran embarks upon that could seem attractive to Vietnamese American youths looking to piece together their own histories. At the same time the comic form remains physically accessible, and the themes remain suitably weighty, for those of older Vietnamese American generations whose language training may limit their attempts to read an academic Vietnamese American history written in English or a literary production filled with poetic phrasing. *Vietnamerica*, then, can stand as a cultural touchstone for intergenerational Vietnamese American understanding, and while the book is not yet translated into Vietnamese, considering the international popularity of graphic narratives, these same accessible formal qualities should eventually foster a transnational following.

Conclusion: Picturing the Past

Because of the war Vietnamese family members have often had to live as strangers. Attending to the work of Bich Minh Nguyen, Le Thi Diem Thuy, and Monique Truong reveals that missing family members is a common and important theme in many examples of contemporary Vietnamese American writing. As families were repeatedly broken apart by the horrors of war and the refugee period, finding the past requires finding missing family members, plotting, and placing them in their absence. While Yen Le Espiritu suggests that Vietnamese American authors must become "tellers of ghost stories,"[15] I propose that Tran goes a step further by locating how the social lives of these "ghosts" are manifest in the gestures, rhythms, and places of the living. The political importance of identifying somatic resonances can be understood through Nguyen-Vo Thu-Huong's call for Vietnamese American artists and scholars to "make the dead tangible," as without this reanimation the war becomes a mere "body count."[16] Spurred on by a need to imagine the lives of the missing, Tran's appeal to visual social bodies and historical contexts of Vietnamese families, then, provides a material orientation of wartime experiences, without reducing the vitality of these times to instrumental geopolitical desires.

As scholarship about the Vietnamese American community often requires looking back to Vietnam to find missing actors, it is no coincidence that many Vietnamese American scholarly and artistic works are transnational in scope. A transnational approach does not need to suggest that borders are now being broken down; rather, it can detail the affective orders produced by national containments and conflicts on a global scale.[17] By setting a vast majority of his story in Vietnam, despite being an American author and actor himself, Tran visually demonstrates both the continuity and discontinuity between Vietnam and its diaspora. This social history necessarily demands that "his" story straddle multiple national and temporal boundaries, yet this does not eliminate his material and political standing. For whether the title's double entendre is read "Viet in America" or the overlapping of country names Vietnam and America, his illustrations consistently place the story within political boundaries that compress, violate, and propel the figures in the text. This material specificity makes Tran's work groundbreaking in its ability to link the colonial, transnational, and Asian American experience by graphically mapping a visible Vietnamese social body that exists across numerous historical and spatial environments.

NOTES

1 GB Tran, *Vietnamerica: A Family's Journey* (New York: Villard Books, 2010).

2 David L. Ulin, "Book Review: 'Vietnamerica' by GB Tran," *Los Angeles Times*, January 30, 2011, http://articles.latimes.com/2011/jan/30/entertainment/la-ca-vietnamerica-20110130.

3 Jade Hidle, "An Interview and Review of GB Tran's *Vietnamerica*," *diacritics*, February 24, 2011, http://diacritics.org/?p=3070.

4 Isabelle Thuy Pelaud, *This Is All I Choose to Tell: History and Hybridity in Vietnamese American Literature* (Philadelphia: Temple University Press, 2010), 8.

5 Nhi T. Lieu, *The American Dream in Vietnamese* (Minneapolis: University of Minnesota Press, 2011), 8.

6 See Andrew X. Pham, Aimee Phan, and Bao Phi, to name just a few.

7 Hillary L. Chute, "Women, Comics, and the Risks of Representation," *Graphic Women: Life Narrative and Contemporary Comics*, ed. Hilary L. Chute (New York: Columbia University Press, 2010), 3.

8 See Elaine H. Kim, *Asian American Literature: An Introduction to the Writings and Their Social Context* (Philadelphia: Temple University Press, 1982).

9 See Timothy Yu, *Race and the Avant-Garde: Experimental Asian American Poetry since 1965* (Stanford, CA: Stanford University Press, 2009); Christopher Lee, *The Semblance of Identity: Aesthetic Mediation in Asian American Literature* (Stanford, CA: Stanford University Press, 2011); Rocío G. Davis and Sue-Im Lee, eds., *Literary Gestures: The Aesthetic in Asian American Writing* (Philadelphia: Temple University Press, 2005).

10 Derek Parker Royal, "Foreword; Or Reading within the Gutter," in *Multicultural Comics: From Zap to Blue Beetle*, ed. Frederick Luis Aldama (Austin: University of Texas Press, 2010), ix.

11 Pelaud, *This Is All I Choose to Tell*, 13–14.

12 Leonard Rifas, "Race and Comix," in Aldama, *Multicultural Comics*, 27–38.

13 See Gene Luen Yang, *American Born Chinese* (New York: First Second, 2006).

14 This corporate backing, of course, raises questions regarding the uneven politics underwriting how transnational Vietnamese literature becomes popular. GB Tran was "discovered" at the popular Comic-Con convention in San Diego, and his book *Vietnamerica* has been reviewed in numerous prominent media outlets. This visibility demonstrates how the Vietnamese diaspora holds a privileged position in defining transnational Vietnameseness for a global audience. The institutional access that a new Vietnamese American artist like Tran has far outstrips what even the most popular mainland Vietnamese author could possibly hope to enjoy. However, in the future Internet culture could cause this promotional imbalance to drastically alter. The digital era has brought new attention to various Vietnamese social bodies through food blogs, television food shows, and YouTube clips, allowing others to stay current with contemporary Vietnamese movements, slang, and gestures. In sum, then, the imbalance certainly remains where the diaspora has an overabundance of power to

construct a transnational audience, but this is a site worth watching as it holds the possibility of changing relations very rapidly if Internet access and freedom of expression in Vietnam are priorities going forward.

15 Yen Le Espiritu, "Toward a Critical Refugee Studies: The Vietnamese Refugee Subject in US Scholarship," *Journal of Vietnamese Studies*, 1, nos. 1–2 (2006): 410–433.

16 Nguyen-Vo Thu-Huong, "Forking Paths: How Shall We Mourn the Dead?" *Amerasia Journal* 31, no. 2 (2005): 183.

17 Lan P. Duong, *Treacherous Subjects: Gender, Culture, and Trans-Vietnamese Feminism* (Philadelphia: Temple University Press, 2012), 15.

PART III

Wading in the Mainstream

12

Paradise, Hawaiian Style

Tourist Films and the Mixed-Race Utopias of U.S. Empire

CAMILLA FOJAS

Pop culture locates Hawai'i as the origin of tiki culture, volcano sacrifices, the friendly and happy native, grass skirts, hula girls, and surfer boys while helping to install the symbolic coordinates of one of the largest, if not the largest, tourist industries in the United States. These ideas and icons are supported by the mainland interpretation of "aloha culture" as embodied by the welcoming native offering up the bounties of Hawai'i to the weary traveler. The idea of the Hawaiian islands as the fruit of the continental (or mainland) United States and its golden bounty dates back to the imperious ventures of the annexationists. In fact, John Stevens, the U.S. minister to Hawai'i, architect of the illegal overthrow of Queen Lili'uokalani, and mastermind of the annexationists, likened Hawai'i in 1893 to a fruit ready for the taking in his persuasive missive to the State Department: "The Hawaiian pear is now fully ripe and this is the golden hour for the United States to pluck it."[1] This language is key to the place of Hawai'i in the U.S. imaginary as a subject waiting passively to be subsumed into the imperial whole. Some decades earlier, in 1823, similar language was used by John Quincy Adams to describe Cuba as "an apple severed by the tempest from its native tree" and thus ready for the taking.[2] None of the other colonies acquired in 1898, save Puerto Rico, held the same fascination or elicited the same covetous gaze as Hawai'i and Cuba, and it is no coincidence that they would become the two sides of a coin in the North American tourist imaginary—Guam, though groomed for tourism, never fully took hold in mass media as a tourist destination for the United States. For both islands 1959 was a pivotal year; as Cuba moved away from the colossus of the North through revolution, Hawai'i was drawn inextricably into the imperial center through statehood. The waning of U.S. tourism to Havana refocused the tourist gaze elsewhere, and one of these places was the island chain of Hawai'i.

The era just following Hawai'i's entry into statehood was a key historical phase of the imperial mood of the United States. The full integration of Hawai'i into the union of states more than compensated for the complete loss of Cuban affiliation and obeisance—tourist relations between the United States and the Caribbean island tempered down in the 1950s in response to accounts of political unrest and soured in 1960 when the Cuban government nationalized all U.S. property.[3] Though tourists to the Caribbean were rerouted to Puerto Rico, Hollywood film and media culture shifted its love affair with all things Cuban to Hawai'i. In popular culture, Hawai'i was not just a safe and stable tourist destination; the island archipelago presented a new frontier of the United States, one that brought expansive economic opportunities and an "exotic" escape from the workaday life of mainland North America. It was also the only island in the U.S. imperial orbit to achieve statehood, to reach a level of political development deemed sufficient for assimilation into the national imaginary.

Post-statehood Hollywood films set in Hawai'i were part of a discourse of celebration of a new era of U.S. hegemony, particularly after the loss in the Caribbean. There were a number of 1960s tourist features—*Blue Hawaii* (1961), *Gidget Goes Hawaiian* (1961), *Girls! Girls! Girls!* (1962), *Ride the Wild Surf* (1964), *Paradise, Hawaiian Style* (1966), and *Kona Coast* (1968)—that made Hawai'i visible as a site of redemption and imperial defiance—that is, where the newest state was brandished as a sign of North American superiority and the gold standard of colonial development. The playboy, beachboy, and surfer protagonists of these films are all part of rebellious youth subcultures dedicated to the pursuit of pleasure and leisure over conventional domestic interests. Yet these icons of defiant youth culture are framed, not as a threat to the mainstream, but as representatives of the maverick spirit that is core to U.S. leadership acumen. Hawai'i is at the crux of these representations; of all the colonies, it was exceptional as the ultimate fulfillment of the imperial narrative about mature capitalist development. Hawai'i was represented as a future model of the United States, a paradise of prosperity, security, and racial harmony. Prophesying this enduring image of the islands, President Dwight D. Eisenhower endorsed statehood for Hawai'i as a place of harmony and integration where "East meets West" and that provides "a unique example of a community that is a successful laboratory in human brotherhood."[4] The islands represented a utopic site of mixed-race relations during the era of racial unrest on the continent.

Hawai'i Tourist Films

By the late 1950s and early 1960s, various events worked together to prop up the visitor business in Hawai'i: the statehood movement, the introduction of jetliners to replace the less reliable DC-6s and DC-7s, and the waning of tourist ventures to other locations of the former U.S. insular empire. At the same time, the Hollywood studios would deliver mass media tourism through the visual itineraries shaped by the likes of Elvis. This genre, which I call "Hawai'i tourist films," emerged in the post-statehood boom period. In these Hawai'i-based films, the year 1959 has symbolic resonance that extends beyond actual historical periodization. They would present an ideal model of transformation from colonial appendage to domestic political-economic integration. The tourist films of the 1960s share many features. Most are a product of the post-statehood euphoria about the newly domesticated Hawaiʻi as a tourist destination. They offer the lay of the land, providing a visual overview of the features of the tourist locale. Often new goods, services, transportation possibilities, hotels, and resorts are featured prominently. The film might itself act as a tour that stands in for the experience of the place or sufficiently piques enough interest to compel viewers to become actual tourists. A major part of the visual tourist experience is that of the "authentic" indigenous performance; in this case, of hula, chanting, or other forms of expression attributed to native cultures.

Overall, the tourist film offers a narrative context for the "tourist gaze," described by John Urry as the objectification of the host culture by the visitor. He borrows the term from Michel Foucault, who writes of the "medical gaze," or a set of looks endorsed and authorized by an entire institutional structure, one that organizes and produces knowledge about the gazed upon object. Urry's gaze is reminiscent of what Laura Mulvey famously describes as the "male gaze" in cinema, an equally objectifying look that presupposes a passive female or feminized body.[5] The gaze in cinema is curious and controlling, in which seeing and knowing are linked in a proprietary fashion. Likewise, the tourist gaze is curious; it demands a novel visual experience, a new or exotic set of scenes, objects, peoples, and landscapes. These various definitions of the "gaze" work together nicely to describe the function of the tourist film narrative and its visual dynamics. The tourist gaze, caught in a dynamic of seeing and being seen, defines that which is seen as "other" or as a colonial and often feminized object. Indigenous cultures and peoples are spectacles for the viewer, the tourist. For Urry, the tourist gaze is socially organized and changes over time and across contexts, affecting space, the peoples who inhabit it, and social practices.[6] The tourist film shapes a gaze through objects and peoples on the screen while it creates an imaginary space from which national entities and individual identities are construed. The images of the host location are shaped according to visitor desires; the landscape and its peoples are framed in stories that are inviting and pleasurable for the mainstream viewer. For 1960s media about Hawaiʻi, tourism is a celebrated site of capitalism and a source of redemption through integration into the mainland economies as a practice of empire. Tourism was considered the key to full domestication and entry into the U.S. imaginary.

Part of the fantasy of any capitalist order is that of the rapid economic class ascension through capital accumulation, one that is accelerated for imperial cultures in the colonies. Post-statehood Hawaiʻi promised mainland Anglo Americans many opportunities for lucrative business ventures and pleasurable leisure activities, and the tourist films presented the notion that these two categories could be easily combined as one. One of the earliest examples of post-statehood films, *Blue Hawaii* (1961), features all of the fantasies about the new state and the entrepreneurial possibilities therein while acknowledging, in passing, the militarization of the islands. The film encourages new capital relations with Hawai'i concealed in the pleasurable discourse of tourism and its adjunct, entertainment culture. Elvis is the perfect tour guide whose successful music career made him an icon of the American Dream—the capitalist fantasy of attainment and redemption.

Elvis is Chad, a soldier returning from peacetime duty who returns to his transplanted Southern family and girlfriend on O'ahu. His girlfriend, Maile, along with his parents, urge him to ditch his beachboy ways and find an occupation that suits him, leading him to find a lucrative venture in the burgeoning tourist industry. *Blue Hawaii* plays with many biographical facts of Elvis's life and is part of his ongoing relationship to the islands. Like Chad, he had just returned from a two-year stint in the U.S. armed forces in 1959. Soon after learning that the Pacific War Memorial Commission was having trouble raising money for the USS *Arizona* Memorial in Pearl Harbor, Elvis offered to do a benefit concert for the project in 1961. He returned in the same year to begin filming *Blue Hawaii*, a year later to film *Girls! Girls! Girls!* and five years later for *Paradise, Hawaiian Style*.

Blue Hawaii exploits Elvis as a figure who mediates between cultures and represents the reconciliation between opposing cultures and values. Elvis brokers the neutralization of contradictions and the integration of conflicting sides: between youth and mainstream, native and white, male and female cultures, and continental U.S. and island cultures. For instance, the very context of the film depicts this idea. Elvis and his family represent the integration of two unrelated geographies in the migration of southern plantation culture to Hawai'i. In fact, the plantation system, its major signifiers and cultural norms, are transplanted from a popular cultural imaginary of the Old South onto the modern plantation of O'ahu. Hawai'i is the new South within a modern capitalist context. The depiction of the plantation system and all of its accoutrements—the Southern belle and her patrician husband and their philandering son—could be from any Civil War–era Hollywood film and provides a familiar template of identification for a mainstream audience. Elvis, as Chad, is the force of change who will reconcile these opposing values and ideas, among other achievements, and he will modernize the image of the old-plantation culture by integrating it with a new industrial formation: tourism.

Elvis Presley, icon of youth culture, commandeers the new relationship of the imperial outpost to its command center, acting as a "personal guide to America's exotic Eden, our Polynesian paradise."[7] The film's trailer is a tourist vehicle that promotes Elvis's "natural" talent for leading tours of Hawai'i. The film is both a preface to an island vacation while it stands in for that same vacation, announcing (in the tagline from the film's trailer) that "Elvis brings you the vacation of your life." The opening sequence begins with a freeze of a well-known postcard image of Waikīkī framed by the peak of Diamond Head accompanied by the crooning voice of our tour guide, who sings the eponymous song. This is followed by a number of such alluring tourist postcard images that entice the viewer to turn visual apprehension into actual experience of the islands, particularly of iconic tourist sites: Hanauma Bay, Tantulus, Ala Moana Beach Park, and the Coco Palms Hotel on Kaua'i.

Blue Hawaii depicts the beachboy subculture, composed of musicians and surfers who hung out on the beach all day acting as "one man tourist bureaus."[8] More true to fact, the beachboy culture was the domain of Native Hawaiians in the Waikīkī surf zone or po'ina nalu, a popular tourist beach, in the early part of the twentieth century. Isaiah Helekunihi Walker argues that surfing is a Hawaiian cultural practice and an assertion of cultural autonomy and resistance to colonial encroachment. The Waikīkī surf boys were composed of mostly Native Hawaiian surfers who would use their skills for remuneration as surf instructors, tour guides, lifeguards, bodyguards, musicians, and local celebrities. They were popular with *haole* women, white women, with whom they would openly violate laws against miscegenation and thus assert their anti-colonial self-possession. Rather than being "passive" and "sexualized," these men were sexual agents and entrepreneurs who operated their own businesses and profited from tourist whims.[9] The Elvis Hawai'i films exploit and dehistoricize this beachboy phenomenon and, in typical Elvis style, adapt it to mainstream culture, emptying it of its political valence. And unlike the Hawaiian beachboys who were deemed a social threat for white women, Elvis is seen as providing a necessary service and protection for all women, one who often crosses racial lines in a manner that does not upset social norms given the popular cultural acceptance of interracial relations of white men and brown women.

The Elvis films are meant to be tours of the islands, giving viewers a visual map of the new "sister state" and an introduction to its different cultural dynamics and mores. For example, In *Blue Hawaii*, we are introduced to O'ahu by Chad's Hawaiian girlfriend, Maile, who gives us an overview of some main tourist areas of Honolulu from the Pali Highway, to Kalākaua Avenue in Waikīkī, to the Honolulu International Airport. Maile is our initial tour guide, but she is actually a stop on the cultural tour of the islands. We soon discover that she is *hapa*, or of French and Hawaiian heritages, a mix that the film represents as a source of internal conflict. Through her character we learn what it means to be Hawaiian. When she catches Chad kissing a flight attendant she is overcome with jealousy; "My French blood tells me to argue with you and my Hawaiian blood tells me not to." Her Hawaiian blood makes her more passive and accepting, less interested in conflict or contestation and more likely to accommodate the offending party. This corresponds nicely with colonial portraits of Hawaiians as welcoming the invading forces of U.S. capitalists and subsequent annexation. It is also a key portrayal of Hawaiians as naturally inclined to the welcoming embrace attendant to tourism. Maile and her fellow Hawaiians are happy and hospitable natives who, in case any viewer might think otherwise, are excited to meet and greet the sojourning tourist. In keeping with the Hollywood practice of using white actors to play the brown member of the interracial couple, the actress who plays Maile is Anglo American; thus the "interracial" intimacy is in compliance with the Production Code. It is not until *Paradise Hawaiian Style* (1966) that the interracial couple is actually played by actors of different races.

Maile's French side is the source of trouble from whence emerges her reason and sense of justice. Yet in this situation, her Hawaiian side wins, which is also a victory for Chad, and she forgives him his transgression. But it is this mix of Euro-Hawaiian heritage (perhaps recalling that of the tragic life of Princess Kaʻialani) that raises Maile above the other Native players in this drama. Unlike others who will be background and servile figures who add color to the story, Maile's mixed identity aligns her more closely with mainstream culture and thus gives her a distinct advantage. It opens the possibility for her to become Chad's aide in his business venture into tourism. Moreover, their mixed-race relationship signals the racial harmony of the islands and the state-level collaboration between the white-dominant mainland and Hawaiʻi.

Chad is our main tour guide to the fiftieth state, our crooning entertainment, and a protagonist who embodies the conflicts and anxieties brewing for his generation in the 1960s—a time of the Cold War, racial unrest, and a revolution in sexual and gendered attitudes. When he returns to Oʻahu from his military service he refuses to return to his privileged place in the tony neighborhood of Kahala and the role already determined for him by his well-appointed family. His refusal of his parents' expectations to take over the family business and settle into a bourgeois lifestyle and "marry a girl of [his] own class" (read: "race") registers as part island malaise and lack of ambition and as part of the rebelliousness of the beachboy counterculture. It is a crisis familiar to the majority of the audience yet something more exotic, a special condition of the tropics. Though Chad is a thoroughly mainland boy who, along with his immediate family, is a relatively recent transplant to Hawaiʻi from the South, he displays many of the cultural values and way of life attributed to the tropics. When a befuddled traveler, seeing Chad kissing another woman in front of his girlfriend, asks where Chad got his basic training, referring to his skilled romantic exploits, the reply is "in Hawaiʻi." Yet Chad's acculturation to the islands is what gives him a distinctive edge as an entrepreneur. This, combined with his appeal to women, builds his business. In the logic of the story, that which would be a negative sign for Hawaiians is a sign of Chad's prowess.

State of Tourism

For Jon Goss, the narrative of the tourist scapes of Hawai'i follows a cyclical arc of "innocence, corruption, and redemption."[10] This story arc is complicit with the official history of Hawai'i from the vantage of the imperial culture in which innocent native culture is corrupted by colonialism but redeemed through its attachment to the United States. In the 1960s tourist films of Hawai'i, this redemption is achieved and displayed through the expansion of the tourist industry and thus economic independence of the former colony. And tourist development coincides with individual character development. In *Blue Hawaii*, Chad describes his assertion of financial independence from his parents as his "declaration of independence." The narrative encodes an allegory about the status of Hawai'i for the mainland viewer, as paradoxically attaining independence as it becomes moored to the united States. In this case, independence is the consequence of ever more tourism. Chad has to reconcile the paradoxes and conflicts in his quest for the pleasures of leisure by shirking the duties of work. His desire is complicit with the tourist desire to throw off the yoke of industrialism and find freedom in the experience of pure pleasure. Or as Maile reminds Chad, whom she finds napping on a surfboard: "You can't spend the rest of your life on a surfboard." Chad will find a way to bring together the opposing forces of leisure and work by making his leisure into work—just as he integrates a number of other oppositions that he encounters.

Chad searches for a viable career in the tourist industry working for a small tour guide company instead of working in agricultural business raising pineapples with his father. His search for a lucrative and independent business allegorizes the shift in Hawai'i from the plantation economy to tourism. His maturation to independence allegorizes what is deemed as the "economic maturation" of Hawai'i. He embodies all of the major industries and institutions on the islands: military, agriculture, and tourism. He refuses the former two for the latter, asserting that "Hawaii has a big future and I want to be a part of it," referring to the major expansion of the tourist enterprise in the islands. The opportunities of agriculture have been fully tapped and are deemed part of an inert past, while tourism promises a whole new range of possibilities. But his initial refusal to join his family business is only transitional and will be revised when Chad realizes that he can combine both industries and integrate the interests of both generations; he fulfills his father's expectations and his own entrepreneurial desires by uniting them. He links his tour company with the work of his father's firm, the Southern Pineapple Company, by offering tours to its employees and arranging incentive trips. His idea is to provide reinvigorating island respites for workers so that they might return to the mainland and work more efficiently.

Chad initially works for another tour company where he learns the ropes of the industry and proves his potential for mature development. His first tour is to take a youngish schoolteacher and four of her teenage students—presumably the ideal audience of the Elvis movie. We are given a tour of the islands with a short educational introduction about the significance of the island of Oʻahu within the archipelago. The tour takes the audience through central Oʻahu and its pineapple fields. The focus of the group of teenage girls is Ellie, a particularly rebellious and intransigent teen. She is detached, sullen, and resistant. She is variously a typical teen and a reminder of the burgeoning youth movement, of which Elvis is a major icon, which will question authority and undermine the status quo. Either way, she stands in for the wayward North American refusing the beneficent lead of those in power—in an ironic twist, the authority in question is Elvis, which is a major part of the ideological work of the story. As it turns out, she's simply misunderstood, and a firm hand by Chad causes her complete rehabilitation and reincorporation into the society of the other teenage girls. He is not just a tour guide but offers moral guidance and discipline for the wayward girls and their caretaker. His maturation and narrative success is dependent on the type of leadership he exhibits. In the process, he proves to Maile that he is mature, dependable, and faithful and asks for her hand in marriage. The film ends with every conflict resolved and everyone coming together for the impromptu but "authentic Hawaiian" wedding ceremony between Chad and Maile. This ending pulls together all of the ideological loose ends under the cover of marriage, allegorizing the complete legal, financial, and cultural integration of the islands—Maile—and the mainland—Chad. For Hawaiʻi, redemption is achieved by adapting to the economies of tourism, not through sovereignty or self-determination.[11]

Much of the tourist media about Hawaiʻi in the 1960s thematized the difficult maturation or coming of age of the protagonist in a story arc that tacitly allegorizes the maturation of the Hawaiian colony through the self-abdication of statehood. Maturation is depicted in socioeconomic and psychosexual terms that are both deeply gendered and heteronormative. Each protagonist in the imperial drama must resolve a moral crisis whose solution can be found in tourism. In *Blue Hawaii* and *Paradise, Hawaiian Style* the tourist film genre overlaps with that of the teen surf picture and the rock-and-roll films made popular by Elvis—the Elvis beach films combine all three subgenres. Though these films have protagonists who are part of rebellious subcultures, they are stories with a clear imperial moral about mature economic development.

In *Blue Hawaii* and *Paradise, Hawaiian Style*, the mark and symbol of U.S. power is in the ability to integrate opposites and gloss contradictions, to commingle leisure and work and private and public spaces for maximum profit. Thus, the Elvis in both films makes his private pleasures into public work for personal gain. In much the same way, the private pleasures of watching a Hollywood film performs the social work of propping up the United States in the Pacific and the world.

Like *Blue Hawaii*, *Paradise, Hawaiian Style* begins with a trip on a United Airlines airplane—though a small detail, this common theme is part of the tourist film promotion of the various communication technologies of the travel industry. We meet Rick Richards, a recently fired airline pilot, as he returns to Hawai'i. Elvis, as Rick, is a bit older than he was in his last Hawai'i-based picture, but he has a very different role than that of Chad in *Blue Hawaii*. Elvis as Rick is a self-centered womanizer who is unable to hold down a job. Rick's playboy exploits are played up for comedy and are not treated as seriously disabling. Rather, he is able to bounce back from being fired from a major airline to starting a new venture with a friend because of his many female connections. In a comical fashion, Rick encounters women with whom he has had affairs all over the islands. They all work in the hospitality industry and serve as business connections promoting his new partnership with his friend Danny—called Danrick Airways.

Rick is less beachboy than playboy. He embodies what Barbara Ehrenreich describes as the "playboy ethic" characterized by a refusal of middle-class expectations.[12] The playboy is part of the postwar economic boom and the sensibility of the leisured class to resist domestic encumbrances for the pleasures of sexual freedom. He is the embodiment of U.S. economic prosperity who explored the freedom and fun of capitalism. Though the film indulges the pleasures of the playboy lifestyle and even shows how it can enhance business opportunities, Rick is not allowed to run rampant for too long. In the end, he must find a way to model the proper kind of playboy disposition, one that is only transitional and temporary and that eventually leads to his reformation.

Like its predecessors, *Paradise, Hawaiian Style* uncovers an ideal liberal democratic order through a new social formation: mixed race relationships. Rick's business partner Danny, played by famed Asian American actor James Shigeta, is initially loath to partner with Rick because his large family is dependent upon his income. When we meet Danny's family, it turns out that he and his blonde wife have five mixed-race children—played variously by Asian and white kids, though Danny, we are to believe, is Hawaiian. By the time this popular tourist film was released, in 1966, mixed-race issues were part of the popular cultural landscape. It was released a year before *Guess Who's Coming to Dinner* (1967) and is unique in its normative depiction of mixed-race relations as simply the status quo in Hawai'i. These films are reminders of the potent symbolic and often overdetermined meanings of mixed-race peoples and relations in popular culture. For example, in war films, particularly those that take place in Hawai'i and the Asian Pacific, interracial intimacies between Asians and Anglos represented strategic alliances and political relationships of the United States to Asian nations—as in *Sayonara* (1957). These romances were typically between Anglo men and Asian women, where the latter were viewed as the spoils of war.[13]

In the 1960s, there was political movement toward a major legal battle that would be won in 1967: The landmark Supreme Court case *Loving v. Virginia* would overturn any remaining state laws against interracial marriage and inaugurate what Maria P. P. Root would call the "bi-racial baby boom."[14] Indeed Danny's family is a major part of this boom. The most prominent "mixed-race" kid, Jan, gets top billing in the film and is featured in several song and dance routines. Donna Butterworth, who played Jan, was born in Pennsylvania but moved to Hawai'i when she was young and learned to sing and play ukelele. Unlike Maile of *Blue Hawaii*, who embodies the conflict between her white and Hawaiian selves, Jan occupies a role similar to that of Elvis as Chad. Both embody the collaboration and harmony between the races and prove that Hawai'i is a future vision of the United States as an exemplary site of the triumph over racial discord.

Paradise, Hawaiian Style introduces new aspects of the maturing tourist industry that, still nascent in the 1950s, had grown exponentially by the late 1960s.[15] By the mid-1960s, new tourist opportunities would involve risk and large amounts of capital to compete in a glutted market. Within an established industry, any new venture has to target a niche market and experience; it has to offer something that others will not or cannot offer. Rick asks Danny to gamble on a partnership offering helicopter tours or short interisland trips delivering people, animals, and goods on relatively short notice. For instance, Rick delivers several uncrated dogs to a dog show on another island, interrupting his ability to fly, causing injury to the dogs and himself, and seriously ruining his female passenger's hairdo. But the tours also offer a specialized tour that is a sign of prestige and attainment. Rick gets the idea about the potential symbolic value of these tours when he shuttles a businessman to a meeting on a neighboring island. The man, Mr. Cubberson, became wealthy selling alligator skin shoes by promoting them as a "symbol of prestige, of wealth, of importance." The new tourist guide is thus able to separate his tour from the volume tours targeting the mainstream tourist; instead, Danrick Airways sells something "prestigious" with a wider profit margin. The new venture involves more risk as the partners must borrow, but the gamble could bring new cultural capital in the form of "prestige."

Though the risk seems great, Rick, exhibits standard North American virtues of being adventurous, risk taking, optimistic, and confident—all virtues of the imperial sensibility. At one point he says, "Where would we be if Captain Cook hadn't taken a chance?" Even as he suffers blows to his ego, losing his job and career, he never admits defeat and willfully redoubles his efforts to attain his goals. Rick, as does Chad in *Blue Hawaii*, turns his vices into virtues and leisure into work. His womanizing is the source of the his business acumen, and he will use each woman as a networking opportunity so, as he tells one woman, he "can combine work with the pleasure of seeing [her]." Women are also stops along the visual tour of the film, they are outposts, island colonies of Rick's playboy empire. This ancillary status of the women hearkens back to the classical structure of narrative and plot as masculine, premised on the journey of Ulysses and the tumescence, climax, and detumescence of plot. Or, in visual tourist narratives, woman is the destination, and her body stands in for the natural bounties of the land and is a pleasurable site for visual exploration.

Rick is the consummate playboy, repaying women for their business connections with the pleasure of his sensual company. His constant refrain, which will come back to haunt him, is "You scratch my back, and I'll scratch yours." The crisis of the story occurs when the exchange relationship is broken and Rick's misadventures catch up with him. Rick flies one of his new girlfriends and his business partner's daughter, Jan, to a picnic on a secluded beach. The girlfriend, using a technique Rick employed with her, throws the helicopter keys away to buy more time with him. Unable to locate the keys, they are all stuck on the beach for the night, causing Rick to miss his business obligations and distressing his partner, Jan's father. It is a fatal mix of business and pleasure. The aim of the film is to reestablish a productive relationship between capital and leisure.

In many ways the film is an allegory of Rick's refrain ("You scratch my back, and I'll scratch yours"), the primary exchange being between Hawai'i's tourist industry giants, particularly the Polynesian Cultural Center and the transportation industry, and the film itself. It is no accident that each film—*Blue Hawaii* and *Paradise, Hawaiian Style*—opens in the same manner: with the main character flying in on a United jetliner. The films publicize and promote all forms of transportation communication from the continental United States to the islands. Rick's refrain signals the transaction between agents of dominant culture that objectify native culture as exchangeable goods. Rick gives his time and attention to various women strategically placed in the tourist industry so they might deliver tourist dollars to his company. In return, the tourist viewers of the film receive all the delights that the islands have to offer.

Rick, for his misadventure during the picnic, is stripped of his pilot's license, but he chooses to fly without it to search for his partner and eventually save him. In a move typical of the North American sensibility, the ends justify the means. He breaks the law in order to do the right thing. He is rewarded for this sense of justice. He seeks out an agent of the Island Aviation Bureau, Mr. Belden, to ask for the reinstatement of his license, not for personal gain but to save the company that he created with Danny. He makes his plea, and his adventurous spirit and assertion of risk is framed as a cardinal virtue and the guiding moral of the narrative. Mr. Belden agrees to have his license reinstated because, "If a man risks his entire future to save a friend, he can't be all bad." Elvis, as Rick, is rewarded on more than one front. He ends up securing the love of the only unavailable woman around him—she claimed to be married as a ruse to throw him off. He does not just get the girl; he sings a song about it as hula dancers perform the lyrics in a performance that takes place at the Polynesian Cultural Center (PCC).

For the first few years of its existence, the PCC had yet to make a profit. Then, fortuitously, Hollywood stepped in with a proposition similar to that which Elvis offered his many women in *Paradise, Hawaiian Style*: a mutually beneficial exchange. In fact, as Rick sets up his contacts, he visits a performer at the PCC to make such an arrangement. Perhaps as a result of its major role in *Paradise, Hawaiian Style*, the PCC finally, in 1967, turned a profit.[16] This product placement would seem to challenge the tax exemption the PCC enjoys, but more significantly, it points to the consumption model of tourism propagated by both entities. The PCC is not overtly cited in the storyline but is given prominent billing in the credits with no ambiguity about how to find it: "Our gratitude to the Peoples of the Pacific at the Polynesian Cultural Center—Laie, Oahu, Hawaii."

In the end, as is typical of musicals, the entire cast of *Paradise, Hawaiian Style* converges on the Polynesian Cultural Center, which is referred to simply by the event that takes place in this locale, the "Polynesian Welcoming Festival." In this spectacle, which showcases all that the PCC has to offer, Elvis takes part in every one of the seven cultural performances on display. The end of *Paradise, Hawaiian Style* converges with the actual final show of the PCC—after a long day of touring each indigenous village, tourists take part in a luʻau and watch a flashy show that gathers all of the various indigenous groups in a summary performance. There is a perfect coordination and integration of the film narrative and the PCC narrative. Each Polynesian culture is showcased with Elvis as the focal point signaling the conflation of the two representational spaces. But even prior to this finale, the PCC is used, not as a space of performance of culture, but as the culture of Hawaiʻi itself. That is, there is no separation from the song-and-dance routines we come to expect from Elvis and the space of the theme park populated by peoples in Native garb. Both are displayed as part of the pure visual pleasure of the narrative. The spectacle with Elvis at the center fully "Americanizes" these performances and exhibits Rick's victory over his own base desires. He transforms his failures and weaknesses into virtues, and the last scene is a showcase of his success and leadership allegorized in his position as the focal point and lead of the spectacular finale.

As in *Blue Hawaii*, Elvis in *Paradise, Hawaiian Style* proves that he can, through his own willful determination, reform his ways and be a successful entrepreneur. In many ways, the Elvis-in-Hawaiʻi films are colonial narratives that tacitly reflect upon the role of the colonies in the U.S. empire. That is, these are stories about how to turn wayward colonial conditions into new industrial formations, making Hawaiʻi a model of the prosperous future of the United States. This idea of forging success from abject conditions is the very stuff of the American Dream. There was no better protagonist to express the rags-to-riches embodiment of the American Dream than Elvis Presley, who transcended his working-class roots to become a major popular cultural icon and movie star. In *Blue Hawaii* this class ascension is depicted as natural to Chad, whose family occupies a tony Hawaiʻi Kai home replete with various Asian butlers and servants. Yet despite his privileged background, Chad aspires to be a "self-made man" and to explore his own route to career success. He is the embodiment of youthful defiance as a key element of the portrait of U.S. exceptionalism and the ideal American as a maverick capitalist. Likewise, in *Paradise, Hawaiian Style*, Elvis's Rick is beset by his weakness for women and pleasure seeking. But he turns these "failures" into a defiant success by turning his personal relationships into business connections.

These films exhibit U.S. exemplarity through their protagonists: Elvis in *Blue Hawaii* is business minded and diplomatic, and the slightly older Elvis of *Paradise Hawaiian Style* finds redemption through his entrepreneurial spirit. Each protagonist faces problems and conflicts and solves them in a way that provides guidance for audiences and proves the capacity for world leadership of the culture that produced them. In these tourist films, Hawai'i is promoted as a sign of the power and messianic duty of the United States to assume global leadership. It represented the best of all that the United States has to offer, where the issues plaguing the mainland have already been resolved. While, in the 1960s, the rest of the United States is dealing with the violence of social unrest and adolescent deviance, Hawai'i, particularly in the Elvis films, is a paradise of racial harmony where rebellious youth cultures are assets to dominant culture. Hawai'i was a model colony to which others fell short; its popular cultural status as mature, developed, entrepreneurial, and amenable to tourist desires gave it the edge over the rest of the islands in the U.S. imperial orbit. It would be rewarded with statehood and a steady flow of tourist dollars.

NOTES

1 Quoted in Tom Coffman, *Nation Within: The History of the American Occupation of Hawai'i* (Kihei, HI: Koa Books, 2009), 127.

2 Quoted in Robert H. Holden and Eric Zolov, eds., *Latin America and the United States: A Documentary History* (New York: Oxford University Press, 2011), 9.

3 Rosalie Schwartz, *Pleasure Island: Tourism and Temptation in Cuba* (Lincoln: University of Nebraska Press, 1997), 203.

4 Quoted in D. W. Meinig, *The Shape of America: A Geographical Perspective on 500 Years of History*, vol. 4, *Global America, 1915–2000* (New Haven, CT: Yale University Press, 2004), 205.

5 Laura Mulvey, "Visual Pleasure and Narrative Cinema," in *Film and Theory: An Anthology*, ed. Robert Stam and Toby Miller (Malden, MA: Blackwell, 2000), 483–494.

6 John Urry, *The Tourist Gaze: Leisure and Travel in Contemporary Societies* (London: Sage, 2002), 1–2.

7 Quoted from the film's trailer; see "*Blue Hawaii*—Trailer," Paramount Movies, YouTube, June 13, 2012, https://www.youtube.com/watch?v=qf-KSYbBRfQ.

8 Robert Allen, *Creating Hawai'i Tourism: A Memoir* (Honolulu: Bess Press, 2004), 16.

9 Isaiah Helekunihi Walker, *Waves of Resistance: Surfing and History in Twentieth Century Hawai'i* (Honolulu: University of Hawai'i Press, 2011), 70–73.

10 Jon Goss, "'From Here to Eternity': Voyages of Re(dis)covery in Tourist Landscapes of Hawai'i," in *Hawai'i: New Geographies*, ed. D. W. Woodcock, 153–177 (Manoa: Department of Geography, University of Hawai'i, 1999), 154.

11 It is not until the television series, *Hawaii Five-o*, that some of the political issues vexing native populations is given some, but never sufficient airtime—within the constraints of entertainment media.

12 Barbara Ehrenreich, *The Hearts of Men: American Dreams and the Flight from Commitment* (London: Pluto, 1984).

13 See Gina Marchetti, *Romance and the "Yellow Peril": Race, Sex, and Discursive Strategies in Hollywood Fiction* (Berkeley: University of California Press, 1994).

14 Maria P. P. Root, *The Multiracial Experience: Racial Borders as a Significant Frontier in Race Relations* (Thousand Oaks, CA: Sage, 1996), xiv.

15 Bryan H. Farrell, *Hawaii: The Legend That Sells* (Honolulu: University of Hawaii Press, 1982), 16.

16 Ibid., 45.

13

Post-9/11 Global Migration in *Battlestar Galactica*

Although it attempts to show us future worlds, science fiction in mass media has much more to say about our contemporary moment. It would seem to be the quintessential genre of escapist fantasy, yet science fiction makes manifest our collective anxieties, transforming and projecting them onto other monstrous and alien bodies. Science fiction has a particular resonance within Asian American studies, not simply because of the stereotypical association of both Asian Americans and science fiction with nerd or geek subcultures, but also because the relatively significant role of Asian people and cultures in mainstream futuristic narratives. Since the first *Star Trek* series, which responded to the racial movements of the 1960s with a multiracial and multinational crew, we've come to expect at least a token Asian character to represent the cosmopolitan future. In *Yellow Future*, Jane Park argues that, when we don't find Asian bodies, we often find the echoes of Asian culture in the mise-en-scene in films like *The Matrix* and *Blade Runner*.[1] These gestures toward Asian-ness reoccur throughout visual culture from cult television shows such as *Firefly* to massive blockbusters such as the *Star Wars* franchise, which dressed its star Padmé Amadala in geisha-esque makeup and kimono-like robes.

Park's work advances other recent scholarship in Asian American studies that draws a direct line between representations of Asians and speculative narratives. The dominance of techno-Orientalism in contemporary depictions of an often dystopic future reinforces popular beliefs about the natural inclination of Asians toward science and technology. Although first coined by David Morley and Kevin Robins to describe depictions of Japan in the 1980s as fears of its economic power was on the rise,[2] the term has been expanded and revised by Asian American scholars to chart the continued anxiety over the so-called Pacific century.[3] Images of Asian culture and, infrequently, minor Asian characters signal the chaotic future, one no longer under the control of the West. In films like *Inception* and *Lucy* the Asian characters mainly exist to coerce the white stars into using morally questionable technology.

The anxiety surrounding technological growth subtends worries about immigration and national boundaries. The racialization of technology revives the long legacy of yellow peril fears about invading hordes of Asian immigrants bent on dominating and erasing European culture. In literary studies, the Winter 2008 issue of *MELUS* was dedicated to untangling the conflation of "Alien/Asian" in both science fiction and popular representations of technology. The "forever foreigner" stereotype discussed in several of the chapters in this book restricts Asians in the United States to the default status of alien with its associative links to both illegality and alienation. The category of Asian American is particularly fraught around the doubled meaning of alien as, literally, otherworldly creatures of science fiction fantasy and the migrant who remains marginal to the national body. When Asians appear in science fiction, then, their symbolic weight overpowers any overtly colorblind narrative.

The genre of science fiction gives us a way to first invoke and then resolve scenes of social chaos and to explore the divisions between society and the Other,[4] and the critically acclaimed, cult, cable television series *Battlestar Galactica* (*BSG*; 2004–2009) functions as an ideal site to examine the representation and resolution of current social contradictions. Race dictates the logic of Asian actors' narratives while the explicit storyline continually denies the significant of race and, in fact, denies its existence in our race-free future. By placing race at one remove, the show, ironically, can speak more directly to race under the cover of narrative necessity. In an earlier article, I focused on the role of the mixed-race child and the trope of interracial romance and transnational adoption in the series. That storyline worked to reconcile some of the contradictions inherent in the shift from early twentieth-century ideals of U.S. colonial and patriarchal domination to the current neocolonial global order. However, the more linear parallel progression of U.S. foreign policy reflected in the show's shift from a story of adoption to the valorization of the biological nuclear family is complicated by the introduction of the character Tory Foster played by the South Asian Canadian actress Rekha Sharma. Tory, when read against the other Asian Canadian reoccurring character, Athena (Grace Park), provides a contradictory image of "failed" assimilation. By refocusing my analysis on this dyad, rather than the mother/daughter pairing in the interracial adoption narrative, competing domestic paradigms of race and national identity come into focus.

Battlestar Galactica was not only the most popular show ever broadcast on the Sci-Fi Channel, it also is one of the few to feature an Asian woman as a central character. The dramatic series, which is based on an earlier, campy, 1970s television series, portrays the aftermath of the near annihilation of the human race by Cylons, humanoid robots. The complicated story follows the remnants of the human colonies in their flight from their Cylon enemies. Like *Star Trek*, the population of the fleet is meant to mirror all of human society, but, again like *Star Trek*, it mirrors the United States more than the global population. The humans search for a new homeland with the Cylons in pursuit. Since the Cylons look like humans, they are able to infiltrate the human colonies, and many of them are not even aware that they are not human. The search to determine who is and is not a Cylon motivates much of the plot of the later seasons. By the end of the series, we come to learn that both of the (only) Asian actresses in the series are Cylons rather than human. Their narrative trajectory once we discover their real identity hinges on their acceptance into human society as they attempt to shed their social status as non-human aliens.

The show highlights the fungibility of Asian American racial formations through the contrast between its Asian female stars. Athena, who transforms through human love, ends up a wife, mother, and loyal soldier. She comes to represent the "good" citizen-subject by embodying an exaggerated feminine ideal and forming an overwhelming affective attachment to a national ideal. Tory, in contradistinction to Athena, is never fully recuperated into human society. Instead of embodying a "post-racial" ideal of Asian upward mobility, the character of Tory develops in response to the increasingly tenuous space of South Asians post-9/11. As other critics both popular and academic have noted, and as one of the show's creators Ronald Moore has stated,[5] *BSG* responds directly to the moral and social and political implications of a post-9/11 world.[6] The show, which first aired in 2004, begins with an explosion that remakes the world of the show's characters, and the subsequent episodes are shadowed by contemporary wars in Afghanistan and Iraq. When read in conjunction with her nonnormative femininity, Tory's rejection of an assimilationist ideal positions her in an ambivalent dialectical relationship with Athena. The inclusion of both characters in the show aptly demonstrates the flexibility of Asian Americans in the service of nationalist racial projects.

Science Fiction and the Pacific Future

The continued resonance of Asia and Asian people for U.S. science fiction media is more than simple generic convention. Generic conventions offer us a familiar narrative to work through reoccurring anxieties over, in this specific case, the place and meaning of the alien Other in our midst. The token Asian character has become a staple of the genre. In fantasy dramas such as *Lost*, *Heroes*, and *The Walking Dead* as well as futuristic adventure shows such as *SGU Stargate* and *Agents of S.H.I.E.L.D.* (both of which star Ming-Na Wen), the inclusion of Asian characters signal our aspirations toward a multicultural future, albeit a multicultural future that still seems to adhere to a normative whiteness. It is significant that all of these examples are ensemble shows with many characters and multiple storylines in each episode. Like workplace dramas that, similarly, include a single Asian character (*Grey's Anatomy*, *The Good Wife*, and *House*), the presence of Asian bodies, even Asian American stars, does little to displace whiteness. These shows, then, are less an opportunity to explore the experience of Asians or Asian Americans than a meditation on the roles of Asians in the symbolic racial economy of the United States.

The deployment of the alien Other as a stand-in for racial and ethnic differ-ence is not new to science fiction.[7] True, race is often absent or limited in science fiction criticism,[8] and discussions of race on television often neglect science fic-tion,[9] but there are notable exceptions. Included among these are scholars who argue that aliens have often acted as metaphors for racialized Others in film[10] and in television.[11] *Star Trek* has been of particular interest to scholars of media and race[12] who argue that representations of alien races in the series parallels the movement from a civil rights era to a "post-racial" one.

Interpreting Cylons as a stand-in for racial differences is a common point of departure for analyzing the *BSG*.[13] The show is explicitly allegorical, end-lessly dissected on discussion boards by fans and in popular print by critics. In an interview with Grace Park she says she first had trouble creating her Cylon character. She continues, "Someone close to me said. 'It's pretty easy. It's just an oppressed race.' As soon as I heard that I was [snaps fingers] 'That's what it is.' And I've been using that a lot."[14] Although the Cylons may look like humans, they have a different religion, family structure, and political system, all of which are emphasized as significant and almost insurmountable distinctions. Analyz-ing the enmity between humans and Cylons through the perspective of race can help us parse the ways in which we conceptualize the relationship between dominant U.S. society and racialized immigrants. As Charles Ramírez Berg writes in his book on Latinos in film, we should view science fiction "with the hope of unveiling what we as a society repress and oppress in regard to immigra-tion."[15] Ramírez Berg argues that understanding aliens as immigrants does not preclude other metaphorical readings and that immigration should be included as an important interpretive lens. While Ramírez Berg's work focuses on Latino immigrants, the inclusion of Asian immigrants into the analysis of science fic-tion allows us to consider multiple facets of the racialized rhetoric of immigra-tion, especially as it is inevitably linked to the issue of assimilation.

Within the world of *BSG* alien/racial differences are often mapped onto national difference. The humans, who serve as our primary point of identifica-tion, reflect the culture and ideals of mainstream U.S. society, but the Cylons' culture is shrouded in mystery and frequently needs to be explained to the audi-ence. Furthermore, as the series progresses and we learn more about Cylon society, it shifts from a primary association with terrorism to a portrayal of a nation-state with specific Cylon characters as migrants. The most explicit of these representations concerns a debate in the last season over the right of Cylons to move freely through the fleet. The storyline closely echoes debates over the rights of immigrants. Late in the series, some Cylons break from their leaders and seek asylum among the humans, occupying largely service positions. A significant portion of them die as they do the hard and dangerous labor of try-ing to repair cracks in the ship's hull. These Cylons eventually demand political representation on the fleet's elected council, prompting public debates about the limits of their citizenship rights.

By understanding Cylons as immigrants and by focusing on Athena and Tory, we can examine differential immigration paths of Asian populations that often follow ethnic lines. *Battlestar Galactica*'s rare inclusion of two Asian characters offers us the chance to examine two distinct and overlapping models of immigration, the East Asian wage laborer and the South Asian skilled laborer. Despite their many similarities—both characters are Cylons, and both begin the show believing that they are human—their plot lines represent two divergent models for understanding Asian American racialization. The primary distinction between them is their positioning in relation to the nuclear, gender-normative, heterosexual, family. If we understand the family as a metonym for nation, then these two models of affective attachment present two different ways of imagining the laboring immigrant body in relation to the nation.[16]

Battlestar Galactica works hard to reconcile some of the contradictions of the United States globally through its explorations of multiple family formations. Although the United States positions itself as anti-imperialist and anti-colonial, dedicated to the democratic self-rule of all countries, it participates in an unequal global economic system. Its image as a multicultural, anti-racist meritocracy belies its system of differential citizenship and immigration, which limits and controls movement across its borders. Even while the barriers between national economies seem to be weakening, national boundaries are becoming ever more rigid.[17] Global migration has been touted as a the ultimate symbol of freedom, liberal individualism, and the transcendence of traditional nation-states, yet the nation still plays a considerable role in differentiating and regulating types of migration. *Battlestar Galactica* provides a storyline that can reconcile both of these contradictions by revising the story of migratory flows from one of capital and labor to one of affective ties. Thus migration is not the result of neocolonial economic policies but a personal choice by those people who are emotionally drawn to the United States and want to move there. Structural inequalities are naturalized and justified along familial lines. In the world of *BSG*, those migrants who adhere to the correct story by forming strong affective ties are rewarded, while those who remain workers, whose primary tie to the humans is as laborers, remain disenfranchised outsiders.

Tory Foster and the Televisual Politics of 9/11

The character of Tory Foster tracks the shifting ground of multicultural rhetoric following the events of 9/11. Analyses of the show as meta commentary on the War on Terror have focused on the way the series rehearses issues such as wartime torture, the limits of political dissent, and the morality of an invasive war.

However, their analyses remain within the logic of the show itself, imagining the Cylons as an alien race fighting against the human race. Yet these two Cylons are played by actors of color, and reading the differences among the Cylons through everyday racial categories opens up an alternative reading. If we step outside of the series' imaginary world and read the bodies on display in the show as racialized bodies, we can see that, in conjunction with the show's overt political commentary, there is also a visual emplotment of the impact of the War on Terror on racialized bodies within the U.S. borders.

At first, Tory is only a minor character in the show. As the assistant to President Roslin (Mary McDonnell), her only significant actions for the first three seasons occur in the context of her morally questionable loyalty to her boss. She first rigs an election to make sure Roslin stays in office and then helps to find a foster mother to care for Athena's kidnapped child. At the end of season 3, Tory discovers that she is not human, as she had always believed, but instead is one of five Cylons aboard the ship, the *Battlestar Galactica*. These five Cylons, named the Final Five, acted as a sleeper cell embedded in the ranks of the human forces. Played by the only South Asian actor in the show, Tory is overdetermined by race, ethnicity, and the force of the narrative in ways that vary widely from the other white Final Five Cylons. So even though the other Final Five Cylons are not people of color, the national hysteria around sleeper cells and the possibility that people might live among us for years before becoming "activated" as terrorists coalesces with long-standing beliefs in the inherent foreign-ness of the Asian Other. Stereotypes of Asian duplicity and inscrutability map easily onto fears of infiltration by terrorists disguised as everyday, if racially marked, people in your very neighborhood or workplace. Tory's moral laxity and her ambivalence about human society cannot be separated from our extratexual visual marking of her, in the context of 9/11, as a threatening racial Other.

The narrative positioning of Tory reverberates with the wider positioning of South Asians within U.S. culture—the epitome of the model minority while also always a potential terrorist. Madhavi Mallapragada captures some of this ambivalence in her study of Indian American high-tech workers who arrive as skilled labor for well-paying jobs.[18] Their economic success, like their academic successes, as noted by Shilpa Davé in her article on spelling bees,[19] appear to tell the classic Horatio Alger story about the value of hard work in a meritocratic society. Never a leader, Tory is, nonetheless, an uncompromisingly hard worker. Indeed, she shows a blind devotion to President Roslin, compromising her own integrity to further her mentor's career. As her character develops, however, we find that her devotion to humankind, embodied by their leader, is merely a convenience.

Her model minority veneer peels away to reveal her inescapable Cylon nature. Of all the Final Five, Tory questions her humanity and allegiance to the humans the most. While the others, all played by white actors, remain committed to their human existence, Tory "returns" to live with the Cylons and tries, unsuccessfully, to convince the others to do the same. As Yuko Kawai argues, the model minority and the yellow peril stereotypes are two sides of the same coin.[20] The very success of the "threatening model minority," in the words of Kent Ono and Vincent Pham, poses a threat to the nation-state as they take the high-paying jobs and places at high-status universities away from their "rightful" owners.[21] Since their success also depends upon their supposedly foreign work ethic, it is also a sign of their clannishness and inability to properly assimilate. Casting the role with a South Asian actor gives additional resonance to our eventual realization of her true Cylon identity. As Sunaina Maira explains, "The national allegiances of Muslim, Arab, and south Asian Americans have come under intense scrutiny for signs of betrayal to the nation, and for any wavering in allegiance to the project of freedom and democracy as defined in the neoconservative vision for the 'New American Century.'"[22] The show leads the audience to constantly question Tory's true beliefs and loyalties. The yellow peril bleeds into the paranoia of the War on Terror, and no matter how consistently the narrative deracinates Tory's female South Asian body, it continues to signify beyond the show's overt storyline.

Nation, Family, and the Yellow Peril

The racialization of Tory extends beyond the repetition of time-worn stereotypes of the model minority and yellow peril. Gender and familial norms also make her storyline legible and meaningful. Tory steps outside of the narrow conventions of the heterosexual nuclear family multiple times. Each time she does she is reminded, along with the audience, of the folly of her ways. Her rejection of domesticity is taken to extremes, and she attacks one of only two nuclear families in the show. In the end, she jeopardizes her standing in human society and, eventually, dies unable to reconcile with either the humans or the Cylons. Tory's sexual deviance, as Deepti Misri argues,[23] resonates with other cinematic representations of the Muslim terrorist. Post-9/11 media differentiates the good Muslim from the bad terrorist by "using the heterosexual family as a template for citizenship." In Tory's case, her sexual deviance serves as evidence of her failure to become a citizen of humanity.

Even before we find out that Tory is a Cylon, the show suggests that she is a part of the non-normative family unit consisting of herself, the female President Roslin, and a single mother known only as Maya (Erica Cerra).[24] This queer family unit is reinforced within the show by the consistent visual pairing of Roslin and Tory during the beginning of the third season when the kidnapping takes place. Although Roslin is romantically aligned with the male Admiral Adama in the narrative, she is more frequently linked visually with Tory since Tory appears nearby or in the background of many of Roslin's scenes while Adama is on a ship far away. Tory, a minor character at that point in the series, is almost exclusively seen in the company of Roslin, and their intimacy is cemented by their shared knowledge of their theft of Athena's child, Hera. The trio of Roslin, Tory, and Maya, then, can be fruitfully read as an alternative, queer, family unit. This adoptive family unit is later shown to be helpless in the face of attacks by the Cylons and is ultimately disavowed by Roslin.

The Cylons' difference and the (il)legitimacy of their culture are both represented by their deviation from human nuclear family formations. In the series, the family, and motherhood in particular, become sacrosanct. One controversial episode during the first season depicts President Roslin after much on-air soul searching deciding to outlaw abortion to help perpetuate the human race. In contrast, the Cylons live in a communal society, and we see them form families with multiple sexual partners of both genders. More damning is their method of reproduction. Because the Cylons reproduce through cloning, they do not depend upon heterosexual coupling. In the season 3 episode "A Measure of Salvation," one character justifies the proposed genocide of the Cylons saying, "No fathers, no mothers, no sons, no daughters." During that same season, the Cylons kidnap a baby girl, but their all-female household is unable to cope with raising the infant, who quickly becomes ill and continues to cry until the adoptive Cylon mother threatens to kill the baby.

Once Tory learns she is a Cylon, she begins to relinquish her human identity, and we, the audience, know the break is complete when she murders the wife and mother of another member of the Final Five. There are only two intact nuclear families on the show, Athena's family, discussed in more detail below, and the family unit of Cally (Nicki Clyne), Cally's son Constanza, and Galen (Aaron Douglas), who is another member of the Final Five. When Tory realizes that the mother, Cally, has discovered the hidden Cylon identities of the Final Five, she follows her to a launch area. Cally, devastated to find out her husband is a Cylon, plans to kill herself and her child. Tory takes the child and shoots the mother into outer space. The camera remains on her impassive and emotionless face as she kills Cally while holding her child. It is also at this point in the series when we first see Tory begin sexual relationships with two other male characters on the show. Significantly, neither of these are love relationships, and both are with men who have other romantic commitments, so their relationships do not even have the potential to become traditional, heterosexual, monogamous parental relationships. As the series ends, Tory is punished for her attacks on the nuclear family. When Galen learns that Tory murdered his wife, he breaks Tory's neck. Each of these elements exist in metonymic relationship to each other—Tory's anti-maternal behavior, her gender non-normative sexual relationships, and her alienations from the human nation. Her resistance to domestication into a rigidly gendered familial bond as much as her threat to the human fleet make Tory an expendable character by the show's conclusion.

From Wage Labor to Affective Labor

Seen in isolation, it might be possible to read Tory's storyline as primarily about the line between human and machine with little to say about race, gender, family, or nation. However, in the context of the other female characters on the show, her singular narrative trajectory reads much more like a cautionary tale for Asian women who attempt to exist outside of strictly delineated traditional gender roles. Tory and Athena, the other character played by an Asian actor, are anomalous in a show widely admired for its strong female characters. The show does develop complex female characters more than most action television series, especially in the science fiction genre, but it also gives far less latitude to its Asian stars. Notably, the central characters of President Roslin and Starbuck (Katee Sackhoff) excel at their jobs and end the show as heroic figures.[25] Even when Starbuck behaves badly—drinking, fighting, lying—her character is a rebel rather than a villain like Tory. In contrast, the "good" Asian Athena is fully entrenched in traditional and normative gender roles, while the "bad" Asian Tory is career driven and emotionally detached from the humans.

Although murder may be Tory's crime, the show punishes her for her failure to emotionally attach to the humans. If we view the series as a commentary on the relationship between our national identity within a network of global labor, then Tory's treatment in the show makes narrative sense. *Battlestar Galactica* provides a storyline that can reconcile the contradiction of a national ethos of opportunity in a land of immigrants existing at the same time as inequitable immigration and labor policies. The Cylon Athena provides a vivid contrast to the Cylon Tory. Athena is one of multiple clones collectively called Eight, all played by the Korean Canadian Grace Park. Conveniently enough, the storyline of *BSG* itself splits Park into two Eight clones who can be aligned with divergent models of female migrant labor. The economic and social system of the United States increasingly depends upon transnational migrant labor while citizenship and sanctioned immigration become ever more unattainable for many of those very workers. While Boomer, another clone, and Athena emerge as central and distinct figures, the masses of other Eight Cylons form an important backdrop to the primary stories. Thus, for the remainder of the essay, the characters played by Park will be either specifically named as Boomer or Athena or will go by the generic name of Eight.

The association of Boomer visually with the global migration of Asian female labor is cemented by an image from the end of the first season. Boomer realizes that she is a Cylon, not a human as she had long believed, when she leaves her spaceship and is surrounded by identical versions of herself. The scene, complete with an ominous soundtrack, is menacing and meant to evoke unease at the uncanny image of indistinguishable replicas of Eights. That image became one the show's defining symbols, as it was included in the opening credits followed by the inter-title, "There are many copies."

The image of multiple Boomers resonates with that of the faceless masses of Asian female "nimble fingers," a term used to objectify and categorize these workers,[26] and Boomer is diminished when confronted with her multiple selves. Factory labor depends upon a flexible and interchangeable workforce, a workforce that is increasingly migratory and transnational.[27] Yet the laboring mass of factory workers, like the "coolie" labor of the nineteenth century, are by their very interchangeability and exploited state poor potential citizens. Boomer fails repeatedly as a citizen-subject of the human colonies and is the character that resembles most closely the criminalized migrant. She remains under the control of her home state, the Cylon nation, throughout the show and is both a traitor and terrorist. As the Cylon model specifically designed for romantic love, the resonances with other images of Asian women seem too obvious to ignore, recalling the Asian woman as wartime prostitute and spy and, during peacetime, as an interchangeable part of the global sex trade.[28] The Eight model of the first season is one of many indistinguishable, uncountable replicas produced as sexual and reproductive capital.

Although Athena begins much like the other Eight Cylons, her divergent path sets her in stark contrast to Boomer. At first, her role in Cylon society, like Boomer, is to seduce humans and produce a Cylon/human hybrid child. Athena is a victim of Cylon society, a point made explicit by a long and unexpected beating by two other Cylons. The camera lingers on the abuse, beginning with a close-up of a fist coming toward the camera and then slowly panning away as she crawls and then kneels while being punched and kicked repeatedly. She is also represented as complicit in her own exploitation by agreeing to perform acts—sex and reproduction—for political ends rather than understanding those behaviors as "naturally" flowing from affective ties. The turning point comes when Athena falls in love with Helo and begins her integration into human society.

Her partial acceptance into human society, however, is also marked by repeated and sadistic punishment. She is abused and shunned by everyone but Helo. As Grace Park says of her character in an online interview with *13Minutes-Mag*, "They do everything to Athena [Eight]. Like she's so brutalized you can't help feeling sorry for her. That's kind of the point."[29] During most of Athena's pregnancy she is kept under observation in a glass-enclosed cell, and many of her most dramatic scenes, including a near gang rape, are filmed through thick glass and wire, distancing the viewer and preventing a clear identification with her. In addition, this state of constant surveillance invites the viewer to assist the ship's crew in keeping her under a punishing gaze. Despite this treatment, Athena remains loyal to the humans and even willingly contemplates Cylon genocide to prove her worth to them. Athena's rehabilitation into an acceptable citizen, then, requires her victimization. It is through her brutalization that she proves her loyalty and gains the goodwill of the humans.

Athena's movement from enemy to a partial citizen also requires her to reject rather than identify with others who labor under the same conditions. Unlike Tory, Athena never associates with other Cylons. Instead, she lives in isolation among the humans who dislike and distrust her. During a fight with Helo, she says, "I have to fight every day on this ship to be accepted" (season 3, episode 14). She not only distances herself from other Cylons but, by the last few episodes, tracks her double, Boomer, and shoots her. She finally annihilates the earlier, undomesticated version of herself, a version that understood her reproductive labor as work rather than being natural and free. The other Eights remain part of the sex trade or, in the last season, are expendable manual laborers engaged in the futile and sometimes fatal attempt to repair the ship.[30] As the series progresses, the other Eights become more easily distinguished from Athena, who dresses almost exclusively in military clothing. The other Eights appear in a variety of flared miniskirts and form-fitting jackets, emphasizing the contrast between Athena, the ultrapatriot, and the rest of the Eights, the sexualized seductresses.

The primary paths for Eights are severely limited to an emotional submission to the humans or exploitation and death. The overarching bootstraps narrative of Athena's partial integration into the professional class of the ship also explains the failure of the majority of the Eights since they are "poor citizens" who do not form families and affective ties to the humans. The figure of Athena and her various copies rewrite distinct migrant groups as part of a teleological progression that renders acceptable the exploitation of one group and the limited citizenship rights of the other.[31] The implication is that the system itself is equitable and fair, and if one only forms the "correct" relationship with both labor and affect, then the movement from low-status to high-status migrant is inevitable.

National Belonging and the Family Romance

Athena begins her transition through a romantic relationship, but she is saved and redeemed by motherhood. When she arrives on the ship *Battlestar Galactica*, the central metropolis in the series, she is spared from immediate execution by announcing her pregnancy. In the episode "A Measure of Salvation," Athena is made resistant to a Cylon disease by the fetal transfer of her hybrid human/ Cylon baby's blood. In that case, the baby literalizes a blood tie that links Athena to the humans. This exemplifies what Lauren Berlant has termed "fetal motherhood," meaning the mother is "becoming more minor and less politically represented than the fetus, which is in turn made more *national*, more central to securing the privileges of law, paternity, and other less institutional family strategies of contemporary American culture."[32]

Figures 13.1 and 13.2. Tory as the driven career
woman, and Athena as the loving mother and wife.

Having a Korean North American embody the role of Athena helps propel the
narrative trajectory by reinforcing the long-held stereotype of Asian women as
naturally and irrevocably feminine and suited to domesticity. Although she is a
fighter pilot, she also seems to be a primary caregiver. She is the only one of the
characters seen in domestic labor, usually related to Hera, folding clothes and
comforting and playing with her.[33] These images recall the inter-racial romances

of post–World War II cinema, in which the excessively feminine Asian woman was represented as a direct rival to independent white women in films such as *The World of Suzie Wong* (1960), *Sayonara* (1957), and *Love Is a Many Splendored Thing* (1955). These images of inter-racial romance helped to reassert traditional gender roles in reaction to the threat of the independent woman, both celebrating the superiority of white masculinity and reprimanding white women for their lack of docility and domesticity.[34] Athena's excessive and dangerous femininity can only be contained through monogamy and motherhood. Her racial difference also reminds the audience of her foreign-ness, her inability to fully assimilate. This places her into a double bind. Like the model minority stereotype, she must excel but is, by her very efforts, set apart from the others. Athena's precarious place within the fleet produces a narrative that demonstrates the ability of the fleet to accommodate difference, but in order to maintain a coherent narrative it must also constantly remind the audience of that very difference.

Athena's acceptance into human society is always tenuous and contingent upon the charity and sponsorship of her husband and her commander. In a scene that was cut from the episode "Maelstrom" but included in the DVD extras, she confronts another woman on the ship and says, "You hate who I am. You hate where I'm from. You hate me because I'm a Cylon. But you won't kill me because I love my husband and I love my child. Because I love this ship and what it means to me" (season 5, episode 17). Although she may be hated and will never be recognized as fully deserving of citizenship, she is allowed to exist through her affective relationships to her family and the state and her embrace of a clearly defined gender role. In contrast, Tory, who does not have a male protector despite having several heterosexual relationships, pays for her deficiencies with her life.

Differential Citizenship in Outer Space

Detaching global migration from capital and labor and yoking it to affect and family also provides a justification and logic to differential citizenship laws. Although citizenship may be couched in terms of universalism and color-blind ideals, in practice, acquiring citizenship is a highly stratified and racially marked process.[35] Retooling labor migration from an economic relation to an emotional one distances and isolates the United States from the economies and politics of other nations by ignoring its role in the global circulation of labor. Instead, we have a familiar "American Dream" story of transnational labor set in space. The explanation of global migration is revised from one of unequal interdependence on a national and global scale to one where women exploited by their home country enter the United States as devalued service labor, including sex workers or mail-order brides or as potentially treacherous skilled labor.[36] The laboring women remain in the host country out of loyalty or love of an obviously superior culture, and a lucky few find their way into "legitimate," middle-class, traditionally gendered, heterosexual families. The family unit helps to reproduce the state's interests with the assumption that the migrant wife will assimilate to the dominant culture, produce children for the state, and remain under the patronage of her male champion. Those who remain ambivalent about their attachments to a single national identity and who maintain an economic but not an emotional relationship are left outside of the national narrative. In our final image of Athena, she strolls with her husband and child as the founder of a new civilization. Tory ends up dead and unmourned at the end of her storyline.

Representations of the heterosexual nuclear family as the natural and ideal reflection of the nation are a key component in resolving the contradictions of global inequalities. The Asian migrant worker who does not qualify for cultural citizenship has not properly assimilated to white dominant culture by abandoning all attachment to other cultures or identities. While Athena's story offers a path toward becoming a recognized national subject, it does so by erasing the structured flow of a specifically racialized and gendered labor force. If the global order is enabled through our ability to imagine and represent its shape, then the fact that the differential narratives of alienation and assimilation in *Battlestar Galactica* would be so familiar and satisfying should give us pause. Mass media representations that naturalize contingent citizenship, heteronormative families, and the structural inequalities of transnational capital and labor are becoming all too commonplace in the struggle to narrate the United States as a global power.[37]

NOTES

1 Jane Chi Hyun Park, *Yellow Future: Oriental Style in Hollywood Cinema* (Minneapolis: University of Minnesota Press, 2010).

2 David Morly and Kevin Robins, *Spaces of Identity: Global Media, Electronic Landscapes and Cultural Boundaries* (New York: Routledge, 2002).

3 For some of the more prominent of these commentaries, see Wendy Hui Kyong Chun, *Control and Freedom: Power and Paranoia in the Age of Fiber Optics* (Boston: MIT Press, 2008); Lisa Nakamura, *Digitizing Race: Visual Cultures of the Internet* (Minneapolis: University of Minnesota Press, 2008); Greta Aiyu Niu, "Techno-Orientalism, Nanotechnology, Post-humans, and Post-posthumans in Neal Stephenson's and Linda Nagata's Science Fiction," in "Alien/Asian," special issue, *MELUS* 33, no. 4 (2008): 73–96.

4 Stephen Neale, *Genre* (London: British Film Institute, 1980); and Vivian Sobchack, *Screening Space: The American Science Fiction Film* (New Brunswick, NJ: Rutgers University Press, 1997).

5 Cited in Brian Ott, "Framing Fear: Equipment for Living in a Post-9/11 World," in *Cylons in America: Critical Studies in Battlestar Galactica*, ed. Tiffany Potter and C. W. Marshall, 13–26 (New York: Continuum, 2008).

6 Luke Howie, "'They Were Created by Man . . . and They Have a Plan': Subjective and Objective Violence in Battlestar Galactica and the War on Terror," *International Journal of Zizek Studies* 5, no. 2 (2011): 1–23; Laura King and John Hutnyk, "The Eighteenth Brumaire of Gaius Baltar: Colonialism Reimagined in *Battlestar Galactica*," in *Breaching the Colonial Contract*, ed. Arlo Kempf, 237–250 (Dordrecht: Springer, 2009); Ott, "Framing Fear"; Juliana

Hu Pegues, "Miss Cylon: Empire and Adoption in 'Battlestar Galactica,'" in "Alien/Asian," special issue, *MELUS* 33, no. 4 (2008): 189–209; Steven Rawle, "Real-Imagining Terror in *Battlestar Galactica*: Negotiating Real and Fantasy in *Battlestar Galactica*'s Political Metaphor," in *Battlestar Galactica: Investigating Flesh, Spirit and Steel*, ed. Roz Kaveney and Jennifer Stoy, 129–153 (New York: Palgrave MacMillan, 2010).

7 The metaphorical use of aliens as racial and ethnic Others is also recognized by mainstream audiences, as evidenced by the popular controversy over the film *Avatar* (2009), which many believed replicated racialized colonial narratives. Even James Cameron, the movie's director, felt compelled to respond to these audience interpretations. See Geoff Boucher, "James Cameron: Yes, 'Avatar' Is 'Dances with Wolves' in Space . . . Sorta," pt. 2 of the "Hero Complex Interview," *Los Angeles Times*, August 14, 2009, http://herocomplex.latimes.com/uncategorized/james-cameron-the-new-trek-rocks-but-transformers-is-gimcrackery.

8 A. C. Roberts, *The History of Science Fiction* (Basingstoke: Palgrave Macmillan, 2006); and Jay Telotte, *Science Fiction Film* (Cambridge: Cambridge University Press, 2001).

9 See Herman Gray, *Watching Race: Television and the Struggle for "Blackness"* (Minneapolis: University of Minnesota Press, 1995); Darrell Hamamoto, *Monitored Peril: Asian Americans and the Politics of TV Representation* (Minneapolis: University of Minnesota Press, 1994); Darnell Hunt, *Channeling Blackness: Studies on Television and Race in America* (New York: Oxford University Press, 2005); Alan Nadel, *Television in Black-and-White America: Race and National Identity* (Lawrence: University Press of Kansas, 2005); Sasha Torres, ed., *Living Color: Race and Television in the United States* (Durham, NC: Duke University Press, 1998).

10 Eric Greene, *Planet of the Apes as American Myth: Race and Politics in the Films and Television Series* (New York: McFarland, 1996); Sara Ahmed, *Strange Encounters: Embodied Others in Post-coloniality* (New York: Psychology Press, 2000); Ed Guerrero, *Framing Blackness: The African American Image in Film* (Philadelphia: Temple University Press, 2012); Adilifu Nama, *Black Space: Imagining Race in Science Fiction Film* (Austin: University of Texas Press, 2010); Charles Ramírez Berg, *Latino Images in Film: Stereotypes, Subversion, and Resistance* (Austin: University of Texas Press, 2009).

11 Sierra Adare, *Indian Stereotypes in TV Science Fiction: First Nations' Voices Speak Out* (Austin: University of Texas Press, 2009).

12 Daniel Bernardi, *Star Trek and History: Race-ing toward a White Future* (New Brunswick, NJ: Rutgers University Press, 1998); Micheal Pounds, *Race in Space: The Representation of Ethnicity in Star Trek and Star Trek: The Next Generation* (Lanham, MD: Scarecrow Press, 1999); Leah Vande Berg, "Liminality: Worf as Metonymic Signifier of Racial, Cultural, and National Differences," in *Enterprise Zones: Critical Positions on Star Trek*, ed. Taylor Harrison, Sarah Projansky, Kent A. Ono, and Elyce Rae Helford (Boulder, CO: Westview Press, 1996), 20.

13 C. Dies, "Erasing Difference: The Cylons as Racial Other," in Potter and Marshall, *Cylons in America*; Pegues, "Miss Cylon."

14 Grace Park, interview, IGN, video, July 19, 2005, http://www.ign.com/videos/2005/07/19/battlestar-galactica-2004-tv-video-grace-park.

15 Ramírez Berg, *Latino Images in Film*, 156.

16 There are too many references to list here, but prominent scholars working at the intersection of gender and race studies have long argued that the representations of family function as a metonym for the nation. See Lauren Gail Berlant, *The Queen of America Goes to Washington City: Essays on Sex and Citizenship* (Durham, NC: Duke University Press, 1997); David Eng, *The Feeling of Kinship: Queer Liberalism and the Racialization of Intimacy* (Durham, NC: Duke University Press, 2010); David Palumbo-Liu, *Asian/American: Historical Crossings of a Racial Frontier* (Palo Alto, CA: Stanford University Press, 1999); Raka Shome, "'Global Motherhood': The Transnational Intimacies of White Femininity," *Critical Studies in*

Media Communication 28, no. 5 (2011): 388–406; Shawn Michelle Smith, *American Archives: Gender, Race, and Class in Visual Culture* (Princeton, NJ: Princeton University Press, 1999); Hortense Spillers, "Mama's Baby, Papa's Maybe: An American Grammar Book," in "Culture and Countermemory: The 'American' Connection," special issue, *diacritics* 17, no. 2 (1987): 65–81.

17 Saskia Sassen refers to this simultaneous movement toward a nationalist ideology and a denationalized global economy as "the opposite turns of nationalism." See Saskia Sassen, *Losing Control? Sovereignty in the Age of Globalization* (New York: Columbia University Press, 1996), 59–64.

18 Madhavi Mallapragada, "Curry as Code: Food, Race, and Technology," in this volume.

19 Shilpa Davé, "Winning the Bee: South Asians, Spelling Bee Competitions, and American Racial Branding," in this volume.

20 Yuko Kawai, "Stereotyping Asian Americans: The dialectic of the model minority and the yellow peril," *Howard Journal of Communications* 16, no. 2 (2005): 109–130.

21 Kent A. Ono and Vincent N. Pham, *Asian Americans and the Media*, vol. 2 (Malden, MA: Polity, 2009).

22 Sunaina Maira, *Missing: Youth,Citizenship, and Empire after 9/11* (Durham, NC: Duke University Press, 2009), 4.

23 Deepti Misri, "Bollywood's 9/11: Terrorism and Muslim Masculinities in Popular Hindi Cinema," in this volume.

24 I'd like to thank Abigail Derecho for pointing out the queer family unit formed by Roslin, Tory, and Maya at a presentation of an earlier version of the paper at the April 2008 "Console-ing Passions" conference, Santa Barbara, CA.

25 The more ambivalent figures of Ellen Tigh and Number Six (also Cylons), who are primarily defined by their (gender non-normative) romantic attachments rather than careers are ultimately redeemed by the series end and live "happy ever after."

26 Laura Hyun Yi Kang, *Compositional Subjects: Enfiguring Asian/American Women* (Durham, NC: Duke University Press, 2002).

27 Piyasiri Wickramasekera, "Asian Labour Migration: Issues and Challenges in an Era of Globalization," International Migration Paper no. 57 (Geneva: International Labour Office, August 2002), http://www.ilo.org/wcmsp5/groups/public/---asia/---ro-bangkok/documents/publication/wcms_160632.pdf.

28 Christine So, "Asian Mail-Order Brides, the Threat of Global Capitalism, and the Rescue of the U.S. Nation-State," *Feminist Studies* 32, no. 2 (2006): 395–419.

29 J. Nguyen and D. Le, "*13MinutesMag* Presents Grace Park: The Photo Shoot!" YouTube, January 18, 2007, http://www.youtube.com/watch?v=vEoFKGzWVTk&feature=related.

30 In a short series of webisodes that aired online between seasons, "The Face of the Enemy," another Eight appears who previously seduced Gaeta (Alessandro Juliani) in order to steal state secrets. She is revealed as a murderer and is, in turn, stabbed by Gaeta.

31 Aihwa Ong argues that the differential success for various Asian groups has more to do with the capital Asian migrants bring into the country rather than how much they make while they are here. She distinguishes between different modes of labor migration that range from the irregular or undocumented migration of low-wage, unskilled workers to capital-rich businessmen and "parachute kids" who move freely across national borders in pursuit of educational opportunities. See Aiwa Ong, *Flexible Citizenship* (Durham, NC: Duke University Press, 1999).

32 Berlant, *The Queen of America Goes to Washington City*, 85.

33 The rare exception is the few occasions we see Cally attempt to care for her child. These scenes usually reinforce the difficulties she has caring for a baby on board the ship.

34 Susan Koshy, *Sexual Naturalization: Asian Americans and Miscegenation* (Stanford, CA: Stanford University Press, 2004); Robert Lee, *Orientals: Asian Americans in Popular Culture* (Philadelphia: Temple University Press, 1999); Gina Marchetti, *Romance and the "Yellow Peril": Race, Sex, and Discursive Strategies in Hollywood Fiction* (Berkeley: University of California Press, 1993); Caroline Chung Simpson, *An Absent Presence: Japanese Americans in Postwar American Culture, 1945–1960* (Durham, NC: Duke University Press, 2001).

35 Ong, *Flexible Citizenship*, 13.

36 V. Gonzalez and R. Rodriguez, "Filipina.com: Wives, Workers, and Whores on the Cyberfrontier," in *Asian America.net: Ethnicity, Nationalism, and Cyberspace*, ed. R. C. Lee and S.-L. C. Wong (New York: Routledge, 2003); Kang, *Compositional Subjects*; Marchetti, *Romance and the "Yellow Peril"*; and Celina Shimizu, *The Hypersexuality of Race: Performing Asian/American Women on Screen and Scene* (Durham, NC: Duke University Press, 2007).

37. Portions of this chapter appeared in the article Leilani Nishime, "Aliens: Narrating Global Identity through Transnational Adoption and Interracial Marriage in *Battlestar Galactica*," *Critical Studies in Media Communication* 28, no. 5 (2011): 450–465.

14

"Did You Think When I Opened My Mouth?"

Asian American Indie Rock and the Middling Noise of Racialization

DOUGLAS ISHII

During the summer of 2012, I talked to members of the Tuesday Night Project (TNP), a volunteer, multidisciplinary art organization in downtown Los Angeles: Traci Kato-Kiriyama, TNP co-founder; Sean Miura, now TNP curator; and R. Scott Okamoto, TNP performer and supporter. Over our conversation, Miura shared how music helped him come into a panethnic Asian Pacific American (APA) consciousness when he started college: "I remember the first thing I did was buy the Magnetic North album, and the second thing was buy a Blacklava T-shirt that my mom wouldn't let me buy because it said, 'I Suck at Math.'" Miura's selection of Magnetic North is no accident, as the New York–based hip-hop duo is known for the APA-identity-affirming sensibility of songs like "We Belong."[1] I, however, came of age listening to Incubus, Our Lady Peace, and The Offspring—all suggestive of rock's white masculinities. I could not express APA solidarity through music until the identities of the biracial Japanese American MC/guitarist Mike Shinoda and the Korean American DJ Joseph Han in the rap/metal outfit Linkin Park became visible and Shinoda released "Kenji," a song that narrates a Japanese American family's internment, through his side project Fort Minor in 2005. I wondered: Do APAs not rock?

Of course we do. My concern is less with APA invisibility and more with the racial power within U.S. music that must be bartered for visibility. Since the 2005 publication of *East Main Street: Asian American Popular Culture*,[2] APAs have made strides in the U.S. music scene, largely owing to the user-driven Web 2.0. The emergence of the Asian American YouTube generation, whose members include Kina Grannis, David Choi, and AJ Rafael, illustrates how APAs have sidestepped the recording industry as producers and consumers.[3] Instead, I ask, What strategies do APAs use to confront, as opposed to circumvent, the gatekeeping conventions of the musical marketplace and its racialized dismissal of APAs as viable artists? I take on this question through the reputed autonomy of indie rock, a form whose identification with the fringe and alternative refuses financial capital but whose status signifies an accumulation of cultural capital—non-financial but consciously acquired characteristics associated with class status and symbolic capital—the intangible value added through prestige and recognition. By attending to Born in Chinese's Asian American compilation album *CompilAsian* (2007) and the Tuesday Night Project as two sites of collaborative creative labor, this chapter explores how these Asian American indie rock productions negotiate Asian Americans' middled and middling position within racial hierarchy and cultural hierarchy to theorize race-conscious independence from the dictates of popular music and indie culture.

"Function under That Control": On Race and Indie Rock

Indie's singer/songwriter image defaults to being racially white even as it appears a democratic identity, exemplifying the simultaneous invisibility and disavowal of race within indie specifically and rock music generally. The form's racialized legacy is evident in the U.S.-based indie anthropologist Wendy Fonarow's column for the *Guardian*, "Ask the Indie Professor," in which she responds to user questions about the music's history, style, and politics. In a January 4, 2011, article about the question, "Why are there so few non-white artists in indie?"[4] she admits that in the United Kingdom, non-white artists, like the audience, represent roughly 1–2 percent of participants. However, she writes: "It's interesting that there isn't a similar ethnic scrutiny of hip-hop or country. Or for that matter, why Balinese gamelan music is disproportionately popular with Balinese people?" Her skeptical comment dodges the reader's question about the exclusions of whiteness by claiming indie rock as an "ethnic" production. Asian-ness can only be evoked through the "traditional" performances of gamelan, rendering Asians foreign to sonic modernity. As seen here, APAs are seen as fundamentally not belonging to a field underwritten by a white/anti-Black hierarchy.

This hierarchy is endemic to the form itself in two mutually racializing ways. First, as Matthew Bannister argues, the spirit of indie rock in the United States maintained white 1960s folk revival projections of "folk" and "authenticity" in which Blackness functioned "as a kind of symbolic marginality, which allow[ed] young whites to imagine themselves as an oppressed minority."[5] This fantasy facilitated white identification with abjected blackness to enable an opting out of postwar U.S. capitalism without addressing the white privilege that made this marginality merely symbolic. This imagining is evident in the works of two of U.S. indie's major influences: Bob Dylan, whose 1962 anthem "Blowin' in the Wind" borrows from the slave song "No More Auction Block" to ask about peace, war, and freedom; and Joni Mitchell, who donned a suit and blackface for 1976 to 1982 Black hipster persona Art Nouveau to confront rock's sexism in an analogy of (white) woman and Black (man).[6] Indie can indeed be seen as the province of whites when such objectification of Black people, even for progressive causes, remains in view.

Second, Fonarow's defensive maneuvers illustrate how cultural capital is racialized and racializes through this white/anti-Black hierarchy. Fonarow shifts her evasion from ethnicity to class as she muses: "The aesthetics of indie: the longing for a golden age, the melancholy, poverty chic, and the overall values of simplicity, autonomy and austerity. This may not be appealing to immigrant or marginalised groups who have already experienced poverty and experience genuine outsiderness as a social class." Though her turn to class evokes the British culture wars, Fonarow cites Cristal, Louboutins, Prada, and diamond grills as the idealized commodities that hip-hop loves and indie loathes. She poses the perceived opulence of the MC, envisioned through these racialized markers, against the asceticism and aestheticism of the indie band. Indie rock has since the 1970s taken up the art attitudes of "high" culture—intellectualism, distance, asceticism, and refinement.[7] Much of this elevation consciously identified musical forms associated with the Black diaspora, such as dance and rap, as "low," commercialized, mass culture, as made evident in critic Kelefa Sanneh's 2004 takedown of "rockism," the dogmatic celebration of a rock ethos to devalue other musical genres: "Could it really be a coincidence that rockist complaints often pit straight white men against the rest of the world? Like the anti-disco backlash of 25 years ago, the current rockist consensus seems to reflect not just an idea of how music should be made but also an idea about who should be making it."[8] Fonarow, like the critics Sanneh indicts, poses (white) artistic value against (Black) financial value, reiterating high/low cultural boundaries via racialization.

In this way, indie rock's dual positioning, as an alternative and elevated aesthetic form, depends on racist projections of Blackness as both an escape route and a trap of capital. The emerging field of Asian American ethnomusicology, with its predominant attention to hip-hop, funk, and jazz, has focused on how APAs have used music to understand themselves as a minoritized collectivity akin to African Americans, which contrasts how APAs enter the class scripts that express whiteness in genres like indie rock.[9] Against these classed plays of white/anti-Black hierarchy, the folk trio A Grain of Sand, made up of Chris Kando Iijima, Nobuko JoAnne Miyamoto, and William "Charlie" Chin, founds a genealogy of Asian American indie rock—not only one that seeks an alternative to hegemonic culture, but also one that contests the racialized spirit so evoked in Fonarow's response.

The group's 1973 self-entitled album, *A Grain of Sand: Music for the Struggle by Asians in America*,[10] is credited as the first musical work of a panethnic consciousness. As Daryl J. Maeda argues, Grain of Sand did not just seek to foster racial pride and cultural nationalism; their songs, written amid their community-organizing experiences, articulated the antiracist and anti-imperialist dimensions of the emergent Asian American identity and its affiliation with progressive politics.[11] Their songs, like the anthemic "We Are the Children" and the pedagogical "Imperialism Is Another Word for Hunger," actively support Yellow Power ideologies of panethnic organizing, self-determination, and critique of systemic oppression. But they also illustrate how Yellow Power as an idea and as a movement developed alongside the struggles of other groups of color in the United States and abroad to develop affinities outside of white supremacy.[12]

Taking up A Grain of Sand's album liner, an essay that is part Marxist theorizing and part APA political manifesto, as a framework, I understand Asian American indie rock as a negotiation of racializing capital, creative labor, and agency. To the pure artist, the liner rejects the assumption of art as apolitical, as this supposed neutrality naturalizes ideology. The group identifies how an artist's commercialist motivations, like fame and prestige, reflect the capitalist hierarchies that oppress in the first place. They write: "To assume one will be able to function under that control and retain the integrity and freedom necessary to grow politically and personally is naïve and one must question whether it is the politics or the 'name' that has priority." The album liner brackets "Art" with quotation marks and capitalization to note "Art"'s construction through exclusionary hierarchies of value and its resultant estrangement from other cultural fields despite its perception as universal. But, to the activist, they argue against the use of music as propaganda and refuse to collapse the aesthetic into ideology: "Music has the power to touch; at the same time it can move people collectively while striking some emotion deep within an individual." In their account, music can create an emotional resonance in the listener that is individualized yet collectivizing—an affective openness that could be harnessed for APA movement organizing. A Grain of Sand worked through "Art" and its capital while critiquing its disciplining effects; they manipulated "Art"'s capacity to entrench its participants in the middle of cultural hierarchy to generate a middling sense of agency.

"A Country Called 'Chinese'": The Racial Grammars of Asian American "Talent"

Part of indie rock's political appeal is its search for networks of production and distribution apart from the institutionalized practices of recording labels and deals—a practice that mirrors A Grain of Sand's critique of "Art" and its institutionalization. One result of such processes is *CompilAsian: A Collection of Asian American Music*, a twelve-track collection of APA rock musicians. The album represents the sole recording by the independent Asian American label Born in Chinese and was released on March 13, 2007. Born in Chinese founder Eugene Song explains that his label's name comes from a question he was asked by an instructor in a college English class:

> During the class discussion, the professor introduced the idea that the poet's [Asian American] cultural background had a profound influence on her work. Then, turning to me, she said, "Well, you would understand, Eugene. . . . Because you were born in Chinese, right?"[13]

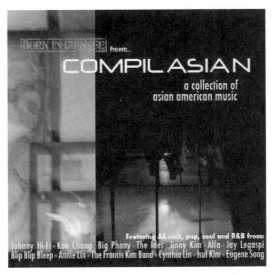

Figure 14.1. *CompilAsian* cover art. Courtesy of
Eugene Song.

Confused, angered, disappointed, and amused by this quotidian racism, Song
found that, as he shared this story, such microaggressions were a common Asian
American experience—a reiteration of the "forever foreigner" narrative that
1960s and 1970s Asian American cultural nationalism sought to displace. Song
repurposed this question, ironizing its casual ignorance, to capture the politics
of his label; he appropriates the glaring phrase to turn injury into an identity-
building opportunity.

Bringing together Song's New York City network of APA musicians, the
album features APA singers and songwriters and APA-fronted bands performing rock, folk, and power pop. Song explains in the album's press release that
CompilAsian has a pedagogical intent: "By helping to promote and expose these
amazing APA musicians, I hope to do my part to spread knowledge and APA
art in the hopes that one day, no one will ever be so uninformed as to think
that having black hair and almond-shaped eyes means I was born in a country
called 'Chinese.'" Born in Chinese's origins story illustrates how Song understands *CompilAsian* as a teaching tool and a political intervention in indie rock
by normalizing the image of the Asian American musician, even though *CompilAsian*'s tracks do not consistently foreground social critique in their lyrics. As
seen in the press release, Song does not see the album as speaking to activists but
rather to a musical public unfamiliar with Asian Americans, reflecting the continuities between A Grain of Sand's 1970s and *CompilAsian*'s 2000s but illustrating
changes in the racial landscape. Even as *CompilAsian* participates in A Grain
of Sand's legacy by using music as an organizing tool, its eschewal of counterpublic analysis makes evident that the album's intervention is to reevaluate APA

musicians' skill as cultural capital, to then include these musicians within "Art"'s symbolic capital.

Manifesting a shared desire for that end, *CompilAsian*'s individual artists qualify their art making primarily using the category of "talent." As Oliver Wang reminds us in his analysis of Asian American MCs, APA musicians have been measured through an abstract notion of talent, "an ill-defined and ambiguous concept most often deployed after the fact (i.e., success supposedly confirms the existence of talent, yet not every talented artist is successful)."[14] Talent as an idea justifies a corporate meritocracy of visibility, as it here speculates and evaluates the ability to accrue financial capital in lieu of demonstrated skill. As Wang illustrates, APAs are seen as alien to popular music and thus are seen as unprofitable, which is cyclically perpetuated through APAs' invisibility in the music scene. Asian Pacific Americans' confrontation with "talent" is thus a racial project as defined by Michael Omi and Howard Winant: an interpretation of racial dynamics that gives "race" its power to explain a distribution of resources.[15] Talent in the abstract not only conceals but also accounts for the a priori exclusion of APAs from having their skill seen as cultural capital; it preserves this exclusion by refusing to recognize APAs owing to their lack of this symbolic capital. Talent in the abstract is thus racialized and racializing.

For example, the singer/songwriter Isul Kim, a featured *CompilAsian* artist, negotiates "talent" discourse through what I call a *model minority racial project*, mobilizing the available terms of the model minority myth to confront racial exclusions. In a 2006 interview with *AA-Profiler*, an Asian American entertainment blog, she explains that her parents have always viewed her music career as a "hobby": "Look, they've got a daughter who went to Harvard and initially embarked on a career in nonprofit and NGO work, and now she spends half of her day collecting tips performing at Fisherman's Wharf in San Francisco."[16] Kim identifies her Ivy League education and her casual source of income as a mismatch and locates her parents' anxieties as evidence of this. As Kim's interview illustrates, she constructs herself as an artist because she has forgone the "good life" of her educational pedigree by existing outside of salaried financial capital and extant cultural hierarchy. In this way, she has countered model minority scripts and instead has focused on her musical acumen. This appeal makes Kim symbolically known as indie by her opting out of the expected payoffs of her education, explaining to the reader why the symbolic capital of artistry should be redistributed to include her Asian American self. While Kim's opting out appears to be affiliated with a colorblind folk ethos that exists outside of capitalism's limitations, the class privilege associated with such a refusal recenters whiteness—locating her Asian American body in proximity and demonstrating how Asian Americans are middled within racialized cultural hierarchies.

Isul Kim's negotiations of model minority imagery and her use of her musical artistry reflect the changed conditions of Asian Americanist critique, also seen in Kim's contribution to *CompilAsian*, "This Fever." The song intertextually references Peggy Lee's "You Give Me Fever," evoking scenes of smoky jazz clubs with its syncopated blues beats. The song's opening verse challenges a lover, the implied addressee of Kim's lyrics: "Never asked you to love a rainbow / never asked you to learn a foreign tongue / but if you're going to keep up this attitude / well, my Eastern Proclamation has just begun." Through tropes of color and language difference, these lines suggest the narrator's deviation from the bodily norm by making visible the contrasting presence of whiteness. They also implicate the toxic fascination of her subject with that deviance. Kim satirizes the sexualized, embodied trope of the fever, both the subjective heat of passion and the "Yellow Fever" of interracial intimacy, as pathological fetish. Throughout, the narrator repeats a probing question: "When you look into my eyes / do you see a slant or do you really look inside?" Kim appropriates the sedimented associations of Peggy Lee's source text—untamable desire and its embodied affects—and uses them to confront the sexualized and gendered scripts that structure ways of seeing Asian American womanhood. Her awareness of these gendered racial grammars reproduces the antiracist poetics that have become the motivating language of Asian Americanist critique.

However, her wish for her addressee to "really look inside," to a space beyond the scripting of her body, yearns for a universal ontology that makes race external to subjectivity—a colorblind fiction. This externalization of race suggests how Kim's awareness of gendered racial grammars uses Asian American indie rock's intangible capital to leverage agency. Joining her first verse's stereotype critique, Kim's second verse asks, in pointed, marcato tones: "Did you think when I opened my mouth / that a sound like this would come out?" Her lyrics implicate her addressee as understanding her body as symbolically alien, and as such refuse to be abstracted away from this material fact of difference. Her narrator acknowledges that, with her "midnight hair" and her "almond eyes," she looks different, literalizing multiculturalism's promise of coming to voice while remarking on the impossibility of that voice being heard apart from how her body is read.

Though her lyrics ultimately wish for freedom through a recognition of her personhood, this imagined universality represents her confrontation with the racialization of "talent." Returning to her *AA-Profiler* interview, Kim explains that her favorite performance memory occurred at a local show when she "could see [the audience] perk up their ears and think, 'What the f*&#@$!?' when they saw this Asian chick get up on stage."[17] Because of the lack of resemblance between "Asian American" and "indie rock," Kim understood the lowered expectations of her audience. This experience of proving the crowd wrong evokes the disjuncture between the racialization of "talent," and its classed white/Black binary, and the body of the Asian American performer. And yet, despite Kim's race-conscious lyrics, her question, "Did you think when I opened my mouth /

that a sound like this would come out?" marks out as the song's only corrective the inclusion of Asian American bodies within the listener's racial frames—a middling vision that does not repudiate the whiteness of indie rock but also does not forget that racial power underwrites racialized life. Beyond Isul Kim, many of *CompilAsian*'s artists self-narrate through model minority racial projects, indicating their awareness of racialization beyond self-identification. Making good on *CompilAsian*'s stated politics as more than a gimmick, the album can be understood as not accepting Asian American racialization as overdetermining these artists' relationship to craft or personhood, using the lyrical and stylistic conventions of indie to carve out an independence.

"Beyond Talent": "Art + Community" in the Tuesday Night Project

The volunteer community arts organization Tuesday Night Project (TNP) creates programs throughout southern California with the mission of "Art + Community"—a mission that defines TNP's project of reflecting and generating APA identity through cultural production. It has also served as a performance site for some of *CompilAsian*'s artists, including Johnny Hi-Fi, who has become a regular featured act. As in *CompilAsian*, this political identity is underwritten by intangible capital. The Tuesday Night Project was founded in 1999 as a "bottom-up" effort to revitalize Los Angeles's Little Tokyo Historic District by creating a local space for APA artists at the Aratani Courtyard of the Union Center for the Arts. These efforts persist as their flagship series, Tuesday Night Café (TNC), which is held on the first and third Tuesday evening of each month in the April to October performance season. Each TNC show is a multidisciplinary program, showcasing featured and open mic performers in spoken word poetry, musical performances, stand-up comedy, short film screenings, and performance art, with onsite vendors and a visual artist who creates during the show. The Tuesday Night Project provides a live stream of shows held at the Aratani Courtyard at www.tuesdaynightproject.org. However, despite the range of acts and participation that TNC invites, TNP remains firmly invested in indie culture's do-it-yourself practices and the disarticulation of community art from payment—an activation of indie rock's aesthetic principles. This analysis of "Art + Community" is based on TNC shows from the thirteenth and fourteenth seasons in 2011 and 2012, my 2012 interview with former TNC host Johneric Concordia, and the 2012 conversation that began this chapter. The Tuesday Night Project's community organizing self-consciously uses "Art + Community" to index "Arts'"s immaterial value and gentrification in Los Angeles as related processes of racialized displacement.

The Tuesday Night Project's most poetic analysts speak directly to APA experiences and anti-Asian racism, such as Kato-Kiriyama's poetry or Concordia's spoken-word and muscial performances with his band, The Fighting Cocks, but

Figure 14.2. Tuesday Night Café promotional banner for the fifteenth season in 2013. Photography: Dustin Hamano. Design: Byron Dote and Candace Kita. Courtesy of the Tuesday Night Project.

my interest is in how the space facilitates this critique. The Tuesday Night Project's ability to give voice to such critics corroborates TNP's statement of purpose, which explains that the

> TN Project's purpose is to build a space for people to connect through the artistic expression of the API [Asian Pacific Islander] and L.A. communities and to provide time for cultural, social, and political awareness with opportunities for involvement, collaboration, real relationship-building and action.[18]

The Tuesday Night Project's call to awareness and action signals the creation of a counterpublic that can contribute to progressive politics. Its emphasis on social connection tangibly networks a community through regular interaction and creates a space of alternative values by using art as edification and entertainment. However, the discourse of art making frames TNP's intentions by accessing the elevation of "artistic expression" as cultural capital and the rarity of this status as symbolic capital; instead of dissent, which can appear polarizing, there is art. The implied universalism of "Art" and its classed connotations create an air of respectability, which enacts the intentionality of the space by legitimizing the local APA community. As such, the space is structured by the capital its alternative status would seek to repudiate—a departure from A Grain of Sand's critique of "Art"'s dissembling uses of intangible capital.

This implication in capital does not invalidate TNP's intervention, as TNP promotes a middled agency within these conditions. The Tuesday Night Project is uninterested in financial accumulation, devoting most of its earnings from its annual fundraisers to equipment maintenance and transportation expenses. Tuesday Night Project co-founder Traci Kato-Kiriyama explained that her inspiration came from her participation in the late 1990s in organizing Art Attack, an annual performance showcase, to respond to the mutual feeling of Kato-Kiriyama and other youth community organizers that "Man, J-Town's dead!" Noting the decreased activity in the ethnic enclave, they assessed the need to make what Kato-Kiriyama referred to as an "API scene." To address this, Art Attack, as TNP would later do, organized a showcase of local artists and performers to establish a social calendar and inviting spaces that would anchor an APA community's group identity in Little Tokyo, as it had been located decades before, and revive the neighborhood's financial viability. However, gentrification scholars such as Arlene Davila and Justin Maher illustrate how the bringing in of "art" to urban neighborhoods increases the cool factor, which turns into the tangible capital that enables imposed redevelopment.[19] Against this displacement, TNP's creation of APA art and an API scene uses these systems of value designation to demonstrate how Asian American ownership of the space is itself valuable. As part of the May 15, 2012, TNC, Kato-Kiriyama and TNP honored Bill Watanabe of the Little Tokyo Service Center, TNP's fiscal receiver. In his recognition speech, Watanabe referred to TNP as "grassroots community development" that "helped make Little Tokyo a little more hip." His reference to TNP as grassroots community development recognizes that, though its methods may mirror top-down urban planning from a consumption perspective, such as bringing in the tourist money of non-residents, TNP makes sure that long-standing businesses and organizations have a voice in how the community will develop and for whom.

These community preservation efforts can be read as adapting the legacy of APA activism that has sustained Little Tokyo to the structural realignment of Los Angeles as a global city, while also suggesting changes in the management of urban space. Bounded by Los Angeles Street, Alameda Street, 1st Street, and 3rd Street, Little Tokyo is one of the remaining three Japantowns in the United States that date to the early twentieth century, and it remains even as Los Angeles continues to invite redevelopment throughout its downtown. The Little Tokyo Service Center was founded in 1979 as a multipurpose social service center as an outgrowth of the 1960s and 1970s Yellow Power activism in Los Angeles that fought the city's attempts to erase its disavowed history of racial segregation through transnational investments.[20] Laura Pulido, James Kyung-Jin Lee, and Scott Kurashige have noted that Little Tokyo's survival throughout Los Angeles's entrée into global capitalism is due to APA organizing like that of the founding of the Little Tokyo Service Center—organizing that also became the material basis of a politicized, panethnic APA identity in the region.[21] The Tuesday Night Project energizes an Asian American subject through this genealogical legacy of APA social movement organizing. However, Lee illustrates how Little Tokyo became packaged as a tourist destination and a commercial investment at the behest of Asian American community organizations just as Asian Americans ascended to model minority status and the Third World Left declined. Evidenced by the high-rise condominiums that continue to rise around the neighborhood's perimeter, the neighborhood's ethnic packaging for ethnographic appeal has facilitated the city's real estate–based gentrification. Little Tokyo's multiracial history, including its transformation into the African American enclave Bronzeville during Japanese American internment, got forgotten in the city's adoption of the earlier activist strategy of narrating Little Tokyo as a Japanese American-cum-Asian American space.[22] The continued use of these affective and symbolic discourses of home making and historic preservation amid their official incorporation can unfortunately participate in the dispossession of other groups seen less favorably by city management.

Inhabiting the tension of what Roderick Ferguson refers to as the conflict between "vernacular insurgency" and "institutional desires," TNP uses discourses of "Art" and "activism" for their recognition value, thus routing performances of APA community through hierarchical frameworks.[23] However, Kato-Kiriyama seemed aware of this in our conversation, as she rebuffed a claim that a skilled performer is all that is needed for social change: "But I think it's also beyond talent, right? Because I think that our intention is bringing out somewhat of a rawness, you know, realness and an honesty. We beg of that in the space, and it's something that is energetic more than explicitly read on a website." Kato-Kiriyama evokes her understanding of what Oliver Wang and *CompilAsian* have identified as the dissembling contradiction of "talent" as a racialized category that at once appears to be universal by posing "rawness" and "realness" as alternatives to "talent." In her discussion, Kato-Kiriyama contrasted the indie rock ensemble, Andrew Figueroa Chiang and the Blazing Rays of the Sun, against the freestyling hip-hop artist SKIM—both of whom are crowd favorites and regular featured TNP performers. With his skinny ties and fashionable suits, Andrew Figueroa Chiang has become known for his polished performance, quirky demeanor, and tight arrangements; SKIM, in contrast, has a reputation for her unpredictable sets, extemporaneous flows, and jam-session approach. As Kato-Kiriyama explained, "talent," expressed by Figueroa Chiang, is the ability to replicate an audience's aesthetic expectations; this exists in a range to "rawness," as illustrated by SKIM, who appears to access subjectivity through her self-conscious refusal of the constructedness of staged performances. "Talent" reveals its dissembling dimensions, while "rawness" offers an immediacy that can disassemble the machinations of aesthetic expectation; "talent" can offer inclusion through intangible capital, while "rawness" can denaturalize that same capital—a praxis that recalls A Grain of Sand's critique that takes advantage of "Art"'s visibility.

"Our Values Then Guide Our Choices": The Taste of APA Community

The Tuesday Night Project thus uses this visibility as a politic within consumer capitalism, such as when Kato-Kiriyama explained that TNP's choice of partners and affiliates reflects "Art + Community":

Those things [like partnerships] guide our values; our values then guide our choices and our actions. So then, if we value building relationships with people, which is how I have been taught for many years to define community organizing, then of course we're going to want to find good people in every sector.

In Kato-Kiriyama's formulation, political orientations to "community" can exceed those to wealth and accumulation. "Community" names an emotional investment, one that cannot be measured financially but comparatively values social capital over financial capital. In line with TNP's definition of community organizing, TNC gives time between performers' sets for groups and organizations to speak to the audience. In the 2012 season, this segment actively became a venue for the Chinatown Community for Equitable Development (CCED), an anti-gentrification league out of Los Angeles's nearby Chinatown. The CCED educated about the potential harms of a proposed Wal-Mart and generated support for their efforts by critiquing Wal-Mart's questionable labor practices and impact on locally owned business.[24] The Tuesday Night Project's solidarity with Chinatown focuses on how consumer agency can maintain the community's spatial autonomy at the level of the subject.

The rhetorical practices of community and autonomy illustrated in this campaign suggest how TNP's community organizing can thus be seen as a self-reflexive development of taste. Pierre Bourdieu argues that taste is based in subjective preferences that indicate how taste-making institutions interpellate consumers as subjects of intangible capital. As such, taste represents how subjects embody the cultural hierarchies of value that maintain commodity production.[25] The Tuesday Night Project works through the same value designations of taste in creating a public performance space that uses "Art" as a legitimizing producer of "community," incorporating its artist selection and community partnerships into its agenda of awareness building and audience education. Both the 2011 and 2012 seasons involved a women-centered show, an LGBTQ show, and a Filipino American show, each of which spotlighted non-profit organizations and cultural organizations; the 2012 season included collaborations with the Los Angeles branch of South Asians for Justice and the Orange County–based, Vietnamese American–centered performance group Common Ground. The Tuesday Night Project shared the stage with these organizations, inviting them to the Aratani Courtyard to promote their programs with TNP's regular audience. Through these collaborations, TNP spends its status' symbolic capital and its "talent"'s cultural capital to redistribute its intangible capital as the energetic quality of the space named by Kato-Kiriyama—an exchange of value that does not guarantee profit but could nonetheless be an investment in a political program.

The Tuesday Night Project's community organizing through "Art + Community" suggests how capital can be reappropriated to create alternative taste—an embodiment of capital that directs its subject away from commodity production and toward community development. "Art + Community" allows for a vision of APA community organizing that, rather than imagining a theoretical existence outside of capitalism as neoliberal arrangements erase communities as we do so, navigates the middlings of APAs in racialized classed hierarchies. As with Isul Kim and *CompilAsian*'s entry into indie rock through model minority racial projects, TNP enters the Los Angeles scene through its self-aware "hipness" and its manipulations of intangible capital—both of which recall the appropriations of Blackness that historically have been a subtext for seeking the alternative. However, instead of Asian American inclusion in a mass public that participates in this racialization, these two projects of indie rock and independence also suggest how to develop an APA counterpublic that acknowledges the need to work through what inclusion and incorporation may dissemble in ways that Yellow Power could not presage. As these artists, organizers, and activists have made apparent, APA panethnic culture offers an energetic blueprint toward a vision in which "Art + Community" equals a social justice agenda.

NOTES

The author would like to thank the editors, particularly Shilpa Davé, for their trust, generosity, and faith throughout the writing process. This project would not have been possible without the Tuesday Night Project's support.

1 I use "APA" as a quality of a political agenda and community, and "Asian American" as a racial label. My use of APA is animated by Yen Le Espiritu's *Asian American Panethnicity* (Philadelphia: Temple University Press, 1993).

2 Shilpa Davé, Leilani Nishime, and Tasha G. Oren, eds., *East Main Street: Asian American Popular Culture* (New York: NYU Press, 2005).

3 For excellent work on this cohort of performers and creators, see Grace Wang's *Soundtracks of Asian America: Navigating Race through Musical Performance* (Durham, NC: Duke University Press, 2015).

4 Wendy Fonarow, "Ask the Indie Professor: Why Are There So Many White Indie Bands?" *Guardian*, January 4, 2011, http://www.guardian.co.uk/music/musicblog/2011/jan/04/ask-indie-professor, accessed January 15, 2013.

5 Matthew Bannister, *White Boys, White Noise: Masculinities and 1980s Indie Guitar Rock* (Burlington, VT: Ashgate, 2006), 34. See also Tom Gruning, *Millennium Folk: American Folk Music since the Sixties* (Athens: University of Georgia Press, 2006).

6 See Murray Leeder, "Haunting and Minstrelsy in Bob Dylan's *Masked and Anonymous*," *Journal of Popular Film and Television* 40, no. 4 (2012): 181–191; and Miles Parks Grier, "The Only Black Man at the Party: Joni Mitchell Enters the Rock Canon," *Genders* 56 (2012), http://www.genders.org/g56/g56_grier.html.

7 Wendy Fonarow, *Empire of Dirt: The Aesthetics and Rituals of British Indie Music* (Middletown, CT: Wesleyan University Press, 2006), 58–60; Bannister, *White Boys, White Noise,* 37–40.

8 Kelefa Sanneh, "The Rap against Rockism," *New York Times*, October 31, 2004, http://www.nytimes.com/2004/10/31/arts/music/31sann.html, accessed December 15, 2013.

9 For example, Kevin Fellesz, Deborah Wong, and Nitasha Sharma interview artists who affiliate with Black struggles and cross-racial communities.

10 *A Grain of Sand: Music for the Struggle by Asians in America* (Paredon Records, 1973).

11 Daryl J. Maeda, *Chains of Babylon: The Rise of Asian America* (Minneapolis: University of Minnesota Press, 2009), 141.

12 See the album liner notes to *A Grain of Sand: Music for the Struggle by Asians in America*, http://media.smithsonianfolkways.org/liner_notes/paredon/PAR01020.pdf. Thanks to Theo S. Gonzalves for this resource.

13 *CompilAsian: A Collection of Asian American Music* (Born in Chinese, 2007); "About Us," Born in Chinese, accessed January 15, 2013, http://borninchinese.wordpress.com/about.

14 Oliver Wang, "Rapping and Repping Asian: Race, Authenticity, and the Asian American MC," in *Alien Encounters: Popular Culture in Asian America*, ed. Mimi Thi Nguyen and Thuy Linh Tu (Durham, NC: Duke University Press, 2007), 36.

15 Michael Omi and Howard Winant, *Racial Formation in the United States: From the 1960s to the 1990s*, 2nd ed. (New York: Routledge, 1994), 56.

16 "*AA-Profiler*: Isul Kim," *AA-Profiler* (blog), AA-Risings: Da Entertainment Resource about Asian Pacific Americans, http://www.aarising.com/aprofiler/isulkim.htm, accessed August 1, 2013.

17 Ibid.

18 "About Tuesday Night Project," *TN: Tuesday Night Project*, http://www.tuesdaynightproject.org/about, accessed January 15, 2013.

19 Arlene Davila, *Barrio Dreams: Puerto Ricans, Latinos, and the Neoliberal City* (Los Angeles: University of California Press, 2004); Justin Thomas Maher, "The Capital of Diversity: Difference, Development, and Placemaking in Washington, D.C." (PhD diss., University of Maryland, 2011).

20 This struggle is detailed in Jim H. Matsuoka's "Little Tokyo: Searching the Past and Analyzing the Future," in *Roots: An Asian American Reader*, ed. Amy Tachiki, Eddie Wong, Franklin Odo, and Buck Wong (Los Angeles: UCLA Asian American Studies Center, 1971), 322–334.

21 Laura Pulido, *Black, Brown, Yellow, and Left: Radical Activism in Los Angeles* (Berkeley: University of California Press, 2006); James Kyung-jin Lee, *Urban Triage: Race and the Fictions of Multiculturalism* (Minneapolis: University of Minnesota Press, 2004); and Scott Kurashige, *The Shifting Grounds of Race: Black and Japanese Americans in the Making of Multiethnic Los Angeles* (Princeton, NJ: Princeton University Press, 2010).

22 An example of this is the November 2005 *Little Tokyo Planning and Design Guidelines*, co-authored by the Little Tokyo Community Council and the Mayor's Little Tokyo Community Development Advisory Committee. The Joint Task Force narrates the neighborhood's multiracial history as a microcosm of Los Angeles until Japanese American settlement in 1904; upon Japanese American internment, Little Tokyo "became a virtual ghost [town] in a matter of months" (8), occluding this sharing of space entirely. See Little Tokyo Community Council and Mayor's Little Tokyo Community Development Advisory Committee, *Little Tokyo Planning and Design Guidelines* ([Los Angeles]: November 2005), http://www.crala.org/internet-site/Projects/Little_Tokyo/upload/LTCDACApprovedGuidelines.pdf.

23 Roderick A. Ferguson, *The Reorder of Things: The University and Its Pedagogies of Minority Difference* (Minneapolis: University of Minnesota Press, 2012).

24 More information is available at CCED (Chinatown Community for Equitable Development), http://www.ccedla.org/.

25 Pierre Bourdieu, *Distinction: A Social Critique of the Judgement of Taste*, trans. Richard Nice (Cambridge, MA: Harvard University Press, 1984).

15

Winning the Bee

South Asians, Spelling Bee Competitions, and American Racial Branding

SHILPA DAVÉ

Although the first National Spelling Bee competition was held in Louisville, Kentucky, in 1925, it is in the twenty-first century that film, television, and Broadway have highlighted the event as the subject of popular narratives. First broadcast on ESPN in 1994, and known since 2006 as the annual Scripps National Spelling Bee competition, it has been telecast live on network television (ABC). The celebrity and media profile of the National Spelling Bee has risen rapidly since the release of the documentary, *Spellbound* (2002), and the competition has become a popular (and commercially successful) representation of the American Dream for diverse populations in American culture.[1] But increasingly, what dominates the narrative of the Spelling Bee is the fact that since 1999, South Asian Americans, and specifically Indian and Indian Americans, have dominated the top spots in competition.[2] The Spelling Bee phenomenon has been embraced so much by the Indian American community in the United States that in the Smithsonian national exhibit on Indian Americans in the United States (*Beyond Bollywood: Indian Americans Shape the Nation*, 2014–2015) there is an interactive Spelling Bee platform where visitors can role-play as a spelling bee participant and champion, allowing visitors to dream of being on stage and in the spotlight.[3] Specifically, the exhibit recognizes that Indian Americans have shaped the modern idea of the American Spelling Bee championship because of their dominance in the competition. Since 2008, Indian Americans have been on a consecutive winning streak in the American national contest that includes (for the first time) Indian American co-champions in 2014 and in 2015. The intersection of the high national profile of the Spelling Bee with the Indian American community creates opportunities to discuss the dual branding or racialized branding of the Indian American community as both a successful immigrant group in the mainstream and as savvy entrepreneurs of American culture in the world of education, commerce, and capitalism.

A champion of the National Spelling Bee not only represents the best and brightest hope of our educational system but also accentuates an image of a young American citizen who is not necessarily a math genius but instead one who speaks and spells English well. Recent headlines in articles about the

Spelling Bee feature questions such as, "Why are Indian Kids So Good at Spelling?" or "Why Indian Americans Reign as Spelling Bee Champs."[4] The headlines and accompanying stories suggest a correlation between being Indian and being a good speller that connotes the successful assimilation of South Asians as Americans through the mastery of the English language.

By framing the headlines as questions or explanations, the articles seek to break down the formula for success and emphasize how kids practice with their parents and train in Indian "minor-league" bees in the United States, where Indian kids of all ages battle fiercely for the top spot of being a champion. Winning the Bee for the contestants is not about proving one's American citizenship (as is often the topic of mainstream articles); instead, it is tied to being the best reflection of Indian American community values that emphasize family and cultural heritage. This idea includes reframing the idea of the Spelling Bee as a pre-professional pipeline to college and saving the prize money for the winner's college education.[5] The Spelling Bee has become an integral part of Indian American community conversation as well as an item of mainstream interest. It is the development of the community narrative of the Spelling Bee in relation to the mainstream narrative that I wish to explore in this essay as Indian Americans have taken an American phenomenon and have re-created a competition to reflect Indian American community needs and interests. Significantly, the complex representations of South Asian Americans in different manifestations of the Spelling Bee competition contests, questions, and illuminates twenty-first century arguments about the political, social, and cultural production of Asian American identity as a central and unifying group identity.

This essay argues that the image of Indian Americans as master spellers in a competitive format accentuates citizenship in an apolitical context. It examines, as a case study, the development of the corporate-sponsored South Asian Spelling Bee (as opposed to the Scripps National Spelling Bee) as a model for combining business and educational interests in a marketing/branding plan to cater to the South Asian community. Additionally, I argue that the result of the participation in the spelling bees is the repackaging of the American success story for both parents and children in the language of business and pre-professional training. The Bee is a competition for young people (between the ages of eight and fourteen) and an opportunity to show off the educational prowess of South Asian American children.[6] Thus the Bee serves multiple functions as a cultural rite of racial performance, a site of corporate branding and marketing, and, finally, a concrete nexus of immigrant aspirations.

The image of the spelling bee champion is part of the story of successful branding of immigrant assimilation to American cultural values by the mainstream media and also an important part of Indian American self-representation for immigrant parents and the younger generation as celebrities in American culture. In the case of the Spelling Bee, it is not adults who reap the fame but the young champions who make celebrity appearances in local and global media markets, including national television shows such as *The Today Show, Late Night with David Letterman, Jimmy Kimmel,* and *The Daily Show*. Their stories and journeys are engaging, compelling, and endearing narratives. It is the celebration of the success of the future generation that specifically attracts the Indian American community at large but also has wide crossover appeal to a mainstream audience.

The national and corporate community spelling bees have become events that draw the diverse South Asian community together for American businesses and advertisers who are targeting a specific audience—the affluent and professional South Asian American demographic market. The unexpected winning streak and domination by South Asians helps to create a unifying narrative for the South Asian community that has been previous difficult to pin down in American racial categories or marketing campaigns.

National and Cultural Branding of the Bee

There is no doubt that the Spelling Bee is a quintessential American event. However, there have been very few scholarly treatments or discussions of the Bee in contemporary culture. In his 1941 article, "The Spelling Bee: A Linguistic Institution of the American Folk," the linguist Allan Walker Read characterized competitive spelling as a popular educational need to show and share reading and writing skills to and with the community.[7] More significant, the Bee represents a competition that has no barriers and is symbolic of the "democratic social condition of America."[8] Participating in the contest, as well as becoming the champion, is emblematic of the American ideals of accessibility applied to competition and education.

Sam Whitsitt, in his 2010 article, "The Spelling Bee: What Makes It an American Institution?" maps out the relationship between language and American identity. He observes that in the United States (as opposed to England) it was a "correctness in spelling, and not in pronunciation" that determined the success for a champion. "One could spell correctly without having to comply with anything else; without having to alter your behavior, your speech, your manners, or who you were."[9] The implication is that the spelling competition offers a fair and equal playing field that is open to all, or at least all who have mastered the English language. However, scholars such as myself note that accent and pronunciation of the English language does influence how success is viewed. In *Indian Accents: Brown Voice and Racial Performance in American Television and Film*, I argue that the ambiguity of the Indian racial position in American culture has made the group difficult to characterize and be represented in popular culture.[10] As a result, mainstream narratives have often focused on Indians as an assimilated minority who speak English well enough to be understood by American audiences but who also speak English differently, which also codes and encapsulates the community as foreign and exotic and not quite American. Indian Americans are simultaneously rendered "other" and assimilable by their command of the English language. Additionally, Indians are also an example of how the relationship between "correct English usage" and American identity are linked through the Spelling Bee. In effect, Indian American racial identity, as represented in the Spelling Bee, is the combination of a mastery of linguistic assimilation and adoption and assimilation of middle-class values of education and economic prosperity. Indian immigrants and their children can dominate the Spelling Bee because they are fluent in English and because the family places an emphasis on educational prowess and success. Thus the narrative of the Spelling Bee emphasizes the family-friendly and non-competitive nature of the contest as opposed to narratives of Asian brown- or yellow-peril discourse of foreigners who are a threat to national security or American employment and labor.

One key difference is that "tweeners" (rather than adults) are the subjects of Spelling Bee narratives. The images of young people are divorced from media depictions of South Asians as suspected terrorists, dubious foreigners, or call-center employees. Instead the spellers are depicted as slightly awkward adolescents (with glasses and braces) who are part of a supportive community of spellers who are enthusiastic, generous, and appreciative of one another. In 2014, co-champions Sriram Hathwar and Ansun Sujoe complimented and showed admiration for each other's spelling skills on the talk-show circuit after their win.[11] The attempts by adults to make them declare one winner showed their grace under pressure and represented that the kids were delighted to be co-champions. Their object was not to beat someone else but to focus on the positives of winning: "I like sharing the victory with someone else," Ansun said. "It's been quite shocking and quite interesting too. It's very rare."[12] Also rare is the opportunity to see and cheer for Indian Americans in live sports, and as writer Sameer Pandya points out, there is a fan element to viewing a geek or freak show with gawky Indian Americans as the academic stars: "They are quiet politically, loud academically—characteristics ostensibly emanating from Asian cultural values. They are perceived as *geeks*, not only in the pejorative sense, but also as studious kids who represent the American ideal."[13] It's a combination of sports and academics that help solidify the image of Indian American kids as model minorities whose racial bodies and presence are depoliticized and offset by their cultural and academic success.

With the title also comes a substantial monetary prize. The Scripps Spelling Bee has steadily increased their prize winnings, from a $1,500 cash prize in 1989 to the current $30,000 prize. Julie Chen, the former host of the television program *The Early Show* on CBS, asked the 2009 Spelling Bee champion Kavya Shivashankar, "What are you going to do with the money and where does the Bee take you?" In her answers, Kavya stated that she wanted to use most of the $30,000 for college and that her goal was to go to medical school and become a neurosurgeon.[14] While her comment could be represented as Asian American "model minority" behavior, her answer is also one that would make any parent and particularly South Asian parents proud because it ties the participation in the American Bee to the specific cultural values of higher education and a prestigious profession prevalent in the South Asian American community. The Spelling Bee thus becomes intertwined with narratives of cultural performance and is also parlayed into the world of American business and advertising.

Spelling Bee culture combines family participation and educational prowess with a sporting event atmosphere that celebrates the democracy of the United States and, I argue, is an example of American cultural marketing and racial branding. In her work on brand cultures, Sarah Banet-Weiser makes an important distinction between commodification and branding. She explains that, while commodification is rooted in economic and market strategy that sells and packages products for the consumer, branding is more intimately connected to our cultural values. Commodification, she says, is "a monetization of different spheres of life, a transformation of social and cultural life into something that can be bought and sold. In contrast, the process of branding impacts the way we understand who we are, how we organize ourselves in the world, what stories we tell about ourselves."[15] Using Banet-Weiser's terms in relation to the Spelling Bee, I would argue that the historical and mainstream narrative of the Spelling Bee is part of a national branding that emphasizes the idea that anyone (no matter how young) can be a success and an American champion. However, the media coverage of the event tends to focus on the commodification of the Bee as a sporting event that draws television audiences and advertisers. The Bee stands at the convergence of the processes of commodification and branding. The insertion of South Asian and South Asian Americans into this convergence complicates the ideas of branding and commodification with the intersecting lines of racial narratives and racial consumers in the twenty-first century.

The cultural areas of our life, such as the way we think of our identity, religion, and creativity, Banet-Weiser argues, are influenced by the cultural phenomena of branding. The brand of the National Spelling Bee competition appeals to a diverse audience by capturing core values of American culture such as participatory democracy, the importance of education, the thrill of competitive sport, and the prevalence and relevance of one national language—English. As dominant champions in the National Bee, South Asian Americans are part of that brand—a racialized brand that identifies the cultural values of an ethnic and immigrant community within the totality of mainstream American culture.

South Asian Cultural Branding and the Community Spelling Bee

The South Asian American community has always been a difficult niche group to target for mainstream advertisers because South Asians (like Asian Americans) have various languages, religions, customs, and generational differences. Not all South Asians celebrate common national holidays such as Indian Independence Day (April 15). Other events such as Gandhi's birthday or the festival of Diwali (Indian New Year, which is celebrated differently within states in India) don't cross all of the demographics (religious or political) in the United States. Besides Bollywood, cricket, and food, what brings the South Asian Diaspora together? How do businesses target South Asian groups outside of restaurants and grocery stores? Advertisers have noted with interest that South Asian Americans, and specifically Indian and Indian Americans, dominate the top spots in the Scripps National Spelling Bee competition held annually in Washington, DC. Rahul Walia (CEO of the public relations firm Touchdown Media) was looking for an event that could bring South Asians together and had an "American feel."[16] In 2006 he developed the idea of a South Asian spelling bee to offer the spelling bee experience outside of the National Spelling Bee event. He worked with advertisers and corporate sponsors to create spelling bee competitions in selected target cities with large South Asian populations as a means to reach the lucrative money-spending demographic in the community: adults aged thirty-five to fifty-five in families with small children.

However, the idea of hosting spelling bee contests to appeal to South Asians is not a new one. Before the emergence of a corporate-sponsored South Asian spelling bee, the Indian and Indian American community had already been organizing educational events for children and teenagers. The North South Foundation (NSF), a non-profit organization started in Illinois in 1989, has over sixty regional chapters all over the United States. According to their website, in 1993, the foundation developed educational contests for Indian American children that coincided with their organizational mission to provide scholarships for children in India.[17] Along with spelling bees, the foundation offers vocabulary, math, geography, essay writing, and public speaking competitions (and pilot programs) for children in grades 1–12. The tagline on the website reads: "Encouraging Excellence in Education," and the site states that all proceeds from the event registration funds contribute to scholarship funds for the less privileged in India. The emphasis is on helping others in India and establishing the practice of volunteering in the Indian community to aid others who are less fortunate. The only award mentioned on the site is not for educational achievement but instead highlights a "role model award." The value of giving back in terms of time, money, and knowledge to the Indian community underscores the basic values of the NSF foundation and is particularly evident as one of the first descriptions on the site is that the organization is a non-profit and volunteer community organization.[18]

The specific online information pages devoted to the spelling bees emphasize that participating in the bees instills ethnic pride in the young Indian people (grades 1–8) but also that competing in the event teaches important academic and professional skills. The site lists some of the following beneficial aspects of participating in the Bee: "Building self-confidence and self-esteem, learning new concepts, meeting other children and making friends in our community, improving communication skills, interacting with a group, and developing discipline." In addition to these concepts of self-presentation and meeting other Indian kids for educational interactions, two other effects of participation are listed on the site. The first says that "recognizing that hard work leads to success more so than just innate intelligence," and the second states that "competing against one's own ability, not against others," is an important value to keep in mind. The ideals behind these goals delineate some of the key characteristics of the community, which is not to beat down others but instead to focus on how you work and represent yourself (as a role model) to others in terms of academic achievement. On its website, the NSF states that these contests are designed to "encourage academic excellence among Indo-American children" and describes the success of participants through academic achievements such as finishing in the top tiers at the National Spelling Bee and gaining admission to Ivy League colleges.[19] The Spelling Bee is one venue that the Indian American community uses to represent educational success and achievement of young people to its own community.

The mainstream press writer James Berger described the NSF bees as "minor league training grounds for the major league" National Spelling Bee.[20] While journalists such as Berger discuss the disproportional representation of South Asians at the national Spelling Bee (11 percent of the participants) as an example of different cultural learning styles (rote learning or memorization associated with Asian cultures), Indian American participants (according to the websites and during informal conversations with me at the 2009 South Asian Spelling Bee in Los Angeles) emphasize that it takes time, effort, and hard work, rather than innate skill. For Indian children of parents who are professionals (mostly engineers and technology specialists) or parents who have been recruited to the United States because of their technical skills (on H-1B visas, etc.), the notion that participation in spelling bees fosters skills such as discipline and improving communication and listening practices while creating a positive experience for them is significant. Many of the immigrant parents have seen how their education has translated into financial security, and they want to pass on the same work values to their children. Mainstream business and advertisers have developed a model to combine business and educational interests in the South Asian community and repackage the narrative of the American Dream for both parents and children. A spelling bee is transformed though increasing popularity and celebrity attention from an Indian American community event produced by the non-profit North South Foundation to corporate-sponsored events with prize money, a televised final event in India, and a red-carpet show for South Asian (not just Indian) American communities. Additionally, a community bee is also preparation for the cross-over of participants to the mainstream recognition, contribution, and domination of the National Spelling Bee.

The Corporate Spelling Bee and South Asian American Consumers

One of the key developments in the advertising business in the twenty-first century is the development and proliferation of ethnic and racial niche advertising firms that consult with the larger firms to create ad campaigns for specific minority populations. In the business world, one industry that showcases the convergence of Banet-Weiser's idea of commodification and branding with racial narratives of Asian Americans is the specialty or boutique-advertising firms that develop campaigns for Asians in the United States. In her study of Asian American advertising firms, the anthropologist Shalini Shankar interviews Asian American advertising executives about how they market their firms and create ad campaigns.[21] Shankar observes that executives engage in what she calls "meta-production," the process by which they transform general marketing data for "commercial consumption" with class or ethnic markers to appeal to Asian American consumers. Meta-production focuses on the content and form of an advertisement, so to tailor the message to fit Asian American narratives, executives have to promote cultural and linguistic aspects of the group. Shankar explains that Asian American ad executives remake Asian Americans from a numbers category, or stereotypes, to "real characters" who have motivations, desires, and dreams. The racial brand depicts Asian Americans as an ideal minority who value a "kid's education and family culture."[22] In addition, Asian Americans are represented as an upper- or middle-class audience made up of good "racial consumers"[23] who are racially distinct without being threatening. Since Asian Americans are a pan-ethnic, multilingual group with diverse religious backgrounds, the aim of Asian American advertising firms are twofold: first, to validate their existence as a niche business that features Asian Americans as an important pan-ethnic block of consumers to mainstream advertisers, and second, to cater to the diverse ethnicities within Asian American communities to create targeted ads for individual groups such as Chinese, Filipino/as, and South Asians in the United States.

One firm that that invited me to different events and that I observed in 2009–2010 is IW Group, Inc., a boutique advertising firm that creates advertising campaigns exclusively for the Asian American market, including South Asians.[24] A South Asian account supervisor remarked that the Spelling Bee attracted the exact demographic that insurance giant Metropolitan Life, or MetLife, was interested in developing and expanding through their multicultural marketing division.[25] Most of IW Group's advertising campaigns for MetLife in the Asian American market focused on the theme of passing down cultural values (respect for elders, reverence for family, blessings for new ventures such as college) and protecting those values by insuring those you love for the future (home, car, and education). The firm and the client were developing campaigns that merged the idea of cultural values and consumer values to create a racial brand designed to appeal to the South Asian American community. The Spelling Bee emerged as an event that marked the convergence of business and educational goals for the parents and the children and the advertisers. The idea that educational success leads to financial success and that financial success leads to a comfortable and secure life is the American Dream for all but is particularly directed at Asian Americans and South Asian Americans. Spelling then becomes part of a racial brand for South Asian American families and an important part of South Asian American identity.

The MetLife South Asian Spelling Bee is a well-crafted marketing event that caters to the educational values of the community and the business interests of the client. The format of the Bee (from the words used to the competition to age limit) follows the National Spelling Bee so it becomes a pre-professional training ground for young South Asian kids to learn the techniques and practices associated with being a good speller. Unlike the North South Foundation website, which tends to deliver information, the South Asian Spelling Bee website is more colorful and interactive, often with scrolling photos of winners (with their trophies and checks) and participants, video links, and the names of corporate sponsors.[26]

Videos on the website for the South Asian Spelling Bee touts the contest as a way for South Asians to compete against the best (themselves) because several South Asians have been national champions in the past and also participate in a family oriented and educational activity.[27] In the South Asian Spelling Bee there is a registration fee, and under the rules and guidelines section a contestant's eligibility to participate is determined by age and racial background. The rules state that "at least one parent or grandparent must be of South Asian descent."[28] In the definition presented, "South Asia" includes Afghanistan, Bangladesh, Bhutan, India, Maldives, Nepal, Pakistan, and Sri Lanka. This is in contrast to the North South Foundation non-profit spelling bee competition, which only invites those of Indian origin to participate. The North South Foundation's spelling bees are open to children of Indian origin from grades 1 to 8 and is in two levels, a junior spelling bee (for grades 1–3) and a senior spelling bee (for grades 4–8).[29] Advertising for the South Asian Spelling Bee is done through ethnic outlets such as South Asian newspapers, South Asian TV and radio stations, and online Listservs. MetLife also has a direct link to the South Asian Spelling Bee on its South

Figure 15.1. South Asian Spelling Bee poster, Los Angeles, 2009.

Asian insurance homepage. Since he started promoting and producing the Bee, Rahul Walia has seen a rise in participation of almost 50 percent as the Bee has grown to over 1,000 participants in twelve cities.[30] He hopes to expand the Bee to other cities such as Toronto and perhaps to even create an international bee.[31]

Both bees offer prize money for the winners. The prize money for the contests are named "scholarship prizes" to further characterize that both spelling bees emphasize that the rewards from the bees should support educational goals rather than a gaming system or a big-screen TV. The North South Foundation bee stipulates that the award money ($1,000; $500; $250) will be redeemable in the first year of college for the winner.[32] Thus the prize reinforces the foundation's mission that these contests are meant to prep children for higher education and are not just monetary enterprises. In promotional video productions for the South Asian Spelling Bee, many of the kids and their parents are interviewed about winning in a "red carpet" runway moment as they enter the competition. Most of the kids (and their parents) talk about how their winnings would go into their college fund, but some of them mention that they might use a portion of their winnings to buy video games.[33] The South Asian Spelling Bee is clearly a more commercialized production but one that also appeals to values of the Indian community because it is depicted as a community event that also offers some of the celebrity status of the National Bee but in specific South Asian markets. Sony TV Asia televises the South Asian Spelling Bee to over 120 countries (except India and Pakistan) in a delayed-tape format. So at its most basic level, the South Asian Spelling Bee is part of the commodification process of the South Asian community for mainstream clients such as the insurance firm MetLife, but simultaneously, the corporate bee also generates business and interest from community media outlets such as ethnic newspapers, radio, and television.

It is important to note that, in addition to the marketing and advertising campaigns, the Bee appeals to the cultural values and community aspirations. The South Asian Spelling Bee in past years has hosted Indian American champions of the Scripps National Spelling Bee as guests of honor, for example, the 2012 champion Snigdha Nandipati from San Diego. In 2009 (including the regional bee I attended), the guest stars included both the Scripps National Bee champion Kavya Shivashankar (from Kansas) and the second runner-up Aishwarya Pastapur (from Illinois). Both young women were present at some of the regional bees to meet with the kids and parents. Aishwarya was an "alumna" of the South Asian Spelling Bee, and Kavya's younger sister, Vanya, was participating for the first time in the South Asian Spelling Bee. In 2015 Vanya was a co-champion in the Scripps National Spelling Bee in Washington, DC.

Significantly, in both the non-profit and corporate events, South Asian American participants and their parents are not one-dimensional or static consumers of the spelling bees; instead, there is a recognition that the community bees do yield success and rewards for Indian American children. Both bees provides images of South Asian American role models for young people and families and also provide an example of how South Asian Americans can participate in extracurricular activities that foster both academic success and personal growth. From personal observation, I noted how excited the young participants were to meet and talk with the National Bee finalists. The winners were role models that the kids had heard about, and as one participant mentioned to me, the finalists were "Indian kids with parents just like me."

The winners act as walking advertisements for both community values and the corporate sponsored bees, but they also represent everyday inspirations of mainstream success to the next generation of South Asian spellers. The narratives for both competitions emphasize that, with community support, Indian Americans can do well in the national competitions. The North South Foundation spelling bees and the MetLife South Asian Spelling Bee (in their promotional materials) present their events as integral steps in the path to participating and being successful at the Scripps National Bee. The goals for these pre-professional

Figure 15.2. The 2009 Scripps National Spelling Bee winner, Kavya Shivashankar.

bees focus on preparing the kids for the big stage of national media and also on educating them in how to discuss their spelling success in relation to their cultural values. This narrative includes discussing cultural practices plus high educational goals. While other non-Indian participants have professional coaches and teachers (as seen in *Spellbound*), the South Asian community competitions resemble a well-planned business model by the sponsors for how their kids can win a spelling bee.

Conclusion

With the development of the corporate-sponsored South Asian Spelling Bee, the emphasis on community support and education is combined/elided with media coverage, prize money, and the interest of global advertisers. The North South Foundation bees are held during the same time as the South Asian Spelling Bee, and so participants have some different options for practicing in anticipation of the Scripps National Bee. Since the South Asian Spelling Bee is inclusive of all South Asians (not just Indians), it has all the appearance being the more marketable bee because it recognizes the diversity within and among the South Asian community.

All the elements of the South Asian Spelling Bee are linked to how children should behave in the competitions because if the young participants are prepared for the situation, they can face anything that happens. This is somewhat in contrast to the journalist James Maguire's observations of the Scripps Spelling Bee in his book *American Bee* as an "individuality-fest. The task is not high drama—the kids are, after all, spelling. No fireworks there. But each speller has his or her variation on the form. This isn't a team sport. Each kid stands at the microphone very much by him-herself. They are forced to rely upon themselves."[34] Like Maguire, you can't help but admire the gumption of the kids standing up and facing each word and finding the inner strength to go on.

However, the idea that South Asians are now developing pipelines of kids trained to compete and win the National Bee does put the ideals of the Bee at odds with the sporting goal of the competition, which is to "win." It also speaks to the privilege of kids who have the means and the opportunity to have specialized attention. It defies the idea that South Asian kids have an innate ability to excel, with the ethnic bees revealing a calculated and planned campaign for South Asians to dominate in the academic arena and to allow young kids to have an opportunity to get into some of the prestigious colleges where they may not have legacy ties. The process is entrepreneurial in that the goal is for individual success (get into college, get on TV), but it is the social community that trains the kids and puts them into position to do well. Thus community values are emphasized as the foundation for success. But the other factor that the kids and the parents stress is that spelling is something that they do together as a family, and when the kids succeed it's not just the individual but the family that also thrives. In 1985, Balu Natarajan was the first South Asian to win the Scripps Spelling Bee, and since that time Indian Americans have become an established presence at the National Bee. Balu (now a physician specializing in sports medicine) emphasizes that family interactions create strong spellers and positive spelling bee results: "It's the collective work [between] the speller and his or her family. Really, that's been the common thread. It's a common thread that transcends race and ethnicity."[35] He emphasizes the family support for the speller. In the past and in the present, other spellers have had coaches and preparatory spell-offs, so why shouldn't Indian Americans create a forum for their kids to help them excel?

The dominant performance of Indian American kids in the Scripps competition and the rise of independent spelling bees such as the North South Foundation bees and the MetLife South Asian Spelling Bee has not gone unnoticed. In April 2013, the Scripps national competition announced that the championship would be judged on both the spelling of the words (the format used in previous competitions) and vocabulary definitions (which would reflect understanding the meaning of the words). The director of the National Spelling Bee, Paige Kimble asserts, in an interview with the Boston Globe, that the Scripps Spelling Bee has been about the centrality of vocabulary and proper English usage: "Our purpose is not only to help students improve their spelling but also to increase their vocabulary, learn concepts, and develop correct English usage that will help them all their lives."[36] It can be argued that the National Bee is addressing its own relevance as either a contest of memory or a contest of vocabulary knowledge (i.e., associating it with the college admission SAT tests). The rule change addresses the charge that spelling winners only memorize words but do not necessarily understand how these words are used or what they mean.

The rule change begs the question, Why now, and does the change have anything to do with the domination of Asian Indians at the Bee? The change to the rule is a fundamental shift in the format and structure of the competition and how the winner is evaluated. The new criteria separate the ability to spell under pressure (and the lights and camera) from the relationship of spelling to vocabulary (which is done in a private and individually written test). Despite the rule change, the 2013 winner was Arvind Mahankali, an Indian American boy from Bayside Hills in Queens, New York, who won on the word "knaidel"—a word derived from Yiddish. And in the following years, the 2014 and the 2015 co-champions were both Indian-Americans who had participated in the National Bee multiple times. In general, the top-ten finalists and winners tended to be the older spellers who have more experience with the bees and also a more extensive vocabulary. There is a layering of multiple narratives around the National Bee about how South Asian American communities are defined in mainstream media, how Indians define and brand their own community interests, and how these narratives tug and pull at each other to complicate the idea of cultural representation, the model minority myth, and citizenship.

NOTES

1 The documentary *Spellbound* (dir. Jeffrey Blitz; New York: Thinkfilm, 2002) followed eight candidates in their pursuit of the championship prize of the 1999 Spelling Bee and also focused on the thematic narrative of how participating in the Spelling Bee was a venue to highlight the American Dream in the stories of tweeners—youth in grades 4–8. The documentary was nominated for a 20002 Academy Award and has won praise and a fierce following among the Spelling Bee hopeful. Among the contestants the documentary follows are two Indian Americans, including the eventual winner Nupur Lala, an African American young woman, a Latina, and four white contestants from various class and regional backgrounds. (The term "tweener" was introduced in the 1940s and used in relation to marketing and broadcast audiences; see the *Oxford English Dictionary*).

2 The first Indian American to win the Bee was Balu Natarajan in 1985 (sponsored by the *Chicago Tribune*) and the second was Rageshree Ramachandran in 1988 (sponsored by the *Sacramento Bee*). The first black Spelling Bee champion was Jody-Anne Maxwell (from Kingston, Jamaica) in 1998, who was also the first champion outside the United States. In 1975 Hugh Toteson from Puerto Rico won the crown.

3 The co-curator of the exhibit, Dr. Pawan Dhingra, explains that, "for *Beyond Bollywood*, I wanted to include the spelling bee because it has become one of the main representations of Indian Americans in popular culture. . . . Bees also would appeal to youth, which is important in an exhibition trying to speak to a variety of audiences" (e-mail response to the author, June 29, 2015).

4 See James Maguire, "How to Win the Spelling Bee," *Wall Street Journal*, June 16, 2009, http://www.wsj.com/articles/SB124398728702579459; and Ben Paynter, "Why Are Indian Kids So

Good at Spelling?" *Slate Magazine*, 2010, http://www.slate.com/articles/arts/culturebox/2010/06/why_are_indian_kids_so_good_at_spelling.html); and Tovia Smith, "Why Indian Americans Reign as Spelling Bee Champs," *Morning Edition*, NPR, May 29, 2012, NPR Morning Edition http://www.npr.org/2012/05/29/153898668/why-indian-americans-reign-as-spelling-bee-champs."

5 Although it is rarely discussed, winning the Scripps National Spelling Bee comes with an instant celebrity stature as well as lucrative monetary prize: a $30,000 check (from 2005 to the present) from Scripps, a $2,500 U.S. Savings Bond from *Merriam-Webster*, and $2,000 worth in reference material from *Encyclopedia Britannica*. In 1989 the winner received $1,500.

6 To qualify to participate in the final, contestants need to be between the ages of eight and fourteen and compete through open school competitions in their city and region before landing in the national bee.

7 Allan Walker Read, "The Spelling Bee: A Linguistic Institution of the American Folk," *PMLA* 56, no. 2 (1941): 495–512.

8 Ibid., 511.

9 Sam Whitsett, "The Spelling Bee: What Makes It an American Institution?" *Journal of Popular Culture* 43, no. 4 (2010): 888.

10 Shilpa Davé, *Indian Accents: Brown Voice and Racial Performance in American Television and Film* (Urbana : University of Illinois Press, 2013).

11 While most news coverage was complimentary, there was talk about some of the negative racial comments posted on social media that asked, for example, "Where are our American kids?" and that equated Indian American kids and Asian American kids as non-white. See Lindsey Bever, "Scripps National Spelling Bee Draws Racially Charged Comments after Indian Americans Win Again," *Washington Post*, May 30, 2014, http://www.washingtonpost.com/news/morning-mix/wp/2014/05/30/scripps-national-spelling-bee-draws-racially-charged-comments-after-indian-americans-win-again.

12 Bill Chappell, "National Spelling Bee: Rare Co-Champions, and a Star Online," *The Two-Way*, NPR, May 30, 2014, http://www.npr.org/sections/thetwo-way/2014/05/30/317336613/national-spelling-bee-rare-co-champions-and-a-star-online.

13 Sameer Pandya, "The Spelling Bee: America's Great Racial Freaks-and-Geeks Show," *Atlantic*, June 11, 2014, http://www.theatlantic.com/entertainment/archive/2014/06/the-spelling-bee-americas-great-racial-freak-show/372528/.

14 *CBSNews*, "Spelling Champ: 'I'm Still Excited,'" May 29, 2009, http://www.cbsnews.com/news/spelling-champ-im-still-really-excited.

15 Sarah Banet-Weiser, *AuthenticTM: The Politics of Ambivalence in a Brand Culture* (New York: NYU Press, 2012), 4.

16 Phone conversation with Rahul Walia, CEO of Touchdown Media, April 1, 2010.

17 See the North South Foundation, "US Contests: General Information," http://www.northsouth.org/public/uscontests/uscontests.aspx.

18 See the North South Foundation home page at www.northsouth.org.

19 See North South Foundation, "US Contests: General Information."

20 Joseph Berger, "Striving in America, and in the Spelling Bee," *New York Times*, June 5, 2005, http://www.nytimes.com/2005/06/05/weekinreview/striving-in-america-and-in-the-spelling-bee.html.

21 Shalini Shankar, "Creating Model Consumers: Producing Ethnicity, Race, and Class in Asian American Advertising," *American Ethnologist* 39, no. 3 (August 2012): 578–591.

22 Ibid., 584.

23 Ibid., 589.

24 Thanks to the Advertising Education Foundation for selecting me for a visiting professor fellowship with IW Group. I would like to offer a special thanks to then-CEO Bill Imada and IW Group for allowing me to observe and ask questions about the advertising business and for generously hosting me in Los Angeles.

25 Phone conversation with Shagorika Ghosh, IW Group, Inc., April 1, 2010.

26 South Asian Spelling Bee, http://southas_10/html. ianspellingbee.com.

27 See "Video," *South Asian Spelling Bee*, https://southasianspellingbee.com/news/video, accessed November 19, 2015.

28 See "Eligibility," *South Asian Spelling Bee*, https://southasianspellingbee.com/get-ready/start-today/eligibility, accessed October 30, 2015.

29 The 2009 winner of the Scripps Spelling Bee, Kavya Shivashankar is a former 2004 junior spelling bee champion who was featured on the North South Foundation homepage in 2010. The second runner-up, Aishwarya Pastapur, is also listed as having been the third runner-up of the Senior Spelling Bee in 2008.

30 The South Asian Spelling Bee has regional competitions in New Jersey, New York, DC Metro, Boston, Los Angeles, the San Francisco Bay area, Dallas, Houston, Chicago, Seattle, Atlanta, and Orlando. The finals are held in August, and TV Asia (Sony Entertainment) broadcasts the competition.

31 The problem for creating an international bee would be in the word choice. Currently the Bee uses *Webster's International Dictionary*, but for competitions in Britain or India, it is the *Oxford English Dictionary* that is the gospel of the English language, and it would change the nature of an American Bee to an activity that loses its cultural value elsewhere.

32 See the North South Foundation at http://www.northsouth.org.

33 The MetLife South Asian Spelling Bee charges a $50 registration fee for each child. In the twelve regional competitions, the winner receives $500, the first runner-up receives $300, and the second runner-up receives $200. The champion receives a check for $10,000 from MetLife. Unlike the North South Foundation contest, there are no conditions placed as to how and when the money will be used, but the assumption is that the award money also supports tuition scholarships.

34 James Maguire, *American Bee: The National Spelling Bee and the Culture of Word Nerds: The Lives of Five Top Spellers as They Compete for Glory and Fame* (Emmaus, PA: Rodale Books, 2006), 38.

35 Meena Thiruvengadam, "The New Global Indian: How Indians Spell S-U-C-C-E-S-S at the Bee," *Wall Street Journal*, June 9, 2009, http://www.wsj.com/articles/SB124451890174497075.

36 Ben Zimmer, "At This Year's Spelling Bee, Make Way for Meaning," *Boston Globe*, April 28, 2013, https://www.bostonglobe.com/ideas/2013/04/27/this-year-spelling-bee-make-way-for-meaning/rQvjgD90iGphHEadNsNtCI/story.html.

16

The Blood Sport of Cooking

On Asian American Chefs and Television

TASHA OREN

It surely is no accident that Asian Americans on television entered U.S. living rooms through the kitchen. The first series regular was Hop Sing, the family cook, played by Victor Sen Yung on the NBC western *Bonanza* (1959–1973), and later, in sitcoms, Noriyuki "Pat" Morita as Matsuo "Arnold" Takahashi, was cook and owner of the local hangout, Arnold's, on ABC's *Happy Days* (1974–1984).[1] Representations of Asian Americans on television sitcoms and dramas has since diversified, however incompletely, yet the recent interest in Asian American cuisine and chefs, so dominant within current trends in innovative cooking and restaurant culture, has refocused and reframed popular attention to the Asian American toiling in the restaurant kitchen. As I write this, cooking magazines, blogs, and the popular press teem with profiles of the latest Asian American celebrity chef sensations. On TV, the ABC network, home of the first- (and second-) ever Asian American–centered sitcoms—*Mr. T and Tina* (1976) and *All-American Girl* (1994–1995)—adapted Chef Eddie Huang's 2013 autobiography, *Fresh off the Boat*, as a family sitcom. Yet, in the unscripted twenty-four-hour food TV-scape that is the Food Network and its cable and network competitors, among the personality-driven programs and ever-expanding constellation of TV star chefs, pie lords, cupcake queens, BBQ pit masters, bacon wranglers, or mercurial restaurateurs, Asian American chefs remain a rarity.

Neither the Food Network nor other commercial cable competitors[2] currently produce or air a single show with an Asian American chef host. However, in one corner of the food TV universe, Asian Americans dominate. In fact, if you are watching an Asian American cook on television, odds are you are watching a cooking competition.

In the last few years, every major food competition from *Top Chef* (three Asian American winners in the last six years: Kristen Kish, Paul Qui, and Hung Huynh) to *The Taste* (won by Filipina American Khristianne Uy in its first season, with Marina Chung and Jeff Kawakami as runners-up in the second), from *Top Chef Masters* (won in 2011 by Floyd Cardoz) to *The Next Food Network Star* (won by Aarti Sequeira in 2013), saw an Asian American chef win, or at least featured a healthy presence of Asian American talent. Amateur home cooks fared just as well: 2013's *MasterChef* (the most popular food television format in the world) was won by Christine Ha, a blind home cook from Houston whose heavily promoted book, *Recipes from My Kitchen: Asian and American Comfort Food*,[3] was recently published. *MasterChef*'s last two seasons featured front-runners Lynn Chyi in 2013 and high school senior Aharn Cho in 2014, and the first ever *MasterChef Junior* iteration of the format saw twelve-year-old Dara Yu advance to the finals.

How do we account for this particular niche of overrepresentation? How do we make sense of it in the context of current culinary and media cultures, both so suffused in a global network of exchanges, world-circulating influences, and trend-driven momentum? How do we understand this moment of Asian American visibility in televisual culinary competitions in tandem with Asian American history and its own global linkages?

One obvious reading offers the world of food TV as simply another manifestation of a two-tiered representational system. Here, the unscripted cooking competition serves as an alternative "way in" to food television for Asian American talent, barred from taking central stage on conventional, chef-led, star-vehicle cooking programs by risk-averse (at best) or racist (at worst) network casting practices.

Another reading readily evoked by Asian American domination of the competition format is a lingering stereotype: that of the head-down, hard-working, driven, and competitive model minority. It also suggests a singular popular rendition of the American image of Asian American labor: that of the perpetually striving newcomer, never the veteran head honcho.

And while such readings are surely relevant and resonate powerfully with a long history of mainstream fantasy and popular representation, deciphering televisual identity politics is often complicated. Together with cultural history and narrative constructions, television's system of representation is beholden to the medium's own economic, technological, textual, and temporal imperatives. Add to that the specific realm of unscripted television the conventions of the competition/elimination format and the richly evocative and specialized world of professional cooking, and you arrive at a finely calibrated sliver of the television universe. As I argue, this segment of American television is important and particularly instructive for tracing how notions of identity, taste, and capital—both economic and cultural—are constructed, remade, and made meaningful. What's more, I aim to illustrate how such a television-centered analysis is inextricably bound with a broader account of Asian American history and, finally, how this particular history, rooted in post-immigration experiences from Asia to the United States, links up in surprising ways to an Asian textual migration that forever changed U.S. television. But before turning to television, we must first consider Asian American immigrant history in light of our current moment of culinary popular culture.

A Particular Unease: Asian American Chefs, Restaurant Labor, and U.S. Food Culture

> I don't believe anybody agrees with what I say or supports what I do because they truly want to love Asian people. They like my fucking pork buns, and I don't get it twisted.
> —Chef Eddie Huang, *New York Magazine*

Asian American chefs are at the vanguard of new American cuisine—as countless laudatory articles, reviews, and profiles attest. This new cuisine is marked by its complex and varied relationship to Asian ingredients and techniques, and (mostly) for the racial identity of the chefs leading the charge—David Chang, Danny Bowien, Roy Choi, Eddie Huang, and others. Characterized by global travel, biographical distinction, hipster-esque swagger, and a deliberate playfulness of style, class markers, technique, and influences, this is an Asian American cuisine. It is an unhyphenated style, set free from both the straitjacket of "authenticity" and tiki-soaked associations with "fusion."

This Asian American style of cooking is often celebrated as a unique historical culmination of an Asian American immigrant experience in the context of popular culture, racial politics, and globalization. In food writer and historian Joshua Ozersky's account, this current emergence of what he has dubbed the culinary "Asian American Funk Collective" tracks perfectly with both American culinary and Asian American immigration histories to produce the moment when Korean American David Chang could hit the American gastro-sweetspot serving personal takes on (Japanese) ramen, (Chinese) pork buns, and (Korean) ssam dishes.

As Ozersky suggests in his account, Asian American immigration history, in combination with the general development of American food culture—specifically the evolving interest and growing familiarity with Asian food and ingredients and the rise of the celebrity chef—produced a current young cadre of skilled, first-generation American-born culinary artists whose ethnic heritage, global sensibility, and native charisma pinged fortuitously with the current cultural zeitgeist.[4]

Writing about this emergence as a "radical reinvention," Nancy Matsumoto draws a distinction from Asian cuisine in America more sharply, emphasizing the new cuisine's vital interaction with popular, urban culture:

> What they're making is not just "modernist" Asian cuisine. It's a type of cooking that has filtered through the multiethnic influences of their upbringings: taco stands, fast food joints, barbecue shacks, hip hop, and graffiti. Theirs is not the "fusion" cooking of the late '70s and '80's, effete creations of European-trained masters who melded cultures with delicacy and nuance. Nor is it the cooking of

Nobu Matsuhisa or Martin Yan, talented newcomers who tutored America in Asian ingredients and flavor combinations. This new wave of chefs is dishing up what I call Asian Soul Food: a gutsy, high-low mash up of street food and haute cuisine, old country flavors and new-fangled cooking techniques.[5]

Matsumoto's laudatory emphasis is instructive here first for her attention to media culture. As she suggests, these shaped earlier U.S. understandings of Asian American chefs as immigrants whose cooking is sourced whole from their "home" countries elsewhere. Even more important, Matsumoto's careful parsing of current Asian American cuisine reveals an anxiety of categories and a deep investment in redeploying the notion of authenticity toward biography and class. In her framing, the cuisine is a cultural dialectic: "mash-up" versus "fusion," "multi-ethnic" versus both Asian and European, "gutsy" versus the "effete," and hip-hop and soul against the pale formalism of the modernist. Matsumoto's efforts to unmoor this cuisine from national and formal associations and cleave it to popular, distinctly American multi-ethnic experience and a youthful defiance of distinctions is nothing if not a response to a long and troubled history—a history that, as Tina Nguyen laments, mars the pleasure in such recent popular successes:

> What is the proper way to react to the Asian American Chef cultural phenomenon? The impulse to celebrate their arrival, and their boldness, and their stereotype-shattering attitude, *should* be a net positive. At the same time, however, such a celebration also serves as a stark reminder of their limitations: why are Asian-American achievements recognized *only* in the food world? And why, despite how integral their heritage is to their food, is their new infamy as the Asian American Chef Cartel (or whatever name they've been given this week) so *dependent* on their race?[6]

As Nguyen's essay reminds us, Asian American politics of food are suffused with cooking's own status as the primary (or even singular) means of Asian American visibility and labor—and a source of persistent stereotypes.

The designation of Asian American as a category, Martin F. Manalansan argues, begins with the toiling body and is inseparable from a history of labor. Asian Americans' labor and immigration histories within the United States, along with food and cooking's high symbolic value, both as articulation of identity and representation of difference, produce "Asian Americans' relationship with the material and symbolic aspects of food . . . as part of their continuing marginal and abject status in the American cultural imagination."[7] These stereotypes, as Anita Mannur and others have pointed out, centered on food and cooking's symbolic value in designating Asian Americans as perpetual foreigners.

Indeed, Asian American stereotypes of foreign-ness are so thoroughly inter-mingled with food that Melissa Hung, founder and first editor of the Bay Area Asian American culture magazine *Hyphen*, vowed to never publish a recipe in the magazine's pages.[8]

Aside from food itself, the site of the restaurant is particularly resonant in the cultural history of Asian American immigration. For much of the last century, the immigrant-run Asian restaurant was often the main (or only) arena of con-tact between (mainly) white majorities and Asian Americans. These material exchanges with non-Asian diners, as Timothy K. August notes, involved not only tailoring an environment and a set of rituals to connote an "authentic" experi-ence but also often the deliberate performance of difference and foreign-ness. As August suggests, this economic relationship itself required such performances of Asianness as a perpetual foreign exotic not only in the restaurant environment but also in the marketing of Asian-branded foods.[9]

These scholarly works, among others, illustrate how food and its prepara-tion—in the domestic setting and the public space of the restaurant—is a par-ticularly potent site of cultural signification for Asian Americans. Yet food and cooking are important not only in their material practices but also in their rep-resentations, and these form the context in which specific practices gain new meaning. Scholars who examine the representation of food and cooking have turned their analytic attentions most closely to cooking in film and novels. Yet cooking on television, particularly unscripted (often mislabeled as "real-ity" TV), remains underexplored as a textual domain where identities and cul-ture circulate within the framework of expertise, competition, economics, and on-camera labor.

The massive popularity of food, restaurants, and cooking culture *as* popular culture was, in no small measure, shaped by its media presence. As I've written elsewhere, the evolving media deployment of culinary consumption and prepa-ration in the United States has always functioned as a marker of identity, class, and mastery—and does so now in tandem with the judgment-as-expertise econ-omy of social media.[10] The particular symbolic closeness of Asian Americans with food in the mainstream cultural imagination—as producers and servers of culinary consumption and bodies marked by culinary difference—thus makes for an interesting and complex cultural dilemma when Asian American cooking meets celebrity culture and reality television.

As we've seen thus far, Asian American chefs' status in the culinary world of restaurants, food blogs, and magazines stands in odd contrast to their rela-tive absence as presenters, instructors, or narrative centers. At the same time, they are *over-represented* as cooking competitors. As I suggested above, common understandings of this imbalance link it to an old tradition of media stereotypes that denied Asian Americans a place of narrative centrality or authority and cast them as perpetually driven new immigrants. These readings are certainly resonant but, as I already noted, lack a specificity. Representations necessarily operate in relation to one another—and certainly do so across media forms and other cultural texts. This intertextual dependence notwithstanding, tracing how medium-specific texts evolve and how particular types of representations gain symbolic currency *within* a given medium and genre are equally important—and crucial to the questions I pose above.

In focusing on the emergence of Asian American chefs and cooks as TV personalities, and their particular intersection with cooking competitions, I'd like to locate their presence within the specificity of the cooking show as an evolving genre and trace how it refigured cuisine into a personality spectacle. My aim here is not to ask how Asian American chefs are represented on TV but, rather, how this representational category is instructive for understanding television as cultural programming—in the fullest sense of the word. And while this account is particular to the medium of television, it is also fundamentally global in its scope.

Food Television and the Cook-Along Format

For years, food television meant simply "cooking instruction" and featured a stable form: a domestic, kitchen-like set and a familiar instructor who addressed the viewer directly while demonstrating the preparation of a particular dish. Imported from its format predecessor on commercial radio, such programing relied on the specific premise of the "cook along." This format hailed the (presumed female) viewer as an apprenticing home cook, an eager (or beleaguered) student, who was invited into the site of easy culinary mastery and urged to watch, learn, and replicate.

As media historian Dana Polan documents, early (pre-national) cooking shows on local networks were often experimental in format, setting, and presentation. They also featured a wide variety of personalities, cooking styles, and international influences.[11] Television's conventional and economic convergence into a nationally based networked system, supported by sponsors and advertisers and driven by day-part distinctions between female homemaker audiences (in the morning), kids (afternoon), and male-led family evening viewing in the early 1950s followed its rapid adaption into the American family home. As Lynn Spigel, David Marc, and George Lipsitz have shown, as television transformed from a largely coastal novelty to a central household medium, it not only shed its experimental openness and multi-ethnic address to embrace conventional formats and ideal, middle-class whiteness but also took on an ideological, pedagogical quality that aimed to educate its viewers in proper consumption and coherent national, class, and gendered identities.[12] The cooking instructional as "homemaker helper" emerged as one such explicit text charged with directing homemakers in the art of nourishing and caretaking of their families, enhancing their skills in cooking for guests and community activities (like church and women's committees), and successfully withstanding the scrutiny of others.

In light of this dire narrative of joyless service, blandness, and conformity, many American food and TV historians herald Julia Child, the French-trained home cook, as a trailblazer, a pioneer who in 1963 single-handedly recalibrated the American palate and revolutionized food TV. Child famously infused the cooking program format with much-needed exuberance, an enthusiasm for new flavors, and an emphasis on the sheer pleasure of tasting, cooking, and eating.[13] In demystifying French cuisine to novice American cooks and whetting her audience's appetite for unfamiliar ingredients on her first PBS hit, *The French Chef*, Child opened the door to new cooking traditions and a diversity of hosts.

Not coincidentally, the first Asian American television chef, Joyce Chen, debuted her own program, *Joyce Chen Cooks*, on Child's same WGBH set in 1966, introducing many audiences to Chinese home cooking. Known as the "Chinese Julia Child," the Boston-area restaurateur and author Joyce Chen is credited with popularizing Peking duck, hot and sour soup, and moo shu pork for American palates as well as coining the term "Peking ravioli" for potstickers.[14] As Polan documents in his book-length study of the program, *Julia Child's "The French Chef*,*"* the modular set, built for Child, would easily "convert" into Chen's with the replacement of the French-themes images at the front of the counter with vaguely Asian designs. The small but significant changes that would produce the proper intimate setting and infuse each woman's performance space with markers of location, psychological comfort, and atmosphere spoke volumes about the status of both cuisines as French and Chinese cooking were undergoing the process of televisual familiarization: "The set was reconfigured into a kind of minimalist space whose backgrounds were bathed in darkness and dotted with curtains, lacquer patterns and Asian pottery."[15] As (verified) lore would have it, Joyce Chen's much more reserved and physically restricted style of movement around the kitchen—especially when compared with Child's demonstrative and expansive presentation method—was also a product of retrofitting: *The French Chef* set was built with consideration of Child's imposing six-foot frame, and the significantly shorter Chef Chen required the use of concealed lifts to fully reach the countertop.

PBS, a precursor to the Food Network with its extensive cooking programming in the 1970s and 1980s, was also the home of the Asian American TV chef and popular personality Martin Yan, who in 1978 starred in the first of several Asian-style cooking shows, *Yan Can Cook*, and later Katie and Leeann Chin's *Double Happiness*, which combined recipes with recollections and conversation about Chinese and Chinese American culinary traditions.

While PBS and its local stations remained strong and prolific producers of the cook-along format, the 1990s saw the introduction of the Food Network, as

Figure 16.1. Joyce Chen at work on *Joyce Chen Cooks*; this set location also served as Julia Child's iconic kitchen on *The French Chef*. Image property of WGBH/available through The New-York Historical Society Digital Archive.

food, eating and gastronomy emerged as strong commercial draws in the rapidly expanding cable marketplace. In the first decade since its establishment in 1993, the Food Network also relied primarily on the how-to, in-kitchen instructional convention. Shot on cozy sets resembling domestic kitchens, the programs featured genial white presenters who, with an eye-level, mostly stationary camera, engaged audiences (addressing them as "you") with a warm, intimidation-free style. As the status of food as a sanctioned mainstream pursuit and a marker of class mobility grew in the late 1990s, the Food Network's programming featured an accompanying shift: the conspicuous move toward higher production values (including sumptuous, soft-focus close-ups of glistening ingredients); younger, attractive presenters for whom food was both a leisure activity and an explicitly sensual pleasure (as I've written elsewhere, the British host and cookbook author Nigella Lawson epitomizes this turn to so called gastro-porn); and a new openness to culinary travel, sampling, and, in the parlance of the time, "fusion" cuisine. This shift to prettier, exotic flavor hunters was personified in the young and handsome restaurateur Ming Tsai's popular *East Meets West* and future culinary stalwart and model Padma Lakshmi's *Padma's Passport*.

Yet another radical change was sweeping through food television in the early 2000s. Friendly, domestic, instructional cooking programs were slowly redelegated to "daytime" and online content. In prime time, on Food Network, and later on Bravo and even network television, food was turning to blood sport.

The Global Genesis of the Cooking Competition Format

The program that transformed the Food Network from a friendly special-interest channel into a pop culture phenomena was *Iron Chef*. Set in a "kitchen stadium," this lavish Japanese cooking competition, featuring professional chefs, celebrity tasters, a mystery ingredient, heroic bombast, and a race against the clock, revolutionized food television in the United States.

In the years following its introduction in 1999—and over a decade later—the leading rating successes in food-related television remain shows in which chefs compete in cooking challenges under strict time restrictions, subjected to often-harsh criticism by a panel of judges, and a win/lose outcome. Weekly one-by-one eliminations are a common feature, as is a high-profile host's dismissal of the dejected chef with a catch phrase ("Pack up your knives and go," "You have been chopped," or "Take off your jacket and leave the kitchen"). On the Food Network, the leading primetime programs for over a decade have all been competition shows (*The Next Food Network Star*, *Iron Chef America*, *The Next Iron Chef* and *Chopped*), and Bravo's *Top Chef* franchise still leads in overall food TV ratings as it, and popular network offerings like Fox's *Hell's Kitchen* and *MasterChef* spawn dozens of similarly structured cooking competitions spanning the cable and network spectrum. In these programs, cooking is not a means for pleasure or social recreation but a technically demanding, sweaty, and stressful display of labor and expertise.

The food TV turn away from the home kitchen and into the public show space has also been marked by a sharp turn toward professionalization. Here, the spectacle of cooking highlights the restaurant as the site of mastery, performance, and artistry and reinscribes it into the explicitly capitalist logic of *cooking as work*—most commonly, competitors are awarded with seed money to start their own restaurant. While *Top Chef*, *Next Food Network Star*, or *Hell's Kitchen* are most notable in their mission to promote and reward young professionals, more startling are shows like *MasterChef* that stress their intent to facilitate the successful competitor's transformation from domestic cook (who cooks for love and pleasure) into professional chef. This explicit drive toward professionalization is most striking and absurd on *Masterchef Junior*, where three professional chef-restauranteurs routinely address fourth graders about their potential contributions to "our industry."

But how did this happen? And how, in an environment so hostile to "foreign" programs as American television, and so averse to radical change, did a Japanese show manage to change everything?

In TV, as in cooking, repetition and recombination of basic recipes—innovation within convention—are the fundamentals. Master these, and you've mastered the form. And in television, no programming type better epitomizes this maxim than the format—and it is impossible to understand the rise of the competition in food television without it.

Format, as I've argued elsewhere, is the essential software of contemporary television and is vital to any consideration of food culture as popular culture.[16] The format industry is the single largest part of the international television market, constituting over 60 percent of all entertainment television worldwide. And, while the skill competition remains the most popular reality format all over the world, the vast legal gray zone between inspiration and imitation allows for as many new unlicensed format-like mutations as the market will bear. Although formats have been a television staple for decades, they rose to international prominence in the late 1990s with the juggernaut success of the Scandinavian formats *Big Brother* and *Survivor* and the *British Idol* franchise. And while the contemporary weekly format of skill-challenge-judgment-elimination that now typifies the highest-rated food-programming competitions traces paternity to these European reality formats, the mother of the American cooking competition is Japanese.

Iron Chef first aired in 1996 on local Bay Area cable station KTSF as part of a Japanese programming block on Saturday evenings. Subtitled versions of episodes began to air a year later, and the show's momentum as an underground local cult hit grew. By 1998, it was the most popular program on the channel and was picked up by other local stations (in Los Angeles, Hawaii, and New York) and spread by word of mouth and illict copies by fans elsewhere online.[17] This is how a Food Network staffer first saw *Iron Chef* and brought it to the attention of programmer Eileen Opatut. Opatut bought the rights to fifty-two episodes of the new "international edition" that Fuji TV produced by dubbing and subtitling the old shows.[18] The episodes began airing in July 1999, making *Iron Chef* the first foreign-made cooking show to air on American television and earning the Food Network a large and unexpected one-third overall jump in ratings that summer.[19]

The show was such an instant hit because more than just home cooks were watching: For the first time in its nascent history, Food Network programming attracted a wide demographic, most notably college students new to the channel and to cooking programs. These young viewers generically associated the program, not with cooking, but with martial art films, manga, video games, and an Asian popular aesthetic just peaking in the United States at the time. Dubbing the program "Late Night College TV," one journalist reported how the show had become a staple of social viewing for college students (complete with *Iron Chef* drinking games); it also represented an important lifeline for the Food Network, whose strategy to broaden viewership (and advertisers) with an "entertainment first" programming shift had finally paid off.[20] Another review highlighted how the show "cloaks earnest competition and serious cooking in the goofiest trappings, including English dubbing that seems modeled on the exclamatory rhythms of kung fu movie translations."[21] Indeed, as Mark Gallagher argues, this practice of English dubbing was deliberately reminiscent of the low-budget style of martial arts films (despite the show's status, in 1999, as the most expensive cooking show ever made) to add comic resonance—and dubbing often altered the actual translation, Gallagher notes, to adhere to a quirky style and a camp aesthetic that would appeal to its western audience.[22]

The status of *Iron Chef* as a pivotal television text and as popular culture thus intersects importantly with Asian American cultural history and the increasingly long global ties that link cultural affinities, tastes, and sensibilities. As many Asian American studies scholars pointed out, the growing presence, circulation, and popularity of Asian goods and culture at the turn of the last century were closely linked to the presence and cultural practices of an emerging generation of Asian American pop culture consumers who functioned as "agents of cool." As Mimi Thi Nguyen and Thuy Linh Nguyen Tu note, these Asian American cultural brokers facilitated the increasing availability, circulation, and appeal of particular goods, texts, and trends.[23] Thus, Asian American college students spearheaded the introduction, and eventual popularity, of Hong Kong cinema in the United States in the early 1990s, the same period that saw the founding and publication of *Giant Robot*, the alternative lifestyle magazine that featured both Asian American and Asian pop culture and quickly became the arbiter and translator of "Asian Cool." Similarly, it was these early fans a few years later whose word-of-mouth admiration for *Iron Chef* first piqued the Food Network's attention. As *AsianWeek* observed, *Iron Chef* was an early U.S. television entrant into the "Cool Japan" trend, already under way with manga and video games.[24]

Dubbed "Pokéman for grown-ups" in the *New York Times*,[25] *Iron Chef*'s over-the top style certainly facilitated its reading as a camp product. Yet its surprising ability to draw previously unrelated audiences not only provided food TV with its most lucrative programming recipe to date, it also coincided with the American TV industry's new openness to so called "reality television," with its promise of low production costs, quick turnaround, and especially in-text advertising opportunities in the form of product placement.

The initial series broadcast of *Iron Chef* was followed by an *Iron Chef America* special in 2002—which broke all Food Network ratings records. A regular *Iron Chef America* series followed in 2004 and was quickly followed by a veritable flood of cooking competition shows all over U.S. cable networks, with Fox's format of *Hell's Kitchen* in 2005, Bravo's *Top Chef* in 2006, and Food Network's own format spin-off *The Next Iron Chef* in 2007 among the early favorites.

The move from the kitchen to "kitchen stadium" (as the arena where iron chefs do battle) is apt, not only as it signaled the move from the domestic to the public and from private to professional, but also as a powerful illustrator for what "worked" as popular television. As I've illustrated in the history of food television above, cooking and food preparation were always linked, in their media incarnation, with particular personalities and paired food genres with specific individuals, settings, identities, and styles. The flamboyant theatricality and combative diegetic frame that *Iron Chef* brought to American food television coaxed these already existing narrative threads to form the cloth from which this new brand of cooking show was cut. As one reporter gleefully described the pleasures of the battle:

> As popular as "Iron Chef" may have been during its six-year run in Japan, it seems to have found its true following in America, where it has become one of the Food Network's most popular offerings. The New York Battle, which pitted US chef Bobby Flay against Iron Chef Japan Masaharu Morimoto, drew unprecedented ratings for the network. It aired on June 25, 2000, with more than 960,000 households tuning in to watch the cocky American cook accidentally cut himself, zap himself on an electric pot, and then jump up on a cutting board at the match's conclusion, to the disgust of his more reserved Japanese counterpart, who handily won the battle. The sizzling contest was popular enough to spark two special rematch programs, which aired this past June.[26]

Importantly, the show's integration into an American imagery included not only the introduction of more specialized ingredients and cooking techniques but also cultural and behavioral modes. This included the adaptation of the Japanese overly formal—and highly performative—style that cast chefs as serious craftsmen (virtually all were male in the show's early incarnations), laying their pride and mastery on the line as part of what T. J. M. Holden has termed the program's "vernacular of power."[27] This dynamic remained in the American iteration, where cooking prowess, mental toughness, resourcefulness, character, and ingenuity were highlighted as marks of culinary mastery. Yet, most important, this new narrative approach to cooking as a battle of skills and wills encouraged its growing audience to think of each culinary style and each chef's personality in symbiotic terms, each as an *extension* of the other.

Identities on the Line: Asian American Performance and Food Competitions

In tracing the recombinant elements that explain how cooking competitions have come to dominate the food TV landscape thus far, I have emphasized the recipe-like structure of television and how the then-nascent European task-and-elimination format of reality TV met the Japanese single-ingredient-cooking-stadium and judging-panel formula to produce, in the United States, a fount of popular food competition variations. Yet what of the Asian American chef? *Iron Chef*'s history and early popularity with a certain segment of Asian American viewers does not, of course, explain current TV competitions' apparent hospitality to Asian American chefs. To understand that, we need to turn to narrative strategies and the new television value of *style as identity*. Here, I highlight the double meaning in the title to this section; for those unfamiliar with commercial kitchen lingo, the term *on the line* refers to the actual workman-like structure of the restaurant kitchen—its military-inspired hierarchical structure and its systematic placement of given cooks and kitchen hands at specific stations (grill, stove, veg, sauce, etc.) as dishes are assembled in rapid repetition. Yet "on the line," of course, also speaks of risks and dangers—the stakes of putting oneself forward and on display.

Who you are, in the logic of reality TV cooking competitions, riffs on Brillat-Savarin's ubiquitous dictum "Tell me what you eat, and I'll tell you who you are," yet here, "what you cook" replaces "what you eat" to arrive at the same insight. In the tightly orchestrated universe of the cooking competition, labor, style, and their results are the key to personality and the ways each chef is distinguished from the others. Cooking *is* identity.

In food studies, the bonds between cooking and national identity are multiple and robust. Priscilla Parkhurst Ferguson, for example, has argued—as a variant alongside Benedict Anderson's focus on print exchange as the binding core of imagined communities—that it was cooking, and specifically Parisian cuisine, that formed a French national identity.[28] Importantly, the emergence of the restaurant is a key locus for this transformation of food production into cuisine—and of public eating and serving into performance. Ferguson's work, among others, stresses how studies of food—shared traditions, knowledge, economy, and institutional structures—are necessarily also geographies of place that bind people to the past, to their location, and to each other.

Television, and specifically the cooking program, can thus be thought of as a site for the contemporary reorientation of cuisine into spectatorship, a text that not only transforms practice into performance but also redefines it as a shared tradition.

What *Iron Chef*'s hyper-competitive cooking format brought to food television was not only the premise of a chef cooking competition as mainstream entertainment, but more important, it reversed representational strategies of cuisine, ingredient preparation, and presentation by positioning East Asian, and specifically Japanese style, as the norm.

More important still, it linked style of cooking with identity and promoted culinary difference as narrative element in a profoundly new way. *Iron Chef* drew from and fed into the then-still-evolving conventions of the reality format to align audience sympathies with competitors' distinct identities—understood purely as extensions of their skill. Thus, on *Iron Chef*, each chef stood as a personification of their culinary specialty (Iron Chef Japanese, Iron Chef Italian) accented in the show's spectacular intro.

Figure 16.2. Iron Chef.

As they emerged on hydrolic platforms onto the raised stage, the chefs, life-sized action figures, were posed in distinct culinary gear, some with their expertise-related culinary "weapons" of choice: a cleaver for the canary yellow–swathed Iron Chef Chinese; a tomato for Iron Chef Italian, clad in red; and (inexplicably) a pear, for Iron Chef French. Perhaps in reference to his maverick status or lack of local exoticism, Iron Chef Japanese (Matzuharo Morimoto, who made a successful transition to the U.S. version) was armed only with his formidable stare as he stood, spread legged and battle ready, at the center of the stage, wearing a silver-and-red-accented outfit and matching cap. Not surprisingly, the nationalist-based culinary classification did not survive in the American-made iterations. However, the iron super chefs still have their own technique and strengths and draw their culinary prowess from a personal history and training lineage. This is no small tweak since, in the American version (as in the slew of competition cooking shows that followed), a chef's cooking styles and preferred flavor profiles are emphasized as crucial components of their individual identity and competitive chops. And it is here that Asian American chefs, steeped in the complex and often fraught centrality of food for Asian American history—and well versed in such reconfigurations of cuisine as unique personal history—excel.

This surge of Asian-inspired flavors and preparations as part of every chef's most basic arsenal of skills is a development that is importantly antithetical to the original *Iron Chef*'s basic premise of nationally defined cuisines. Nonetheless, within the television cooking universe, it is a direct descendant and lives comfortably alongside the muscular, nostalgic, and aggressively juvenile food TV reliance on BBQ, diner fare, and EBB (everything better with bacon). This change is also reflected back in the larger culture of restaurant styles from food trucks to fine dining. Thus, we can see food TV's influence in the meaningful recalibration of Asian flavors, techniques, and ingredients. Pried free from the reductive violence and polar construction of authenticity and fusion—the latter's now abject status in restaurant trends is a turn that cannot be understood without cultural theory—"Asian American" cuisine claims a categorical right of place and creative ownership for Asian American chefs.

Before closing, I'd like to return to the construct of the television cooking competition and circle back (again) to the question we started with: What are we to make of the fact that it is only in the confines of the competition that this work of palate and culture realignment is done?

Asian American Soul Redux

Addressing the representational potential offered by the cooking competition format, Timothy K. August suggests that it

> creates the possibility that disparate kinds of subjectivities can be displayed, which is particularly notable for Asian Americans, who in television, film and theater have been limited to playing familiar symbolic and secondary roles, racially disqualified from playing more meaty roles written with white bodies in mind. In this arena, the Asian American is no longer forced on screen or in the restaurant, to play the role of the invisible waiter or deliveryman; rather the contestant . . . can take full advantage of this gaze to accrue cultural capital by exhibiting his skills as a master chef. . . . This form offers opportunities for Asian Americans to exceed prefigured representations and use the theoretically unscripted nature of the medium to constitute positions and personalities that run counter to prefigured types. Or so it would seem.[29]

In reading a particular episode of *Top Chef*'s third season, August points to a pivotal exchange between then-frontrunner Hung Huynh and head judge Tom Colicchio. In it, Colicchio acknowledges the French-trained chef's technical skill as the best in the show but, referring to his Vietnamese birth, complains that Huynh has not shown the judges more of himself—meaning, his Vietnamese culinary roots. Huynh's reply, a warmhearted and judge-moving tribute to his mother, grandmother, and "bloodline" tradition of cooking with love is, as August convincingly suggests, little more than a performance of strangeness, designed to assure the judges by recasting himself according to familiar constructs of Asian-ness and racial legibility. "I grew up in the kitchen," Huynh tells the judges, without a hint of the brash and cutting style that has characterized his performance thus far, "sleeping in the kitchen. . . . When I think of my mom's food I get so emotional, I get tingly because it's all about soul." His reply moves the judges, and, in the formal logic of the show, is constructed as a watershed moment of emotional release. Huynh goes on to win.

Indeed, as August demonstrates, the problem of conflation among culture, cuisine, and identity (or "soul") is problematic, to say the least—Huynh, the first Asian American to win a televised cooking competition, was also taken to task for being "too competitive" and "not a team player." However, as I suggested, cooking competitions do not trade in the promise of ethnic tabula rasa; rather, they narratively rely on a compulsory symbolic symbiosis between chef/identity and style/technique. This new form of "soul," with its decentering of the national for the personal and experiential—the injunction for a "biography on a plate"—coalesces neatly with Matsumoto's labored definition of Asian American cuisine. Yet this requirement, like all media texts' relationship to legibility, is perfunctory and productively unstable.

Doubtlessly, Asian Americans' over-representation in this particular niche of food television aligns easily with the stereotypes of industriousness, ambition, hard-working compliance and a perpetual new immigrants' drive. Yet, considering the evolution of the food competition format as a dynamic cultural mechanism of representation complicates this ready reading. Instead, it suggests that the format's own history, narrative roots, and emphasis on style, expertise, and skill as markers born of personal experience and unique history better account for the cooking competition's particular hospitality to representational difference. It is in the productive tension among these countervailing processes of meaning making that Asian American representation in culinary competition shows gain cultural legibility. This often-contradictory process further reveals how various pressures of identity, capital, and history, arranged within a particular medium and narrative form, circulate certain formations while adjusting and disrupting others.

NOTES

1 While *Happy Days* aired for seven seasons, Pat Morita's character was a regular in the third season only (1975–1976).

2 The publicly funded PBS remains an exception, as it has been historically.

3 Christine Ha, *Recipes from My Kitchen: Asian and American Comfort Food* (Emmaus, PA: Rodale, 2013).

4 Joshua Ozersky, "Talented, Young and Asian American," *Time Magazine*, June 20, 2012, http://ideas.time.com/2012/06/20/talented-young-asian-american.

5 Nancy Matsumoto, "Stinky, Spicy, and Delicious: The Radical Reinvention of Asian American Food," *Atlantic*, July16, 2012, http://www.theatlantic.com/national/archive/2012/07/stinky-spicy-and-delicious-the-radical-reinvention-of-asian-american-food/259864.

6 Tina Nguyen, "Is the Media Coverage of Asian American Chefs a Good Thing?" *Braiser*, July 27, 2012, http://www.thebraiser.com/asian-chefs-media-coverage.

7 Martin F. Manalansan, "Cooking Up the Sense: A Critical Embodied Approach to the Study of Food and Asian American Television Audiences," in *Alien Encounters: Popular Culture*

in Asian America, ed. Mimi Thi Nguyen and Thuy Linh Tu (Durham, NC: Duke University Press, 2007), 180.

8 Jeff Yang, "Asian Pop/Believe the Hyphen," *SFGate*, August 28, 2007, http://www.sfgate.com/entertainment/article/ASIAN-POP-Believe-the-Hyph-2507656.php.

9 Timothy K. August, "The Contradiction in Culinary Collaboration: Vietnamese American Bodies in *Top Chef* and *Stealing Buddha's Dinner*," *MELUS* 37, no. 3 (Fall 2012): 97–115.

10 Tasha Oren, "On the Line: Format, Cooking and Competition as Television Values," *Critical Studies in Television* 8, no. 2 (2013): 20.

11 Dana Polan, *Julia Child's "The French Chef"* (Durham, NC: Duke University Press, 2011).

12 Lynn Spigel, *Make Room for TV: Television and the Family Ideal in Postwar America* (Chicago: University of Chicago Press, 1992); David Marc, *Demographic Vistas: Television in American Culture* (Philadelphia: University of Pennsylvania Press, 1996); George Lipsitz, "The Meaning of Memory: Family, Class, and Ethnicity in Early Network Television Programs," *Cultural Anthropology* 1, no. 4 (1986): 355–387.

13 Polan, *Julia Child's "The French Chef."*

14 Rain Robertson, "Joyce Chen," *The Cambridge Historical Society: Culinary Cambridge*, http://cambridgehistory.org/discover/culinary/joycechen.html.

15 Polan, *Julia Child's "The French Chef,"* 141.

16 Tasha Oren, "TV Strikes Back: Reiterational Texts and Global Imagination," in *Global TV Formats: Understanding Television across Borders*, ed. Tasha Oren and Sharon Shahaf (New York: Routledge, 2012).

17 Gabriella Lukacs, "*Iron Chef* around the World: Japanese Food Television, Soft Power and Cultural Globalization," *International Journal of Cultural Studies* 13 (2010): 409.

18 Steve Johnson, "Cooks Trash Talk, Settle Foes' Hash on 'Iron Chef,'" *Chicago Tribune*, March 15, 2000, http://articles.chicagotribune.com/2000-03-15/features/0003150366_1_iron-chef-kitchen-stadium-eel.

19 Ibid.

20 D. Bell, "*Iron Chef* Continues Reign of Late-Night College TV," *American Intelligence Wire*, April 6, 2003, 62–66.

21 Julie Salamon, "Critic's Notebook; Chefs Battle Like Samurai in a Cult Hit," *New York Times*, June 19, 2000, E1, http://www.nytimes.com/2000/06/19/arts/critic-s-notebook-chefs-battle-like-samurai-in-a-cult-hit.html.

22 Mark Gallagher, "What's So Funny about *Iron Chef*?" *Journal of Popular Film and Television* 31, no. 4 (2004): 176–184.

23 Mimi Thi Nguyen and Thuy Linh Tu, "Introduction," in Nguyen and Tu, *Alien Encounters*, 20.

24 Emily Leach, "Cool Japan: Why Japanese Remakes Are So Popular on American TV, and Where We're Getting It Wrong," *AsianWeek*, September 13, 2008, http://www.asianweek.com/2008/09/13/cool-japan-why-japanese-remakes-are-so-popular-on-american-tv-and-where-we%E2%80%99re-getting-it-wrong.

25 Salamon, "Critic's Notebook; Chefs Battle Like Samurai in a Cult Hit."

26 James Norton, "WWF Meets Haute Cuisine on 'Iron Chef,'" *Christian Science Monitor*, October 3, 2001, http://www.csmonitor.com/2001/1003/p16s1-lifo.html.

27 T. J. M. Holden, "The Overcooked and Underdone," in *Food and Culture: A Reader*, 3rd ed., ed. Carole Counihan and Penny Van Esterik (New York: Routledge 2013), 119–136.

28 Priscilla Parkhurst Ferguson, *Accounting for Taste: The Triumph of French Cuisine* (Chicago: University of Chicago Press, 2004).

29 August, "The Contradiction in Culinary Collaboration."

PART IV

Migration and Transnational Popular Culture

17

Curry as Code: Food, Race, and Technology

MADHAVI MALLAPRAGADA

According to the *Urban Dictionary*, "stindian" is slang for "a stinky Indian, typically an IT professional on H1B visa status."[1] Launched in 1999, the *Urban Dictionary* is a user-generated database of slang and popular terms. "Urban dictionary is *written by you*"—so goes the slogan for the site, which allows users to offer definitions for existing words or, better still, create their own words and define them.[2] "Stindian" is one such coinage. Defined by a user in 2007, the entry has since been voted "up" 135 times and voted "down" 32 times by the *Urban Dictionary* community. The communal evaluation is based both on the definition of "stindian" as well as the detailed description that follows it: "A Stindian commonly eats the stinkiest of the stinky foods, such as chicken vindaloo (extra curry) and curry fried okra. Usually the stindian forgets that showers exist in the universe, or has a very short memory when it comes to the last time he or she bathed. Their olfactory senses are overly non-existent, thus they don't know how enormously bad they smell to the rest of the world. Common stindian names include: Subbu, Ambarish, and Naranayananananan."[3] Completing the entry are the seven associated tags of "ambarish," "indian," "it," "smelly," "stinky," "software developer," and "subbu." While Subbu and Ambarish are popular names for South Indian men, "Naranayanananananan" is an exaggerated name for possibly Narayan or Narayanan. The most iconic example of this strategy—exaggerating Indian immigrant last names to highlight their length—is "Nahasapeemapetilon," the last name given to the fictional animated character Apu in the television series *The Simpsons*.

"Stindian," however, refers to real, not fictive, Indian immigrants, and through its tags and detailing it conjures up a template for the "stindian" figure: a male immigrant in the United States on a temporary work visa known as the H-1B, of South Indian nationality, employed in the information technology (IT) sector, and possessing a stinky body odor due to a combination of factors—excessive consumption of Indian curry, poor personal hygiene, and a lack of self-awareness about the body's unpleasant effects on the surroundings.

This opening example lays out the key topics I address and engage with in this essay—the representation of Indian curry as a stinky food, Indian immigrant IT workers on the H-1B visa, and online narratives that link the "overwhelming" and "unpleasant" smell of curry with the "unwanted" presence of Indian immigrants in the information and technology sectors of the United States. A Google search for the term "stindian" did not yield any additional result besides the original citation at the *Urban Dictionary* (to the best of my knowledge). But a search for the tags or metadata organizing the "stindian" entry—Indian, smell, stinky, and curry—yields an astonishing number of results *and* a range of contexts in which narratives linking smelly Indian bodies and Indian food circulate online. For example, on *Yahoo! Answers*, the user-generated question-and-answer website, we find references to curry-smelling Indians in diverse groups such as "Food and Drink," "Do-It-Yourself," "Society and Culture," "Travel," and "Home and Garden." Here is a sample of the kind of questions posed by the site's users: "Why do Indian people always smell of curry, without fail?" "Do Indians really smell like curry?" "Does the smell of Indian curry bother you?" "Why do Indians really smell like curry?" "Why do Indian people smell bad?" "Why do Indians smell so much?"[4] Oftentimes users seek input from the community to help get rid of the smell of curry from one's body, clothing, or residential space: "How can I stop a curry smell?" "Getting rid of the curry smell?" "My house smells like curry, help!!!" "Neighbors cooking smell [of curry] in my bathroom," "No Offence: Why do some Indians not wear deodorant and smell like curry?" "Previous tenants were Indian, how can I get rid of the curry smell permanently?"

The association of a place with the smell of curry also appears very frequently in online reviews of either residential or business spaces. For example, on *City-Data*, the social networking site with data and information forums about U.S. cities, users express how the undesired sensory encounter with curry smells not only leads to a loss of privacy (in the sense of "I don't want to smell the curry but have no choice") but also material loss ("I had to spend $$$ on cleaning and deodorizing solutions," "I am being asked to pay extra $$$ by landlord to get rid of curry smell") and bodily harm (by concluding that migraines, headaches, and nausea are the side effects of inhaling the intense spices of curry).[5] It is also common to see reviews of Indian-owned businesses commenting on the overpowering smell of curry that permeates the office space, thus making any business interaction in that space a challenge for potential customers. As one reviewer of an Indian-owned Econo Lodge in Dumas, Texas, writes on *TripAdvisor*, a travel website company, "There is a very nice Indian family that owns/runs the hotel, and they live on the first floor in their own apartment within the hotel. It smells like curry every hour of every day. I was in the furthest room away, and the smell was nonstop."[6] Be it one's apartment, a neighboring home, or a large hotel, all these spaces seem to be equally vulnerable to the overpowering presence of Indians and their food. Relatedly, references to the lingering smell of curry—exemplified through queries such as "previous tenants were Indian, how can I get rid of the curry smell permanently?"—bring up the notion that an encounter with the curry smell (or Indians who smell like curry) are in fact sensorial experiences that one is forced to have against one's wishes.

Against this general context of online narratives about curry as "smelly" and "stinky" Indian food and Indian immigrant bodies as "curry smelling," the rest of this chapter explores how references to curry emerge in online spaces devoted specifically to the U.S. information technology and software industry, its workplace cultures, and its workforce. It focuses in particular on examples and descriptions from online discussion forums, news coverage, and social media references in which references to the labor and work cultures of immigrants are mediated by allusions to their food cultures—including the practices of cooking, packaging, and consumption of food.

Curry, I argue in this chapter, operates as a code—a metaphorical and covert form of representation—that produces a discourse about Indian immigrants as foreign, unwelcome, unwanted, yet nevertheless a lingering presence in the U.S. workplace. Curry hence functions as a metaphor for the "Indian" body that, in turn, becomes visible in time and space predominantly through the sense of smell. I further argue that the politics of curry in the information technology workplace makes the racialized minority location of Indian immigrants visible. In other words, curry marks the outsider status of the immigrant not just within the "national" framework ("Indian not American") but also within the racial hierarchies of American culture ("not white" and not a desirable "ethnic" group within multicultural United States).

The Politics of Reading Curry as Code

My intention behind reading curry as code is twofold. One, by considering how ideologies of race mediated through the metaphor of "ethnic" food operate within the U.S. software and information technology industries, one can help dismantle an long-abiding narrative about technological neutrality and, in particular, of digital technologies being inherently neutral.[7] In other words, a popular construct about software, computing, and digital code is that they are purely technical details based on mathematical calculation and algorithms. Questions relating to cultural politics, power relations, and ideological bias still continue to be popularly viewed as outside the realm of technology. A common idea we encounter in public discourse is that what we do with digital technology is cultural; technology per se, be it coding, software programming, or hardware, is about "neutral" facts and scientific truth. This myth of technological neutrality also helped shape a dominant discourse about the presumed neutrality of the U.S. software and IT industries that apparently were immune to the social and cultural divides in the rest of society. A good example of this discursive production is the stereotype about Silicon Valley as a place where only talent, ability, performance, and innovation are the prerequisites for success and recognition or, as one industry heavyweight puts it, "a natural meritocracy."[8] Such ideal and utopian images of Silicon Valley continue to circulate and abide despite a series of critical assessments of the gender, race, and class gaps in this so-called place of equal opportunity. In this context, reading curry as code for the racializing space of the technology workplace allows us to intervene critically into idealizations and decontextualized narratives about the people, places, and practices in the IT industry. Wendy Chun has argued that decoding race through software and, inversely, seeing software as racialized are particularly difficult because of two overlapping concepts: that, if it is not seen or made visible, race does not exist, and that software is a symbolic code, which cannot be made visible unless it is connected to hardware.[9] Chun's insight can be applied to the politics of curry, and particularly curry smells, in that much like software the smell cannot be made visible unless it is connected to the bodies of Indian Americans; through that, curry makes the racialized minority location of Indian Americans visible.

Two, my intention behind reading curry as code is also to consider how race and racism intersect with the construction of the United States and especially its (IT) workplaces as a vision of multiculturalism for the contemporary age. Indian immigrants are rendered as a "curry menace," a smelly horde of invaders, in many of the discussions online. Such representations must be understood within a larger historical context spanning the nineteenth and twentieth centuries, when Indian and Asian migrants were demonized as a "peril" and a "menace" to white, American national culture and citizens.[10] The curry menace imagery is then a contemporary take on a historical imaginary that has shaped hegemonic U.S. culture's interaction with its Asian "Other."

Here, a crucial element is the role of "curry" as a symbol for Indian identity. While curry is popularly considered a cornerstone of "authentic" Indian food, it is actually a British colonial invention.[11] While Indian cuisine uses a variety of spices or masalas, and the proportion of the different spices varies based on the dish, the British version of curry relied on offering a standard, fixed mixture of spices—and authenticating it as quintessentially Indian. Scholars examining the politics of food in colonial and post-colonial contexts have noted that the fabricated version of curry assuming greater currency in the West is an expression of food imperialism, whereby the British who colonized India were able to shape the production and dissemination of an English invention and offer it as "authentic Indian food." The production of the curry menace image in American work spaces with a heavy Indian immigrant presence thus reveals the new pathways whereby issues of cultural difference, ethnic identity, labor, race, and nationalism are being imagined and negotiated from a conservative, neoimperial American perspective.

Curry Racism: Targeting the Indian IT Professional on the H-1B Visa

Dice (www.dice.com) is a career website for technology professionals in the United States that was created in 1990, the same year the U.S. Citizenship and

Immigration Services created the H-1B visa program. *Dice* has been described as the "most prominent site in the Silicon Valley high-tech recruiting industry"[12] in one account and is popularly viewed as a leading resource for locating jobs and information about hiring companies in the IT sector. The site's discussion forum, "Tech Talk" is a particularly interesting space to explore the themes covered in this chapter because, while the intention behind most posts are to discuss jobs, the labor market, or company management, they often lead to significant debates about the politics of hiring immigrants, the relationship between U.S. immigration policies and job scarcity for American workers, and the highly competitive software industry, where one needs to constantly hone's one skills to keep one's job.[13] The Indian technology professional working in the United States for an American company and doing so while being on the temporary work visa known as the H-1B is a frequently referred to in the posts.

The H-1B visa program's inauguration at the beginning of the 1990s decade was shaped by an urgent need to accommodate U.S. demands for specialized foreign labor in several sectors. In this period, the sectors that were booming and creating unprecedented demand were technology, science, and medicine related.[14] Although it is a temporary, non-immigrant visa that could be availed upon for a maximum of six years, the H-1B is also a dual-intent visa, which means that persons who are allotted the H-1B visa and enter the United States can come in with another intention, namely to become immigrants, provided their U.S. employers can sponsor their transition from temporary H-1B visa holders to permanent residents (green card holders) and legal immigrants.[15]

During the 1990s–2000s period, the H-1B category became increasingly associated with information and software sectors of labor in the United States while the Indian male "techie" became the dominant symbol of the H-1B visa holder as well as the symbolic face of the United States's immigrant workforce in Silicon Valley and other centers of technological innovation, such as the Boston, New York's Silicon Alley, and Austin's Silicon Hills.[16] Over the years, the H-1B visa has been allotted to Indian nationals more than any other national group. Indians dominate the H-1B visa category by receiving approximately half of all the visas allotted annually; for example, of the 269,653 H-1B visas issued in 2011, Indian citizens received 156,317, or 58 percent of the total visas allotted.[17] Although the U.S. Congress had in the past issued an annual cap of 65,000 H-1B visas, the actually allotted numbers have fluctuated quite a bit, especially during the 2000s (e.g., 217,340 in 2003 and 287,418 in 2004).[18] While during the 1990s, fears of the Year 2000 problem (Y2K) ensured a steady increase in the number of H-1B visas issued to foreign workers—most of whom, not surprisingly, were involved in the fields of computing and information technologies—the 2000s have highlighted increasing tensions among legislative, political, and industry (especially the IT industry) bodies over the continuing influx of the kind of foreign labor attracted by the H-1B policy.[19] In its twenty-four-year history, the H-1B has been subject to several reforms and amendments. In 2015, when immigration reform was yet again a primary topic of congressional hearings, the H-1B visa and proposed changes to its structure were at the center of a national debate.

In this context, the linking of Indian professionals on the H-1B visa to their curry-eating habits, *Dice*'s "Tech Talk'"'s threads that are ostensibly about technology or IT jobs is very illuminating. In 2012, Indian American entrepreneur Vivek Wadhwa's book, *The Immigrant Exodus: Why America Is Losing the Global Race to Capture Entrepreneurial Talent*, made an ominous prediction that the United States will no longer be able to attract the best entrepreneurial minds from around the world if it continued to sustain policies that were anti-immigrant. In the book, Wadhwa advocates for H-1B visa reform by suggesting that the visa quota be increased rather than decreased (as many critics of the H-1B were suggesting) and, furthermore, for giving the H-1B visa holder a greater number of incentives to continue to stay in the United States. Wadhwa's narrative, echoed by industry stalwarts like Bill Gates, entirely rejects the notion that the H-1B is an anti-American policy and instead seeks to argue that the United States will suffer a "brain drain" (a depletion of intellectual and knowledge capital) if it does not act quickly to retain the large incoming foreign labor force. Not surprisingly, the book's key arguments drew the attention and, in some cases, the ire of discussants on "Tech Talk" forums.[20] While many discussants stated that they disagreed with the book's conclusions, one member, noting that Vivek Wadhwa an Indian American who was writing about a visa program that favored Indians, offered the following title as more appropriate to convey the book's key points: "My Pet Goat. 101 recipes for goat curry, and how to really annoy your co-workers by putting such culinary creations into a microwave oven and subsequently destroying said microwave oven and causing the building to evacuate."[21] Derailing a thread that is a serious conversation about policy issues, economic realities, and labor-market fluctuations and redirecting it via an outburst to the food cultures and eating practices of Indian workers is a very common strategy adopted by forum participants who advocate a very staunch culturally nationalist position of American capital and economy despite the realities of global capital, information, and labor flows. These members frequently remind the forum participants at large that American jobs are for American citizens; from their perspective, an immigrant workforce only depletes the resources of the American economy rather than contributing to it. In this line of thought, immigrant workers weaken the role of the American nation and jeopardize the prospects of American workers to be employed and to secure a competitive salary. No surprise, then, that when Groupon announced its plans to recruit a hundred engineers from Silicon Valley in 2012, there was considerable criticism of the company's move by forum members.[22] One participant dubbed it a "world-wide Indian conspiracy," and noted that Groupon would probably use the H-1B visa category to allot the new jobs, which in turn would end up being given to Indian men. Another member introduced the term "H-1B army" as a gesture of solidarity with the discussants who called attention to a sense of feeling besieged by a combination of factors—job scarcity because of a slow economy and the growing Indian labor force that is being courted with plum jobs courtesy of the H-1B visa policy. It was not too long before the motif of an invasion by large numbers of immigrants was tied to an image of curry as weapon of mass destruction, as the following post reveals: "Lord knows they have a cache of chemical weapons. Anyone who's ever smelled that god awfull curry . . . they indiscriminately throw in a microwave knows what I'm talking about."[23] Curry here is equated to a toxic, deadly chemical that would inflict great harm, even annihilate the human bodies of "American" workers. The simultaneous presence of curry and Indians is deemed as nothing short of a peril to American workers who rightfully belong in the American workplace.

Similarly, in a post from 2010, the peril narrative is constructed through a discussion about the "filthy habits" of Indian co-workers in IT firms. The original post featured a link to a media report that suggests that H-1B workers in the United States are "virtually enslaved."[24] The report notes that H-1B visa holders are often overworked and underpaid but cannot really complain because they would then jeopardize their jobs and ultimately their immigrant status. H-1B visa holders cannot secure a job on their own; they need to find a U.S. company that is willing to sponsor their stay in the United States. They remain legally in status in the United States only as long as they are sponsored employees; this precarious arrangement in turn keeps H-1B visa holders chained to the exploitative labor practices of contemporary capitalism. The language of indentured labor, servitude, and corporate slaveholders is repeatedly used online to bolster the case for a more open labor and immigration rule structure governing the H-1B category. On the "Tech Talk" forum, however, while some members tried to offer a rationale for reference to virtual enslavement, for others, it offered an opportunity to redirect the metaphor and position themselves as the group being threatened. While for one member the presence of Indians is nothing less than an "infestation," for another having Indian co-workers gives rise to the feeling of being trapped. While arguably the underlying message is one of suffocation (or fear of) as a result of shared intimacy of work life with H-1B visa professionals, it is expressed through their encounter with Indian curry. Noting that Indians take long lunch breaks "with 20 [other] Indians," the respondent connects his sense of feeling trapped to the fact that the smell of curry never leaves the office building, "as the windows are sealed."[25] This notion that, while Indian workers leave the building at the end of their working day, the smells and odors associated with them—notably curry—never leave but linger is remarkably similar to examples (cited earlier) in which new tenants complain about the unrelenting presence of Indian tenants who had lived in those spaces previously. Even though the Indian immigrant in both instances is not physically inhabiting a place at the time, reminders of his past presence (a previous tenant) or of his continual presence (gone at the end of the working day but will be back the next day) are created through an olfactory memory.

On a site like *Dice*, along with other related job boards such as *Cafepharma* (www.cafepharma.com), a job and discussion board for the medical and pharmaceutical industries, the association of Indians with H-1B armies and the smell of curry is reiterated so often that the use of "curry" seems like a code word, a word whose meaning, the posters assume, is common knowledge. Indeed, the use of "curry" in a racist, pejorative way is very widespread and prolific online. *Urban Dictionary*, which gave us the term "stindian," offers definitions for over a hundred variations of the term "curry." The site, once listed by *Time* magazine as one of the top fifty websites in the United States,[26] defines "curry" as a referent for both Indian food and an Indian person. "Curry muncher" is described as both a person who eats a lot of curry and as an insult to a person of Indian origin. The term frequently appears in racist content online along with other racist epithets such as "curry head" and "curry town." Other variations of the term indicate that, in addition to racist interpretations of curry, there are explicit sexual, patriarchal, and elitist meanings attached to it. In a 2011 weblog about San Diego's technology industry, which suggested that the city was a financially rewarding place for technology workers, an anti-immigrant response cynically suggested that the returns are going to an Indian outsourcing firm and "its curry eating buddies."[27] When another poster challenged the comment's underlying racism, the respondent asserted that "the comment about the curry smell can be verified as fact by anyone who has had to work around a shop where there are a clan of H-1B Indians employed. It indeed DOES smell like curry and it's pretty annoying to the nose of people not acclimated to it."[28] Additionally, the poster urged forum members to conduct an online search with the phrase "indian smell like curry" and witness for oneself how pervasive the distaste for curry and Indians who smell like it is.

The association of filth, stink, distaste, threat, and uncouth hordes with the figure of the Indian immigrant professional in the IT industry contributes to the building up of a discourse of the "curry menace." In fact, following the unprecedented influx of Indian professionals into Silicon Valley in the 1990s and early 2000s, a reporter making a case for thinly veiled racism among the digerati in the Bay Area argued that the swarming armies of technology workers from India are perceived as nothing less than a "curry menace."[29] Though the reporting was focused on addressing why people in the IT world were being racist toward Indian engineers, it concludes that "technology workers who heap scorn on their Indian counterparts aren't necessarily doing it because they think Indians are racially inferior. More to the point, they're pissed off because strangers are taking their jobs away—strangers who didn't go to the same schools as they did and grew up in places they can't locate on a map."[30] In other words, people who are

CURRY AS CODE: FOOD, RACE, AND TECHNOLOGY | 271

not from "here." While the problematic of racial inferiority cannot be addressed, let alone solved, by the simple assertion that it doesn't appear to exist (as the reporter's quick dismissal of the racial hierarchy seems to indicate), the narrative in this article points to a common strategy in mainstream culture in which underlying issues of racial and cultural difference and racism are displaced onto economic factors or hegemonic imaginations of the familiar space of (national) belonging. I argue here that what is threatening or menacing has perhaps less to do with fear of losing one's job and more to do with losing one's sense of the familiar, dominant mythology of who and what belongs within the American nation. The encounter with the racial Other results in deploying the difference as a presence that is overwhelming but cannot be tolerated—it is a menace that needs to be removed. Furthermore, in resorting to a food metaphor that stereotypically renders Indian immigrants as foreign and "ethnic," the discursive politics of "curry menace" connects with a longer history of racist and Orientalist constructions of Indian and South Asian labor in the United States. In the early 1900s, popular national magazines such as *Collier's* and *Forum* featured reports in which Sikhs working in lumber mills and railroad construction on the West Coast were regarded as a "Hindu invasion" and a "horde of Hindus." One oft-cited report, "The Tide of Turbans," describes Sikhs as "swarms of swarthy people from the ancient lands of the Orient" and a "threatening inundation of Hindoos over the Pacific Coast."[31] Racist terms such as "turban heads," "towel heads," and "rag heads," which have gained greater currency in the United States after the attacks of September 2001, were widely used in the early twentieth century to present the Sikh laborer as both racially "inferior" but also threatening. "Curry menace," in this context, offers a new take on racist representations of Indian immigrant labor. As with references to the "Hindoo invasion" in the 1900s, references to curry as a menace as a result of the influx of Indian IT workers must be understood as a deployment of a cultural sign of the racial Other, whose presence cannot be tolerated by normative, white American culture.

"Ethnic" Lunches in "American" Offices

As the presence of Indian immigrants in the U.S. workforce threatens national and racial hierarchies underpinning the idea of "America," we find that discussions about bringing "ethnic" foods as office lunches are quite prolific online. The conversations surrounding such topics often rest on deciding whether it is appropriate to bring certain foods that are fine to eat at home out into the public. These dialogues give us an insight into how cultural anxieties and struggles exist within the multicultural office environments of the IT industry, quite contrary to the utopian images associated with them.

Ideal narratives about leading technology firms such as Google and Microsoft (also leading employers of Indian immigrants on the H-1B visa, by the way!), for example, emphasize the global and ethnically diverse cuisine served in their office cafeterias while also suggesting that the diversity of food is an acknowledgment of the different cultural backgrounds of the companies' workforce.[32] While mainstream media coverage applauds the multicultural kitchen of the Googleplex, articles like the one titled "Why Your Co-worker's Smelly Lunch Makes You Feel Bad" on *The Kitchn* blog remind us that there is a lot more to the story than company-sponsored free lunches. The article concludes that "smelling other's lunches in the office can make people feel as if they have 'lost control over their personal environment.'" While the article lists fish and burritos as the leading "smelly foods that get the most complaints," it frames the story visually by including an picture of Indian curry. One also finds online a number of think pieces that reflect on the fact that increasingly lunch in the office means eating lunch at the desk and, therefore, "one person's food choices can affect everyone."[33]

On the technology forum *AnandTech*, a member with a post titled "Apparently, I Am "THAT Guy" (Food Smell in Cafeteria)" asked fellow discussants to weigh in on an incident in which heating curry in the office microwave solicited disapproval from the member's co-workers.[34] While not identifying himself racially, the member mentioned that the food was cooked by his Indian girlfriend; likewise, while not identifying the race of the disapproving co-workers, the member nevertheless indicated that they were American—a conclusion one can make based on his remark that "funny how the Arabs, Indians and other foreign coworkers don't mind and some even came over to ask and compliment how delicious the food smelled." The member also confided that his desire to poll the forum community on this issue was triggered when his sister "also" thought that "I have no consideration for my coworkers and I should bring in something 'less offensive.'" The community's response ranged from reiterating that the post member was indeed "that guy," to earnest discussions of what smells might work better in an office environment, to encouraging him to ignore the haters in the office. Others offered deeper readings of the debates over office lunches. One member noted that the different food smells reminded the "haters" of their expectations "to actively preserve the little bubble of purity that they carry around with them, or believe they do. That they have some kind of right to live as if no one else exists in the world." Another member viewed the olfactory resistance as "Americans [being] resistant to new things from other cultures" while cynically adding that since "most Americans eat cold sandwiches for lunch, microwave smells remind them of their poor lunch choice."

The following view by another user foregrounds a commonly expressed argument that immigrants need to leave their "ethnic" food at home when they go to work. "You are definitely in the wrong; you are at work, this is not your house. We have actually had HR put signs up in an attempt to dissuade this problem and they have even had to speak to certain people specifically." The cultural politics of such censure is made more apparent in the following post, which states, "You don't have a right to invade the whole area with your nasty fish and curry smell. It isn't a cultural norm here." As the conversations got increasingly unreserved (with one mini-thread comparing the act of heating curry to be as rude as farting in public), one post offered that U.S. citizens unhappy in the IT industry because of the "curry" factor should to "switch over to the arms industry [in which] there is plenty of work for software developers [and because] those jobs usually require US citizenship with ties to foreign government/corporations. As a result, non-American cuisine in the break room should be very rare, unless you count Panda Express, Taco Bell, and Olive Garden." The inclusion of three popular and commercially successful food chains that serve Americanized ethnic food (Chinese, Tex-Mex and Italian, respectively) brings into sharp focus the use of food as code for imagining a national "authentic" American culture or a hybridized version that can be safely incorporated (and Americanized) within the multicultural "melting pot."

Conclusion

Food is mostly understood as an embodied, sensorial experience, while technology is often stereotypically understood in terms of the machinic, the disembodied, and—in the age of computing—as code. Yet when we encounter the use of curry as a referent for Indian technology workers, we witness the mapping of a sensorially charged subjective field of understanding (I eat, smell, touch, see, and feel curry) onto a community of immigrant workers in the information industry who, it is not unreasonable to say, are rendered as "virtual" subjects. Working behind the machine, writing software, and populating the offices of high-tech companies, they are mostly understood in popular culture as stereotypes—the Indian who is a programmer, an IT technician, or software consultant. They are, in this context, rendered virtual, and not real, because mainstream culture (including the IT world) rarely recognizes them as embodied subjects with lived culture and everyday practices. Although mainstream America needs its immigrant workforce to keep the digital capitalist system working smoothly, it is as if it will not be forced into a serious engagement with what that association means for its shifting cultural identity. The presence of a transnational labor force in the United States changes not just the political and financial domains of work but also, and perhaps most crucially, the cultural and social dimensions of work cultures and workplace practices. As the various examples discussed in this chapter tell us, while immigrant labor can be represented invisible in popular accounts of the information technology industry, their food is what seems to make them suddenly "real" and visible. And it is precisely at this point of putting the two together—"real" food and "virtual" workers—that a sharp expression of the theme of race and difference in the contemporary United States emerges.

Curry, I argue, is a very crucial code for the racialized Indian immigrant in the information economy, a code that illuminates a larger picture about belonging and exclusion for Indian immigrants in the United States.

NOTES

1 *Urban Dictionary*, s.v. "stindian," http://www.urbandictionary.com, accessed January 10, 2008.

2 *Urban Dictionary*, http://www.urbandictionary.com.

3 *Urban Dictionary*, s.v. "stindian."

4 For example, "Why Do Indian People Always Smell Like Curry, without Fail?" *Yahoo! Answers*, n.d., http://answers.yahoo.com/question/index? qid=20101102024723AAQ8pC7.

5 See, e.g., "Being Charged $100 for 'Curry Smell' by Landlord at End of Lease (Foreclosure, Hotel)," *City-Data*, May 4, 2009, http://www.city-data.com/forum/new-jersey/636479-being -charged-100-curry-smell-landlord-11.html, accessed April 13, 2011.

6 "Bad Room Repairs and Smells like Curry 24/7," *TripAdvisor*, December 7, 2009, http://www .tripadvisor.com/ShowUserReviews-g55769-d124472-r50819283-Econo_Lodge-Dumas_ Texas.html, accessed January 3, 2014.

7 An early excellent critique of the notion of technological neutrality in the field of computer science is Abbe Mowshowitz, "Computers and the Myth of Neutrality," in *Proceedings of the ACM* [Association for Computing Machinery] *Twelfth Annual Computer Science Conference and SIGCSE* [Special Interest Group on Computer Science Education] *Symposium* (New York: Association for Computing Machinery,1984), 85–92, available through the ACM Digital Library (paywall), http://dl.acm.org/citation.cfm?id=808144 , accessed February 22, 2013.

8 Peter Bell, quoted in Andrew Keen, "Keen on . . . Peter Bell: Yes, Silicon Valley Is a Natural Meritocracy (TCTV)," *TechCrunch*, November 10, 2011, http://techcrunch.com/2011/11/10/ keen-on-peter-bell-yes-silicon-valley-is-a-natural-meritocracy-tctv, accessed April 1, 2014.

9 Wendy Chun, "Race and Software," in *Alien Encounters: Popular Culture in Asian America*, ed. Mimi Thi Nguyen and Thuy Linh Nguyen Tu (Durham, NC: Duke University Press, 2007), 304–333.

10 See Ronald Takaki, *Strangers from a Different Shore: A History of Asian Americans* (Boston: Little, Brown, 1989).

11 Uma Narayan, *Dislocating Cultures: Identities, Traditions and Third World Feminism* (New York: Routledge, 1997).

12 Chris Benner, *Work in the New Economy: Flexible Labor Markets in Silicon Valley* (Malden, MA: Wiley-Blackwell, 2002), 120.

13 Since I wrote this, *Dice* has moved the "Tech Talk" discussion forums to a sister site, *Slashdot* (http://slashdot.org); it appears that the organization of content has changed in the wake of the website change, and this information may no longer be available.

14 U.S. Citizenship and Immigration Services, Department of Homeland Security, "H-1B Specialty Occupations, DOD Cooperative Research and Development Project Workers, and Fashion Models," http://www.uscis.gov/working-united-states/temporary-workers/h-1b -specialty-occupations-dod-cooperative-research-and-development-project-workers-and -fashion-models, accessed September 7, 2011.

15 Ibid.

16 See Anna Lee Saxenian, "Silicon Valley's New Immigrant Entrepreneurs" (San Francisco: Public Policy Institute of California, June 1999), http://www.ppic.org/content/pubs/report/ R_699ASR.pdf, accessed October 14, 2015.

17 U.S. Citizenship and Immigration Services, "Characteristics of H-1B Specialty Occupation Workers: Fiscal Year 2011 Annual Report to Congress, October 1, 2010–September 30, 2011" (Washington, DC: U.S. Department of Homeland Security, March 12, 2012), 7, http://www.uscis.gov/sites/default/files/USCIS/Resources/Reports%20and%20Studies/H-1B/h1b-fy-11-characteristics.pdf, accessed November 3, 2015.

18 U.S. Citizenship and Immigration Services, "Characteristics of Specialty Occupation Workers (H1-B): Fiscal Year 2004" (Washington, DC: U.S. Department of Homeland Security, November 2006), http://www.uscis.gov/sites/default/files/USCIS/Resources/Reports%20and%20Studies/H-1B/h1b_fy04_characteristics.pdf, accessed November 3, 2015.

19 Christine M. Matthews, "Foreign Science and Engineering Presence in U.S. Institutions and the Labor Force" (Washington, DC: Congressional Research Service, October 28, 2010), https://www.fas.org/sgp/crs/misc/97-746.pdf, accessed October 14, 2015.

20 Vivek Wadhwa, *The Immigrant Exodus: Why America Is Losing the Global Race to Capture Entrepreneurial Talent* (Philadelphia: Wharton Digital Press, 2012).

21 "Tech Talk: Mr Wadhwa Wrote a Book," *Dice*, n.d., http://techtalk.dice.com/t5/Tech-Nation-Discussion/Mr-Wadhwa-Wrote-a-Book/m-p/313246/highlight/true#M47671, accessed September 13, 2013.

22 "Tech Talk: Groupon Is Hiring an Army of Engineers in Silicon Valley," *Dice*, http://techtalk.dice.com/t5/Tech-Nation-Discussion/Groupon-Is-Hiring-An-Army-Of-Engineers-In-Silicon-Valley/m-p/295118/highlight/true#M42481, accessed December 10, 2012.

23 Ibid.

24 "Tech Talk: H1B Workers Virtually Enslaved in Silicon Valley," *Dice*, http://techtalk.dice.com/t5/Tech-Nation-Discussion/H1B-Workers-Virtually-Enslaved-in-Silicon-Valley/td-p/200349/highlight/true/page/2, accessed December 10, 2012.

25 Ibid.

26 *Time*, "50 Best Websites, 2008," http://content.time.com/time/specials/2007/article/0,28804,1809858_1809955_1811527,00.html, accessed November 3, 2015.

27 Don Bauder, "Comparatively, Tech Workers Haul in Bucks in San Diego," *San Diego Reader*, January 6, 2011, http://www.sandiegoreader.com/weblogs/financial-crime-politics/2011/jan/06/comparatively-tech-workers-haul-in-bucks-in-san-di, accessed May 2, 2012.

28 Ibid.

29 Annalee Newitz, "The Curry Menace," *AlterNet*, July 14, 2003, http://www.alternet.org/story/16410/the_curry_menace, accessed January 11, 2012.

30 Ibid.

31 Herman Scheffauer, "The Tide of Turbans," *Forum* 43 (June 1910): 616–618.

32 See Adam Roberts, "Lunch at the Googleplex," *Amateur Gourmet*, October 22, 2012, http://www.amateurgourmet.com/2012/10/lunch-at-the-googleplex.html, accessed December 17, 2013.

33 Anjali Prasertong, "Why Your Co-worker's Smelly Lunch Makes You Feel Bad," *The Kitchn*, http://www.thekitchn.com/why-your-coworkers-smelly-lunc-154564, August 8,2011, accessed January 7, 2013.

34 "Apparently, I Am 'THAT Guy' (Food Smell in Cafeteria),"*AnandTech Forums*, http://forums.anandtech.com/archive/index.php/t-2202823.html, accessed December 17, 2012.

18

Bollywood's 9/11

Terrorism and Muslim Masculinities in Popular Hindi Cinema

DEEPTI MISRI

Why should we attend to "Bollywood's 9/11," as this chapter proposes we do?[1] The global reach and impact of Bollywood cinema is by now well known: The most popular film industry in the world, Bollywood films famously command massive audiences not only across India but also among South Asian diasporic audiences as well as other viewers in the United States, the United Kingdom, the Middle East, Australia, and Canada, as well as East Africa and Southeast Asia. These facts, combined with the indisputably global impact of 9/11 itself—over a decade of war in Afghanistan and Iraq, the widespread conflation and vilification of Arabs, Muslims, and brown people (men, in particular), and the indefinite detention of hundreds of such men without trial in the U.S.-run Guantanamo Bay prison—compel an examination of how this powerful domain of Hindi cinema has represented the events of 9/11 to its vast global audiences, whose cultural comprehension of this global historical event should certainly be of as much interest to us as our own.

Bollywood cinema offers a perspective on 9/11 that is not available in either U.S. mainstream media or that other cinematic behemoth known as Hollywood. Transnational feminists have observed how U.S. media coverage after 9/11 "focused exclusively on losses suffered by white, middle-class, heterosexual families even though those who died or were injured include many people of different races, classes, sexualities, and religions and of at least ninety different nationalities."[2] Popular Hollywood films about 9/11 have reproduced these erasures. Films ranging from *United 93* (2006), to *Reign over Me* (2007), to *Zero Dark Thirty* (2012) have been at best uninterested in the impact of 9/11 on non-white subjects in America. At worst, as several critics noted of *Zero Dark Thirty*, they have been "neutral" or even validating of the U.S. state's interrogation techniques that landed hundreds of innocent South Asian and Middle Eastern men in U.S. prisons in the hunt for Osama bin Laden. Bollywood cinema has presented a significant counterweight to these representations, exploring the aftermath of 9/11 from the minority perspective of immigrant South Asians and South Asian Americans in the United States.

In this chapter we will closely consider one Bollywood blockbuster, Kabir Khan's *New York* (2009), a thriller centering broadly on a Muslim-led terror plot to bomb a federal building in New York City. Released and reviewed in India as well as the United States, *New York* is one of a handful of recent films from South Asia that explore the experiences of South Asian Muslim men in the United States, who after 9/11 were subject to large-scale illegal detentions under the Patriot Act. Declared a box-office hit in its opening week, *New York* performed well in both the Indian and overseas markets, faring particularly well in the Middle East. It was the opening film at the Cairo International Film Festival that year and was reported to have also circulated widely in pirated form in Syria, Jordan, Egypt, and Saudi Arabia, countries from which large numbers of U.S. detainees hailed. As a point of comparison, we will also consider *Kurbaan*, another post-9/11 film from the same year, also set in the United States, but one that evinces certain stock Islamophobic tropes that *New York* expressly attempts to avoid.[3] Unlike *New York*, *Kurbaan* was declared a definite flop despite favorable reviews by some Indian critics. Rather than simply understanding *New York* as a "good" example compared with *Kurbaan*, we will see how both films offer resolutions that reinscribe the conditionality of Muslim male belonging in the nation-state, albeit to different degrees. Yet, if we read closely, we may find within *New York* some signs of discontent that contradict the terms of minority integration seemingly endorsed by the film.

New York: Recasting Post-9/11 Media Tropes

Like the later film *My Name Is Khan* (2010), and to some extent the earlier Pakistani film *Khuda Ke Liye* (2007), *New York* sets out to problematize the criminalization of Muslim masculinities in post-9/11 U.S. discourse while seeking to reintegrate these subjectivities through the production of "good" Muslims. In the course of this attempt, *New York* speaks to some key tropes through which cultural anxieties about Muslims in general and Muslim men in particular have been managed in both the U.S. and Indian nationalist discourse, often in remarkably similar ways.[4] In particular, two dominant tropes in U.S. media discourse following 9/11 were the "drama of nationalist domesticity," in which U.S. national community was repeatedly cast in the image of the white heterosexual family, and the figuring of the Muslim terrorist as a primitive, monstrous, and sexually deviant "monster-terrorist-fag."[5] These tropes resonate in significant ways with the depiction of the Muslim terrorist in Bollywood cinema. The Hindu family has, of course, long served to model the nation in Bombay cinema, also emblematizing what is under threat from Islamist terrorism. In *Aamir* (2008), for example, as the suit-wearing, educated "good Muslim" protagonist considers whether to follow the terrorist's orders to place a bomb on a bus, the camera focuses repeatedly on a bindi-wearing mother and her son—the iconic image of what is at stake.[6] Aamir decides to sacrifice himself and save those on the bus, in a resolution that confirms Shahnaz's claim that "the only acceptable Muslim man in the increasingly nationalist India is a dead one."[7]

While the second trope, that of the terrorist's sexual deviance, has not always characterized the Muslim terrorist in Hindi cinema, it appears to have traveled. In Khan's earlier film *Kabul Express* (2006), for example, we hear a joke about the homosexual proclivities of the Taliban within minutes of the opening frames. In *Khuda Ke Liye* (a Pakistani film, but sharing many of the same formal features and audiences as Bollywood cinema) the innocent Mansoor, when asked yet again in interrogation, "What is your relation with Osama bin Laden?" replies in frustration: "I don't know. Maybe he's gay and he likes me?" Such moments evince a knowingness in South Asian cinematic discourse about this particular American trope of Afghan/Muslim/terrorist (these being frequently conflated categories) sexual deviance.

New York recasts these twin tropes via two formal maneuvers. First, the film routes the main terror plot through a device familiar from the Bollywood buddy film genre: the heterosexual love triangle featuring an intense male friendship (*dosti*). Second, the film reworks what some critics have called the "cinepatriotic genre" in Hindi cinema.[8] Much like the post-9/11 media discourse in the United States, Hindi cinema's cinepatriotic genre sorts good Muslims from bad Muslims via the figure of the Muslim terrorist, while using the heterosexual family as a template for citizenship. *New York* fuses and adapts these genres in order to rescript the figure of the Muslim terrorist *through* a particular management of Muslim male sexualities. This attempt brings the film to an unusual resolution, both to the erotic triangle and to the film itself—an imperfectly "queer" resolution that is connected to the film's project of reintegrating alienated Muslim masculinities into U.S. national space.

Love, *Dosti*, and 9/11

Ten minutes into *New York*, we are introduced to the buff John Abraham, one of Hindi cinema's best-known stars and its only Christian male star, playing the role of an Indian-born, all-American college student named (of course) Sam. Sam is first shown embarking on an "annual challenge," a furious footrace with another student who is white, blonde, and male. The two men set off, bounding across hallways, lunchrooms, and terraces, clearing hurdles on their way to the finish. Even when held back physically by his white opponent, Sam pushes forward smilingly. Cheered on by a largely white college crowd, as well as the Indian-American Maya (the film's female lead) and the fresh-off-the-boat Indian student Omar, the two men finally disappear into a tower, out of sight. As we look on at the empty tower, a brown hand emerges into sight, takes hold of a rope, and gradually raises the American flag as the crowd cheers wildly below.

This spectacular display of patriotism is an early cue to Sam's eventually revealed Muslim identity, for the scene draws on a tradition of sentimental representations of Indian Muslims in Hindi cinema in which that otherwise "undecidable" figure is called upon to ritually perform national loyalties that cannot simply be taken for granted.[9] This idyllic moment of Sam's patriotic triumph is situated firmly within a flashback narrative, recounted by Sam's onetime friend Omar in a police lockup. Arrested under false charges at the very beginning of the film under the Patriot Act, Omar (a distinctly Muslim name) is being interrogated by Roushan, another South Asian Muslim man working with the FBI. It is as Omar reconstructs his memories of Sam for Roushan that we learn that "Sam" is short for Samir Shaikh, a Muslim terror suspect sought by the FBI. The moment this is revealed, the significance of the flag race comes more fully into focus: Could this uber-integrated South Asian man possibly be a terrorist, or is he an innocent patriot, scapegoated by the FBI like his friend Omar?

The scene ends with the first triangulation between the main players in the love triangle: the uber-masculine, all-assimilated Indian American Sam; the shy, newly arrived Indian Muslim student Omar; and semi-assimilated Indian American woman Maya (whose unmarked communal status through the film betrays a distressing elision of the effects of racial profiling for South Asian women). Descending from the flag tower, Sam flirtatiously solicits a hug from Maya; rebuffed, he turns to Omar, lifting the smaller man off the ground in a bear hug. When the fresh-off-the-boat Omar introduces himself with the words "I've just come," Sam replies with cosmopolitan wit: "What, with just a hug?" The joke "outs" the multidirectional libidinal energies that sustain the first half of the film. Just as Maya flirts playfully with both men, the latter also arguably romance each other in ways both secret and open, through the many other codes that cinema employs to disguise and reveal the "secret politics of our desires."[10] At the same time, the explicit reference to homosexuality also serves to mark Sam as a modern Muslim subject, running against popular attributions of Muslim conservatism and homophobia in the United States. Indeed, one of the narrative arcs of *New York* concerns the transformation of Omar into a properly cosmopolitan modern Muslim subject who can be assimilated into the nation.

In the erotic triangle that quickly forms, although Maya is ostensibly the common object of male desire, it is Sam who occupies the apex of that triangle, as evoked in that early scene where Sam stands heroically atop the flag tower, as Omar and Maya watch admiringly from the lawns below. In representing the evolving friendship and romance between Sam, Omar, and Maya, *New York* replays several conventions well familiar from the buddy film, which critics have often identified as a genre that has always simmered with homoerotic potential.[11] In both Bollywood and Hollywood cinema, this genre typically entails an idealization of male homosocial bonds, or *dosti*, combined with marginal heterosexual pursuit and palpable misogyny. What distinguishes the Bollywood buddy genre, however, is its rootedness in conventions that historically have barely distinguished between romantic love and friendship. As Shohini Ghosh reminds us, "Bombay cinema rarely represents romance through sexual explicitness. Therefore, the cinematic devices used to represent love are similar, even identical, to those depicting friendship."[12] As a result, friendship becomes readable as romantic love. This is the light in which we might consider the frequent embraces between Omar and Sam on the football field; Omar, the smaller man, at one point leaping jubilantly into the tall and well-built Sam's arms after scoring a touchdown, as the song "Hai Junoon" (There's a passion in the heart) plays in the background.

But notably, the queer dynamic between Sam and Omar becomes visible as a function not only of resistant spectatorial practices—whereby queer audiences pick out the sexual subtext in the manifest heterosexual narrative of a film—but also of what Thomas Waugh calls "winking semiotic play."[13] Waugh points to a growing sexual playfulness in the Bollywood buddy film in the nineties, in films like *Main Khiladi Tu Anari* (1994) which while adhering to heterosexual romance at the level of plot, "winked" at queer spectators via image, choreography, and song lyrics. *New York* similarly "winks" rather more openly today, repeatedly constructing the muscular Sam as "top" to Omar's "bottom" masculinity.[14] In one scene, a woozy Omar runs out of a bar following his bravado in drinking games and returns in a limp faint, borne in the manly arms of Sam. Thus the homoerotic vibes between Sam and Omar exist not merely in the queer eye but are being signaled actively on screen. On the football field, in the bar, and in Sam's sweeping embraces, the smaller Omar is humorously constructed as a feminized partner to the hyper-masculine Sam, as Maya watches on smilingly.

This multidirectional tapestry of desires is consolidated in the shadows of the twin towers and swiftly undone by 9/11. Visually and libidinally in the long-ish song sequence "Hai Junoon," the towers literally bind the trio together in an improbably idealized pre-9/11 past of perfect racial integration, youthful sexual energy, and hope. Throughout the song, Sam, Maya, and Omar play with their (white) American friends on the football field as the twin towers glisten as backdrop, walk amid the city's bright lights and tall skyscrapers, and finally end up at the song's conclusion sitting by the Hudson, the threesome framed against the city skyline at night facing the World Trade Center. If it seems surprising that the phallic pillars of capitalist patriarchy visually anchor the non-heteronormative bonding between three brown protagonists in America, it soon becomes clear that this can be the case only so long as that symbol of phallic power is fully erect. As long as the towers stand, the threesome holds together. As soon as the towers fall, however, the trio, too, disintegrates.

In the film, 9/11 comes about exactly as Omar begins to realize that Maya and Sam are in love with each other. It is as he questions Maya about this that a shriek is heard, and they both rush into a room, to hear the breaking news of

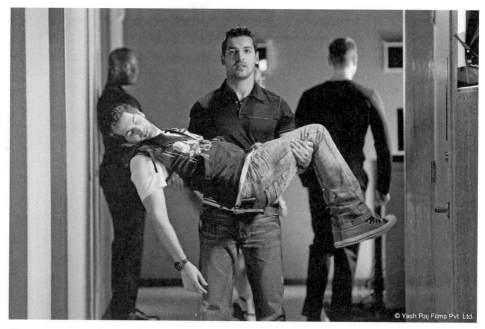

Figure 18.1. Omar presented through codes of "bottom" masculinity. Image courtesy of and copyright Yash Raj Films Pvt. Ltd. (www.yashrajfilms.com).

9/11 on television. The scene registers a dawning separation between the immigrant Omar, who remains standing at the liminal space of the doorway, and the other students in the room, most of all Sam and Maya. As the television anchors detail the events, and the image of the first plane crashing into the World Trade Center is seen, the shocked Maya, tearing up, leaves Omar's side, moving closer to the television but also toward Sam, seen standing nearby. As the second plane crashes into the second tower, the camera gives us a close-up of a white, blonde couple, the distressed but composed man supporting the openly weeping woman—before cutting back to Sam and Maya, establishing them as the mirror image of the white couple, at least in the way they respond to the event. Omar stands back, looking alternately at the explosions on TV, and then at Sam and Maya, locked in embrace with their backs to Omar.

The scene emphasizes their heterosexual convergence as simultaneous with the fall of the towers. If their grief draws Sam and Maya closer and also bonds them in identity to the collective grief of the students around them, Omar's separates him absolutely, from his closest friends as well as the community of mourners in the room. Nowhere is Omar's status as an outsider more explicitly marked than in this moment of national and heterosexual bonding. Cast outside the newly bonded American heterosexual dyad as they experience a moment of national crisis, Omar leaves the city for Philadelphia that very evening, breaking off all contact with them. As one suitor exits the scene and the trio falls apart,

Figure 18.2. Sam and Maya respond to 9/11. Omar stands in the liminal space of the doorway. Image courtesy of and copyright Yash Raj Films Pvt. Ltd. (www.yashrajfilms.com).

it seems that the love triangle has been brought to the predictable heterosexual resolution in a moment of national mourning. But even that does not survive in the aftermath of 9/11.

Terrorism, Muslim Masculinities, and Cinepatriotism

New York now takes a darker turn, drawing increasingly on conventions from the cinepatriotic genre. With Omar's departure from the city, we are now returned to the present, seven years after 9/11, back to the prison cell where Omar is pressured to spy on Sam. Under Roushan's close watch, Omar reunites with Sam and Maya (now married with a son named Danyal). Soon he learns, after some false leads, that the exemplary Sam *is* after all the terrorist the FBI had thought him to be.

The sudden revelation of the seemingly integrated Sam as Muslim terrorist risks reinforcing the troubling and widely criticized narrative of "going Muslim"—a phrase coined in 2009 by the New York University business professor Tunku Varadarajan to describe how "a seemingly integrated Muslim-American . . . discards his apparent integration into American society and elects to vindicate his religion in an act of messianic violence against his fellow Americans." The suggestion, therefore, was that every Muslim-American is a terrorist in the making.[15] This is complicated, however, soon after the film's intermission, when the narrative provides a detailed backstory for Sam's evolution from model citizen into "Muslim terrorist." This is a departure, it should be noted, from many other representations of terrorism in Bollywood, which give barely a nod (if at all) to the historical production of figures who appear as either heartless or misguided Muslim terrorists.

Here a comparison with the Muslim terrorist figure in *Kurbaan* is instructive. The "going Muslim" storyline is all too evident in *Kurbaan*, a film that also dips into an entrenched paranoid Hindu narrative in India, whereby hypervirile Muslim men trick Hindu women into love, marriage, and bearing Muslim children. Ehsaan, a flirtatious professor in New Delhi, pursues Avantika, a Hindu woman visiting from the United States and persuades her—against her initial resistance and the reservations of her father—into marrying him. Seemingly liberal, he offers generously to follow her back to the United States, where they move into a South Asian neighbourhood, next door to a sinister, domestic violence–prone Muslim family. Ehsaan's liberal façade is soon torn down as he is revealed to be in league with them, a terrorist who had tricked Avantika in order to gain papers to enter the United States and carry out a series of bombings.

Kurbaan's mapping of domestic violence onto terrorism trades wholeheartedly in the tropes of victimized Muslim women and abusive Muslim men that had been used to legitimize the U.S. invasion of Afghanistan in 2001.[16] Yet it also features some striking dialogues that voice opposition to the U.S. wars in Iraq and Afghanistan. Consider the debate in which the "good Muslim" American journalist Riyaz expresses a harsh and well-historicized critique of U.S. foreign policy at a public lecture by Ehsaan. It is a strangely ambivalent moment: While in the scene the xenophobic white students at the lecture appear incapable of acknowledging Muslim suffering, Riyaz is also simply rehearsing this line of argument only to win Ehsaan's trust and infiltrate his terrorist circle. His own loyalties to the U.S. military and nation-state have already been laid down in an earlier scene where he returns from Iraq and gives his girlfriend an account of losses suffered by U.S. troops, with no account whatsoever of civilian casualties in Iraq (these are later mentioned by his father, with whom Riyaz clearly disagrees).

Perhaps partly because of this scene, the Indian film critic Gaurav Malani counted *Kurbaan* among films on terror that take a "neutral stance on global terrorism." As Malani approvingly noted, "Though *Kurbaan* is sensitive towards the victimization of innocent Muslims (that might have provoked them towards terrorism), it doesn't focus on their detailed background accounts through extended flashbacks [as *New York* does]. *That saves the ordeal and it only makes sense to avoid the obvious*."[17] Arguably, such moments may paradoxically contain the very critique they articulate, whereby the devastation of the U.S. invasions are acknowledged precisely in order to be neutralized by an overall vision of monstrous, essentially violent Muslim others. Thus in *Kurbaan*, the acknowledgment of Afghan suffering is balanced out primarily through the device of burqa-clad women subjugated by their controlling and abusive terrorist menfolk, as they call out to the Hindu woman Avantika for rescue. Indeed the "balanced" picture of "American excesses" for which reviewers commended *Kurbaan* also lends credibility to the caricature of the misogynist Muslim terrorist family in that film.

Compared to *Kurbaan*—or, indeed, other Bollywood terror films like the 2006 *Fanaa*, the 2008 *Aamir*, and the 2008 *A Wednesday* (which acknowledge in passing the horrors suffered by Muslims in Kashmir, Afghanistan, Iraq, and within India)—*New York* presents the Muslim terrorist rather differently. First, it depicts, rather than simply glossing, the impact of state atrocities on Muslim men. Second, it traces the construction of the Muslim terrorist to the abuses of an authoritarian state in the aftermath of 9/11. In this it departs clearly from Varadarajan's framing of Muslim Americans as terrorists-in-waiting. *New York* puts on display the process of dis-integration through which once-integrated Muslim citizens become unhitched from the national imaginary *through* the gendered racial profiling of the U.S. state: the criminalization of Muslim men, their disappearance and illegal incarceration, and their torture and humiliation in custody based on perceptions of Muslim masculine subjectivities.

In this, *New York* both draws on and reworks what Amit Rai, following Manisha Sethi, identifies as the "cinepatriotic genre" in Hindi cinema. Within this genre, the figure of the "bad" Muslim terrorist becomes crucial for the production of "good" Muslim citizens by serving as a foil. Moreover, in this genre, the trope of the heterosexual family is mobilized to integrate the Muslim other into an ostensibly secular but really Hinduized India. On the surface, *New York* appears to replay stock cinepatriotic tropes by producing Sam as the misguided terrorist, positioning Omar and Maya as foils to the "bad Muslim," and drawing upon the minority woman (Maya) to anchor the misguided terrorist via the normalizing dream of the heterosexual family unit via marriage and childbearing. Despite these cinepatriotic impulses, however, *New York* cannot but also register the repeated *failure* of the heterosexual family to anchor the misguided Muslim terrorist—a failure that it traces explicitly to the interruptions of the state.

For instance, Sam traces his own path to terrorism back to the state's interruption of the just-begun romance with Maya. Ten days after 9/11, Sam recounts, he was picked up by the FBI at Union Station, on his way to visit Maya in Washington, DC. In a sequence of scenes visually referencing the abuses of Guantanamo and Abu Ghraib, we see a naked and bound Sam with a bag over his head, interrogated, falsely implicated, incarcerated, tortured, and humiliated in prison.[18] Finally he is released for lack of evidence, but he emerges from prison a broken man. The film mourns over his wounded masculinity as he fails to find a job and is plagued by the persistent trauma of his torture in prison. Maya's efforts to reintegrate him into "normal" family life via marriage and child bear little reward; Sam is able to enter a state of normalcy only in the brotherhood of men, when he joins a sleeper cell in Brooklyn. While women and family may offer the possibility of redemption to the misguided terrorist in a film like *Mission Kashmir* (dir. Vidhu Vinod Chopra, 2000)—where, as Rai observes, "secure heterosexuality [in the form of the terrorist's love interest Sufi] calls the liminal Muslim back from the edge of ruinous, monstrous violence into the folds of domesticity"—in *New York*, that attempt fails. Toward the film's ending, as Sam gets ready to detonate the FBI building, Maya arrives on the scene and attempts to dissuade him by reminding him of home and family. Although Sam drops the trigger, the FBI, breaking its promise to Maya, shoots at him, and Maya falls in the line of fire as well. Both die, as the state once again interrupts the heterosexual resolution that Sam and Maya had, like model citizens, attempted after 9/11.

Queering the Love Triangle

It is in its final moments that *New York* completes its unusual resolution to the heterosexual love triangle, as well as to the drama of the film at large. The final scene is set on a baseball field, and it establishes Omar as adoptive parent to Danyal, the son of the dead Sam and Maya. As Omar watches Danyal play and acknowledges the compliments of another parent in the bleachers, Roushan enters the picture and seats himself next to Omar, seeking a reconciliation. The exchange that follows is the last debate between the two characters, where, in the tradition of cinepatriotic films, the violence of the state is weighed against the violence of the terrorist. When Omar bitterly demands why the innocent Maya had been killed along with Sam, the indignant Roushan replies: "A Muslim child whose father was a terrorist is playing on an American team! *That* is what was achieved!" In addition to producing a fiction of seamless Muslim integration, Roushan's response also seems to suggest that, for Danyal to "play on the American team," Sam's death alone would not have been sufficient; Maya's removal was necessary, too.

And so it happens that Roushan and Omar are the last couple standing (in nearly identical beige jackets), marked as Danyal's new parents by their joint attendance at the baseball match in the company of other parents. The scene recalls an earlier moment in the film that also takes place on a baseball field, explicitly positioning Omar, Maya, and Danyal as the family that might have been. Indulging the young boy, Omar drops the ball after catching Danyal's pop fly—an avuncular concession that is noted by the beaming Maya, who has just been interrogating Omar about his still-single status. Omar jokingly reminds Maya of that "Hindi film scene" from years ago when Sam had run after a thief to retrieve Maya's bag and so won the girl, leaving Omar as the "side hero." Had Omar run after the thief, he would have been in Sam's place in this idyllic family. Omar's invocation of the Hindi film love formula here primes the viewer to anticipate how the situation might end once the main hero steps out of the picture: Will Maya be handed over to Omar, in the tradition of films like *Sangam*

(1964), *Dostana* (1980), *Qurbani* (1980) and *Kal Ho Na Ho* (2003)? The moment is cut short by Sam. Omar's interrupted family fantasy can only now be completed in the film's concluding scene, once again on the baseball field—via a necessary reconfiguration in which it is Roushan, the state-allied Muslim, who steps in to complete the family circle.

And so at the film's conclusion, in the exact moment typically reserved for the happy ending of heterosexual pairing, *New York* leaves the viewer with an all-male Muslim family composed of Roushan, Omar, and Danyal. This resolution queers the heterosexual Hindi film love formula that Omar had invoked with Maya in the previous baseball scene. Instead of one of the male rivals expectedly exiting the love triangle to make way for the other's successful heterosexual union, *New York* "kills off" both Samir and Maya and introduces Roushan where Maya should have been slotted, by genre conventions and by heterosexual mandate.

Rather than Maya being passed on to Omar, it is Omar who is passed on to Roushan. The resolution reveals that the more significant triangle has all along been that between Sam, Omar, and Roushan, with Omar being the bone of contention between the hyper-masculine, disenchanted Muslim American citizen Sam and the state-allied "good Muslim" Roushan, who seeks Omar's compliance with the crushing protective and conditional embrace of the sometimes Machiavellian but essentially recuperable American state.

Conclusion

Why does the film end up in this "queer-ish" place—both in its abjuring of the heterosexual resolution to the love triangle and in its presentation of the Muslim male characters through the codes of the global gayness? It is tempting to read the film's resolution as a radical resistance to the incitement to heteronormativity following 9/11. But I see it rather as an outcome of the film's perhaps unwitting exposure of the *impossibility* of certain kinds of patriotic participation on the part of Muslim Americans. Although Sam and Maya, like good American citizens, willingly take up their parts in the heterosexual drama that was supposed to cohere Americans after 9/11, *New York* cannot but reveal the inevitable failure, indeed the impossibility, of that idealized union for Muslim Americans. Their deaths are the result of a fatal innocence about the differential interpellation of racialized citizen-subjects by the post-9/11 scripts of American patriotism. That day, watching the drama of 9/11 unfold on television in the company of fellow Americans who seemed to mirror their own grief, Sam and Maya fail to realize that the heteronormative mandate relayed in post-9/11 public discourse was never meant for them. *New York* registers how that mandate extends largely to white citizen-subjects even as it fears heterosexual—and significantly, reproductive—bonds among Muslims.

It is the unattached Omar who is allowed to survive and who, along with the state-allied Muslim Roushan (the taller man frequently positioned behind Omar in the film), will oversee the upbringing of the terrorist's son. Marked explicitly as "bottom" masculinity, it is Omar who represents the possibility of integration into the nation. It is worth noting, too, that the well-heeled gay-coded Muslim male protagonists of this drama are a far cry from the primitivized sexual deviants of the post-9/11 visual landscape.[19] On a global landscape where a tolerance for homosexuality functions as a kind of Muslim "immigration test" in the West (sometimes literally, as in the Netherlands), *New York*'s verbal and visual citations of homosexuality around Muslim male bodies perhaps function to qualify these subjects for "western" citizenship through a disavowal of homophobia (while never openly embracing homosexuality).[20] In this way the film participates in the "simultaneous engendering and disavowal of populations of sexual and racial others who need not apply"—Muslims, queer or otherwise, who do not fall into the neoliberal frameworks within which a particular model of gayness has lately come to be marked as cosmopolitan, modern, worthy of (selective) assimilation into the nation.[21] *New York* thus risks creating space for the Muslim citizen only by "narrow[ing] the space of dissent that such minority subjects can occupy."[22]

Rather like *Kurbaan* (where the state-loving Riyaz is the sole surviving Muslim while every other Muslim dies: the "bad Muslim" male terrorists and their female supporter Aapa, the hapless Muslim womenfolk in the terrorist family, and even Riyaz's liberal girlfriend Rehana, who dies in a terrorist attack on a plane), *New York* provides multiple audiences in India and abroad with the solace of the integrated minority subject who knows his place. But *New York* nevertheless also hints at the costs of integration on such terms.

Consider the film's final scene, where Roushan delivers a patriotic lecture to Omar, arguing that Muslims must forgive and forget. On the face of it, the film appears to merely endorse the liberal "good Muslim" narrative, but a closer attention to Omar's reaction hints at a much darker reading than such an interpretation allows. Omar responds at first with anger, but following Roushan's exhortations, we see his lips twitch into a half-smile, as Roushan stands imposingly behind him (as he does so very often in the film). Roushan's exhortations to forgive and forget are met with a hesitant silence that casts a pall upon the apparent harmony of the final scene of the two men walking together with Danyal across the park. Omar is not convinced, and underlying Roushan's offer of friendship and the façade of reconciliation palpably lurks the warning of continued surveillance and the suppressed dissent of the disgruntled minority subject.

NOTES

1 This chapter is a revised version of an earlier article, "Queer Resolutions: 9/11 and Muslim Masculinities in New York," *South Asian Popular Culture* 11, no. 2 (2013): 157–167. I am grateful to the editors for their suggestions on this chapter. I am also thankful to Himika

Bhattacharya, Huma Dar, Shilpa Davé, Danika Medak-Saltzman, and Beverly Weber for thinking through key aspects of the film with me.

2 Paola Bacchetta et al., "Transnational Feminist Practices against War," *Meridians* 2, no. 2 (2002): 302.

3 The actor Irrfan Khan, who plays FBI agent Roushan in *New York*, reportedly turned down the role of the Muslim terrorist played by Saif Ali Khan in *Kurbaan*. Both actors are Muslim in a film industry in which many of the top male stars are Muslims who play predominantly Hindu characters on screen.

4 It is worth bearing in mind that the position of Muslims in Hindu-dominated India is somewhat analogous to that of Muslims and indeed South Asians more broadly in the United States—these minority populations in both states exist at the sufferance of the majority community (Hindus in India, non-Muslims in the United States). Thus, for audiences of these films in India, the alienated Muslim protagonists of these films are likely to recall similar struggles of identity and assimilation.

5 Bacchetta et al., "Transnational Feminist Practices against War"; Jasbir Puar and Amit Rai, "Monster, Terrorist, Fag: The War on Terrorism and the Production of Docile Patriots," *Social Text* 20, no. 3 (Fall 2002): 117–148.

6 The bindi serves as a visual code for "Hindu" as much as beards and caps do for "Muslim" in Bombay cinema.

7 Shahnaz Khan, "Nationalism and Hindi Cinema: Narrative Strategies in Fanaa," *Studies in South Asian Film and Media* 1, no. 1 (2009): 92.

8 Amit Rai, "Patriotism and the Muslim Citizen in Hindi Films," *Harvard Asia Quarterly* 7 (2003): 4–15.

9 Sumita S. Chakravarty, "Fragmenting the Nation: Images of Terrorism in Indian Popular Cinema," in *Terrorism, Media, Liberation*, ed. J. David Slocum (New Brunswick, NJ: Rutgers University Press, 2005), 238.

10 Ashis Nandy, *The Secret Politics of Our Desires: Innocence, Culpability and Indian Popular Cinema* (London: Zed Books, 1999).

11 Thomas Waugh, "Queer Bollywood, or 'I'm the Player, You're the Naive One': Patterns of Sexual Subversion in Recent Indian Popular Cinema," in *Keyframes: Popular Cinema and Cultural Studies*, ed. Matthew Tinkcom and Amy Villarejo (New York: Routledge, 2003); Shohini Ghosh, "False Appearances and Mistaken Identities: The Phobic and the Erotic in Bombay Cinema's Queer Vision," in *The Phobic and the Erotic: The Politics of Sexualities in Contemporary India*, ed. Brinda Bose and Subhabrata Bhattacharyya (London: Seagull, 2007).

12 Ghosh, "False Appearances and Mistaken Identities," 421.

13 Waugh, "Queer Bollywood," 292.

14 The star body of John Abraham is far from incidental to such winking, of course—particularly following his 2008 hit *Dostana*, a tongue-in-cheek buddy film that treats its own heterosexual triangle like the pretext it is, while providing an abundance of purple-hued, naked-male-torsoed pleasures to spectators and sealing John Abraham in the public imagination as a "gay" icon with polysexual appeal.

15 For a full critique of this article, see Huma Dar, "'Going Deeper' Not 'Muslim': Islamophobia and Its Discontents," *PULSE*, December 3, 2009, http://pulsemedia.org/2009/12/03/going-deeper-not-muslim-islamophobia-and-its-discontents.

16 See Lila Abu-Lughod, "Do Muslim Women Really Need Saving? Anthropological Reflections on Cultural Relativism and Its Others," *American Anthropologist* 104, no. 3 (September 2002): 783–790.

17 Emphasis mine. See Gaurav Malani, "Kurbaan: Movie Review," *Economic Times*, November 20, 2009, http://economictimes.indiatimes.com/news/news-by-industry/media/entertainment-/entertainment/Kurbaan-Movie-Review/articleshow/5249742.cms.

18 Conspicuously absent from this repertoire of abuse is the sexual torture of brown men so explicitly documented in the photographs from Abu Ghraib.

19 Puar and Rai, "Monster, Terrorist, Fag."

20 Gopinath notes how such citations constitute Bollywood's way of managing nationalist anxieties around male queerness, typically by containing them within diaspora, while at the same time marking the rising cosmopolitanism of Bollywood cinema as it adapts its codes to the international market. See Gayatri Gopinath, *Impossible Desires: Queer Diasporas and South Asian Public Cultures* (Durham, NC: Duke University Press, 2005).

21 Jasbir Puar, *Terrorist Assemblages: Homonationalism in Queer Times* (Durham, NC: Duke University Press Books, 2007), 2.

22 Rai, "Patriotism and the Muslim Citizen in Hindi Films," 16.

19

Hybrid Hallyu

The African American Music Tradition in K-Pop

CRYSTAL S. ANDERSON

The year 2012 was a significant year for contemporary Korean popular music, or K-pop. Korean rapper Psy achieved unprecedented recognition the world over for his catchy hit, "Gangnam Style." His fame propelled him into the spotlight in the United States in a way that surpassed the previous efforts of other K-pop stars, including Rain, BoA and Se7en, who gained fame around the world but failed to break into the mainstream of American music. Psy found himself appearing on television shows ranging from *Ellen* to *The Today Show*, hobnobbing with a slew of American celebrities, receiving offers to work with pop superstars like Justin Bieber, and even performing for President Barack Obama. Within a matter of months, Psy had horse-danced his way into the American popular consciousness and propelled a K-pop single infused with rap, a musical tradition nurtured by African Americans, to mainstream recognition.

In the same year, Big Mama, the former labelmate of Psy and a veteran Korean vocal group with a reputation for drawing on rhythm and blues (R&B), another black musical tradition, quietly released their final single, "Cleaning Drawers," to much less fanfare but certainly to the notice of longtime global K-pop fans. The release came months after the group—described by Jangta, a blogger for *Green Tea Graffiti*, as the foremost female vocal group in K-pop, whose "musical style and vocals have influenced many Korean R&B singers"[1]—announced its breakup after nine years. While Big Mama's breakup and final single barely a registered ripple in the wake of Psy's global popularity, it marked the departure of the most high-profile Korean R&B vocal group from the K-pop music scene.

While a world-famous Korean rapper and a relatively unknown Korean female group may seem worlds apart, they reveal how black musical traditions such as R&B and hip-hop travel to distant locations such as South Korea and are redeployed to global audiences in new forms. Some see the impact of such circulation of cultural production as superficial at best. While both Psy and Big Mama partake of black musical traditions, they are not seen as legitimate practitioners, largely because their status as Korean artists constructs them outside of genres that many view as solely the purview of black artists. Global audiences respond to Psy's comedic antics, but many do not consider him to be a "real" rapper. Some individuals recognize Big Mama as part of a tradition of singers, but more general global audiences exclude them from the genre of R&B. Richard J. Ripani asserts that "it has remained difficult . . . for any person outside the African American community to produce an acceptable black vocal style."[2] These characterizations of Psy and Big Mama may be related to the degree to which they are deemed authentic in relation to black musical performance. A narrow mode of authenticity excludes both from black musical traditions because they are not black, nor do they share the black cultural and historical context of the music. In other words, few recognize how black musical traditions migrate to South Korea and play a central role in K-pop, making it part of these musical traditions.

However, as K-pop artists, Psy and Big Mama's engagement with the aesthetics of black musical traditions reflects the transnational and hybridized nature of K-pop, a musical culture that invites us to revise our definitions of authenticity. Before the rise of Hallyu, or the Korean wave, South Korea experienced an influx of African American musical cultures as part of a significant American military presence following the Korean War. Since the 1990s, K-pop has subsequently circulated not only to East Asian locales such as Japan, China, the Philippines, and Malaysia but also to Western locations such as the United States, Europe, and Latin America. Thus, K-pop is both the result of circulating cultures and is itself a musical culture that circulates. That circulation invariably brings up questions regarding its relationship to the African American musical cultures that inform it.

Reflecting a fusion of African American and Korean musical sensibilities, K-pop's hybridity goes beyond reductive scripts of authenticity generated by discourses of cultural misappropriation and imitation. K-pop artists like Psy and Big Mama draw on the aesthetic elements of black musical traditions, thereby making them part of these musical traditions. Psy engages with the well-developed genre of humor-based hip-hop, while Big Mama's performance depends on the polytonal vocals key to various genres of R&B. Such performances are deemed authentic by global fans well versed in the black musical genres that inform such performances, fans whose knowledge draws on the aesthetic meanings of these musical traditions. Such black music aesthetics attends to aspects of the music inherent to the genre beyond a particular black experience. Rhythm and blues and hip-hop are black musical genres, not because of who performs them, but because the genres themselves contain elements that reflect black aesthetics. An examination of music aesthetics does not completely ignore cultural and historical context. Rather, such an examination shifts the emphasis to understanding how such elements are used in a transnational context and complicates authenticity by arguing that Korean artists participate in hip-hop and R&B traditions authentically because their performances reflect the aesthetics of these genres.

Black Musical Circulation and K-Pop

Korean hip-hop and R&B represent two of the most recognizable modes of cultural production in Hallyu, a globally directed cultural movement. Anthony Faiola notes that the term was coined by Beijing journalists "who were startled by the growing popularity of South Koreans and South Korean goods in China."[3] Initially, Hallyu described "*regional* popularity of South Korean cultural products such as cinema, television drama, popular music and fashion within Asia," but it has since spread to Western countries.[4] Much Hallyu cultural production is hybrid, the result of mixing American—notably African American—and Korean cultures, beginning in earnest in the 1950s and culminating in the latter half of the twentieth century. When the Korean War brought an American presence to South Korea in the 1950s, John Lie notes that it also "brought popular American music . . . [including] pop and rock via the U.S. Armed Forces radio and television."[5] Americans also brought black musical traditions such as rhythm and blues, which dominated pop to the point where "*Billboard* ceased publication of its rhythm and blues chart altogether, simply because it was apparently so similar to the general popular music chart ('Hot 100') as to be deemed unnecessary."[6] However, this cross-cultural exchange is made more complicated by U.S. intervention into Korea. After initially neglecting Korea in the wake of World War II, the U.S. embarked on a campaign that, according to Charles K. Armstrong, was designed to orient Koreans toward "American-style liberal democracy" using cultural production.[7] For example, Motion Picture Program Abroad, a program initiated by the U.S. military to produce documentary films for occupied territories in 1948, promoted American films that functioned as soft propaganda, promoting the everyday life of Americans in a desirable light and encouraging Koreans to emulate it.[8] This use of American culture had ramifications for African American culture, which simultaneously functioned as nationalistically and ethnically informed cultural production. Pointing to a similar spread of American culture in Europe in the 1960s, Reinhold Wagnleitner proposes that African American cultural production can be seen as "a global extension of the American empire."[9] So African American culture is contextualized by issues of U.S. occupation that must also be read against the backdrop of cold war politics.

Political and social changes played a large role in the reception of African American music in the twentieth century as well. The 1980s and 1990s witnessed a shift from the repressive regime of Park Chung Hee, South Korea's last dictator, to a more democratic and culturally tolerant environment ushered in by Kim Young Sam in 1992. Rhythm and blues and hip-hop represented musical traditions that spoke to the creative possibilities opening in Korean society. Hae-Kyung Um notes that "the relaxation of state censorship on popular music . . . allowed songwriters and singers to explore their artistic freedom and creativity," thereby providing "the contexts in which hip-hop in Korea could take its roots as part of local youth culture from the 1990s onward."[10] Such freedom was also fed by the influx of Korean American artists in early Korean R&B groups who were well versed in African American musical styles. Several went on to become producers. Teddy Park (Park Hong Jun), a member of the Korean hip-hop group 1TYM, became a successful producer for YG Entertainment, making music for Taeyang and G-Dragon, members of the globally popular group BigBang. Jae Chong, a member of the first Korean R&B group Solid, is currently the producer behind pop group Aziatix. While R&B and hip-hop have spread the world over, they resonated with South Korean artists because they spoke to the development of creative possibilities in Korea and became a vehicle for greater creative expression.

Black Musical Authenticity and K-Pop

K-pop, as a part of Hallyu, redirects this hybridized cultural production back out to the world to a mixed reception. Some global fans enjoy seeing African American genres in K-pop. In online surveys conducted with global fans of K-pop, I found that respondents often identify African American genres of music as part of the appeal of K-pop, as this respondent comments: "I really love group harmonies and while K-pop is mostly pop, my favorite groups collaborate on a range of genres, from funk, soul, and R&B. The lyrics are often more poetical with great imagery, and the music more complex than American pop."[11] At the same time, K-pop is routinely criticized for cultural misappropriation. Mark, a writer for the K-pop media site *seoulbeats*, opines that it "becomes problematic when certain elements are added simply for the sake of upping an artist's 'cool' factor while it's being culturally appropriated in a way that is disrespectful (not to mention laughable) to the original product."[12] Such critiques read the use of African American musical styles by K-pop artists as uninspired instances of imitation or outright theft.

Such critiques assess the merit of K-pop's cultural borrowing using a narrow mode of authenticity, what John L. Jackson calls a reductive script that "presupposes a relation between subjects (who authenticate) and objects (dumb, mute and inorganic) that are interpreted and analyzed from the outside because they cannot simply speak for themselves."[13] For black music, that script bases authenticity on a recognition by audiences and critics of a historical experience of African Americans rooted in racism and discrimination or a resistance to dominant powers that oppress based on race and ethnicity. Such experience need not be lived, but the African American context must be acknowledged in some way. In hip-hop, authenticity describes a "realness" inextricably linked to certain African American experiences that respond to threatening dominant cultural forces. Tracing the contemporary discourse of authenticity in hip-hop to the 1990s, Kembrew McLeod notes that, when hip-hop fans speak "in terms of being 'true,' 'real,' or 'keepin' it real,'" it is in response to "the sense that hip-hop culture faces the threat of being erased and transformed into something that is undesirable."[14]

Individuals are measured by the authenticity that emerges from this reductive script that defines "realness" in hip-hop, even outside of the United States. For example, one might assert that global youth participate in hip-hop authentically when they gravitate to its critical impulse, as when Tony Mitchell notes that hip-hop and rap "are also used in different local contexts to espouse the causes of ethnic minorities . . . and to make political statements about local racial, sexual, employment and class issues."[15] Similarly, the authenticity of Korean artists' use of hip-hop is measured by how closely they conform to a U.S.-based hip-hop defined by discrimination and racism. Um employs this script when describing the song "Do You Understand What Is Real Hip-Hop?" from the 1999 *Year of the Tiger* album by Drunken Tiger, the Korean hip-hop duo made up of Korean American DJ Shine and Korean-born but Los Angeles–raised Tiger JK: "The transnational Korean hip-hop with the emphasis on rapping and sampling was perceived to be authentic because it adhered to or emulated the American hip-hop genre rules and styles."[16] While the track has aesthetic elements of hip-hop, Um focuses on its emulation of "a quintessentially African American cultural form and diasporic expression" informed by "nationalism and Afrocentrism."[17] Under a script that revolves around a particular African American experience, Drunken Tiger is authentic because the group's performance is placed within the racial politics of the United States.

This script overlooks black aesthetics not overtly related to such historical and cultural contexts. Such a script employs what Theodore Gracyk calls the "social relevance thesis," which excludes aesthetic readings of black popular music in favor of "that listener's social, historical and institutional positions."[18] However, Gracyk argues that "attending to the cultural location of music does not require a suspension of aesthetic discrimination."[19] Black popular music has meaning beyond the way it may speak to social realities. Ralf von Appen asserts the goal of musical aesthetics is "to understand on a widest-possible basis the significance and meaning aesthetic practice may have for individuals."[20] This does not eliminate the consideration of social and cultural contexts but suggests that "agreeing that music is always social practice does not demonstrate that music is *only* social practice."[21] Aesthetic readings are especially pertinent to K-pop's embrace of black music traditions and the appeal of K-pop to non-Korean-speaking audiences because "music has a purely sensual attraction": "Apart from melodies, rhythms, harmonies and their combinations, lyrics may also be heard as pure sound without attention to their meaning."[22] Music aesthetics also recognizes K-pop's hybridized and complex cultural production and, as Eun-Young Jung asserts, moves us away "from the problematic qualities of essentialism and exclusionism inherent in notions of cultural 'purity' and 'authenticity.'"[23] Even the mantra of "keeping it real" can have multiple meanings. Imani Perry notes that meanings can range from "genuine love, emotional authenticity, and depth" to "an authenticating device" that recognizes origins."[24] McLeod found that "'keepin' it real' and various other claims of authenticity do not appear to have a fixed or rigid meaning throughout the hip-hop community."[25]

Thus, approaching K-pop with a wider script allows us to consider elements beyond social relevance, including aesthetic concerns.

When we expand authenticity to include aesthetics as well as historical and social meanings, it becomes clear that Korean artists create authentic music in the tradition of black musical culture because they employ black musical aesthetics that reflect the same musical meanings as music produced by black artists and audiences recognize those aesthetics and meanings. For example, some see sampling and mixing as generic creative choices, but Andrew Bartlett states that "the art of digital sampling in (primarily) African American hip-hop is intricately connected to an African American/African diasporic aesthetic" that involves "a high-tech and highly selective archiving, bringing into dialogue by virtue of even the most slight representation . . . any range of 'voices.'"[26] When we extend the script of authenticity to the aesthetics of mixing, sampling, and rapping, we see how Korean artists may reflect the aesthetics of black musical performance or the political and social ramifications of the music.

In addition to the presence of aesthetic elements, an authentic performance also depends on recognition by an audience that is familiar with those elements. This audience does not need to be African American, but they are usually familiar with the defining elements of the musical culture. Such knowledge allows them to confer legitimacy onto a particular performance. Paul C. Taylor argues that the aesthetic experience represents "the collection of related perceptions and appraisals that emerges from a certain kind of interaction between an observer and an object."[27] In other words, if individuals are perceived as performing the aesthetic elements of a genre of art, then that performance is authentic for an audience that knows the musical tradition. Allan Moore argues that "it is the *success* with which a particular performance conveys its impression that counts, a success which depends in some part on the explicitly musical decisions performers make."[28] Rather than a restrictive script, Moore suggests a mode in which success is defined by participation in the genre. Similarly, Jackson uses the concept of sincerity to emphasize "a liaison *between subjects*—not some external adjudicator and a lifeless scroll. Questions of sincerity imply social interlocutors who presume one another's humanity, interiority, and subjectivity."[29] Both Moore and Jackson link performance, which represents an engagement with aesthetics, and audiences to open up the possibility of K-pop artists adapting black musical traditions in ways that also allow for their unique voice and perspective.

Hip-hop represents a complex cultural production that resists rigid authentication and encourages the kind of cultural borrowing engaged by Korean artists. In addition to lyrics, other elements of African American music can be used to ascertain the nature of K-pop artists' engagement with black music traditions. In hip-hop, the music over which MCs rap is of equal importance to their dexterity in rhyming. Robert Farris Thompson notes the significance of the break beat, the best part of the song that may last for only seconds: "How to restore the delicious length of live music breaks in a mechanical turntable situation? . . . [DJ Kool] Herc took a conga drum break and extended it across two copies of the same record on two turntables. As soon as one break ended, he switched to its beginning on the second record, and the beat went on."[30] Dick Hebdige notes that, unlike lyrics that depend on a knowledge of the language, the musical composition is accessible to anyone: "The cut 'n' mix attitude was that no one owns a rhythm or a sound. You just borrow it, use it, and give it back to the people in a slightly different form."[31] The focus on rhythm means that meaning, enjoyment, and participation can be achieved apart from lyrics. While global audiences may not understand the wordplay in Korean hip-hop, they respond to the use of rhythm and beat that defines the hip-hop genre.

Black Musical Aesthetics in K-Pop: Psy and Big Mama

If we include aesthetics in our appraisal of K-pop's engagement with hip-hop, we can see that Psy is a Korean rapper who engages in the aesthetics of hip-hop. Born Park Jae Sang, Psy opted to study at Boston University, flouting expectations that he would work in his father's semiconductor company. While he eventually left Boston University and Berklee College of Music without securing a degree, he decided to pursue a career in the music industry, with hip-hop as his chosen genre: "With his leftover tuition money, he purchased a computer, an electric keyboard, and a MIDI. He started listening to hip-hop (Tupac, Dr. Dre, and Eminem were his favorites), and the burgeoning rap genre gave him hope for his own future in music. 'I thought, wow, [by] just saying the words fast I can be a singer.'"[32] Upon his return to Korea, Psy joined LNLT Entertainment and in 2010 moved on to YG Entertainment, one of the "Big Three" Korean music agencies, which prides itself on its production of unique music and is known for artists who engage in black musical performance. YG Entertainment's CEO Yang Hyun Suk sees a difference between the artists at other agencies and his artists, who use hip-hop modes of expression like rapping: "I watched TV and wondered what would happen if pretty girl groups such as Girls' Generation, Fin.K.L and S.E.S performed hip hop songs like YG. Wouldn't it be fun if they went through the entire stage rapping 'intensely'?"[33] Psy's reputation as a rapper was enhanced by his move to YG Entertainment.

Psy's early work, such as his first single "Bird," from his debut album, *PSY from the Psycho World!* reflects several elements of hip-hop. It features Psy rapping over a sample from "Venus" by Bananarama. One could also argue that he engages in the rebellious spirit of hip-hop with the lyrical content of the song:

"Despite the stir caused by 'Bird,' Psy was forced to pay a fine due to the album's explicit language. The next year, he released two albums, *Ssa 2* and *3 PSY*, but *Ssa 2* couldn't be sold to people under 19 due to inappropriate content."[34] Even without understanding the lyrics, one can observe his dexterity in his ability to rap and the effective use of sampling and mixing.

While captivated by Psy's performance, many fail to associate it with the aesthetics of comedy hip-hop, a genre that blends humor with rap. His performances of "Bird" and "Gangnam Style" follow the hip-hop tradition popularized by such icons as Digital Underground and the Fat Boys. Noting their "comic style" and "onstage antics," William Eric Perkins argues that their "outrageous funny lyrics reminded the mass audience that rap could maintain an innocence while being true to its roots."[35] However, reductive scripts of authenticity exclude Psy from hip-hop. Global audiences do not recognize Psy's performance of hip-hop aesthetics because it falls outside of a range of more popular personas adopted by men in hip-hop, including the gangster, the pimp, and the scholar-intellectual. Such roles represent a "self-assertion" represented by vocal performance as well as "the visual symbolism of dress and body decoration," which "marks one way of challenging a sense of race and gender powerlessness."[36]

Psy's visuals do not correspond to any of these archetypal roles of hip-hop. Instead, they mark Psy's performance as comic or pop oriented. Max Fisher notes the impact of the visuals over the song's musical quality on its popularity: "The things that made the song such a K-pop outlier—*the satirical silliness and near-subversive self-mockery*—are the opposite of the genre's typical earnestness and practiced wholesomeness."[37] Fisher not only focuses on the visuals associated with the song, he also contextualizes Psy's rise, not as a hip-hop star, but as a counter to mainstream K-pop. Writers describe Psy as a response to what they see as overmanufactured K-pop idols. While Psy is often nominally identified as a Korean rapper, commentators do not connect his viral hit "Gangnam Style" to the comic hip-hop genre.

While global audiences may not identify Psy with hip-hop aesthetics, Big Mama is routinely described as an R&B vocal group by a smaller audience of K-pop fans. Like hip-hop, R&B functions as a genre with identifiable aesthetics. Authentic performance in R&B rests with the voice, which itself is complex. Mark Anthony Neal traces the essence of R&B music, particularly soul music, to polytonal expression "in which complex and varying meanings were conveyed via vocal tones."[38] Such songs "conveyed rich, textured, and nuanced meanings that were primarily conveyed via tonal qualities as opposed to specific narrative content."[39] In short, soul singers are defined by their ability to reflect the polytonal quality of soul music. Gerri Hirshey notes that "the sound—the story—of soul music is contained in those voices and the infinite change-ups they worked on twelve notes and an equally basic set of human emotions. . . . Style may have linked clusters of artists. . . . But direct, standout *vocal* expression is the touchstone."[40] Hirshey and Neal both describe the centrality of voice in ways that make it accessible to anyone who engages the aesthetic of the vocals associated with R&B.

Korean R&B singers adapt this polytonal vocal quality, which appeals to the centrality of the voice in and represents a departure from traditional Korean music. Lie notes that in the 1970s and 1980s, traditional Korean popular music used a pentatonic scale: "The register of Korean and Japanese musical sensibility remained stubbornly rooted in traditional musical meters. Performers usually stood still, dressed in traditional ethnic garb or conservative 'western' outfit and projecting an utterly respectable appearance."[41] Singers such as Cho Yong-pil "sang without moving, employed melismatic and *pansori* singing techniques, and relied on his vocal skills, rather than on his looks to achieve stardom."[42] Pansori is a traditional Korean genre of singing that features a singer and drummer and focuses on storytelling. However, he represented a distinctly traditional Korean aesthetic: "Cho's music signified Korean-ness, which rendered it alien to those uninitiated to the national culture and the dominant musical style."[43] Korean popular music has a tradition of centralizing the voice, but in ways that are grounded in Korean culture and the pentatonic scale.

However, Koreans embraced the polytonality of R&B, which was new and resonated with the country's youth. Neal notes that "soul music represents the construction of 'hypercommunity' in that both physical and metaphysical notions of space and community, and all the political and social meanings that underlie such formations converge within its aesthetic sensibilities. . . . The soul singer emerges as the popular representation of an emerging postcolonial sensibility."[44] In light of the social dimensions of soul music, this genre may have also represented a vehicle to express emotions rooted in Koreans own experience with dominance. Eun Mee Kim and Jiwon Ryoo link hybrid cultural production of the Korean wave with nationally informed emotion: "Hallyu led to the dissolution of the long-held Han [bitterness, anger] after centuries of being invaded by surrounding super powers, colonialism, and war."[45] Through collective forms such as protests and desires for economic advancement, "suddenly centuries-old 'Han' was lifted as South Koreans were ridding themselves of the deep-held resentment and forced sense of inferiority vis-à-vis its neighboring super powers of China and Japan."[46] In global cultural terms, "Hallyu cut the Gordian knot of the historical tragedy and colonial legacy, putting South Korea on par with Japan."[47] These factors suggest that the aesthetics of soul music plus the centrality of the singer in Korean popular music make it ideal for speaking to the way Koreans feel about their local conditions.

However, Korean R&B singers may also be subject to charges of inauthenticity even while emulating R&B's polytonality. Neal notes that "the commodification of soul reduces blackness to a commodity that could be bought and sold—and this is important—without the cultural and social markers that have defined blackness."[48] This commodification opens up the performance of soul to anyone but also makes it possible to level charges of inauthenticity at performances by non-black performers.

However, R&B music also has a tradition of non-black performers participating and contributing in an uncontested way. Neal argues "for a separate category known as 'white chocolate'—that which 'looks different (and for all intents is different since white chocolate isn't really made of chocolate) but contains all the 'flava' and texture of the original."[49] This category revolves around artists "who challenge essentialist arguments about who is *allowed* to sing black music . . . and who also provide examples of white performances of black pop that transcend simple appropriations (and in the worst case theft) and legitimately add to the tradition."[50] Neal locates such transcendence in an artist like Teena Marie, who "was ultimately rooted in her comfort with and convincing performance of black vernacular traditions of the late 1970s and 1980s" and her honesty "about her musical influences and her intent to be 'just' an R&B artist."[51]

Like Psy who uses the aesthetics of mixing and rapping, Big Mama emulates the aesthetics of R&B through its consistent employment of vocals in a variety of R&B genres. Consisting of Shin Yeon Ah, Lee Young Hyun, Lee Ji Young, and Park Min Hye, Big Mama debuted in 2003 as group defined by their vocals. Individually active within the music industry, the members came together under YG Entertainment. Their appearance drew even more attention to their vocal ability: "In a world where female musicians are critiqued by their outward appearances, Big Mama came out blazing with their enormous vocal talent. Unfortunately, it was their 'full-figured bodies' which garnered more attention than their music."[52] Over their nine-year career, the group released five studio albums, two compilations, and their final single, "Cleaning Drawers," in 2012. Over the years, writers not only routinely cite their vocal ability but also discursively place them in the company of American R&B singers. Jangta writes: "By today's standards, Big Mama singing, style, and image defy the common norm. . . . Instead of finding inspiration from American pop stars—such as Britney Spears and Christina Aguilera—they'd rather pattern their music to Soul/R&B legends Ella Fitzgerald, Stevie Wonder, and Whitney Houston."[53] Such descriptions show how, as Moore suggests, audiences recognize how performers embody different types of polytonal vocals. They associate the way that vocals overlap in black music genres such as gospel and R&B.

The group solidified their participation in the R&B genre by engaging in various genres of R&B music, showing a versatility that covered major styles of black music that emphasizes vocals. Their first album, *Like the Bible*, features songs that range from upbeat R&B pop to gospel covers. "Breakaway," the popular hit from the album, is an eighties-style R&B romantic ballad, with a slow tempo and jazz overtones. It also features the characteristic blending of Korean and English lyrics found in mainstream K-pop. "Refusal" is an upbeat seventies-style pop song that uses horns to complement the members' voices. "Nae Ani Neo" is a slower song with minimal instrumentation that places the lead vocal in the forefront.

In addition to these pop-friendly offerings, *Like the Bible* also includes less-mainstream styles of R&B. "Ray's Rock House" is a doo-wop-inflected track. The English song begins with a simple beat and finger snaps, then leads into a simple but effective piano rhythm. Initial verses feature a vocal that follows the steady rhythm of the piano, followed by choruses peppered by a more improvised vocal reminiscent of doo-wop: "The R&B ballads and up tempo numbers of doo wop are characterized by those harmonies but also by the nonsense syllabus that formed the backbone of the backup vocals."[54] The album also includes a cover of "His Eye Is on the Sparrow," sung in English. This track proves to be a departure for a K-pop album, but it places Big Mama squarely within the tradition that informs so much of R&B. "His Eye Is on the Sparrow" is a gospel standard that many singers have covered, including Mahalia Jackson, Marvin Gaye, and Whitney Houston, and the arrangement on *Like the Bible* emphasises the vocals. The song begins with a pared-down electric piano intro, which leads into a single, mid-range vocal for the first verse. The next verse is taken up by a slightly higher vocal, which is accompanied by subtle yet distinct strings and, later, subtle orchestration. In the third verse, additional vocals emphasize single words, along with a swelling of the strings. By the final verse, all of the members sing with such power that it suggests a full choir. The way that the voices are multilayered shows that the song partakes of the aesthetics of gospel. The arrangement retains the hymn's slow buildup to the climax of the song, and like other renditions, it showcases a soloist performing vocal gymnastics against the backdrop of a full-voiced choir. In reflecting these details of a gospel performance, Big Mama emulates the aesthetics of the genre. Throughout their careers, the members focused on genres of black music that centralize the voice, including R&B and gospel. Black music is not a passing fad with them, and their releases are always informed by black musical genres, so that the group is known for its R&B vocals.

Conclusion

"Gangnam Style" introduced K-pop to the world on a massive scale, increasing the profile of K-pop in an unprecedented way. While many commentators and scholars marvel at its global spread, few focus on how it is possible for a Korean rapper to engage in black music on the global stage in the first place. Such a focus on rapid fame obscures the initial influx of African American musical cultures made possible by political and economic shifts within South Korea. These historical circumstances allowed access to black musical cultures that later result in Psy's aesthetic connections to comic hip-hop, which remain a hallmark of his career. It also completely overlooks the ways in which black musical culture has affected artists like Big Mama, who clearly align themselves with vocal R&B genres. Rather than relying solely on potential connections between Korean artists and the historical and social conditions of African Americans, an examination of the aesthetics of the performances of both K-pop artists reveals how K-pop bears the imprint of transnational black cultures, which circulate the globe and are redeployed in new, hybridized forms. Focusing on music aesthetics extends the script of authenticity to account for the ways that these Korean artists adopt and adapt black musical culture. These K-pop artists also show us how the circulation of cultures affect reception, for it is the fans who are familiar with black musical cultures who mark K-pop performances as authentic. Such recognition is yet another by-product of the circulation of cultures, which raises the ability of fans to see one culture in a variety of global contexts. Knowledgeable global audiences may also construct meaning from music aesthetics that transcends cultural and historical context. Gerald Early argues for the transcendent nature of the Motown sound, "The Sound of Young America," in the 1960s, describing it as something "beyond and before words."[55] Thus, examining K-pop artists' engagement with black musical aesthetics reveals the impact of traveling cultures, which transcend national boundaries in new and exciting ways.

NOTES

1 Jangta, "How Big Mama Went against All Odds in the Korean Music Industry," *Green Tea Graffiti*, February 9, 2010, http://www.greenteagraffiti.com/Music/Korean/Seoul-Singers .html, accessed Janurary 6, 2013.

2 Richard J. Ripani, *The New Blue Music: Changes in Rhythm and Blues, 1950–1999* (Jackson: University of Mississippi Press, 2006), 190.

3 Anthony Faiola, "Japanese Women Catch the Korean Wave," *Washington Post*, August 31, 2006, http://www.washingtonpost.com/wp-dyn/content/article/2006/08/30/AR2006083002985.html, accessed January 21, 2013.

4 Sun Jung, *Korean Masculinities and Transnational Consumption: Yonsama, Rain, Oldboy, K-pop Idols* (Hong Kong: Hong Kong University Press, 2011), 1.

5 John Lie, "What Is the K in K-pop? South Korean Popular Music, the Culture Industry and National Identity," *Korea Observer* 43, no. 3 (2012): 343.

6 Ripani, *The New Blue Music*, 8.

7 Charles K. Armstrong, "The Cultural Cold War in Korea, 1945–1950," *Journal of Asian Studies* 62, no. 1 (2003): 80.

8 Ibid., 79.

9 Reinhold Wagnleitner, "'No Commodity Is Quite So Strange as This Thing Called Cultural Exchange': The Foreign Politics of American Pop Culture Hegemony," *Amerikastudien/ American Studies* 46, no. 3 (2001): 454.

10 Hae-Kyung Um, "The Poetics of Resistance and the Politics of Crossing Borders: Korean Hip-Hop and 'Cultural Reterritorialisation,'" in "East Asian Popular Music and Its (Dis) contents," special issue, *Popular Music* 32, no. 1 (2013): 53.

11 Crystal S. Anderson, "Noona, Unnie, Oppa, Hyung: Research Shows Adults Like K-pop for the Music," *KPK: Kpop Kollective* (blog), September 16, 2012, http://kpopkollective.com/

2012/09/16/noona-unnie-oppa-hyung-research-shows-adults-like-k-pop-for-the-music, accessed October 14, 2015.

12 Mark, "Aegyo Hip Hop: Cultural Appropriation at Its Messiest," *seoulbeats*, January 5, 2013, http://seoulbeats.com/2013/01/aegyo-hip-hop-cultural-appropriation-at-its-messiest, accessed October 14, 2015.

13 John L. Jackson, *Real Black: Adventures in Racial Sincerity* (Chicago: University of Chicago Press, 2005), 14–15.

14 Kembrew McLeod, "Authenticity within Hip-Hop and Other Cultures Threatened with Assimilation," *Journal of Communication* 49, no. 4 (1999): 148.

15 Tony Mitchell, "Another Root—Hip-Hop outside the USA," in *Global Noise: Rap and Hip-Hop outside the USA*, ed. Tony Mitchell (Middletown, CT: Wesleyan University Press, 2001), 10.

16 Um, "Poetics of Resistance," 57.

17 Ibid., 52.

18 Theodore Gracyk, *Listening to Popular Music, Or, How I Learned to Stop Worrying and Love Led Zeppelin* (Ann Arbor: University of Michigan Press, 2007), 48.

19 Ibid., 2.

20 Ralf von Appen, "On the Aesthetics of Popular Music," *Music Therapy Today* 8, no. 1 (2007): 7.

21 Gracyk, *Listening to Popular Music*, 1.

22 von Appen, "Aesthetics of Popular Music," 11.

23 Eun-Young Jung, "Transnational Korea: A Critical Assessment of the Korean Wave in Asia and the United States," *Southeast Review of Asian Studies* 31 (2009): 71.

24 Imani Perry, *Prophets of the Hood: Politics and Poetics in Hip Hop* (Durham, NC: Duke University Press, 2004), 87.

25 McLeod, "Authenticity within Hip-Hop," 139.

26 Andrew Bartlett, "Airshafts, Loudspeakers, and the Hip Hop Sample: Contexts and African American Musical Aesthetics," in *That's the Joint! The Hip-Hop Studies Reader*, ed. Murray Foreman and Mark Anthony Neal (New York: Routledge, 2004), 393, 401.

27 Paul C. Taylor, "Funky White Boys and Honorary Soul Sisters," *Michigan Quarterly Review* 36, no. 2 (1997): 328.

28 Allan Moore, "Authenticity as Authentication," *Popular Music* 21, no. 2 (2002): 220.

29 Jackson, *Real Black*, 15; emphasis in original.

30 Robert Faris Thompson, "Hip Hop 101," in *Droppin' Science: Critical Essays on Rap Music and Hip Hop Culture*, ed. William Eric Perkins (Philadelphia: Temple University Press, 1996), 216.

31 Dick Hebdige, "Rap and Hip-Hop: The New York Connection," in Forman and Neal, *That's the Joint!* 226–227.

32 Marlow Stern, "Psy Talks Gangnam Style, Growing Up, and His Next Single," *Newsweek*, October 29, 2012, http://www.newsweek.com/psy-talks-gangnam-style-growing-and-his-next-single-65393, accessed October 14, 2015.

33 Elle, "Yang Hyun Suk Believes That the Idol Fad Is Over?" *YG United*, September 30, 2012, http://ygunited.com/2012/09/30/yang-hyun-suk-believes-that-the-idol-fad-is-over, accessed July 22, 2014.

34 Stern, "Psy Talks Gangnam Style."

35 William Eric Perkins, "The Rap Attack: An Introduction," in Perkins, *Droppin' Science*, 15.

36 Perry, *Prophets of the Hood*, 122.

37 Max Fisher, "Visual Music: How 'Gangnam Style' Exploited K-pop's Secret Strength and Overcame Its Biggest Weakness," *Worldviews* (blog), *Washington Post*, October 18, 2013, http://www.washingtonpost.com/blogs/worldviews/wp/2012/10/18/visual-music-how

-gangnam-style-exploited-k-pops-secret-strength-and-overcame-its-biggest-weakness, accessed October 14, 2015. Emphasis in original.

38 Mark Anthony Neal, *What the Music Said: Black Popular Music and Black Public Cultures* (New York: Routledge, 1999), 38.

39 Ibid.

40 Gerri Hershey, *Nowhere to Run: The Story of Soul Music* (Boston: Da Capo Press, 1984), xiv–xv.

41 Lie, "What Is the K in K-pop?" 344.

42 Ibid., 345.

43 Ibid., 212, 345.

44 Neal, *What the Music Said*, 40–41.

45 Eun-mee Kim and Jiwon Ryoo, "South Korean Culture Goes Global: K-pop and the Korean Wave," *Korean Social Science Journal* 34, no. 1 (2007): 142.

46 Ibid.

47 Ibid., 143.

48 Neal, *What the Music Said*, 95.

49 Mark Anthony Neal, "White Chocolate Soul: Teena Marie and Lewis Taylor," *Popular Music* 24, no. 3 (2005): 372.

50 Ibid.

51 Ibid., 376.

52 "They Will Even Hear Sound of Our Breath," *Dong-A Ilbo*, August 29, 2001, http://english .donga.com/srv/service.php3?biid=2007082953018, accessed October 14, 2015.

53 Jangta, "How Big Mama Went against All Odds."

54 Vladimir Bogdanov et al., *All Music Guide to Soul* (San Francisco: Backbeat Books, 2003), 839.

55 Gerald Early, *One Nation under a Groove: Motown and American Culture* (Ann Arbor: University of Michigan Press, 2004), 108.

20

Transnational Beauty Circuits

Asian American Women, Technology, and Circle Contact Lenses

LINDA TRINH VÕ

In the early 1990s, controversy surrounded the Olympic figure skater, Kristi Yamaguchi, a fourth-generation Japanese American, because of the lack of endorsement contracts she received compared to other gold medalists of her stature. Although publicly she was reluctant to attribute any discrimination to corporate America, critics noted that after Yamaguchi won the gold medal, she received few commercial mega-multi-million-dollar endorsements compared to the Anglo American bronze medalist Nancy Kerrigan, who received numerous offers, including a lucrative advertising contract as the face of Revlon, an established cosmetics company. Wholesome and telegenic, Yamaguchi was popular and relatively well liked by the public, but racially she did not quite fit the "all-American" image, so she was perceived as less marketable to American consumers.[1]

Moreover, the racial controversy was heightened when Yamaguchi accepted an offer to become the spokesperson for a prescription color contact lenses company. She appeared in print ads for DuraSoft Colors contact lenses with copy that read, "*When I want a little change I go green, violet, or gray,*" so one can change their eye color "even if you don't need visual correction." At a promotional event in New York in 1992 that also featured another spokesperson, the model and actress Brooke Shields, Yamaguchi stated, "I change my eye color to match my clothes, or sometimes just to match my mood." Questions were raised about altering a physical characteristic as one would change clothing, but the debates had a layered racial component given Yamaguchi's ethnic background. She was criticized for opting to endorse a product that muted her ethnicity by wearing color contacts that match Caucasian eye colors. Others defended her right to promote beauty products that were intended to enhance facial appearance, thereby downplaying any racial overtones with wearing color contacts. The controversy diminished as the Yamaguchi advertising campaign disappeared and attention shifted to new beauty products.[2]

These controversies highlight the reoccurring theme of women of color positioned outside the societal norms of beauty by corporate America and point to how transformations of their physical characteristics can become racialized.

Bodily features such as eye color or skin color are often politicized, since racial ideologies are attached to them, so biological characteristics are imbued with societal values and meaning.[3] Similar to the ways that hair has become a contentious racial identifier for African Americans, eyes and noses have become visible and magnified racial markers for Asian Americans. They are used as tangible demarcations of racial difference, in which certain characteristics are desirable or undesirable; in this case, Asian "flat noses and slanted eyes" are perceived as racially defining characteristics that are inferior to Caucasian "bigger noses and rounder eyes." There is often a conflation of aesthetic and moral judgments associated with altering the appearance of the eyes. Some critics, including Yamaguchi's, regard any alteration to the Asian eyes as artificial or unnatural and marred by psychological afflictions of internalized racism or an inferiority complex, labeling such acts as white emulation or condemning them as an enslavement to Eurocentric standards of beauty.

Although the Yamaguchi case has faded from the American imagination, the issues it raises resurfaced with the emergence of a contemporary and global case involving circle contact lenses. With the Yamaguchi case, contact lenses offered colors to match Caucasian eyes, but circle contact lenses provide a varying range of colors and patterns that not just cover the iris but extend beyond its borders, creating the illusion of larger, rounder eyes. Initially used by young women in Asia and popular worldwide, these stylistic alterations to the Asian eyes are not geographically isolated acts, nor are they discrete cultural activities; rather, they are interconnected with other forms of cultural production and transcend national boundaries of consumption. The transmission of cultural aesthetics does not simply emanate from formidable trendsetters in dominant regions of the West to passive receptors in subordinate nation-states, so they do not merely replicate unidirectional models of cultural assimilation and dominance. Approximately 70 percent of the Asian American population is foreign-born, so first-generation immigrants transfer their beauty practices from Asia, and those who are U.S. born are influenced by Asian practices through beauty culture that is transmitted through movies, televisions shows, and new technologies. This chapter analyzes more nuanced and complex back-and-forth flows of fashion and cultural influences between Asia and the United States and cultural exchanges between Asian countries, complicating processes regarding the diffusion of racial aesthetics.

This chapter also examines the multi-dimensional and variegated social agency that young Asian American females have in digitally transforming the commodification of popular culture and influencing consumer desires. Youth, females, and people of color are categories routinely dismissed or overlooked in analyses of who can potentially control or redirect the capability of digital cultures and social media.[4] With the advent of the Internet and social media, diverse groups are able to access, engage, and redirect technology and popular culture, and this chapter illustrates how Asian American women's beauty consumption is multi-layered, multi-directional, and interconnected.

The Circulation of Circle Contact Lenses

Larger than regular color lenses, circle contact lenses are color tinted or patterned, not only in areas that cover the iris of the eye but also in an extra-wide outer rim that covers some of the white part of the eye, resulting in the illusion of a larger iris and making the eye appear larger. They are 14–17 mm in diameter, which is at least 2 mm larger than the average iris diameter. These decorative lenses are part of the makeup routines that can be used along with mascara, eyeliner, eye shadow, and fake eyelashes to give the impression of rounder, larger eyes. Part of the global multi-billion-dollar beauty and fashion industries, circle contact lenses, or big eye contact lenses, are popular with fashion-conscious girls and young women, and sometimes with males as well. Trendy in China, Japan, Malaysia, the Philippines, Singapore, South Korea, Taiwan, and Thailand, they have made their way to Australia, Europe, the Middle East, and North America.

For the most part, over-the-counter sales of circle contact lenses, prescription and non-prescription, are technically illegal in the United States, but online sales of this product is difficult to regulate.[5] Medical experts from the United States and overseas warn about the dangers of infections and vision impairment, but this has not deterred young female consumers from purchasing the lenses. A host of manufacturers, vendors, bloggers, and consumers counter the negative media reports about the lenses by praising their beautification benefits, touting the cost savings, and minimizing or equating the dangers to those of wearing regular contacts.

Circle contact lenses increased in popularity partly because of their lower price point compared to regularly obtained prescription contact lenses, the variety of appealing designs, and availability through the Internet, which created new global circulations of mass-produced goods and product endorsements. Customers can purchase them directly from online sellers and can choose the strength of their lenses as well as the color, pattern, and size, so the variety of choices and immediate access is part of their appeal. They can be bought online for $20–$30 a pair directly from overseas producers such as GEO or sellers such as Eyecandy or Korea Bigeyes. Given their relative affordability and the constant unveiling of new designs, consumers are encouraged to purchase multiple lenses. They come in shades such as black, blue, brown, green, gray, and pink with a range of geometric or artistic patterns with catchy names such as Angel, Bella, Diamond, Flower, Nudy, Princess Mimi, Shimmer, Trend, Twilight, and Wing. While some of these lenses are prescription-strength corrective lenses, others are merely decorative. Some online distributors do not openly list their business locations, others such as TokyoWink, based in Hong Kong, Candylens, based in

Figure 20.1. Online companies promote their products with prominent images of Asian female models, in this case Japanese model Tsubasa Masuwaka.

Malaysia, Contactlens Xchange, based in Singapore/Malaysia, and Angel Contacts, based in Canada name their locale. These sites claim to distribute their lenses to clients throughout Asia, including China, Hong Kong, Japan, Malaysia, the Philippines, Singapore, South Korea, Taiwan, and Thailand and nations in Europe and Latin America as well as Australia, Canada, Iran, Turkey, United Arab Emirates, and the United States.

Although these lenses are sold in different continents, it is striking that the online companies promote their products with prominent images of Asian female models. Generated by the producers of circle contact lenses, these online advertising images are used by distributors to market them, so the same images are duplicated on multiple sites. Notably, the advertisements feature Asian models who emulate "Caucasian" beauty standards with their starkly angular faces, dyed blondish hair, very light skin, and sharp noses, features that in some cases appear to be surgically enhanced.

Online stores, retailers, and distributors market big eye contact lenses as a novel beauty enhancement tool that will make the wearer's eyes appear "gorgeous, luminous, bigger, sexier, and more alluring." One of the more popular sites remarks on their popularity that, "in fact, here in Asia, they are so widespread that girls consider them as makeup staples like eyeshadow or false eyelashes!"[6] These evocative advertising slogans promote a "normalized" beauty standard that speciously treats physical traits as if they are as interchangeable as clothing. They recommend adding that "pop of color to your eye" to match your natural eye color, skin tone, eye shadow, or outfit, reminiscent of the Yamaguchi advertising campaign for DuraSoft. The distributor website *Eyecandy's* suggests, "Why not make a statement by transforming your brown eyes with blue contact lenses, or get dolled up by putting on a pair of black lenses? If you prefer a natural look, choose alluring browns and sultry greys that will give you a subtle twinkle in your eyes. Green colored lenses give a sexy look; opt for violet for sweet, girly charm."[7]

Beyond just improving appearances, these advertisements make claims about emotional and personal enhancement. The *Pinky Paradise* website states, "Circle lenses are more than colored contact lens, but they are also [a] fashion trend, confidence booster, and a new way to present yourself. Make a change and make a different [sic] today!"[8] These messages focus on beauty enhancement for the younger generation who has leisure time and wants to make a fashion statement. The companies also concentrate on delivering psychological messages emblematic of the cosmetic industry around improving self-confidence and boosting popularity. Slogans for self-empowerment and self-confidence are interwoven in these ads. These messages are restricted to promoting a specific beauty standard that involves changing the color of the eyes and making them appear larger, reinforcing the message that altering the inadequate Asian eyes can transform one's state of mind and outlook and affect how others might perceive the wearer of the contact lenses.

The Trajectories of Gyaru and Ulzzang Style

The circle contact lens fad in Japan is part of the gyaru, or kogyaru, subculture, which started in the early 1990s and has attracted imitators in other nations. "Gyaru" is a Japanese word that translates into the English word "gal," which originated with the 1970s Wrangler brand of jeans called "gals" that used the advertising slogan "I can't live without men." The style has a number of variants and has mutated over the years but is characterized by girly-glam style, with fans favoring dyed-blonde or reddish hair, sexy clothing, and bedazzling colors. A staple has been fake, decorated nails and big eyes achieved by using eyelid glue or tape (and sometimes plastic surgery), dark eyeliner, fake eyelashes, and circle contact lenses. Mixing the cheap and glitzy with the luxury-brand items has been one of its trademarks, so one standard look has included a private school uniform with a Burberry scarf and loose socks. W. David Marx explains that the gyaru style was initiated by privileged schoolgirls and gained widespread popularity among the mainstream masses of teens who co-opted this trendy pop culture style.[9]

The adoption of the gyaru style has been noted for contesting cultural ideals of Japanese womanhood as well as traditional social protocol or decorum and is regarded as a sign of youthful rebellion. Japanese and overseas media have featured sensationalized stories of the younger generation's provocative fashion choices and liberated lifestyles, especially their sexualized and promiscuous behavior. Social critics have denounced the youth for promoting excessive materialism and superficiality as well as immoral decadence, blaming them for a decline in national character. In contrast, as Marx notes, "Radical voices and feminists saw the young women as cleverly negotiating their own position in a male patriarchal world."[10] These activists perceived them as contesting gender discrimination in the workplace and challenging gender and social norms.

As gyaru style dominated consumer culture with its innovation and followers, these fashionable youth caught the attention of marketers. Shibuya, the modern center for youth in the center of Tokyo, became the main attraction for those desiring gyaru accessories, especially the Shibuya 109 multi-story shopping mall. By the late 1990s, as gyaru fashion became widespread, kogyaru girls were hired as sales clerks at 109 shops and became the "authoritative power" on fashion branding and styles, influencing customer preferences, and these in-store transactions with customers created fans and followers. These trendsetters became a valuable business asset for moving merchandise, essential for the commercialization and commodification of gyaru style, displacing the power entrusted formerly only to big-brand stylists or magazine editors.[11]

Once shunned or accused of being rule breakers, the "gals" were being courted "for their spending power, their adventurous mindset and even as a cultural export."[12] Mihoko Nishii, of Japan's largest advertising group Dentsu, says that studies show that about 12 percent of women between eighteen and thirty-four are devoted gyaru "gals," but over half of the women surveyed share similar fashion tastes: "They may not look like gals but they also want to make their eyes look bigger and they like bling products."[13] She mentions that colored contact lenses and fake eyelashes are examples of "secret weapons" that have been adopted by ordinary women. One of the most popular gyaru models is Tsubasa Masuwaka, who has her own brand of makeup called "Candy Doll," a line of false eyelashes called "Dolly Wink," and a series of circle contact lenses called "Bambi" in Japanese markets and "Princess Mimi" overseas. She has extensive images on the Internet and is often used in online ads to sell circle contact lenses. Although its popularity has declined in Japan and has been curtailed by the global financial crisis, gyaru style has spread to China, Taiwan, and other Asian markets as well as to other continents.[14]

Influenced by Japanese gyaru fashion, the ulzzang style was popularized in South Korea, and these transnational cultural influences on style have spread to other countries, such as China, Japan, the Philippines, Singapore, Thailand, Vietnam, and North America through visual images easily found on the Internet.[15] The rise of ulzzang style extends gyaru fashion and parallels the popularity of Korean popular culture, or the K-Pop phenomenon, which is exporting a global celebrity fashion that includes circle contact lenses and its accoutrements through movies, televisions series, and the entertainment industry. "Ulzzang," or "uljjang," roughly translates to "best face" or "good-looking" in Korean. Through Internet portal communities, girls compete for the ulzzang title through contests in which girls post their headshots and are judged by the global online community. For example, the *Ulzzangasia* web site created what it refers to as a "netizen community" online that allows individuals to post photos and invites peers to vote for those they consider most attractive, with some winners achieving ulzzang celebrity status and garnering fans from global subscribers.[16]

As gyaru style dispersed across national borders through the Internet, it was adapted to local cultural forms; for example, while the visual imagery in Japan is highly sexualized, in South Korea the emphasis is on a childlike innocence and the style is less flamboyant. Although ulzzang subculture is about fashion that includes hair and clothing, its emphasis on facial features helped to popularize circle contact lenses. As one report describes the ulzzang style: "Huge, delicate bambi-like eyes with double lids and a tiny, delicate nose with a high bridge are a prerequisite. Smooth, pale snow-white skin, and rosebud lips are also a must. So is a small and sharp chin to achieve the perfect "*V-line*" face, which should ideally be no bigger than the size of your palm."[17] The "fairy-like" or "princess-like porcelain doll appearance," which includes the large "doe-eyed" look, is achieved with circle contact lenses and eyelid glue, fake eyelashes, eye shadow, and eyeliner. Talk shows, YouTube tutorials, and web sites feature makeup techniques, showing followers how to attain this look, which is likened to Japanese anime. Dissimilar to the gyaru that emphasizes the artificial style, the ulzzang rendition emphasizes "innocent," "natural," or "pure" beauty, even though the ethereal appearance is actually achieved through unnatural means such as circle contact lenses and plastic surgery or skin-whitening products, as well as retouched or edited photos. Young Asian female youth fueled the popularity of circle contact lenses through gyaru fashion in Japan and ulzzang style in South Korea, so what originated in Asia spread though the Internet to Asian American youth, who followed a similar trajectory to become style makers and influential figures in popularizing circle contacts lenses to U.S. consumers as well as redirecting cultural flows.

Lady Gaga, Michelle Phan, and Internet Beauty Gurus

Online culture, as an accelerated form of communication and an expansive form of social networking, has been instrumental in circulating consumer trends across national borders and popularizing circle contact lenses among Asian American young women in the United States. An informal overview indicates that a high percentage of bloggers and users that post photos of themselves wearing circle contact lenses, and many of their fans posting comments, are Asian or

Asian American females. These online venues allow Asian American women to dispense instantaneous beauty knowledge to other young women in a largely unregulated global marketplace. Early adopters of the lenses, some who were gyaru or ulzzang devotees and others who extracted elements of the fashion subcultures, discuss it on their websites, review it on their blogs or message boards, provide YouTube video testimonials, and post Facebook or Instagram photos of themselves wearing the lenses.[18] These makeup artists, both amateur and professionally trained, are referred to as "beauty gurus." Many use English as a medium; however, language is peripheral in the tutorials, since they rely heavily on visual images to reveal how to apply makeup and which products to use. Geography and location is inconsequential, since amateur fashionistas with basic computer equipment can film themselves in their bedrooms or bathrooms demonstrating beauty techniques and discussing style secrets that can easily be uploaded on YouTube, which gains them instantaneous popularity. They have generated additional fans and consumers of the circle contact lenses worldwide, who then promote it further through their online networks.

What once might have originated as a hobby to create how-to videos simply to share their knowledge or to garner attention has become for some a full-time entrepreneurial enterprise that has gained these "beauty gurus" notoriety. It is reported that "viewers watch more than 120 million how-to and beauty videos every day on YouTube" and "makeup videos are now the most frequently searched how-to content on the platform," so marketers began recognizing its potential.[19] Companies, domestic and international, have sought these style makers out for endorsements, product placements, and sponsorships as well as requesting their expertise on predicting fashion trends or surveying them to test out new products. The beauty gurus promote circle contact lenses products by showing the brands prominently in their videos, evaluating and recommending them and listing them in the description of their videos. In turn, companies offer bloggers and YouTube beauty gurus sponsorship opportunities, inviting them to contact the company and to send links to their websites or blogs. The promotional placements can be direct advertisements or appear in subtle forms on the fashion guru sites, with the young females wearing circle contact lenses while they feature accessories, clothes, hair, nails, shoes, or other style tips. Company websites prominently feature YouTube reviews and how-to videos by the beauty gurus that show purchasers how to open vials and how to wear and wash the lenses as well as rating their comfort level and displaying the latest designs. On the beauty guru sites, companies offer the viewers discounts through codes that can be used to buy the lenses or provide them with a free gift with their purchase.

Asian American young women have created their own cultural niche and launched their careers by providing makeup instructions tailored to Asian facial features, including their skin tones, the shape of their eyes, or their cheekbones. Through the Internet, Asian American fans are finding tips on how to wear clothes that fit their physique or how to style their hair. The Internet provides alternative avenues for Asian Americans to purchase cosmetic products, shifting from the importance of traditional malls, department stores, drugstores, and cosmetic or beauty shops that ignored ethnic consumers. Similarly, U.S. beauty and fashion magazines have rarely included advertisements, fashion spreads, or advice columns that cater to those with Asian facial features. Using social network media and video-sharing platforms, Asian American young women use their innovation and expertise to influence consumers, generate demand, and promote trends.

Michelle Phan, one of the most popular and successful of the beauty gurus, and other Asian American beauty gurus have created their own fashion venues and found their own consumer base. Phan, who is in her early twenties, is a Los Angeles-based self-taught makeup artist who debuted her first how-to makeup videos in 2006 using her laptop. Raised by her mother, a Vietnamese refugee who worked as a manicurist, Phan grew up in her mother's beauty salon in Florida. In 2010, with over 160 videos that had been viewed over 479 million times and with over one million subscribers, she became the number one most subscribed female on YouTube.[20] Increasing her subscribership to five million worldwide, and with her first video logging over ten million views, Phan has been instrumental in using these online videos to spread beauty trends, including the use of circle contact lenses.

The rising sales of circle contact lenses in the U.S. market were widely reported after the trendsetter Lady Gaga appeared with big, round eyes in her "Bad Romance" music video. However, the performer's enlarged pupils were computer generated, and it was Phan's tutorial "Lady Gaga Bad Romance Look" that actually led to increased U.S. sales of circle contact lenses. Phan showed how to replicate the "googly eyes" look using makeup and circle contact lenses, along with a blonde wig, to complete the transformation.

In this case, mainstream popular culture and Asian American beauty guru cultures converged with a fashion trend originally popularized in Asia to increase the appeal of circular lenses. Phan has popularized other "Caucasian" fashion looks, often using circle contact lenses with her wide-eyed "Barbie Transformation," "Lady Gaga Poker Face," and Disney princess characters such as her "Snow White" tutorials. Phan's tutorials often pop up on websites for circle contact lense companies globally that also feature still images of Asian models wearing their products, so presumably they are marketing to an Asian or Asian American consumer base. Some that are repeatedly featured are her "Brighter Larger Looking Eyes," "Aurora Eyes," "Avatar Inspired Look," and "Metallic Knight Look," makeup tutorials in which she wears color contact or circle contact lenses.

Phan seems aware of the damaging racial messages that women of color receive about beauty ideals, and in some respects, she has used her personal experiences to attract attention to Asian and Asian American women's beauty

Figure 20.2. Michelle Phan's Lady Gaga Bad Romance tutorial video, showing how to use circle contact lenses to replicate the singer's "googly eyes," was uploaded to YouTube on January 18, 2010, and has since received over 46 million views.

culture; however, she has been criticized for simultaneously reinforcing racial hierarchies through her visual tutorials. She reflected in an interview how growing up in a racialized environment affected her perception of beauty: "Western beauty is considered the dominant beauty in the world. . . . Tall, blond, blue eyes. I always felt a little self-conscious because I wanted to be more Caucasian. I tried to get bigger eyes. . . . I would dress preppy."[21] It seems her largest and most-dedicated fan base is in Asia, especially in Japan, where she ranks at the top for YouTube viewers, and she sources online information for makeup trends in China, Japan, Korea, Vietnam, and other parts of Asia, which is how she spotted the "puffy eye" or "kewpie doll eye" phenomenon in South Korea and created a make up tutorial for it.[22] In this way, racial aesthetics are reappropriated and recirculated across national borders in a circuitous fashion. Given her racial background, she attracted an Asian American viewership, some of whom are critical of the racial overtones in her makeup tutorials, such as online commentaries of her being "fake" or "wanting to look white with her color contacts" rather than embracing her Asian features, which is similar to the Yamaguchi controversy. Although young Asian and Asian American women are reshaping narrow definitions of racial beauty and can be influential cultural trendsetters, they may simultaneously reinforce ideologies of beauty that are infused with racial hierarchies.

The popularity of Phan's online tutorials gained her a contract in 2010 to be the first-ever video makeup artist representing Lancôme cosmetics, a subsidiary of the L'Oreal corporation, and they also supported the launch of her own makeup line, em Cosmetics, which can be shipped all over the world. She is also featured in a Diet Dr. Pepper television commercial, which played during prime-time programming, showing her in front of her laptop filming herself putting on makeup and highlighting a montage of images from her beauty videos, including her "Bad Romance" video. The commercial casts her as a waitress, her real-life former job, in an all-American diner serving the diet soda, saying at the end, "I'm Michelle Phan, and I'm one of a kind." She is one of the rare beauty gurus who has been able to transfer her Internet status to gain entrée into the main-stream beauty industry, as well as leveraging it to gain contracts to endorse other products and business ventures. In 2014, she reached a milestone of one billion views on YouTube and released a book, *Make Up: Your Life Guide to Beauty, Style and Success—Online and Off.*[23] As fashion trendsetters who employ the latest technology, young Asian and Asian American women have found pathways to becoming pivotal figures of attention and influence, while concurrently being co-opted and marketed by global capital; thus the operations of cultural trans-mission is multi-faceted and multi-directional.

Manga, Anime, and Transnational Cultural Circuits

Circle contact lenses extend color and patterns beyond the iris, providing an innocent doe-eyed or doll-like look that has been popularized by the gyaru or ulzzang style, which cultural commenters remark is reminiscent of Japanese manga (graphic novels) or anime (animation).[24] Michelle Phan is also aware of the transnational connections and references Asian popular cultural forms, remarking that, "in Asia, it's all about the eyes in makeup. . . . They like the whole innocent doll-like look, almost like anime."[25] In her videos, she transforms her "almond-shaped" eyes to look like anime art, explaining that "you want your eyes to look like a cartoon, so it's all right to be a bit dramatic. . . . lining your waterline with white will give you an appearance of larger-looking eyes."[26] In their Facebook pages, fans of circle contact lenses in Asia and the United States merge global cultural forms as well, often listing in the "Like" section of their "About" pages the names of companies that produce circle lenses as well as links to anime, manga, and Michelle Phan. The media has picked up on these linkages in reporting the anime connection to circle lenses, with one editorial warning in its title that "Unapproved Contacts to Emulate Japanese Anime Look Not Worth Risk to Vision."[27]

These contemporary linkages to anime have historical roots that reveal transnational cultural interconnections. With the post–World War II defeat of Japan and the subsequent American Occupation, Western cultural forms were introduced to Japan, which reshaped contemporary Japanese traditional and national aesthetics as it remade itself into a global economic power. Dispropor-tionately large eyes are considered a staple of manga and anime styles popular in Japan; however, there are distinct U.S. influences that shaped what is considered a Japanese cultural form that has been transplanted to the United States. In the early 1950s one of the most influential founding fathers of anime, Osamu Tezuka, was inspired by the enormous eyes of the famous U.S. cartoon character Betty Boop, along with Walt Disney's Mickey Mouse and Bambi animation characters.[28] These animal and human images have been noted for influencing his most famous creation, Astroboy/Astro Boy, who has large, round eyes. Betty Boop originally appeared as a dog-like cabaret singer in the Max Fleischer short animation *Dizzy Dishes* in 1930 and was eventually transformed into a humanized female who was portrayed as a sexualized and "glamorous international icon" with her big, round eyes and long eyelashes.[29] Her cartoon shows are lesser known, but her image is still marketed to sell a variety of consumer products. Astro Boy was originally created in 1951 for a Japanese boy's magazine and evolved into a humanized robot with large eyes and a powerful horsepower engine and rocket jets for legs, who promoted ways in which humans and technology can co-exist peacefully. The manga was adapted into a Japanese television series that aired in 1963, then in the same year became the first Japanese animated program to be shown on U.S. television.[30]

Other Japanese artists emulated Tezuka's style, which morphed into characters who are identified as "Japanese" but have exaggerated eyes that can be blue or green.[31] The cultural intermixing is reflected in Japanese manga comic and anime characters which are drawn with large, round, eyes and blond, brown, orange, or red hair.[32] For more than two decades, U.S. television networks have imported Japanese anime, such as Robotech, Voltron, Sailor Moon, Hamtaro, Pokémon, Naruto, and Yu-Gi-Oh, and these shows are popular with American children. In the United States, the "big eyes" look is associated with Japanese manga and anime and, by extension, Japanese popular culture. Hayao Miyazaki's animated Japanese feature films, *Princess Mononoke* (1997), *Spirited Away* (2001), *Howl's Moving Castle* (2004), and *Ponyo* (2008), which were successfully distributed in the United States, also created more anime fans.

Through on-demand television cable networks, computers, and mobile devices, many different genres of anime have become a chief cultural export for Japan, such as the online Anime Network, which is a broadcast and digital distributor of Japanese animation in North America.[33] Anime and manga continues to gain popularity with an avid fan base of children and adults through comic or anime conventions, videos, gaming, and film festivals; however, this subcultural form has also gained widespread aesthetic appeal among those who may not read manga or watch anime. In an age of global digital connectivity, whether this is through print media, television shows, or films, these animated images are now reinforced via the Internet in computer games and online video formats.

While some bloggers and fans counter the criticism that these characters with their large orbs privilege whiteness, others argue they are "raceless" and that the eyes merely depict traits such as innocence and allow them to be more expressive. Defenders regard the intermingling and intersecting of Western and Japanese aesthetics and the fantasy spaces they create as representative of a transnational or stateless culture, characterized by a global hybridity that is a merging of global and local cultures that is neither purely Western or Japanese. Rejecting the idea of American domination of mass culture in which Japanese culture is subsumed into a hegemonic global culture, others regard the popularity of Japanese anime and manga as forms of cultural resistance to the dominance of Western culture.[34]

The repeated ways in which anime and manga characters with large orbs are displayed is instrumental in creating an acceptable aesthetic for circle contact lenses in Japan and abroad. Producers and distributors of circle contacts lenses have capitalized on the popularity of manga and anime to their predominantly female consumers. Noticeable is that, in these fantasy or science fiction theme narratives, there are female superheroes or cyborgs who are shown as independent and powerful, while sometimes simultaneously depicted with sexualized or cute features. This imagery counters the prevalent stereotypes of submissive females and the constraining gender roles imposed upon women in modern Japanese society, somewhat reflective of the ways in which the gyaru fashion intermixes sexuality and independence.[35] One circle contact lenses distributor Kawaii (meaning "cute" in Japanese), attempts to capitalize on this connection between their product and anime to an audience outside of Japan, stating that "cuteness is a national fixation in Japan and it is certainly one of the defining aesthetics of manga and anime."[36] In their "be beautiful" video commercial, another distributor, Pinky Paradise, shows a cartoon girl with large square eyes, but small irises, looking at *Popteen*, a popular Japanese fashion magazine. She then decides to use circle lenses, which enlarge her irises, giving her anime-like eyes, and as a result of her transformation, colorful images of rainbows, flowers, hearts, butterflies, and stars suddenly appear.[37] Some companies are selling anime-inspired circle contact lenses that are named after popular characters, and the advertisements show the anime characters with an accompanying picture of the contacts that replicate in color and design their exaggerated irises. Thus female fans can emulate the fashion style of their favorite characters, including the use of circle contact lenses to copy their prominent facial features.

The imaginary spaces of manga and anime are transmuting idealized standards of beauty, notably influencing the desire for racialized reconfigurations of the body. Anime and manga, which are based on narratives of science fiction or fantasy, have generated avid global devotees who are imitating the anime look. Even White women are emulating Japanese anime characters, or similarly transforming themselves to resemble living dolls, and are further popularizing circle contact lenses, which engenders public fascination and, sometimes, repulsion.[38] This complicates a merely straightforward mimicry of whiteness and highlights the circularity of transnational cultural forms. Anastasiya Shpagina from Ukraine uses the name "Anime" and is known for transforming herself into a Japanese-inspired living doll. Already watched by millions of viewers, her "Flower Fairy" makeup tutorial on YouTube shows how to create the "giant, doe-eyed look" with circle contact lenses along with thick applications of eye shadow, liquid eyeliner, and false eyelashes. Another "human Barbie" who has become a YouTube sensation and embraces the wide-eyed look of a doll is Venus Palermo of Britain, with her numerous Barbie makeup tutorials. She shows fans how to achieve a porcelain-like complexion with rosy accents and the illusion of a narrow nose along with circle lenses for the doll-like look. She dresses in frilly rompers and speaks in a childish voice that some perceive as a feigned Japanese accent. Others are critical of these artificial physical enhancements, such as one blogger who critiques plastic surgery and "dangerous contact lenses" in which "being *human* is apparently no longer desirable" and sets an impossible frame of beauty that women are supposed to now achieve with the perfect look of fantasy and comic characters derived from a digital world.[39] These reappropriations of circle contact lenses in sites beyond Asia and the United States illustrates the complex circuits of racialized cultural forms and also present a critique of how digital imaginations can also shape beauty standards for real women.

Conclusion

This chapter explores the interconnection between four primary cultural sites of production—gyaru fashion, ulzzang style, digital beauty gurus, and anime/manga—which have shaped and contributed to the popularity of circle contact lenses. Although it is assumed that pop culture trends that originate in Japan or in the West can be redistributed globally, this chapter explores the ways in which cultural transmission and transmutation can be simultaneously multi-directional and multi-faceted. The cultural origins of beauty culture is complicated to trace, given the processes of cross-fertilization or cross-pollination and the high speed at which digital circuits re-circulate visual imagery across national boundaries. None of these can be reduced to either a single point of origin or as simply acquiescing to Western beauty standards. Circle contact lenses have expanded beyond Asian American communities and have multi-racial appeal with African American, Latina, and White women promoting them on their beauty tutorials and blogs too. Circle contact lenses as a cultural practice have multiple influences, so transformations to the female body are infused by ideological beliefs and cultural traditions that have divergent origins, rendered more complex by the Internet, which has made beautification practices and products more accessible to audiences worldwide.

Although economic and social inequalities or disparities produced by global capitalism and the commercialization of the Internet are still prevalent, this analysis shows the malleability of new technologies and possibilities for cultural interventions. Undeniably savvy in employing new technologies, Asian American women resist their disenfranchisement on the peripheries and attempt to democratize the marketplace and redistribute technological resources through online consumption and the dispensation of beauty cultures to dictate what is fashionable. Online technologies allocate more control to consumers who can redirect the capitalist economy and dictate trends in the marketplace. Producers and vendors are able to communicate directly with their buyers and receive instantaneous feedback on products as well as promote and sell directly to buyers across transnational borders. While Asian American young women are neglected in mainstream marketing, these transnational circuits have repositioned their economic spheres of influence, increased their clout in setting trends, and allowed them a space to redefine women's beauty culture that is more racially inclusive. Nonetheless, there are limitations to this analysis of inclusive communities and repositioning, since it is also driven by self-interest and economic profit. These young girls and women are still confined by the limiting dictates of a global beauty culture that caters to making them appealing to the opposite sex, places primacy on superficial or frivolous aesthetics of self-enhancement, and emphasizes the homogenization of beauty standards.

Circle contact lenses emerged at a time when technological advances via the Internet allowed young consumers to converse directly with one another globally and fostered the creation of virtual communities. These lenses are a fashion fad that will be replaced by the next obsession with bodily and facial modification; however, even as a temporal product, it is suggestive of the ways in which transnational cultural markets and emerging technologies can evolve to bring new possibilities for intervention, once unimaginable, by Asian and Asian American cultural producers and innovators. It also illuminates the complexities of how racialization figures into these questions of transnational consumption and cultural production in a digital age.

NOTES

1 Elena Tajima Creef, *Imaging Japanese America: The Visual Construction of Citizenship, Nation, and the Body* (New York: NYU Press, 2004), 167–171; Thomas S. Mulligan, "Yamaguchi's Endorsement Deals Prove Good as Gold," *Los Angeles Times*, March 17, 1992, http://articles.latimes.com/1992–03–17/business/fi-4044_1_endorsement-deals, accessed March 27, 2014; Glen Macnow, "Different Shade of Gold—Racism Could Prevent Yamaguchi from Cashing In," *Seattle-Times*, March 8, 1992, http://community.seattletimes.nwsource.com/archive/?date=19920308&slug=1479888, accessed March 4, 2011; Laura Zinn, "To Marketers, Kristi Yamaguchi Isn't as Good as Gold," *Business Week*, March 08, 1992, http://www.bloomberg.com/bw/stories/1992–03–08/to-marketers-kristi-yamaguchi-isnt-as-good-as-gold, accessed April 27, 2014. Commentators note that fears about the economic competitiveness of Japan created an atmosphere of anti-Japanese bashing at the time that might have hindered Yamaguchi's endorsement opportunities.

2 Darrell Y. Hamamoto, *Monitored Peril: Asian Americans and the Politics of TV Representation* (Minneapolis: University of Minnesota Press, 1994), 243–244; Nelson Wang, "From Tennis Rackets to Tinted Contacts," *A. Magazine*, October 31, 1994.

3 Kobena Mercer, *Welcome to the Jungle: New Positions in Black Cultural Studies* (New York: Routledge, 1994), chap. 4.

4 Rachael C. Lee and Sau-Ling Cynthia Wong, "Introduction" in *AsianAmerica.Net: Ethnicity, Nationalism, and Cyberspace* , ed. Rachel C. Lee and Sau-Ling Cynthia Wong (New York: Routledge, 2003), xiii–xxxv; Alicia Headlam Hines, Alondra Nelson, and Thuy Linh N. Tu, "Introduction: Hidden Circuits," in *Technicolor: Race, Technology, and Everyday Life*, ed. by Alondra Nelson and Thuy Linh N. Tu with Alicia Headlam Hines (New York: NYU Press, 2001), 1–12.

5 Juju Chang, Chris Strathmann, and Sabrina Parise, "Eye-Popping New Fashion Trend Could Carry Dangers, Docs Say," *ABC News*, July 6, 2010, http://abcnews.go.com/GMA/Consumer News/circle-lenses-dangerous-docs/story?id=11093873, accessed January 22, 2013.

6 "Which Color Suits Me?" *Eyecandy's*, http://www.eyecandys.com/which-color-suits-me, accessed January 20, 2012.

7 *Eyecandy's*, http://www.eyecandys.com, accessed March 25, 2013.

8 "Wear and Care Guide for Beginners," *Pinky Paradise*, video, http://www.pinkyparadise.com/Video_s/1893.htm, accessed January 22, 2013.

9 W. David Marx, "The History of the Gyaru—Part One," *Néojaponisme*, February 28, 2012, http://neojaponisme.com/2012/02/28/the-history-of-the-gyaru-part-one, accessed April 15, 2013.

10 W. David Marx, "The History of the Gyaru—Part Two," *Néojaponisme*, May 8, 2012, http://neojaponisme.com/2012/05/08/the-history-of-the-gyaru-part-two, accessed April 15, 2013.

11 Ibid.

12 Mariko Oi, "Japan Harnesses Fashion Power of Gals," *BBC News-Tokyo*, August 29, 2012, http://www.bbc.co.uk/news/world-asia-19332694, accessed January 23, 2013.

13 Ibid.

14 Misha Janette, "Where Have All The *Gyaru* Gone?" *Japan Times*, October 14, 2011, http://www.japantimes.co.jp/text/fl20111014r1.html, accessed January 23, 2013.

15 Julieann de Lacy, "Ulzzang!" *Scene Project Online Magazine*, n.d., http://sceneprojectonline mag.weebly.com/fashion-ulzzang.html, accessed January 23, 2013.

16 "About," *Ulzzangasia*, http://www.ulzzangasia.com/about, accessed January 23, 2013.

17 Elizabeth Soh, "Korean 'Ulzzang' Beauty Mania Comes to Singapore," *Singapore Showbiz, Yahoo! Entertainment*, October 29, 2012, http://sg.entertainment.yahoo.com/blogs/singapore-showbiz/korean-ulzzang-beauty-mania-comes-singapore-072253957.html, accessed February 23, 2013.

18 Catherine Saint Louis, "What Big Eyes You Have, Dear, but Are Those Contacts Risky?" *New York Times*, July 4, 2010, A1, http://www.nytimes.com/2010/07/04/fashion/04lenses.html, accessed October 16, 2015.

19 Stephanie Buck, "Michelle Phan: Behind the Makeup of YouTube's Fairy Godmother," *Mashable*, August 23, 2014, http://mashable.com/2013/08/23/michelle-phan, accessed June 7, 2014.

20 "About," Michelle Phan website, http://www.michellephan.com/about, accessed March 30, 2012.

21 Stephanie Hayes, "Michelle Phan, a Youtube Sensation for Her Makeup Tutorials, Has Transformed Her Life," *Tampa Bay Times*, August 23, 2009, http://www.tampabay.com/features/humaninterest/michelle-phan-a-youtube-sensation-for-her-makeup-tutorials-has-transformed/1029747, accessed October 16, 2015.

22 Stephanie Buck, "Michelle Phan."

23 Michelle Phan, *Make Up: Your Life Guide to Beauty, Style and Success—Online and Off* (New York: Harmony Books, 2014).

24 "Unapproved Contacts to Emulate Japanese Anime Look Not Worth Risk to Vision," *Seattle Times*, July 9, 2010, http://www.seattletimes.com/opinion/unapproved-contacts-to-emulate -japanese-anime-look-not-worth-risk-to-vision, accessed January 23, 2013.

25 Catherine Saint Louis, "What Big Eyes You Have."

26 Hayes, "Michelle Phan."

27 See "Unapproved Contacts."

28 Art Young, "Why Circle Contact Lenses Are So Popular," *Helium*, July 7, 2010, http://www .helium.com/items/1883360-why-circle-contact-lenses-are-so-popular, accessed January 23, 2013.

29 Fleischer Studios, "Part One: Betty's Rise to Fame," http://www.fleischerstudios.com/betty1 .html, accessed November 2, 2015.

30 Charles Solomon, "Astro Boy was Role Model Who Revolutionized Manga," *Los Angeles Times*, October 23, 2009, http://articles.latimes.com/2009/oct/23/entertainment/ et-astroanime23, accessed January 21, 2013.

31 Rachael Rainwater-McClure, Weslynn Reed, and Eric Mark Kramer, "A World of Cookie-Cutter Faces," in *The Emerging Monoculture: Assimilation and the "Model Minority,"* ed. by Eric Mark Kramer (Westport, CT: Praeger, 2003), 221–233.

32 Andrew Lam, "Are Asians Increasingly Undergoing Plastic Surgery to Look White?" *New America Media* at *Alternet*, March 31, 2007, http://www.alternet.org/story/49894, accessed March 5, 2011.

33 "About Us," *Anime Network*, http://www.theanimenetwork.com/about-us, accessed January 23, 2013.

34 Susan J. Napier, *Anime from Akira to Howl's Moving Castle: Experiencing Contemporary Japanese Animation* (New York: Palgrave MacMillan, 2005), 9.

35 Ibid., 31–33.

36 *Kawaii.Love.Beauty*, http://kawaiilovebeauty.com/shop/index.php?main_page=page_2, accessed January 24, 2013.

37 "Wear and Care Guide for Beginners," *Pinky Paradise*, video.

38 Ingrid Schmidt, "Top 10 Beauty Videos on Youtube," *Los Angeles Times*, January 2, 2013, http://www.latimes.com/features/image/alltherage/la-ar-top-10-beauty-videos-on-youtube -20130102,0,3361513.story, accessed January 23, 2013.

39 "Female Ideal Now Cartoons?" *hse1976* (blog), November 23, 2012, https://hse1976.wordpress .com/2012/11/23/female-ideal-now-cartoons, accessed January 24, 2013.

21

Making Whales out of Peacocks

Virtual Fashion and Asian Female Factory Hands

CHRISTOPHER B. PATTERSON

For about three months in early 2014, my brother and I met online every Sunday to play the video game *Saints Row IV* (Volition 2013), a carnivalesque satire of American masculinity that gives the player godlike powers in order to obliterate gang members and aliens in a sandbox-style open world. However, we spent most Sundays spending the virtual money we had earned from violent in-game activities on colorful clothing for our avatars, items satirically advertised as "eco-friendly." Though my avatar looked nothing like myself, watching her complete in-game missions in clothing I had personally selected gave me what Petri Lankoski has called an "empathetic engagement" with my avatar, in which I could recognize her desires and attitude as products of my imagination and thus parts of myself (Lankoski 2011, 1). Indeed, tossing yellow scarves over her black jumpsuits seemed to fulfill such an inner glee that at the end of every play session, my brother and I would compare our new outfits by taking in-game snapshots. Soon enough, we were so immersed in the game's cosmetics that we were paying for virtual clothing, not with in-game currency, but with real cash.

In the last ten years, virtual fashion has emerged as both an ethical alternative to real fashion and as an ideal business model for gaming. In the early 2000s, reality television series like *Project Runway* and later *Fashion Star* popularized fashion as both a form of art and a democratic ideal, as most designs were for everyday wear and designs could be voted on by non-experts. But the 2007 economic recession created a rupture in fashion discourse, one that allowed virtual clothing to insert its way as a popular substitute. Massive online games like *Second Life*, *World of Warcraft* and *Guild Wars* allow players to purchase limited-edition clothing made by real designers for only a couple U.S. dollars or for simply liking a Facebook page. Game companies like CCP (Crowd Control Productions) partner regularly with fashion designers to ensure quality fashionable items, hoping to make big-money "whales" out of "peacocks"—players like myself and my brother, who were both willing to use real money to purchase virtual clothing. This narrative, which began to take hold in 2005 with the popularity of *Second Life* in the United States and *Maple Story* in Korea, has heralded virtual fashion as a means of satisfying the urge to "peacock" without spending a large amount of money and without the need for exploitative sweatshops.

By wearing the mark of "art" and "newness," fashion has long stitched up its ethical contradictions to maintain a notion of glamor that dictates the shape of women's bodies and distances consumers from the laborers who make the products. In contrast, the potentials of virtual fashion seem benevolent, as such fashions are shaped as a means of transcending gender and sexual and other social norms found in real-life fashion. Even though the majority of video gamers are now women (Juul 2010), the emergence of virtual fashion came from men—mainly teenagers—who were willing to pay for in-game "cosmetics." Virtual fashion forms seem just as common in violent, male-dominated games like the *Saints Row* series as they are in casual games catered to women. Such fashions are taken up then more as a means of play than for art or beauty. With a seemingly infinite amount of clothing to choose from, players are free to experiment and often establish personal connections with new fashions after dozens of hours of gameplay. According to Yohei Ishii, the director of business development at CCP, "As a designer, you can create clothes that you wouldn't be able to in the real world because of physics or economics. As a gamer, you can be whomever you want to be" (Moore 2011). Game universes allow players to purchase virtual clothing that fits their athletic avatars, clothes that defy gravity, and clothes that perfectly mimic the latest fashions because they are designed by real fashion designers (Wu 2007). In this narrative, even the overweight and elderly can fit in with the latest fashions, and all without the potential guilt of not quite knowing where the clothing came from.

The narrative of virtual fashion as a form of benevolent consumption seems typical of discourses about information technology, which shape information technology devices as futuristic and as part of a global apparatus of innovation that promises to solve all the problems created by the "past" innovations, such as industrial plants, reliance on fossil fuels, and underage, unsafe factory work. As a narrative that explicitly offers the creative technology of the past through the "egalitarian" technology of the present, virtual fashion acts as a means of resolving real anxieties about exploitation and empire without actually changing the means of producing fashion products or information technology. Virtual fashion, for all its potential, does not enable users to stop wearing real clothes manufactured in real factories. Despite the popularity of online gaming, fashion companies like H&M, The Gap, and Zara have increased revenues even as they have publicly relied upon factories that defy state and international labor laws. As the Asian American popular culture critic Thuy Linh Tu writes, the fashion industry "operates through a logic of distance" that "works not to mask or deny the labor of clothing production, but to isolate it from the here and now of fashion making" (Tu 2011, 27). Since clothing production is often associated with Asian countries like Bangladesh, China, and Indonesia, this isolation further obscures Asian factory labor and removes mental images of Asian sweatshops from the products themselves.

In video games, the logic of distance is facilitated through a narrative of virtual fashion that operates by comparing the innovation of information technology to "older" industries like fashion, which are marked as expensive, vain, and exploitative. In emphasizing virtual fashion as an alternative to exploitative factory work, online games like *Guild Wars 2* and *Lord of the Rings Online* now make more money by selling cosmetic items than by charging users to play. Yet as thinkers like Lisa Nakamura and Aihwa Ong have pointed out, information technology, too, relies on the intensive labor of Asian factory hands. Even so, the narratives of progress that shape their commodification focuses the production process almost entirely upon celebrity innovators living within the Global North. Furthermore, the form and gameplay of these games mark them as politically progressive, as players are free to gender bend and experiment and as clothing is bought almost entirely through "micro-transactions" of less than twelve U.S. dollars, thus eliminating the conspicuous consumption and class structure so commonly tied to the fashion industry. Indeed, the particular forms of interactive storytelling result not merely in distancing players from manufacturing processes but in a complete disavowal of Asia and Asian factory labor as well, marking (white) designers as the sole creators within the production process.

This essay investigates how the experience of playing in virtual fashion worlds shapes information technology as a benevolent commodity bestowed from creator (designer) to player. Such gameplay experience de-values and erases Asian factory and development work through the rules and boundaries of gameplay, which produce affects of redemption that alleviate capitalist guilt. The erasure of Asian factory hands is solidified through consumption processes of microtransactions that offer virtual fashion as a "merely cosmetic" way of providing free games. In all of these gameplay mechanisms, "Asia" as a space of production is made invisible, excluded from an otherwise "benevolent" process of production as it directly contradicts the ethical narratives of information technology characterized, for example, by the charity of Bill Gates and the innovation of Steve Jobs. My aim here is to trouble these narratives by exploring how virtual fashion speaks to anxieties between the sweatshop and the ethical consumer. How does the narrative of virtual fashion allow users to ignore the emerging labor market in Asia, where cellphone assembly lines, microprocessor factories, and call centers are becoming just as ubiquitous as garment factories?

Boundaries in a Simulated Universe

Until the 2000s, video game fashion could be read as similar to fashion in literary texts, films, and photography. The styles, references, and patterns were symbolic, trendy, or simply cute and were meant to enhance the player's experience by making the game universe more convincing and stylistic. But with the appearance of massive multiplayer online games like *World of Warcraft* in the early 2000s, the growth of the fashion industry in video gaming became a unique experience all its own. As games like *World of Warcraft* and *Guild Wars* are embedded into players' social networks, a player can wear expensive clothing while maintaining an "innocence" and playfulness that seem different from the romantic and alluring world of fashion. If a gamer purchases a Louis Vuitton bag for her avatar, the symbols of the virtual image attract a different set of meanings than if the player herself were to tout a real Louis Vuitton bag. Even if both items were of the same value, the virtual item is free of the baggage of consumer and imperial anxiety that the real bag might represent to more critical or ethically minded audiences. While some audiences might find the virtual bag silly, none would consider how the bag—indeed, how the image and the device they are viewing the image on—was produced through a transnational exploitative process. When comparing the real thing to the virtual item, the first injunction is to praise the virtual item as a symbol reflecting the free and diverse virtual world through which it is rendered.

The emergence of fashion as a significant mechanic in shaping narratives of game production is tied directly to the experience of playing these games, particularly in experiencing their shared rules and boundaries. As I discussed in my previous work on BioWare games (Patterson 2015), the meanings made through the game's rules and boundaries are not merely meant to facilitate the story but are persuasive, ideological mechanisms in themselves. For the video game scholar Ian Bogost, the gameplay form contains a "procedural rhetoric" in which the art of persuasion occurs "through rule-based representations and interactions rather than the spoken word, writing, images, or moving pictures" (Bogost 2007, ix). For game designers like Jonathan Blow, creator of *Braid*, the most popular indie game of all time, meanings based on the game's form or "dynamics" can rarely be attributed to the designer's intentions or attempts to manipulate the player (Blow 2009). A game's persuasive meaning, rather, is most often unintentional and grows out of gameplay elements that are not necessarily coded with intended meanings. The persuasive grammar of games then comes in the collaboration between the player and the game's rules, its boundaries, and its means of consumption.

The importance of fashion in a game's dynamic meanings is in facilitating the player's subject formation so that the player feels powerful interacting within a supposedly free world. Yet games characteristically limit the player's power and freedom through its gameplay boundaries. Unlike a game's "rules," which are meant to challenge the player and to mediate their relationship to others, "boundaries" in games function similarly to social norms in that they establish limitations upon a social practice ideologically constructed as free and of the player's choice. Any given gameworld contains boundaries, from the spatial boundaries of the game's "map" to imagined boundaries restricting the player's experience of "free play," like a virtual tree, fence, or wall that allows arrows to pass right through. Such boundaries may cause the player anger, resentment, or disappointment, but they are excused as part of the game's artistic design, and in the free social utopia of the gameworld, they are seen as necessary constraints.

Games in which virtual fashion plays a prominent role often feature the telepresence of multiple players who interact within open worlds. Players then feel free not only to interact in a scripted story but also to create their own narratives within the rules and boundaries of gameplay. This goes well beyond the scope of interactive fiction, instead employing the everyday practices of performance. Subject formation is not only coded and encrypted in the narrative but is also embedded in the player's social practices of healing; homemaking; combat; driving cars, ships, and helicopters; and in the clothing they choose for their avatars. The social world of online games is constructed as both "free" and "egalitarian" in that one can imagine interacting with a limitless diversity of other players and can feel their anonymous telepresence as they accomplish every mission. This feeling of anonymity turns the online space into a utopic gameworld, where players are only identified by their freely opted, individual choice—their chosen class, their chosen race, and their chosen means of play. Of all these choices, however, the player's fashion is the most diverse, as players can choose from thousands of separate garments, all for around the same micro-price.

Against the utopic narrative that virtual fashion helps produce, we can trace a game's boundaries in online games to index various incidences of racial and class exclusions. This has been the case in the growing market of Asian players, as the use of an Asian language, especially Chinese, marks players as possible "gold miners," real-life factory workers whose sole job is to perform repetitive in-game tasks to collect as much in-game money as possible (or to level their character). The banning of Chinese gold miners in games like *World of Warcraft* forms a boundary across players who are otherwise celebrated as anonymous. Game administrators seek out these groups through linguistic cues and rely on the online community of players to surveil each other, thus producing groups of players identified as "non-play," who enter the gameworld not out of leisure but out of economic need. For Lisa Nakamura, these unwanted Chinese subjects "depict Asian culture as threatening to the beauty and desirability of shared virtual space" (Nakamura 2009). Indeed, the focus on Chinese gamers particularly speaks to a social erasure of "Asia" within the gameworld, even as players are free to dress their avatars in traditional Chinese fashions, from cheong-sams to Mao suits. In including fashionable cultural symbols worn among anonymous players (who could be any race, sex, or nationality), such games read as diverse and utopic, despite the boundaries excluding the people of those cultures themselves.

The logic of egalitarian play informs the process of clothing manufacturing in online games, while the game's boundaries reveal the player's subject formation by virtue of what a boundary excludes. In the massive multiplayer online game *Guild Wars 2* (ArenaNet 2012), players are meant to work together to obtain objects needed for manufacturing their own virtual clothing. In my own play of the game, I encountered virtual fashion not as exploitative factory work but as a traditional, pre-modern craft, one that demanded I spend hours "grinding" (earning in-game gold) for virtual objects. The labor process is laid out from the beginning. I spend hours gathering raw materials, discovering their locations, then mining and chopping to store them in my backpack. Then I head to cities, often traveling vast distances, to find guilds and teachers who will help me refine the items. Then I must build my skill tree to bind, sew, and dye my new garments. Many hours pass before I can wear my first piece of clothing: a piece of armor made from wool and cotton scraps that resemble a child's attempt to cut a dress out of a burlap sack. Though I could have easily bypassed all that labor by simply purchasing the in-game item with real money, the game's boundary in craftwork keeps me from finding real-world methods to secure the items, such as stealing the items from other players or finding cheap knockoffs made in exploitative factories. The boundary reinforces virtual fashion as a more ethical practice, as its objects function as symbols of earned achievement. In turn, players become intimate with the virtual object by investing it with their own personal experience of producing it.

The in-game craftwork process of gathering wood and ore stands in stark contrast to the real process of obtaining raw materials for video games. In order to manufacture the PlayStation 2, celebrated as the most successful game console ever released, Sony had to obtain its raw material in a process deeply embedded in slave labor, massacre, and rape. The PlayStation 2 used a rare raw material iron, coltan ore, which Sony imported from mining companies in the Eastern Democratic Republic of the Congo. As the ethnographer James Smith has pointed out, the dispossession of land, the enslavement, and deaths (five million) resulting from the ongoing civil war in the Eastern Congo can be traced to Sony's need for coltan ore. As Smith writes, "In late 2000, Sony's efforts to meet the Christmas demand for PlayStation 2, along with intense dot-com speculation, caused the price of coltan to increase tenfold overnight" (Smith 2011, 18). The price hike and Sony's willingness to work with any group that provided the ore "greatly intensified the violence in the Eastern Congo and encouraged multiple groups and nation-states to implicate themselves in the conflict in the hope of making a killing" (Smith 2011, 18). The long-term effects of the price hike was "spectacular violence on Congolese civilians" as women "were 'raped' and 'cursed' from marrying and bearing children, crops and livestock were stolen, and ordinary people were forced into slave labor for militias" (Smith 2011, 19). While companies like Sony, Nintendo, and Apple have "implemented measures" to divest from the Congo, they continue to purchase capacitors that use Congo coltan, relying more and more upon their customers' virtual gameplay experiences to erase real production processes (Parra 2010).

The arduous process of in-game "grinding" forms the player's ethical identity, so that the hours spent "earning" the virtual items produces feelings of redemption. Their "grind" causes the player to feel more aware of the long process of production in "craft" yet directly contradicts the industrial mode of production and the violent processes of obtaining raw material. Even though the object obtained is merely virtual, and thus cannot substitute for the player's real need to wear clothing, its process of grinding gave me, as is characteristic of video games, an impression of freedom and choice. Crafting the item formed my new role in opting to purchase and appreciate virtual clothes rather than real clothing. But, of course, the object in front of me was not a product of the garment factory, but of Asian factories and of raw materials derived from Africa. My guilt as a first-world consumer was gone, and my anxiety about the tenuous egalitarian narrative of gaming, resolved. The game absolved me, and I was ready to participate in the larger global network.

Much has been written about how video games induce feelings of guilt upon players. While being immersed in a game, players may find themselves giddily choosing to kill an animal, only to gasp in horror when they realize that the deed is far more traumatic than it had appeared when the option came in a clickable bubble on their screen. Yet, as my experience in *Guild Wars 2* shows, games also have the power to alleviate guilt, to absolve the player. Attention to a game's boundaries remind us that games cannot simply be read as a text, nor can their stories be read solely as narratives. Indeed, the boundaries reinforce games as "play," as the "grind" required to manufacture clothing produces feelings of alleviation while suturing anxieties concerning players' positions as both consumers and as citizens of the Global North. In accepting these simulated feelings of redemption uncritically, I, too, accept a dream world that denies real manufacturing processes of Asian labor, a labor not merely distanced or obscured but completely excluded, forgotten, erased.

Freemium and the "Merely Cosmetic"

The narrative that tethers virtual fashion to ethical notions of a world without sweatshops has allowed virtual goods to operate as the primary method of gaining profit for many video game companies, despite the fact that such virtual items are merely bits of data. Popular games like *Second Life* and hundreds of casual games can be downloaded completely for free ("free-to-play"), making companies seem benevolent since they only ask for payments through optional micro-transactions (defined as transactions less than $12) that purchase virtual items (Tassi 2013). Gaming communities have celebrated this turn in gaming, and massive online role-playing games like *Guild Wars 2* and *Star Wars: The Old Republic* have abandoned monthly subscriptions to charge only for optional in-game purchases. So long as the ability to purchase in-game content is restricted to fashion designs, or the "merely cosmetic," gamers seem to uniformly hail this shift in payment form. Not only does virtual fashion allow gamers to wear their favorite styles without the cut, make, and trim assembly lines, but it does so without creating unfair gameplay, since such micro-transactions affect only the look of the avatars, not their advantage within the game (Tassi 2013). Indeed, this narrative of virtual fashion has been so successful that it diverts attention away from the possibilities of producing real-world fashion *without* the use of sweatshops. Rather, the turn to virtual fashion sees *all* fashion manufacturing as suspect, turning the gaze of critical suspicion from information technology onto "lingering" forms of factory work. These virtual goods, absent from real-life material, are thus categorized as a "service" that absolves the player. Indeed, the ethical advantage of virtual goods allows some virtual items to carry the same price or to be even more expensive than the real garment, setting a high price for one's ethical affiliation. The often-cited example of this is the massive multi-player online game, *EVE Online*, which sold very realistic cosmetic clothing items for characters that "far outstripped the value of what the actual physical item would cost in the real world, from t-shirts to monocles" (Tassi 2013).

The contemporary shift toward casual games on iPhones and Android devices has propelled virtual fashion to audiences who identify less as gamers and more as consumers but who may also be concerned by the faults of the fashion industry. As the game scholar Jesper Juul points out in his book, *A Casual Revolution*, micro-transactions have become more profitable for casual game companies because their players "often [do] not think of themselves as playing video games (even though they clearly [are])," and the growth of virtual fashion is less from video games becoming cool than from becoming normal (Juul 2010, 1). Juul defines "casual games" as games that are purchased online, can be played in short time bursts, and generally do not require an intimate knowledge of video game history or genre in order to play. Indeed, as Juul points out, game companies now no longer see themselves invested in young, adolescent boys, but in "women over 35" (Juul 2010, 9).

Social networking companies have also capitalized on the trend in virtual fashion by featuring avatars as mascots for users, a strategy that has been most successful in Asia, where the social networking service Tencent QQ (known simply as QQ) has generated over one hundred million dollars in a single yearly quarter, with over 65 percent of revenue coming from the purchase of virtual items (Wu 2007). These virtual items have become more expensive as more users have joined the service, as any item purchased carries the potential to be seen by any of the eight hundred million active QQ accounts. The similar Finnish social networking company Habbo Hotel makes 90 percent of its $60 million+ yearly revenue from virtual goods, while the American social network Gaia Online employs "3 people whose sole job it is to open snail mail envelopes full of cash that people send in for virtual goods" (Wu 2007). Noting that billions of dollars have been spent buying virtual fashion on Facebook, the casual game company CCP partnered with real fashion designers to create "limited-edition avatar outfits" (Moore 2011). While most virtual fashion is sold through micro-transactions, intense or hardcore gamers have turned from "peacocks" to "whales" by purchasing cosmetic items within the hundreds or thousands of dollars range. The most expensive cosmetic item ever sold was for the male-dominated strategy game *Dota 2*, and it made $38,000. The item sold was "a Pink Ethereal Flames Enduring War Dog, a rare variant of the Enduring War Dog . . . available for purchase in the Dota 2 store for $12" (Miozzi 2013). Since *Dota 2* is billed as a balanced competitive game, the $38,000 War Dog costume is "entirely cosmetic" and merely changes the appearance of "a donkey that transports goods to and from the shops to players on the field" (Miozzi 2013).

The temptation to purchase virtual clothing from in-game auction houses may seem like an amusing sub-culture to most, but to many gamers the system that combines free-to-play games with in-game micro-transactions that are "merely cosmetic" assumes a bright future for gaming, where anyone can play any game for free, so long as those who have money volunteer to pay for their cosmetic items and, ultimately, to pay for everyone else. Free-to-play is thus enabled by virtual fashion. Those who play for free are supported by those who pay-to-dress. In 2006, only a year before the economic recession made this system more popular, this business model became known as "freemium," a combination of the words "free" and "premium," in which games would be provided free of charge but micro-transactions (known as "premiums") were made for virtual goods.

Perhaps the freemium form of free-to-play video games can offer some possible answers as to how the narrative of information technology maintains its innocent glaze and its erasure of Asian factory hands. If a game's persuasive power comes from a combination of rules, limitations, and formal attributes, as Ian Bogost and Jonathan Blow remind us, then we can say that the freemium system produces persuasive meanings that affect how players may see the outside world and that, because these meanings are embedded into a particular payment form, they cut across multiple genres. The stark discourse of gratitude from tech industry experts is made explicit by the *Forbes* magazine reporter Paul Tassi when he writes:

> Games who focus their microtransactions on cosmetic upgrades with literally no impact on gameplay are the golden standard when it comes to the system [of freemium games]. . . . Leading the pack is League of Legends, the current most popular game in the world. League allows you to buy champions and runes with

real money, but also lets you purchase them with enough earned XP [experience points]. The only thing locked behind a paywall are cosmetic upgrades for your characters which have no bearing on gameplay, and they're bought for fun, for vanity, or just to say job well done to a company who has given you a great game for free. (Tassi 2013)

Like many gamers, Tassi interprets the free-to-play/pay-to-dress freemium system as a symbol of the benevolence of the game company and of information technology in general, rather than as a strategy that produces feelings of gratefulness in order to make more money through micro-transactions than they would otherwise. Paying for virtual fashion items thus becomes a matter of alleviating one's guilt or showing one's gratitude toward a seemingly benevolent host of designers and computer programmers.

Narratives of Asian Labor and Information Technology

In May 2013, the familiar narrative of garment factory exploitation was reinvigorated following the collapse of the Rana Plaza factory building in Bangladesh. News channels reported the deaths of more than eleven hundred factory workers, almost all of whom were young women who worked in "garment-making companies linked to well-known Western brands" (Motlagh 2014, 64). As news spread of the factory's low wages ($60–$110 dollars a month) and its horrid working conditions (twelve to sixteen hour days with very few days off), the Rana Plaza tragedy sparked a series of short-lived protests for a global minimum wage for garment workers and heated backlash against companies affiliated with factories in Bangladesh.

While the inhumane conditions in garment factories have been a familiar practice for hundreds of years, people in the Global North are often shocked to find similar working conditions in factories that produce information technology. From 2010 to 2012, a slew of scandalous articles emerged against Apple concerning the treatment of Chinese workers in factories owned by its Taiwanese contracted manufacturer, Foxconn, one of the largest private employers in China. These scandals began in 2010 when eighteen Foxconn employees attempted suicide, resulting in fourteen deaths and reporters took pictures of Foxxconn factories where nets had been strung up to keep workers from committing suicide (Chan et al. 2013). Though Apple received most of the negative press, Foxconn produces game consoles and gaming computers, as well as Apple's iPads and iPhones (George 2012). In fact, all three major console companies—Sony, Microsoft, and Nintendo—had their most recent "next-generation" consoles (PlayStation 4, Xbox One, and Wii U) produced by Foxxconn.

Both of these labor-related tragedies—the factory collapse in Bangladesh and the suicides at Foxconn—speak to different means of obscuring Asian factory work. While the collapse of the garment factory was met by competing companies like Wal-Mart and American Apparel producing more ethical ad campaigns to reel in ethical publicity, the suicides at Foxconn resulted in a narrative of exclusion and erasure. Twenty universities in China, Hong Kong, and Taiwan wrote an eighty-three-page report that detailed the Foxconn suicides and labor conditions in factories, which they called an "inhumane" "labor camp" (Tam 2010). Yet economists and sources from Apple were still skeptical that suicides represented a problem, since, considering the number of workers at Foxconn, the overall suicide rater there was lower than that of China or the United States (Beaumont 2010). Indeed, for Apple, profits only increased after the scandal. Attempts to erase the Asian production process in information technology are often analogous to the boundaries of gameplay, where limitations are ignored to instead celebrate the freedom and egalitarianism of gameplay. Similarly, the exploitation of Asian female factory hands is met with skepticism, as it directly contradicts the dominant discourse of information technology as a source of progress, innovation, and benevolent consumption.

While in fashion the consumer is distanced from factory work through the representation of clothing design as a form of artistry, in information technology the obscurity around the production of iPhones, computers, and game consoles has been deeply embedded in the narrative of progress and innovation. As Aihwa Ong has pointed out in her investigation of microprocessor factories in Export Processing Zones in Malaysia, information technology companies have used this narrative to exploit rural areas with a surplus population of non-working females (Ong 1987, 103). Such factories employ already existing structural violence to produce a population of low-wage factory laborers and have a heavy hand in intensifying gender and race hierarchies within their operative spaces. According to Lisa Nakamura, information technology factory work has always relied upon racialized notions of women's bodies (Nakamura 2014). She traces the emergence of information technology factories to Navajo Indian reservations in 1965, when the Fairchild Corporation's semiconductor division used ethnic associations of Navajo women with "blanket weaving . . . and jewelry making," to make the women seem naturally fitted to build electronic devices and integrated circuits (Nakamura 2014). Fairchild was one of the largest private employers in the United States until 1975, when protestors who accused the company of sweatshop labor occupied and shut down its plant. Fairchild then joined the exodus of information technology corporations by outsourcing manufacturing to female workers in Asia.

Whereas in garment work labor crises such as the Rana Plaza collapse in Bangladesh can benefit clothing companies like American Apparel and Wal-Mart, who bill themselves as more ethical, there are few to no information technology companies that would adequately frame a narrative about the exploitation of female women in Asia without also being implicated in it, making the erasure of Asian factory work a common interest for all companies involved. While, for example, the hardware company Dell Computers may have emerged as an alternative to Apple products, not long after the Foxxconn incidents information also emerged about Dell-contracted factories. According to an undercover investigation by Danish and Chinese labor watchdogs, "Chinese workers at factories making Dell computers are being forced to work seven day, 74 hour weeks under appalling conditions" and for below minimum wage (Miller 2013). Such conditions involved breathing toxic fumes, standing up for entire twelve-hour shifts, and having access to one toilet for every fifty-five workers. These hardware factories are largely owned by or contracted to one of the top-ten or even top-five hardware companies. Lenovo, Dell, Hewlett-Packard, Acer, Apple, and Toshiba dominate the market. Because these brand names are so idealized as notions of progress, ethics, and innovation, the processes of just how these products are made, assembled, and transported comes across as trivial.

Besides the work of scholars like Aihwa Ong and Lisa Nakamura, literary writers have also wrestled with exposing the exploitation in information technology manufacturing. In Lawrence Chua's 1998 novel *Gold by the Inch*, the queer Asian American narrator travels to the island of Penang in Malaysia, where his distant cousin Martina works for a multinational microchip factory. When he visits Martina, she describes the factory as a space masked with progress and human development; as she says, she was "awed and intrigued by the equipment she had to use" in the factory, equipment such as a microscope, which "she had only seen scientists and professors use on television" (Chua 1998, 93). Martina's awe for the machine is developed through the symbolic resonance of information technology as the forefront of human development. Due to her exhausting work hours, Martina realizes that the space of "human development" demands that her body be cast off once her labor power has been exhausted.

Transpacific literary works like *Gold by the Inch* expose the microprocessor factory and challenge its narrative as non-exploitative. And as I have tried to show throughout this article, reading games critically can also participate in the same anti-imperial project. Understanding the persuasive rhetoric of games in their rules, boundaries, and modes of consumption can reveal how games shape our inhabited social space as egalitarian, progressive, and futuristic. At stake in reading games critically is the opportunity to expose what such narratives seek to exclude or erase—for example, how the microprocessor factory reproduces the conditions of the garment factory by employing young, female, rural Asian women and in exploiting them through overtime work, housing them in on-site dorms, paying low wages, and creating unsafe working conditions. Indeed, the labor of the microprocessor factories and the computer-welding plants seems to suggest that, despite innovation and progress, forms of debt slavery and hazardous working conditions do not go away; they are not merely "lingering" forms of labor. Rather, they are crucial processes to getting that iPhone or that keyboard or that video game controller into our hands.

REFERENCES

ArenaNet. 2012. *Guild Wars 2*. Online role-playing game. Bellevue, WA: NCsoft.

Beaumont, Claudine. 2010. "Foxconn Suicide Rate Is Lower than in the US, says Apple's Steve Jobs." *Telegraph*, June 2. http://www.telegraph.co.uk/technology/steve-jobs/7796546/Foxconn-suicide-rate-is-lower-than-in-the-US-says-Apples-Steve-Jobs.html, accessed August 20, 2015.

Blow, J. 2009. "NYU Game Center Lecture Series: Jonathan Blow." *NYU Game Center*. http://gamecenter.nyu.edu/2009/10/nyu-game-center-lecture-series-jonathan-blow, accessed June 14, 2014.

Bogost, I. 2007. *Persuasive Games: The Expressive Power of Videogames*. Cambridge, MA: MIT Press.

Chan, J., N. Pun, and M. Selden. 2013. "The Politics of Global Production: Apple, Foxconn and China's New Working Class." *New Technology, Work and Employment* 28:100–115.

Chua, L. 1998. *Gold by the Inch*. New York, Grove Press.

George, R. 2012. "iPhone, Wii U Manufacturer Admits to Employing Children." *IGN*, October 17. http://www.ign.com/articles/2012/10/18/iphone-wii-u-manufacturer-admits-to-employing-children, accessed August 19, 2014.

Juul, J. 2010. *A Casual Revolution: Reinventing Video Games and Their Players*. Cambridge, MA: MIT Press.

Lankoski, P. 2011. "Player Character Engagement in Computer Games." *Games and Culture* 6:291–311.

Miller, D. 2013. "Appalling Conditions of Factory Workers Who Make Dell Computers Who Are Forced to Work Seven-Day, 74-Hour Weeks and Live in Dorms with No Hot Water." *Daily Mail*, November 8. http://www.dailymail.co.uk/news/article-2492998/Revealed-Appalling-conditions-factory-workers-make-Dell-computers-forced-work-seven-day-74-hour-weeks-live-dorms-hot-water.html, accessed June 16, 2014.

Miozzi, C. J. 2013. "Dota 2 Cosmetic Item Sold for $38,000." *Game Front*, November 7. http://www.gamefront.com/dota-2-cosmetic-item-sold-for-38000, accessed June 15, 2014.

Moore, B. 2011. "Fashion Diary: Designers Look to the Virtual World." *Los Angeles Times*, September 18. http://articles.latimes.com/2011/sep/18/image/la-ig-diary-celebrity-20110918, accessed June 16, 2014.

Motlagh, J. 2014. "The Ghosts of Rana Plaza." *Virginia Quarterly Review* 90:44–89.

Nakamura, L. 2009. "Don't Hate the Player, Hate the Game: The Racialization of Labor in World of Warcraft." *Critical Studies in Media Communication* 26:128–144.

———. 2014. "Indigenous Circuits." *Computer History Museum*. http://www.computerhistory.org/atchm/indigenous-circuits, accessed 11 October 2014.

Ong, A. 1987. *Spirits of Resistance and Capitalist Discipline: Factory Women in Malaysia*. Albany: State University of New York Press.

Parra, J. R. 2010. "Congo: The Coltan Conflict Is in Our Hands (and Cellphones)." *Global Voices: Africa*, February 20. http://globalvoicesonline.org/2010/02/20/congo-the-coltan-conflict-is-in-our-hands-and-cellphones, accessed August 19, 2014.

Patterson, C. B. 2015. Role-Playing the Multiculturalist Umpire: Loyalty and War in BioWare's Mass Effect Series. *Games and Culture* 10:207–228.

Smith, J. H. 2011. "Tantalus in the Digital Age: Coltan Ore, Temporal Dispossession, and 'Movement' in the Eastern Democratic Republic of the Congo." *American Ethnologist* 38:17–35.

Tam, Fiona. 2010. "Foxconn Factories Are Labour Camps: Report." *South China Morning Post*, October 11. http://www.scmp.com/article/727143/foxconn-factories-are-labour-camps-report, accessed August 20, 2015.

Tassi, P. 2013. "The Ten Commandments of Microtransactions." *Forbes*, November 25. http://www.forbes.com/sites/insertcoin/2013/11/25/the-ten-commandments-of-microtransactions, accessed June 14, 2014.

Tu, T. L. N. 2011. *The Beautiful Generation: Asian Americans and the Cultural Economy of Fashion*. Durham, NC: Duke University Press.

Volition. 2013. *Saints Row IV*. Video game. Champaign, IL: Deep Silver.

Wu, S. 2007. "Virtual Goods: The Next Big Business Model." *TechCrunch*, June 20. http://techcrunch.com/2007/06/20/virtual-goods-the-next-big-business-model, accessed June 19, 2014.

22

Failed Returns

The Queer Balikbayan *in R. Zamora Linmark's* Leche *and*
Gil Portes's Miguel/Michelle

ROBERT DIAZ

On any given day of the week, diasporic Filipinos watching their favorite shows on The Filipino Channel (TFC) can come across a short, kitschy, but no less entertaining segment called *Star Balikbayan* during the commercial breaks. *Star Balikbayan* follows fortunate *balikbayans*, or transnational returnees, as they become "celebrities for a day" during their most recent visit to the Philippines. These individuals occupy front row seats to local variety and talk shows that they have been religiously following abroad. They also interview famous celebrities backstage as guest correspondents. Participants in turn extol the benefits of a TFC cable subscription, which costs between ten and twenty dollars per month. As Geraldine Yumpit, a devoted customer from Burbank, California, declares after she interviews her idol Toni Gonzaga, "If not for TFC, Filipinos living abroad would not be happy. TFC: the best!" Yumpit's comments exemplify *Star Balibayan*'s effectiveness as a marketing strategy for the growing cable network. The show encourages viewers to imagine their homecoming as tantamount to achieving international fame. It thus conflates the ruse of stardom with the *balikbayan*'s perceived economic success and nostalgia for return. The show reminds us that, in period of heightened transnational movement, returnees play a significant political, cultural, and economic role in the articulation of globalized Filipino/a subjectivities locally and abroad.

For Filipinos in the diaspora, *balikbayans* embody the intricate relationship among labor migration, cultural nationalisms, and contradictory affective affiliations to people and place. Transnational returnees—particularly overseas foreign workers—enable government-sponsored narratives of nationalism by serving as *bagong bayani*, or "new heroes" to the nation-state. They also redefine coalitional politics amid unequal forms of migration and movement, as they engender ambivalent feelings from the local population that range from pride to envy.[1] Cultural discourses valorize heteronormative ideals of familial patronage, sacrifice, and support through returnees. These discourses insist that the act of return ultimately index the *balikbayan*'s unseverable bonds to the family and the nation-state. Discussing the link between return politics and nationalism, Eric

Estuar Reyes suggests that dominant narratives of return are in fact "fictions of return" since they often reproduce metonymic connections to a homeland that rely on "unproblematic rootedness" and "imagined fixity" (Reyes 2011, 115). In other words, precisely because returns are often articulated through nationalist identity politics, these moments mark the limits of celebrating "homecomings" as embodiments of national responsibility.

Given these characteristics, the *balikbayan* figure is crucial to the institutionalization of what I call "redressive nationalisms" within a Filipino diasporic context. Redressive nationalisms involve the strategies deployed by the nation-state to justify monetary, symbolic, and political forms of redress. Redressive nationalisms, despite their articulation as positive affects of filiation and attachment, often circulate as disciplinary mechanisms for consolidating state power and for furthering transnational capital's expansion. Redressive nationalisms valorize specific identities in the name of repairing past dictatorial, colonial, and imperial violence, even as these nationalisms occlude certain subjectivities and communities in the act of animating such reparative sentiments. Redressive nationalisms reproduce and espouse normative kinship structures and ultimately delineate which subjects are worthy of inclusion in the wholesale attempt to "repair" the broken nation-state.

Yet are all returns that simple or reparative? Are all returns universal in their espousal of positive affect, familial responsibility, and national affinity? I engage with these questions as I examine how queer returnees subtend limited articulations of "homecoming." In particular, I analyze Gil Portes's film *Miguel/Michelle* (1998) and R. Zamora Linmark's novel *Leche* (2011a). Both works bring the richness of postcolonial and queer returns into stark relief. *Miguel/Michelle* chronicles the life of a labor migrant who leaves the Philippines as a biological male (Miguel) and who, after seven years of absence, returns to her conservative hometown as a postoperative female (Michelle). Michelle returns in order to gain the acceptance of her family, close friends, and community members. Yet despite possessing the typical *balikbayan* traits often celebrated in popular culture—she is wealthy, she has given back to her community, and she has a successful career—Michelle's identity as a trans woman causes a crisis of signification for those around her. Her trans body forestalls the axiomatic embrace of her as a successful arbiter of economic success and American modernity. She fails to perform the ideal *balikbayan* that both her hometown and the nation-state ultimately demand.

Similar to *Miguel/Michelle*, *Leche* follows the travails of a queer *balikbayan* whose return is anything but simple. The novel narrates the experiences of a gay man, Vicente De Los Reyes or Vince, as he returns to the Philippines after thirteen years of absence. Vince navigates an alien and chaotic metropolitan Manila and ends his journey by returning to his hometown San Vicente. Vince returns to the Philippines not because of an aching desire to reclaim his ancestral roots.

Rather, he returns because the trip is his consolation prize for failing to win the Mr. Pogi (Mr. Handsome) beauty contest in Hawaii. While the contest winner is sent to various "little Manilas" in the U.S. mainland as a goodwill ambassador, Vince is sent to the Philippines to visit the "real" Manila to his chagrin. Comedic and satirical at every turn, *Leche* displays the ambivalences inherent in a queer return, particularly when the protagonist is unable to fully map onto Manila's many cacophonies. Manila becomes an important space to negotiate what Martin Manalansan calls the "wayward erotics" of return. According to Manalansan, such returns are often characterized by messy, inconclusive, and contradictory attachments to homeland that refuse to follow heteronormative scripts (Manalansan 2012, 35).

Rather than exist within seamless narratives of return, queer returnees in *Miguel/Michelle* and *Leche* enact homecomings full of false starts, incorrect assumptions, bad judgments, and definitional misfires. In failing to fully incorporate into their social milieu (whether the small town or the city), Michelle and Vince challenge the very terms that define them as appropriate diasporic returnees. They move beyond the recuperative logics that *balikbayans* must often recite. They challenge the conflation of return with national responsibility by exposing how such a conflation relies on the maintenance of normalized (and often untenable) ideals of cultural citizenship.

Recuperating Returns

"Sir, uuwi po ba kayo?" (Sir, are you going home?), the officer at the Toronto Philippine consulate asked as I was renewing my passport. I was at the consulate to prepare for an impending trip to the Philippines during the 2013 holiday season, one of the busiest tourist seasons of the year. After learning about my plans, the officer gestured to a stack of flyers advertising a government-endorsed excursion called "Winter Escapades." This weeklong trip involved going to six key destinations in the Philippines so that guests may enjoy their sights, festivals, and beaches. The brochure also included a letter from the Philippine ambassador to Canada, Leslie B. Gatan, which affirmed one of the trip's major benefits: the opportunity to meet the current president, Benigno Aquino, Jr., during a courtesy call to Malacañang Palace. To be clear, "Winter Escapades" did not cater to diplomats, dignitaries, and public officials. Nor did it cater to Filipinos/as based in the Philippines. Instead, the trip targeted *balikbayans* in Canada willing to pay the price. This trip thus offers yet another example of the role *balikbayans* play in local Philippine politics. Ironically, the tour that the current administration so willfully supports owes its existence to policies instituted during Ferdinand Marcos's regime, a regime that presidents such as Aquino vehemently criticize. These political and historical nuances are all but forgotten and, to an extent, rebranded by a post-Marcosian institutional apparatus that is willing to gain from the returnee's economic and political potential, much the same way as Marcos did during his time.

Indeed, one cannot fully understand the returnee's significance to Filipino diasporic culture without acknowledging the Marcos government's role in institutionalizing this figure in all aspects of everyday life. After the declaration of martial law in 1972, Marcos needed to assuage the negative effects of dictatorship, particularly for Filipinos living abroad. As a way to alleviate such concerns, Marcos focused on tourism in order to produce a more welcoming or positive image for the Philippines. By expanding the local infrastructure for returnees, Marcos was then able to physically mold the metropolis in the spirit and ethics of his "new society." The historian Linda Richter notes that, as a result of such changes, "the country which only eight months earlier was reputedly seething with violence, declared tourism to be a priority industry eligible for a variety of tax incentives and customs concessions" (Richter 1980, 242).

The *balikbayan* program was an important cog in such a recuperative gesture. Implemented in 1973, the *balikbayan* program materialized the government's efforts to increase both tourism and investment. Aside from its economic benefits, the *balikbayan* program created a bureaucratic structure for occluding the harmful images of martial law. Yen Le Espiritu writes that such *balikbayan* initiatives "must also be understood as an example of transnational politics, designed to secure the endorsement of the overseas population for the regime" (Espiritu 2003, 81). Through the *balikbayan* program, the government tried to assuage the resistance of a growing population of overseas Filipinos living in the United State who have now begun to establish themselves as migrants, workers, and full participants in their respective societies.

The returnee thus sutured particular cracks caused by the historical traumas of dictatorial rule. The creation of a tourist industrial complex during Marcos's time was first and foremost an attempt to "repair" the human rights abuses and limits to freedom effected by dictatorship. Encouraging tourism was a strategic move by the regime to pick an area of growth that would garner the least amount of resistance through what Marcos saw as an industry "relatively unconcerned about political freedom" (Richter 1980, 243). The negative effects of dictatorial rule were repackaged and delivered as something economically viable for the nation-state.

After deposing Marcos, Corazon C. Aquino's administration did not abolish the *balikbayan* program. Despite the fact that Aquino abolished most of Marcos's policies, why, we might ask, did she maintain the *balikbayan* program? I would argue that Aquino continued it because her government saw this figure's potential for reasserting the nation's new political trajectories. Espiritu suggests that the new government enshrined the program into law as a way to entice Filipinos to return and fulfill their nationalist purpose of helping rebuild a new democratic society postdictatorship (Espiritu 2003). The *balikbayan* program thus became Republic Act 6768, which gave more economic incentives for *balik-bayans* than previously established. At this critical historical juncture, when the Philippines was going through major political and economic shifts, *balikbayans* were needed to continue their role as nationalist intermediaries that validated the ethical nature of the new government in power. Such policies require the reiteration of nationalist identity, albeit in new form. They required the re-articulation of travel to and from the "homeland" as the ideal Filipino/a citizen's primary responsibility.

Transing the *Balikbayan*

In their introduction to the groundbreaking issue "Trans-" in *Women's Studies Quarterly*, Susan Stryker, Paisley Currah, and Lisa Jean Moore suggest that, aside from indexing multiple forms of gender-crossing, the term "trans" in transgender also refers to the "potentially porous and permeable spatial territories" that characterize gender itself (Stryker, Currah, and Moore 2008, 12). "Trans," they argue, calls forth the vexed ways in which gendered bodies are situated across different material, geographic, and political contexts. To "trans" our understanding of the world is thus to necessarily commit to seeing the complex ways that gender is articulated alongside other identity constructs and along various hierarchies of difference.

Such a spatial, psychic, and performative interpretation of "trans" provide a useful entry point for examining the experiences of the transgender *balikbayan* in Gil Portes's film *Miguel/Michelle*. At the most fundamental level, the film embodies the many meanings of "trans" by arguing that Michelle's biological transition and journey to "self-awakening" is synonymous with her travel back to her "place of origin." Writing about the prevalence of "journeys" to transgender representation in film and literature, Jay Prosser suggests that such narratives provide a trenchant critique of "originary" stories and their teleological characteristics. Prosser writes that these tropes "contain important ambivalences about home and territory, belonging and political affiliation" (Prosser 1998, 177). This ambivalent framing of "origins"—both biological and geographic—is similarly invoked in *Miguel/Michelle*. *Miguel/Michelle* re-contextualizes the transgender journey and turns this trope on its head. More specifically, the movie imagines a postcolonial and transgender subject whose psychic and material journeys are disciplined by the tenets and affects of flexible citizenship. The film presents a story about the chains of meaning that create the ideal *balikbayan*, such as economic stability, appropriate respectability, and familial commitment, while also foregrounding how such ideals police Michelle's acceptance as a woman. The film thus provides a stark reminder of how departures and returns are disciplined by the pressures that postcolonial labor migrants systematically face.

Figure 22.1. Miguel gazes at an object beyond the screen while his family celebrates his departure. *Miguel/Michelle*, 1998.

By narrating the experiences of a transgender returnee who "fails" to live up to what is expected from a "male" labor migrant, *Miguel/Michelle* exposes how heteronormative "fictions of return" are maintained through state, familial, and communal "fictions" of gendered Filipino/a citizenship. Michelle's body becomes the paradoxical site where such norms take material meaning. It also serves as an example of how diasporic subjects enact multiple forms of bodily, geographic, and affective crossings despite such disciplinary limits. Michelle's trans identity produces an opportunity to unravel the tenuous scripts the have defined what "homecoming" means for particular Filipinos/as in the first place. As Martin Manalansan writes in his analysis of the film, "Michelle's predicament unleashes an avalanche of intersecting desires that disrupts the easy connections between body and modernity, and between mobility and stasis" (Manalansan 2012, 42).

For example, precisely because Michelle's value as a *balikbayan* is intimately linked to her being a "male" labor migrant, her departure and return are haunted by the specter of Miguel. *Miguel/Michelle* begins with a crucial moment of departure. Before the opening credits, the camera provides a close-up of Miguel gazing at an unknown object beyond the screen (fig. 22.1). The shot then pans out to reveal Miguel taking a picture with his immediate family and close friends at the airport (fig. 22.2). The scene conveys a feeling of euphoria and excitement.

Adding to the moment's celebratory atmosphere, other people from Miguel's hometown have also accompanied the family to bid their goodbyes and well wishes. They serve as onlookers, as they cheer Miguel on with elation. After taking their family picture, Miguel's mother Tinay reminds him to make sure he is settled first before sending remittances to the Philippines. His father Nano interrupts by proudly saying that, as a "junior," Miguel is as strong and tough as he. Nano also reminds Miguel that "he" cannot disappoint the family. One of the community members then implores Miguel to marry a blonde woman before he returns. She states, "Naku Miguel, mahahaluan na ng puti ang lahi niyo" ("Wow Miguel, your family's race will be mixed with whiteness").

Even before Miguel has left for the United States, family, friends, and community members have already interpolated him as an exemplary model for Filipino citizenship. As a male labor migrant, Miguel is expected to uphold the values of the traditional nuclear family and to embody quintessential American modernity. He is also expected to support his family. However, by envisioning Miguel's departure as a literal "re-staging" of the family for the sake of the photographer's lens (thus making it a performance within the film), Portes simultaneously gestures to the compositional nature and performativity of this departure and of the familial or institutionalized expectations around Miguel's gender identity. The unsustainability of such expectations comes to the fore when Michelle returns

Figure 22.2. Miguel taking a picture with his family at the airport. *Miguel/Michelle*, 1998.

as a postoperative female, thereby causing a sensation in her hometown to her family's embarrassment. Michelle fails to return as the beacon of heterosexual male promise. She does not marry a blonde woman and has instead transitioned into a woman herself.

The "Americanized" modernity that the community so desires the *balikbayan* to possess, and to boast about with pride, becomes the source of their shame. Emphasizing her inability to reconcile her daughter's transgender identity with her *balikbayan* status, Tinay asks, "Uso ba yan sa America?" ("Is that the fad in America?"). Before they attend mass, Tinay also tells Michelle: "Don't flaunt it too much, try not to put too much makeup." Tinay's entreaties contradict the usual practice of welcoming *balikbayan* family members. Such practices often involve displaying the returnee's accomplishments to other members of the community. Tinay's cautiousness is justified in the film, however, as Michelle and her family are systematically ostracized. In another moment of disavowal, members of Tinay's church group implore the parish priest (Michelle's childhood best friend) to restrict Michelle from going to church. Even though the priest lectures them about the virtues of tolerance, the church members continue to complain. One of them voices her irritation by attacking Tinay: "Tinay acts like a big shot. Just because she has a son that works in America, she behaves like they are different. But in reality, they are indeed different."

These moments of disavowal occur with almost manic repetitiveness in the film. Such moments enable Portes to trace Michelle's struggles for acceptance amid seemingly insurmountable obstacles. Indeed, acceptance forms the primary impetus for the entire film's plot. Acceptance becomes the primary gauge for ascertaining whether Michelle has succeeded in fulfilling her personal objectives as a returnee. Acceptance also becomes the site where the film critiques the limits of inclusionary rhetoric. Despite the movie's continuous attempts to portray a fully resolved story of inclusion, it ends up highlighting the tenuous grounds with which such an acceptance is ultimately proffered. There are two main examples of such a problematic embrace of Michelle. The first involves her father Nano, and the second involves her previous high school. One of Michelle's primary reasons for returning is to gain her father's acceptance. The movie thus stages a scene of violence that both father and daughter experience in order to enact such a resolution. The scene begins with the family having dinner at a lakeside restaurant. Michelle excuses herself to go to the restroom. The audience then hears ominous music. The film shows four men following Michelle in the restroom. They taunt her, as one of the men lifts her skirt up and states: "Miss, my friends doubt whether you're a real woman. Maybe we can see what under your skirt?"

Before they are able to continue, Nano enters the room and demands that the men release Michelle. He states, "Bitiwan niyo siya" (Release her/him).[2] Nano

Figure 22.3. Michelle's flashback: Nando teaches Miguel how to box. *Miguel/Michelle*, 1998.

then defends Michelle, and an altercation ensues. While watching her father come to her aid, Michelle remembers a time when he had taught her boxing (fig. 22.3). This childhood memory then propels Michelle to defend herself. She uses the same boxing moves that her father taught her. Upon witnessing this, Nano becomes convinced that despite the difference in appearance, the Miguel he once knew had never truly left Michelle's body. In other words, even though the film presents this moment as a concrete example of the growing understanding between Michelle and her father, it also inevitably suggests that Michelle could only be accepted after she performs as the version of Nano's son that he demands her to enact. Even amid the scene's almost hyperbolic restaging of the reunion between father and daughter, one gets a sense that the film cannot escape relying on overwrought displays of masculinity, maleness, and heteropatriarchy in order to get to such an acceptance.

Even the movie's penultimate moment of communal acceptance is inherently incomplete and unresolved. By the end of the movie, Michelle's former high school is undecided whether to award her with a distinguished medal of service for financially supporting one of the school's brightest scholars. This crisis comes to the fore, as the scholar is required to deliver the school's graduation speech. Despite the fact that Michelle's *balikbayan* status and her financial support make

Figure 22.4. Michelle's high school celebrates an anonymous benefactor, represented by an empty seat. *Miguel/Michelle*, 1998.

her worthy of positive recognition, the graduation committee is unwilling to condone her transgender identity by celebrating her on stage. They thus resolve this dilemma by asking that Michelle be mentioned as an anonymous benefactor during the graduation ceremonies. She is also not allowed on stage and is represented by an empty seat (fig. 22.4). As the town applauds Michelle's generosity, it is difficult to ascertain who or what exactly is being celebrated. Ultimately, for Michelle to be included during this celebration, she has to be disembodied, literally erased. That is the only way that she can be seen as a legitimate returnee worthy of all the accolades accompanying such an identity.

As the film *Miguel/Michelle* deftly demonstrates, for the transgender *balik-bayan*, returns involve painful processes of negation, disavowal, and fleeting moments of agency. Through Michelle's struggles, the film visualizes what Dean Spade calls "critical trans politics." Spade argues that despite the many modes of erasure that transgender subjects experience, such occlusions paradoxically produce a "specific political potential—a potential to formulate demands and strategies to meet those demands that exceed the containment of neoliberal politics" (Spade 2011, 41). *Miguel/Michelle* embodies such politics precisely when the film critiques the very tenets that define and discipline acceptable gendered Filipina citizenship, tenets that often also rely on neoliberal constructs around transnational travel, diasporic return, and national responsibility.

Disorienting Desires

Leche confronts the complexities of return by centering on the figure of a queer *balikbayan* who, through his various travels across Manila, experiences similar moments of disorientation and confusion. The novel begins with an entry from an imaginary text, *Decolonization for Beginners: A Filipino Glossary*. Penned by the nationalist scholar Bonifacio Dumpit, the glossary defines *balikbayan* as follows:

> *balikbayan, noun* 1. Coined by the Marcos regime in 1973 for US-based Filipinos returning to visit the motherland and witness its vast improvements, attributed to martial law. 2. unwitting propagator of martial law propaganda. 3. potential savior of the Philippine economy. (Linmark 2011a, 1)

Serving as the novel's epigraph, these definitions provide the historical, political, and economic contexts with which readers of *Leche* can frame Vince's return. Even before traveling to Manila, Vince is already struck with the imperative power of a Filipino definitional project. During one of the novel's flashbacks, he recounts attending a lecture by Dumpit, where the professor suggests that, "regardless of birthplace, current residence, or nationality, a Filipino is not a Filipino until he has climbed into a jeepney and paid his share of the ride" (Linmark 2011a, 152). Upon hearing Dumpit's definition, Vince remembers his fascination with the jeepney as a child and the fact that "one's identity could depend solely on a Technicolor ride Dumpit described as 'part lounge, part church, part historical museum, part kitsch, part kunsthaus, but purely Filipino'" (Linmark 2011a, 152).

By centering on the jeepney as one of the key markers for hybrid Filipino identity, Linmark deceptively utilizes an artifact that has undergone various iterations in material and popular culture. The jeepney—which coincidentally also graces the novel's cover—serves as a quotidian form of mass transportation and as a consumerist object that has achieved iconic status in the West (one need only look at the presence of the jeepney in the music video for the song "Bebot," or in the most recent installment of the movie *Bourne Identity*, to get a sense of such iconicity).[3] By rooting Vince's notions of Filipino identity through such a nostalgically mediated and iconic object, Linmark is able to highlight the precarious and often pejorative understanding of belonging that such an image calls forth. So, by the time he arrives in the city, Vince is unable to draw from these memories and icons to effectively navigate Manila's chaos. If anything, these memories underscore his privilege as someone who does not live in the Philippines and whose imagined version of Filipino identity hails from his temporary presence in the country.

Throughout the novel, Vince grapples with the realization that despite his preconceptions about the city, and despite the fact that he had initially thought that he would easily assimilate, the population sees him as an outsider. Even his interview with Kris Aquino—the celebrity daughter of the Corazon Aquino—and with Sister Marie—the feminist nun turned movie star, reiterates these dissonant versions of return. In one of the longest exchanges in the novel, Vince attends Kris Aquino's talk show to discuss his thoughts about being a runner-up in the Mr. Pogi pageant, specifically, and to discuss how he feels about returning to the Philippines after many years of absence, generally. During the interview, Vince mentions his lack of desire to return to the Philippines, since he can access Filipino culture by going to "little Manilas" in the United States. Sister Marie then jumps into the conversation. She criticizes Vince, noting that these "little Manilas" are mere reproductions no different from the Filipino villages established during the St. Louis World's Fair in 1904. For Sister Marie, such spaces are fueled by nostalgia yet are removed from the realities of life in the Global South. Interrupting their conversation, Aquino then ruminates on the differences between Filipinos who have left as permanent emigrants and Filipinos who are forced to temporarily leave the country as overseas workers in order to send remittances back to their families. The dialogue continues:

KRIS: And, in my opinon, which I'm entitled to, these Filipinos are our heroes because of their daily sacrifices and the monthly money remittances then send to their families.
VINCE: What if they don't come back? What if they decide to start a family, a new life elsewhere?
. . .
KRIS: Then they're blank-blank-blankholes.
VINCE: But don't their assholes remain Filipino? Once a Filipino asshole, always a Filipino asshole right?
SISTER MARIE: *(Makes sign of the cross).* Ay my ears!
VINCE: Isn't your definition of Filipino too narrow, too specific, too literal?
KRIS: Of course, otherwise it won't be a definition right? (Linmark 2011a, 233)

The dialogue between Vince, Kris, and Sister Marie is illuminating because it places particular emphasis on the contradictory dynamics of return. Through a seemingly trite and banal exchange, Linmark reflects on how discourses of return produce "good" returnees in the image of the overseas contract worker and "bad" returnees in the image of the disinterested visitor. Because Vince does not conform to these identities fully, he is forced to chart a relationship to the city and to his hometown characterized by a disoriented version of return. As we soon learn in the novel, one way in which he is able to orient his idea of the city is through his longing and desires.

In *Leche*, Vince is continually confronted with an inability to translate, to understand, and to navigate Manila. He gathers his information about the city from postcards and tour guides that depict various attractions and national monuments. These postcards (which are included as pictures in the novel) illustrate a gamut of scenes, from images of key periods in the country's history, to Spanish, American, and Japanese colonial relics, to images of "national" birds, flowers, and churches. They are meant for foreigners and provide brief snippets of information essential to tourists. By making the postcards the main source of information for Vince, Linmark foregrounds the almost alienating effect such artifacts have on him as a *balikbayan*. As Vicente Rafael notes, for *balikbayans*, artifacts made for tourist consumption were meant to streamline local culture, to create packaged "fragments of the *bayan* available for purchase" (Rafael 2000, 207). Rafael further notes that, through these objects, *balikbayans* "encounter commodified versions of their origins now similarly rendered alienable as tourist objects destined for other places" (Rafael 2000, 207).

Yet for Vince, these postcards do not merely serve as flashpoints to a past colonial history he once knew. These postcards also become palimpsests and canvases onto which he can articulate his sexual desires, unrequited needs for intimacy, and often "inappropriate" longings for those who are of a different class background than him, such as his taxi driver and his tourist guide Jonas. The postcards thus become a queer archive of repurposed images that live beyond the "official" images that they are meant to portray. For example, one of the postcards depicts the most sacrosanct religious spaces in the city dating back to Spanish colonization: Quiapo Church. Instead of discussing the church, however (which is usually the type of "tourist story" that is written at the backs of such cards), Vince writes about the novel's namesake *Leche*, a combination sex club/movie set/school/bomb shelter/disco. Vince writes to his siblings:

> Guess where I came from? Hint: Bino Boca shoots his movies there. #2: Marcos kept his mistress there, including your former crush, Dovie Beams. #3: It's a museum, but not really. #4: It's a sex club, but not really. Might as well tell you because the hints are never going to run out: Leche. That's right. (Linmark 2011a, 298)

This layered description of Leche's history threads seemingly disparate histories such as colonialism, martial law, and post-Marcosian Filipino life. Despite the fact that it is set during Corazon Aquino's tenure—one of the few Filipino

American works of fiction to focus on such a period in Philippine history—*Leche* queers vestiges of colonial and dictatorial history by depicting a protagonist who does not merely re-valorize his role as a *balikbayan*—instead of exuding success, he stumbles through the city, sometimes caring more about his sexual desires and his longings than the actual "tourist" attractions he is supposed to enjoy.

Aside from the postcards, Vince's tour of Intramuros (the Spanish walled city in Manila) also becomes an opportunity to articulate his sexual desires. His tour guide Jonas serves as his object of affection. After they finish with the tour, Vince and Jonas dine together. Vince uses their time together as an opportunity to ask Jonas about his life and to possibly ask Jonas to accompany him to Leche. In the process, the two end up discussing the differences that exist between them, despite the fact that they are both diasporic Filipinos. According to Jonas, their differences are characterized by how they both navigate and remember Manila. Vince concurs: "What's so frightening—and fascinating—about memory is that I sometimes wonder if what I'm remembering really happened, or if I'm making it up", to which Jonas replies: "But not all memories come from first hand experiences. . . . Memories are what keeps us as strangers from each other." In the end, their difference influences Jonas's decisions. He abandons Vince by failing to appear at Leche during their meeting time. While reflecting on Jonas's decision afterward, Vince realizes that, for Jonas, he represents an outsider looking in. For Jonas, Vince is an interloper who, like the typical Western tourist, will eventually leave: "*My* country. *My*, not *our*. It's obvious: To Jonas, I'm an outsider. A cliché. . . . Because Jonas's reality is my disorientation. And my chaos his order" (Linmark 2011a, 248). Vince's desire for Jonas, despite its seemingly quotidian role initially, becomes a pivotal source of knowledge in the novel. This desire exposes the material differences that exist between Vince as a *balikbayan* and Jonas as a person living in Manila. Such a desire contextualizes Vince's confusion by making him realize that belonging, particularly as a transnational subject, may be an impossible ideal.

When I interviewed R. Zamora Linmark for *Leche's* book launch, I asked him about the significance of these postcards and other found objects to the novel's overarching themes. In response, Linmark noted that "the postcards, the nightmares, the tourist tips—these are all windows to Vince's complex world. From them we get a sense of his character—his sense of humor, his thoughts, his anxieties, his frustrations, his fears, his desires, his sadness."[4] In other words, the postcards, tour guides, fleeting sexual desires, and celebrity gossip that Vince encounters provide an image of what queer returns might look like for a Filipino American, gay, and postcolonial returnees. Rather than see Vince's attempt at self-acceptance as a futile endeavor with no purpose, I would argue that it is precisely failure, disappointment, and desire that allows the novel to foreground new epistemologies about return, beyond the overwrought and untenable notions of kinship, memory, and national filiation that the state demands of returnees.

FAILED RETURNS | 349

On Failed Returns

What would it mean to depict *balikbayans* who are not invested in the same recuperative gesture as the state? Writing about queer returns, Martin Manalansan suggests that, for queer Filipino migrants, "homecoming is not about final closures, redemptive endings, rosy futures, or ontological completion" (Manalansan 2012, 50). Queer returns thus compel critics to re-evaluate how the experience of travel differs for those who may already be abject from the ideals of belonging and appropriate cultural citizenship. As Jasbir Puar asserts, the experience of travel and return for racialized queer subjects involve "returns to visit family; to rediscover and/or reinforce culture; to reacquaint oneself with tradition, especially by locating queer heritage and connection; and, most important, somehow to be queer or to negotiate a queer self in the homeland" (Puar 2012, 113). In other words, such returns present new challenges and new opportunities for imaging queer diasporas differently. They provide alternative versions of return that recodify and, to an extent, expand our understanding of travel and tourism beyond the globalizing capitalist formations often enjoyed by predominantly white, upwardly mobile, gay men. For queer racialized subjects, returns require that we imagine alternative routes to belonging.

In this regard, *Leche* and *Miguel/Michelle* imagine *balikbayans* that subtend, as they foreground, institutionalized narratives of Filipino/a "homecoming." In the process, both works challenge the ease with which readers and filmgoers from the West can identify with the returnee by making this figure culpable in orientalizing practices encouraged by the postcolonial state. Ultimately, the novel and the film mobilize failure as a way to imagine what alternative forms of return might feel or like for queer *balikbayans*. Judith Halberstam suggests that, for queer subjects, failure can puncture the "toxic positivity of contemporary life" (Halberstam 2011, 3). She further writes that, "if success requires so much effort, then maybe failure is easier in the long run and offers different rewards" (Halberstam 2011, 3). Failure thus produces new epistemologies that counter the disciplinary, unsustainable, and often violent narratives of accomplishment placed on the backs of sexual minorities in order calcify certain forms of citizenship.

This reflection ends with Halberstam's imagining of failure, since such productive and political forms of "failure" saturate Linmark's and Portes's work. *Leche* and *Miguel/Michelle* envision returns that are characterized by misunderstandings, unreciprocated advances, and experiences of disappointment. Yet amid such "failed" versions of "homecoming," these cultural sites provide alternative forms of world making that emphasize the role of sexuality, desire, and erotics in the performance of returns. Ultimately, *Leche* and *Miguel/Michelle* suggest that amid a period of expanding global capitalism, our concept of Filipino agency must be seen as dialectically tied to struggles that Filipinos across the diaspora experience, whether as *balikbayans* dealing with the pressures of return or as Global South inhabitants reckoning with the fact that departures can ultimately be elusive.

NOTES

1 Scholars in Filipino studies have examined the significance of the returnee across numerous cultural and political contexts. See Rodriguez (2002) for a discussion of heroism in relationship to returnees, Rafael (2000) for the resentment locals articulate about *balikbayans*, and San Juan (2001) for the role the *balikbayans* play in articulating contemporary cultural nationalisms.

2 In Tagalog, the personal pronoun *siya* can stand in for both the male and female subject. Thus, it becomes less certain whether Nano meant to refer to Michelle as a male or female. Such interchangeability lends to the problematic nature of this scene.

3 For an analysis of the jeepney as a form of urban or metropolitan folklore and as an articulation of cultural nationalism, see Meñez (1988).

4 For the full text of this interview, see Linmark (2011b).

REFERENCES

Espiritu, Yen Le. 2003. *Home Bound: Filipino American Lives across Cultures, Communities, and Countries*. Berkeley: University of California Press.

Halberstam, Judith. 2011.*The Queer Art of Failure*. Durham, NC: Duke University Press.

Linmark, R. Zamora. 2011. *Leche*. Minneapolis: Coffee House Press.

———. 2011. "Spotlight on: *Leche*". Interview by Robert Diaz, 2011. *Coffee House Press*, http://coffeehousepress.org/blog-posts/spotlight-on-leche-by-r-zamora-linmark, accessed September 3, 2014.

Manalansan, Martin. 2012. "Wayward Erotics: Mediating Queer Diasporic Return." In *Media, Erotics and Transnational Asia*, ed. Purnima Mankekar and Louisa Schein, 33–52. Durham, NC: Duke University Press.

Meñez, Herminia Q. 1988. "Jeeprox: The Art and Language of Manila's Jeepney Drivers." *Western Folklore* 47, no. 1:38–47.

Portes, Gil, dir. 1998. *Miguel/Michelle*. Film. Makati City, Philippines: Forefront Films.

Prosser, Jay. 1998. *Second Skins: The Body Narratives of Transexuality*. New York: Columbia University Press.

Puar, Jasbir. 2002. "Circuits of Queer Mobility: Tourism, Travel, and Globalization." *GLQ: A Journal of Lesbian and Gay Studies* 8, nos. 1–2:101–137.

Rafael, Vicente. 2000. *White Love and Other Events in Filipino History*. Durham, NC: Duke University Press.

Reyes, Eric Estuar. 2011. "Fictions of Return in Filipino America." *Social Text* 29, no. 2:99–117.

Richter, Linda. 1980. "The Political Uses of Tourism: A Philippine Case Study." *Journal of Developing Areas* 14, no. 2:237–257.

Rodriguez, Robyn M. 2002. "Migrant Heroes: Nationalism, Citizenship, and the Politics of Filipino Migrant Labor." *Citizenship Studies* 6, no. 3:341–356.

San Juan, E. 2001. "The Filipino Diaspora." *Philippine Studies* 49, no. 2:255–264.

Spade, Dean. 2011. *Normal Life: Administrative Violence, Critical Trans Politics, and the Limits of Law*. Boston: South End Press.

Stryker, Susan, Paisley Currah, and Lisa Jean Moore. 2008. "Introduction: Trans-, Trans, or Transgender?" In special issue "Trans-." *Women's Studies Quarterly* 36, nos. 3–4:11–22.

Ahmed Afzal received his BA in Third World Studies at Vassar College, an MSc in Cultural Geography at the London School of Economics and Political Science, and an MPhil and PhD in Cultural Anthropology at Yale University. He is the author of *Lone Star Muslims: Transnational Lives and the South Asian Experience in Texas* (NYU Press, 2014). He has taught at Colgate University and Purchase College and is currently a lecturer in the Department of Anthropology, Geography, and Ethnic Studies at California State University, Stanislaus.

Crystal S. Anderson is Director of the Office of Student Research and Associate Professor of English at Longwood University. She is the author of *Beyond the Chinese Connection: Contemporary Afro-Asian Cultural Production* as well as several book chapters on Afro-Asian cultural dynamics. Currently, she is completing a book manuscript on the impact of black music on Korean popular music (K-pop).

Constancio Arnaldo is Visiting Assistant Professor in the Asian/Asian American Studies Program at Miami University of Ohio. He is a co-editor with Stanley Thangaraj and Christina Chin on an Asian American anthology titled *Asian American Sporting Cultures*, contracted with NYU Press.

Timothy K. August is Assistant Professor of Comparative Literature at Stony Brook University. He is currently working on a book manuscript that examines the emergence of refugee aesthetics in Southeast Asian American literature and film.

Shilpa Davé is Assistant Dean of the College of Arts and Sciences and an Assistant Professor of Media Studies and American Studies at the University of Virginia. She is the author of *Indian Accents: Brown Voice and Racial Performance in American Television and Film* (2013) and is co-editor of the collection *East Main Street: Asian American Popular Culture* (NYU Press, 2005). She has chapters in *Keywords for Asian American Studies* (NYU Press, 2015), *The Colorblind Screen: Television and Postracial America* (NYU Press, 2014) and *Transnational Perspectives on Graphic Narratives* (2013).

Robert Diaz is Assistant Professor in the Faculty of Liberal Arts and Sciences at OCAD University in Toronto. His first book project is *Reparative Acts:*

Performing Queer Redress in Philippine Nationalisms. Diaz is also editing *Diasporic Intimacies: Queer Filipinos/as and Canadian Imaginaries*, which brings together artists, scholars, and community workers in order to examine the contributions of queer Filipinos/as to Canadian culture and society.

Camilla Fojas is Vincent de Paul Professor of Latin American and Latino Studies and Director of the Critical Ethnic Studies Program at DePaul University. Her books include *Cosmopolitanism in the Americas* (2005), *Border Bandits: Hollywood on the Southern Frontier* (2008), *Mixed Race Hollywood* (NYU Press, 2008), co-edited with Mary Beltrán, and *Transnational Crossroads: Remapping the Americas and the Pacific* (2012), co-edited with Rudy Guevarra. Her most recent book is *Islands of Empire: Pop Culture and U.S. Power* (2014).

Douglas Ishii is Chancellor's Postdoctoral Fellow in the Department of Ethnic Studies at the University of Colorado at Boulder. He is currently working on a manuscript on how Asian Pacific American arts activism has been shaped by the diverging influences of 1960s and 1970s Yellow Power movement culture and the class norms of post–civil rights racial politics.

Julia H. Lee is Associate Professor of English and Asian American Studies at the University of California, Irvine. Her book, *Interracial Encounters: Reciprocal Representations in African and Asian American Literatures, 1896–1937*, was published in 2011 by NYU Press and was awarded Honorable Mention by the Association for Asian American Studies for Literary Criticism. Her new work examines the formative role that certain social spaces—such as the railroad—play in the articulation of racialized identities.

Lori Kido Lopez is Assistant Professor in the Department of Communication Arts at the University of Wisconsin–Madison. She is the author of the forthcoming book *Asian American Media Activism: Fighting for Cultural Citizenship* (NYU Press, 2016) and a co-editor (with Vincent Pham) of the forthcoming *Routledge Companion to Asian American Media*.

Daryl Joji Maeda is Chair and Associate Professor of Ethnic Studies at the University of Colorado Boulder. Maeda is the author of *Reconsidering the Asian American Movement* (2012) and *Chains of Babylon: The Rise of Asian America* (2009) and co-editor, with Arturo Aldama, Elisa Facio, and Reiland Rabaka, of *Enduring Legacies: Ethnic Histories and Cultures of Colorado* (2011). He is the South and Interior West region representative on the Board of the Association of Asian American Studies.

Madhavi Mallapragada is Associate Professor in the Department of Radio-Television-Film in the College of Communication at the University of Texas at

Austin. She is the author of *Virtual Homelands: Indian Immigrants and Online Cultures in the United States* (2014).

Deepti Misri is Associate Professor at the University of Colorado Boulder, where she teaches in the Women and Gender Studies Department and the Center for Asian Studies. She is the author of *Beyond Partition: Gender, Violence, and Representation in Postcolonial India* (2014).

Konrad Ng is the Executive Director of the Shangri La Center for Islamic Arts and Cultures, a museum that explores the relationship between art, design, and culture. Ng was formerly the Director of the Smithsonian Institution's Asian Pacific American Center, where he led the development of exhibitions, public programs, and digital initiatives about the Asian American experience. Ng was also a professor in the Academy for Creative Media at the University of Hawai'i-Mānoa and the Curator of Film and Video at the Honolulu Museum of Art. His scholarly work explores the cultural politics of Asian and Asian American cinema and digital media.

Leilani Nishime is Associate Professor of Communication at the University of Washington. She is the author of *Undercover Asians: Multiracial Asian Americans and Visual Culture* (2014) and is the co-editor of *East Main Street: Asian American Popular Culture* (NYU Press, 2005). She also has chapters in *Mixed Race Hollywood* (NYU Press, 2008), *American Visual Cultures* (2005), and *Asian North American Subjectivities* (2004). She is currently editing a collection on race and ecology.

Kent A. Ono is Professor and Chair of the Department of Communication at the University of Utah. He has published widely in the area of communications, media, and Asian American Studies, including *Contemporary Media Culture and the Remnants of a Colonial Past* (2009); *Asian Americans and the Media*, with Vincent Pham (2009); *Shifting Borders: Rhetoric, Immigration, and California's Proposition 187*, with John Sloop (2002); *Asian American Studies after Critical Mass* (2005); *A Companion to Asian American Studies* (as editor, 2005); and *Critical Rhetorics of Race*, with Michael Lacy (as editor, NYU Press, 2011).

Tasha Oren is Associate Professor of English and Media Studies and teaches in the Media, Cinema and Digital Studies Program at the University of Wisconsin—Milwaukee. She is the author of *Demon in the Box: Jews, Arabs, Politics and Culture* (2004) and *Food TV* (2017). She is the co-editor of *Global Television Formats: Understanding Television across Borders* (2013), *The Routledge Handbook of Contemporary Feminism* (2017), *Global Currents: Media and Technology Now* (2004), and *East Main Street: Asian American Popular Culture* (NYU Press, 2005).

Celine Parreñas Shimizu is a filmmaker and Professor of Asian American Studies at the University of California, Santa Barbara. Her books include *The Feminist Porn Book* (2013), *Straitjacket Sexualities* (2012), and *The Hypersexuality of Race* (2007). Her award-winning films include *The Fact of Asian Women* (2004) and *Birthright: Mothering across Difference* (2009).

Christopher B. Patterson is Assistant Professor of English at the New York Institute of Technology in Nanjing, People's Republic of China. His work appears in the anthology *Queer Sex Work* (2015). He writes book reviews for *Asiatic* and hosts the podcast *New Books in Asian American Studies*. His fiction, published under the name Kawika Guillermo, has appeared or is forthcoming in *Feminist Studies*, *The Hawai'i Pacific Review*, *Drunken Boat*, and *Mothership: Tales from Afrofuturism and Beyond*.

Vincent Pham is Assistant Professor in the Department of Civic Communication and Media at Willamette University. His publications include *Asian Americans and the Media*, with Kent A. Ono (2009); "'Artfulbigotry and Kitsch': A Study of Stereotype, Mimicry, and Satire in Asian American T-Shirt Rhetoric," in LuMing Mao and Morris Young's *Representations: Doing Asian American Rhetoric* (2009), and book reviews in the *Quarterly Journal of Speech*.

Cathy J. Schlund-Vials is Professor in English and Asian American Studies at the University of Connecticut (Storrs). She is currently the Director of the Asian American Studies Institute at the University of Connecticut and is the author of two monographs: *Modeling Citizenship: Jewish and Asian American Writing* (2011) and *War, Genocide, and Justice: Cambodian American Memory Work* (2012).

Wendy Sung is a doctoral candidate at the University of Michigan, Department of American Culture and Asian/Pacific Islander American Studies.

Linda Trinh Võ is Professor in the Department of Asian American Studies at the University of California, Irvine. She is the author of *Mobilizing an Asian American Community* (2004), co-author of *Vietnamese in Orange County* (2015). She is co-editor of *Contemporary Asian American Communities: Intersection and Divergences* (2002); *Asian American Women: The "Frontiers" Reader* (2004); *Labor versus Empire: Race, Gender and Migration* (2004); and *Keywords for Asian American Studies* (2015).

INDEX

Aamir (film), 277–78, 284

Abraham, John, 278, 288n14

advertising, 235–36

African Americans: immigrants' racist attitudes toward, 95; imperialist use of culture of, 292; indie rock and, 215–16; and K-pop, 11, 290–301; and LA riots, 89–102; masculinity associated with, 32, 116; Pacquiao and, 32, 36

Agents of S.H.I.E.L.D. (television show), 199

Ahn, Philip, 3, 47

Ali, Muhammad, 25

The Amazing Race (television show), 5, 75, 78–86

American Apparel, 331

American Dream: Asian Americans and, 236; Elvis Presley as model of, 186, 194; global labor and, 209; Korean Americans and, 94; spelling bees and, 9, 228, 234, 241n1

AnandTech (website), 272

Anderson, Benedict, 256

Andrew Figueroa Chiang and the Blazing Rays of the Sun, 224

anime, 314–17

Anzaldúa, Gloria, 97

APA. *See* Asian Pacific American (APA) consciousness

Appadurai, Arjun, 86n13, 155

Apple, 326, 330–31

Aquino, Benigno, Jr., 337

Aquino, Corazon C., 338, 347–48

Ark, Wong Kim, 143

Armstrong, Charles K., 292

Art Attack, 222–23

Asian American cuisine, 246–49, 258. *See also* Asian cuisine and restaurants; fusion cuisine

Asian American indie rock, 9, 214–26

Asian American literature, 169

Asian American women: in *Battlestar Galactica*, 9, 198–210; beauty and fashion norms among, 304–18; stereotypes of, 208–9, 220, 316

Asian cuisine and restaurants, 153–54, 248. *See also* Asian American cuisine

Asian Pacific American (APA) consciousness, 214–26

Asian Pacific American Heritage Month, 142, 143, 146

Asians and Asian Americans: category of Asian American, 142–43, 146–48, 162n4, 198, 247; as forever foreign, 198, 218; in Hollywood films, 46–59; masculinity associated with, 34, 37–39, 46–59, 101, 116; as model minority, 32, 38, 48, 61–62, 72, 80–81, 95, 116, 202–3, 219, 231–32, 245; motherhood of, 61–72; as neoliberal model, 6; online popular culture of, 139–49; as potential terrorists, 202; reality television's representation of, 78–79; in science fiction, 197–200; sexuality of, 46–59. *See also* stereotypes

assimilation: in *Battlestar Galactica*, 198–200, 203, 209–10; of Indian Americans, 229, 231; role of race in, 95–97

Astroboy/Astro Boy, 315

August, Timothy, 7–8, 248, 258–59

authenticity: of African American–influenced K-pop, 291, 293–99; of Asian American food, 7, 152, 154–58, 160–61; curry and, 266; of Hawaiian culture, 185; of hip-hop, 293–94; in indie rock, 215; of musical performance, 295; in R&B, 297–99

Avatar (film), 211n7

Azhar (radio host), 128

Aziatix, 293

AZI Fellas, 116

Baker, Caroll, 56

balikbayans (returnees), 12, 335–50

Banet-Weiser, Sarah, 98, 99, 232, 235

Banksy, 99

Bartlett, Andrew, 295

Basco, Dante, 85

Battlestar Galactica (television show), 9, 198–210

Baumann, Shyon, 155

Beam, Louis, 175

beauty gurus, 311–14

Belen, Jun, 157

Berger, James, 234

Berlant, Lauren, 207

Bessire, Lucas, 128

The Big Boss (film), 16–18, 21, 26

Big Mama, 11, 290–91, 297, 299–300

Blade Runner (film), 197

Blow, Jonathan, 324

Blue Hawaii (film), 186–90, 194–95

BoA, 290

body, the: Jordan's, 35; Pacquiao's, 34, 37; in Tran's *Vietnamerica*, 168, 170–74, 176–78

Bogost, Ian, 324

Bollywood films, 11, 276–87

Bonanza (television show), 244

Born in Chinese, 215, 217–18

Bourdieu, Pierre, 225

Bow, Leslie, 95

Bowien, Danny, 246

Boxer Rebellion, 19

boxing: Filipinos and, 34; masculinity associated with, 34; moral narratives associated with, 30–31; Pacquiao and, 27–41; in *Way of the Dragon*, 23–26

branding, 232. *See also* racial branding

Brando, Marlon, 48

Bravo (television network), 252

Bridge to the Sun (film), 46, 47, 56–58

Britain, and curry, 266

Brokaw, Tom, 66, 67

buddy films, 279–80

Bulosan, Carlos, 142

Butterworth, Donna, 192

Cafepharma (website), 270

Cajayon, Gene, 46

Cambodian American rap, 107–21

Cambodian Americans, 6, 107–9, 175

Candylens, 306

Carradine, David, 15

Catholicism, 32–33

CCP. *See* Crowd Control Productions

Cerra, Erica, 203

Cha, Theresa Hak Kyung, 65

Chang, David, 246

Chang, Jeff, 98, 141

Chang, Jung, 65, 69

Chang, Lan Samantha, 65

chefs, 9–10, 244–59

Chen, Joyce, 250, 251

Cheng, Anne Anlin, 52, 53

Child, Julia, 250

Chin, Katie and Leeann, 250

Chin, Vincent, 143

Chin, William "Charlie," 216

China, nationalism in, 19

Chinatown, 73n18

Chinatown Community for Equitable Development, 224

Chinese Alien Wives of American Citizens, 52

Chinese Americans: attitudes toward, 62, 63–64; community of, 52–53; in Hollywood films, 49–56; identity formation of, 62; motherhood of, 61–72; racial identity of, 67–72; racism aimed at, 63–64; sexuality of, 64, 73n18

The Chinese Connection (film), 19

Chinese Exclusion Act, 64

Chinese gamers, 325

Cho, Aharn, 245

Cho, Erwin and Godwin, 78

Cho, Margaret, 63, 65–66, 87n25

Choe, David, 5, 89–102

Choi, Annie, 65

Choi, David, 214

Choi, Roy, 246

Chon, Justin, 85

Chong, Jae, 293

Chopra, Vidhu Vinod, 285

Choy, Christine, 94

Chua, Amy, 4–5, 61–72

Chua, Lawrence, *Gold by the Inch*, 332

Chuck D, 110

Chun, Wendy Hui Kyong, 140, 266

Chung, Hye Seung, 3

Chung, Marina, 244

Chyi, Lynn, 245

cinepatriotic genre, 278, 282, 284–85

citizenship: Asian Americans as forever foreigners, 198, 218; in *Battlestar Galactica*, 201, 206–7, 209–10; Chinese Americans and, 62–64; civil rights subject and, 102n9; cultural experience of, 141; family as criterion for, 71, 203, 209–10; Korean Americans and, 95; marriage as means of, 48, 52; spelling bees and, 229

civil rights subject, 94, 102n9

Clavell, James, 49

Clough, Wayne, 148

Clyne, Nicki, 204

Cohen, Cathy J., 90, 100–101

Cold War, 52, 62, 292

Colicchio, Tom, 258

Collier's (magazine), 271

colonialism: and curry, 266; U.S.-Hawaiian, 183, 188–89, 194–95; U.S. martial arts knowledge derived from, 21; U.S.-Philippine, 33–34 coltan ore, 326–27

commodification, 232

Common Ground (Vietnamese-American performance group), 225

community, 5–8; APA performances and, 221–26; *The Big Boss* and, 18; Chinese American, 52–53; Indian American, 229–41; K-pop and, 298; radio as basis of Pakistani American, 124–36; YouTube as tool for building, 75–76

CompilAsian (album), 215, 217–21, 224

computer-mediated communication, 7

Concordia, Johneric, 221

Congo, 326–27

convergence. *See* media convergence

cooking. *See* television cooking shows

Cordoz, Floyd, 244

Cotera, Maria, 97

Crimson Kimono (film), 46, 47

critical race theory, digitization as vehicle for, 140–42, 148

Crowd Control Productions (CCP), 321, 329

Crowther, Bosley, 56

Cuba, 183–84

culinary tourism, 153–54, 173

Currah, Paisley, 339

curry, 10, 263–74

Davé, Shilpa, 9, 202

Davila, Arlene, 223

Davis, Mike, 92

Debussy, Claude, 67–68

De La Hoya, Oscar, 33, 34

Democratic Republic of the Congo, 326–27

Denny, Reginald, 94, 102n6

deportation, of Cambodian Americans, 115

diaspora: in *The Big Boss*, 16–18; Filipina/o, 28–29, 39; Pakistani radio in Houston and, 127–29; South Asian American, 233; Vietnamese, 165–78, 178n14; *Way of the Dragon* and, 22–23. *See also* immigrants; migration

Dice (website), 266–70

digital humanities, 140–49

Digital Underground, 297

Disney, Walt, 315

DJ Shine, 294

dosti (male friendship), 278–82

Dota 2 (online game), 329

Double Happiness (television show), 250

Douglas, Aaron, 204

Douglas, Susan, 130, 135

drone strikes, in Pakistan, 134–35

Drunken Tiger, 294

Dubrofsky, Rachel, 79

DuraSoft Colors, 304

Dyer, Richard, 3

Dylan, Bob, 215

Dyson, Michael Eric, 35

Early, Gerald, 301

East Meets West (television show), 251

eCurry (blog), 161

Ehrenreich, Barbara, 191

em Cosmetics, 314

Enter the Dragon (film), 15, 22

España-Maram, Linda, 34

Espiritu, Yen Le, 177, 338

EVE Online (game), 328

Faiola, Anthony, 292

Fairchild Corporation, 331

Fairey, Shepard, 98, 99

family: as basis of spelling bee competitions, 240; in *Battlestar Galactica*, 198, 201, 203–4, 207–10; in *New York*, 284–85; as symbol of nation, 201, 204, 207–10, 277–78. *See also* motherhood

Fanaa (film), 284

fashion: facial beauty and, 304–18; labor in relation to, 322–23, 327–28, 330–31; virtual, 321–33

Fashion Star (television show), 321

Fat Boys, 297

Ferguson, Priscilla Parkhurst, 256

Ferguson, Roderick, 224

Filipina/o Americans: diasporic community of, 28–29, 39; fight night spaces for, 28–29, 40; identity formation of, 28–29; and Pacquiao, 27–41; as returnees, 12, 335–50

The Filipino Channel (TFC), 335

film. *See* Bollywood films; Hollywood films

Firefly (television show), 197

Fisher, Daniel, 128

Fisher, Max, 297

Fist of Fury (film), 19–20, 22, 23, 26

Fists of Fury (U.S. film release), 16, 19

Fleischer, Max, 315

Flickr, 146

Flower Drum Song (film), 46, 47, 48, 52–56, 58

Fonarow, Wendy, 215–16

food: Asian American immigrant experience associated with, 246–49; Asian-Latino, 145; curry, 10, 263–74; in Tran's *Vietnamerica*, 170–73. *See also* chefs; food blogs; television cooking shows

food blogs, 7, 151–62

Food Network, 250–54

food trucks, 145
forever foreigners, Asian Americans as, 198, 218
format shows, 253
Foucault, Michel, 185
Fox (television network), 252
Foxconn, 330–31
freemiums, 329–30
Fresh off the Boat (television show), 244
Fuller, Samuel, 47
Fung Brothers, 83
fusion cuisine, 160, 162, 246–47, 251, 258. *See also* Asian American cuisine

Gaia Online, 329
Gallagher, Mark, 254
Gambito, Christine, 76, 86n12
gameplay form, 324–27
Gapultos, Marvin, 156–57
Gatan, Leslie B., 337
Gates, Bill, 268, 323
gaze, the, 185
G-Dragon, 293
Ghosh, Shohini, 280
Giant Robot (magazine), 99, 254
gold miners, 325
Gonzaga, Toni, 335
The Good Wife (television show), 199
Google, 271
Goss, Jon, 189
Gracyk, Theodore, 294
graffiti, 98–100
A Grain of Sand, 216–18
Grannis, Kina, 214
graphic narratives, form and content in, 168–77
Gray, Herman, 94, 102n9
Grey's Anatomy (television show), 199
Groupon, 268
Guam, 183
Guild Wars (online game), 321, 324
Guild Wars 2 (online game), 12, 323, 326–28
gyaru style, 308–10, 314

Ha, Christine, 245
Habbo Hotel, 328
Halberstam, Judith, 349
Hallyu, 291–93, 298
Han, Joseph, 214
Happy Days (television show), 244
Harlins, Latasha, 94,
Harvey, David, 71
Hathwar, Sriram, 231

Hatton, Ricky "Hitman," 31
Hawai'i, 8, 183–95
Hawaii Five-o (television show), 196n11
Hayakawa, Sessue, 3, 47
HBOLab, 74, 86n11
Hebdige, Dick, 296
Hee, Park Chung, 292
Hell's Kitchen (television show), 252, 254
Heroes (television show), 199
heterosexuality: in *Battlestar Galactica*, 9, 201, 203–4, 210; family and nation associated with, 11, 201, 203, 210, 277, 284–85; in *New York*, 278, 280–82, 284–86; in Shigeta's films, 46–59
Hidle, Jade, 166
Hi-Fi, Johnny, 221
hijab, 134
hip-hop: authenticity of, 293–94; comedy hip-hop, 297, 300; elements of, 122n15; global reach of, 112; K-pop and, 290–301; Pacquiao and, 33, 35–36, 39; problematic aspects of, 39; street art and, 98. *See also* Cambodian American rap
Hirshey, Gerri, 297–98
Holden, T. J. M., 255
Hollywood films: Asian American men in, 46–59; Hawai'i in, 8, 184–95; 9/11 in, 276
homecoming stories, 12
homosexuality: in Bollywood films, 288n14; in *New York*, 279–80, 286–87; stereotypes of, 24. *See also* queer
H-1B visas, 263, 267–71
Hong Kong, Lee's films in, 15–26
Hooking Up (webseries), 74, 86n11
hooks, bell, 50
Houston, Texas, 6–7, 124–36, 137n7
Hsu, Ron and Christina, 78
Huang, Eddie, 244, 246
Hung, Melissa, 248
Huynh, Hung, 244, 258–59
Hy, Sambath "Sam," 107, 109–21
hybridity: *Fist of Fury* and, 19, 20; of K-pop, 291–94, 301; *Way of the Dragon* and, 23–26
Hye, Park Min, 299
Hyphen (magazine), 248
Hyun, Lee Young, 299

identity: in Asian American cooking shows, 256–58; Chinese American, 62, 67–72; Filipina/o, 28–29; Hawai'i's role in U.S., 139–49; Muslim, 134; racial, in digital environment, 139–49
Iijima, Chris Kando, 216

immigrants: aliens in science fiction as, 200; Asian American cuisine and, 246–49; Cylons in *Battlestar Galactica* as, 200–201; Indian, 263–74; in IT and software industries, 267–74; radio programming and, 124–36; resentment toward, 268–73. *See also* diaspora; migration
Immigration and Nationality Act, 109, 121n14
imperialism. *See* colonialism
India, 132–33, 138n12, 288n4
Indian Americans: and curry, 263–74; in information technology sector, 10; and spelling bees, 9, 228–41
indie rock. *See* Asian American indie rock
Indochinese Act, 122n14
information technology sector: Indian Americans in, 263–74; labor conditions in, 326–27, 330–32
Ingraham, Chrys, 50
Inosanto, Dan, 20–21
Instagram, 146
Internet memes, 146
internment camps, for Japanese Americans, 143–44
interracial romance, 48, 56–58, 187–88, 191–92, 209, 220
Iron Chef (television show), 252–57
Iron Chef America (television show), 254
Ishii, Yohei, 322
iStardom, 74
Itoh, Makiko, 154, 157
IT sector. *See* information technology sector
I Want the Wide American Earth (exhibition), 142–44
IW Group, 235–36

Jackson, John L., 293, 295
Jangta, 290, 299
Japan, beauty and fashion norms in, 308–9, 314–17
Japanese Americans: in Hollywood films, 56–58; internment of, 143–44; marriage and citizenship of, 48
Japantowns, 223
jeepneys, 345
Jenkins, Henry, 77, 139
Jews, 95–96
Jih, Tamara and Victor, 78
Jing Wu school of martial arts, 19
Jobs, Steve, 323
Joffe, Roland, 114
Johnson, Susan Lee, 49
Johnston, Josee, 155

Jordan, Michael, 35
Joyce Chen Cooks (television show), 250, 251
Jung, Eun-Young, 294
Juul, Jesper, 328

Kabul Express (film), 278
Kaʻialani, Princess, 188
Kaing Guek Eav, 114, 122n34
Kaplan, Amy, 62
karate, 23–26
Kashmir, 133, 138n12
Kato-Kiriyama, Traci, 214, 221–25
Kawai, Yuko, 203
Kawaii, 316
Kawakami, Jeff, 244
Keller, Nora Okja, 65
Keogan, Phil, 80
Kerrigan, Nancy, 304
KevJumba. *See* Wu, Kevin "KevJumba"
Khan, Amir, 34
Khan, Irrfan, 288n3
Khan, Kabir, 277, 278
Khan, Shahnaz, 278
Khekashan Ke Sitare (radio program), 126, 127–31
Khieu Samphan, 114, 122n34
Khmer American rap, 107–21
Khmer K.I.D., 116
Khmer Rouge, 109, 114–15, 120. *See also* Killing Fields era
Khoeun, Samkhann, 117
Khuda Ke Liye (film), 277, 278
Khut, Felix Sros, 118–20
Killing Fields era, 113–17, 119–20, 122n29
Kim, Amy, 161
Kim, Claire Jean, 95
Kim, Elaine, 94, 169
Kim, Eun Mee, 298
Kim, Isul, 219–21
Kim, Jodi, 62
Kim, Ronyoung, 65
Kimble, Paige, 240
Kim-Gibson, Dai Sil, 94
King, Rodney, 89, 102
King, Yolanda, 119
Kingston, Maxine Hong, 62–65, 69
Kish, Kristen, 244
The Kitchn (blog), 272
Klein, Christina, 52, 55
Kogawa, Joy, 65
Korea: beauty and fashion norms in, 309–10; K-pop in, 290–301
Korean Americans, 89–102

Korean tacos, 145
K-pop, 11, 290–301, 309–10
Ku, Robert Ji-Song, 145
Kuan, Diana, 161
Ku Klux Klan, 175
kung fu, 23–25
Kunreuther, Laura, 128
Kurashige, Scott, 48, 223
Kurbaan (film), 11, 277, 283–84, 287

labor: Asian Americans associated with, 247; in *Battlestar Galactica*, 205–6; fashion in relation to, 322–23, 327–28, 330–31; global, 11, 12, 209; in information technology industry, 326–27, 330–32; migration for, 212n31, 339–41; U.S. relationship with, 205, 209; visa programs and, 267–70
Lakshmi, Padma, 251
Lancôme, 313
Lankoski, Petri, 321
Latinas/os, 144–45
Latorre, Guisela, 98
Lawson, Nigella, 251
Leche (Zamora), 336–37, 345-49
Lee, Bruce, 4, 15–26
Lee, James Kyung-Jin, 223
Lee, Julia, 4
Lee, Peggy, 220
Lee, Quentin, 59
Lee, Robert G., 48, 64
Lie, John, 292, 298
Liliʻuokalani, Queen, 183
Lin, Jeremy, 2
Lin, Justin, 85,
Linkin Park, 214
Linmark, R. Zamora, 336–37, 345–49. See also *Leche*
Lipsitz, George, 249
Little Tokyo, Los Angeles, 223–24, 227n22
LNLT Entertainment, 296
Long, Lucy, 153
Lon Nol, 114
Lopez, Lori Kido, 7
Lord, Jack, 49
Lord of the Rings Online (game), 12, 323
Los Angeles riots (1992), 5, 89–102
Los Angeles Times (newspaper), 166
Lost (television show), 199
Love Is a Many Splendored Thing (film), 209
Loving v. Virginia (1967), 191–92
Low, Bee Yinn, 154, 158
Lowell, Massachusetts, 107–9, 118

Lucy (film), 197
Lui, Elaine, 65

Maeda, Daryl Joji, 216
Magnetic North, 214
Maher, Justin, 223
Main Khiladi Tu Anari (film), 280
mainstream media: crossover to, 74–77, 83–86; portrayal of LA riots in, 90, 92–94
mainstream U.S. culture, 8–10
Maira, Sunaina, 203
makeup, 304–18
Malani, Gaurav, 283
Mallapragada, Madhavi, 1, 202
Manalansan, Martin F., IV, 145, 247, 337, 340, 349
manga, 314–17
Mannur, Anita, 145, 162, 247
Maple Story (online game), 321
Marc, David, 249
Marcos, Ferdinand, 337–38
Margarito, Antonio "El Tijuana," 30–31
marriage: citizenship of Asian Americans through, 48, 52; eastern vs. western conceptions of, 53; in Hollywood films featuring Asian Americans, 46–59; interracial, 48, 56–58, 191–92
martial arts, 15–26
Martin, Trayvon, 102
Marx, W. David, 308–9
masculinity, 4; African American, 32, 116; Asian/Asian American, 34, 37–39, 46–59, 101, 116; assimilable, 30–32; boxing and, 34; Catholic, 32–33; and *dosti* (male friendship), 278–82; graffiti and, 100; Muslim, 136, 277–87; Pacquiao and, 27–28, 30–37; stereotypes of Asian, 4, 37–39, 116, 176
Mashburg, Tom, 115
Maslin, Janet, 61
MasterChef (television show), 245, 252
MasterChef Junior (television show), 245, 252
Masuwaka, Tsubasa, 307, 309
maternity. *See* motherhood
The Matrix (film), 197
Matsumoto, Marc, 158, 161, 259
Matsumoto, Nancy, 246–47
Maxwell, Jody-Anne, 241n2
Mayweather, Floyd "Money," 39–41
"Mayweather/Pacquiao: At Last" (documentary), 37
McCarthy, Nobu, 49
McDonnell, Mary, 202
McGuian, Barry, 34

MC Jin, 116
McLeod, Kembrew, 293–95
McPherson, Tara, 140
media convergence, 75–77, 83–86, 139
Melamed, Jodi, 62
Microsoft, 271, 330
micro-transactions, 323, 327–30
migration: *The Big Boss* and, 16–18; Chinese American, 64; labor, 212n31, 339–41; mixed martial arts arising from, 21; U.S. role in controlling, 201. *See also* diaspora; immigrants
Miguel/Michelle (film), 336–37, 339–44, 349
misogyny, 101
Misri, Deepti, 203
Mission Kashmir (film), 285
Mitchell, Joni, 215
Mitchell, Tony, 294
Miura, Sean, 214
mixed-race relations. *See* interracial romance
Miyamoto, Nobuko JoAnne, 216
Miyao, Daisuke, 3
Miyazaki, Hayao, 315
model minority, Asians as, 32, 38, 48, 61–62, 72, 80–81, 95, 116, 202–3, 219, 231–32, 245
Moore, Allan, 295, 299
Moore, Lisa Jean, 339
Moore, Ronald, 199
Morimoto, Matzuharo, 257
Morita, Noriyuki "Pat," 244, 259n1
Morley, David, 197
motherhood: in *Battlestar Galactica*, 204, 207–9; Chinese-American, 4–5, 61–72. *See also* family
Motion Picture Program Abroad, 292
multiculturalism: Asian American online life, 139; Chinese Americans and, 62; IT sector and, 266; LA riots and, 89–90, 101–2; Pacquiao and, 36; science fiction and, 199; and voice, 220. *See also* post-racial society
multimedia migration, 75
Mulvey, Laura, 185
museums, digitization and, 7, 140–49
music. *See* Asian American indie rock
Muslims: in Bollywood, 288n3; "good" vs. "bad," 11, 203, 277–78, 284, 287; in Hindi cinema, 277–87; identity of, 134; in India, 288n4; masculinity associated with, 136, 277–87; misogynist, as stereotype, 283–84; Pakistani, 127; in post-9/11 world, 127, 134, 203, 276–87; racism against, 134; sexuality of, 203, 278; as terrorists, 127, 203, 282–84
My Name Is Khan (film), 277

Nabeel (radio host), 131–33
Nakamura, Lisa, 76, 139–40, 323, 325, 331, 332
nationalism: Chinese, 19; Filipino, 12, 335–36; Lee's, 19–20; Pakistani, 133–34; redressive, 336; U.S., 268–69, 272–73, 277
National Museum of American History, 143
National Spelling Bee, 9, 228–41, 242n5
Neal, Mark Anthony, 297–99
neoliberalism: and Asian American online life, 139; Asian Americans as model for, 6; Chinese American motherhood and, 62, 71
New York (film), 11, 277–87
New York Times (newspaper), 52, 56
The Next Food Network Star (television show), 244, 252
The Next Iron Chef (television show), 254
Ng, Fae, 65
Nguyen, Andrea, 161
Nguyen, Bich Minh, 177
Nguyen, Mimi Thi, 34, 111, 254
Nguyen, Tina, 247
Nguyen, Viet, 159
Nike, 29, 32, 33, 36
9/11 attacks. *See* post-9/11 world; war on terror
Ninh, erin Khuê, 72
Nintendo, 326, 330
Nishii, Mihoko, 309
Nishime, Leilani, 8–9
Nixon, Richard, 114
Norris, Chuck, 22, 24
North South Foundation (NSF), 233–40
nostalgia, 128–29
NSF. *See* North South Foundation
Nuon Chea, 114, 122n34

Obama, Barack, 2, 98, 141, 290
Okamoto, R. Scott, 214
Omi, Michael, 102, 219
Ong, Aihwa, 212n31, 323, 331, 332
Ongiri, Amy, 25
online exhibits, 7, 142–49
Ono, Kent, 203
Opatut, Eileen, 253
Oren, Tasha, 9–10
Orientalism, 67–68, 176. *See also* techno-Orientalism
Osgood, Will, 31–32
Ozersky, Joshua, 246

Pacifica radio station, 126
Pacific War Memorial Commission, 186
Pacquiao, Manny, 4, 27–41
Pacquiao fight night spaces, 27, 28, 39, 40

Padma's Passport (television show), 251
Padoongpatt, Mark, 154
Page Act, 64
Pakistani Americans, 6–7, 124–36
Palermo, Venus, 317
Pandya, Sameer, 231
Paradise, Hawaiian Style (film), 190–95
parenting. *See* motherhood
Park, Grace, 198, 200, 205
Park, Jane, 197
Park, Teddy, 293
Parker, Ed, 21
Pastapur, Aishwarya, 238, 243n29
patriarchy, 48, 50–51, 53–55, 58, 101
Pavlik, Kelly "The Ghost," 31
Pavloski, Daine, 32
Pelaud, Isabelle Thuy, 175
The People I've Slept With (film), 59
Perkins, William Eric, 297
Perry, Imani, 294–95
Pham, Vincent, 5, 203
Phan, Michelle, 83, 312–14
Philippines: colonization of, 33–34; nationalism in, 12, 335–36; Pacquiao and, 27; returnees to, 12, 335–50
Pinky Paradise, 316
playboy culture, 191–93
PlayStation 2, 326
Plokhii, Olesia, 115
P.M. Dawn, 111
Polan, Dana, 249, 250
Polynesian Cultural Center, 193–94
Pond, Arn Chorn, 119–20
popular culture: Asian American cooking shows as, 253–54; digitization of, 139–49
Portes, Gil, *Miguel/Michelle*, 336–37, 339–44, 349
post-9/11 world, 11; *Battlestar Galactica* and, 199–210; in Bollywood films, 276–87; Cambodian Americans in, 115; Muslims in, 126, 134, 276–87; Pakistani Americans in, 127, 134–35; U.S. responses in, 276. *See also* war on terror
post-racial society: Asian Americans as example of, 139, 199; Jordan as example of, 35; media as evidence of, 8, 139; Pacquiao as example of, 27, 35; *Star Trek*'s portrayal of, 200; United States as, 2. *See also* multiculturalism
praCh, 116
Prashad, Vijay, 36, 96–97
Presley, Elvis, 8, 184, 186–95
Project Runway (television show), 321

Prosser, Jay, 339
Psy, 2, 11, 290–91, 296–97, 299–301
Puar, Jasbir, 135, 349
Public Broadcasting System (PBS), 250
Puerto Rico, 183–84
Pulido, Laura, 223
Punyaratabandhu, Leela, 158, 160
Purdy, Patrick, 175

queer: in *Battlestar Galactica*, 203–4; Bollywood films and, 289n20; Filipina/o returnees as, 12, 336–50; in *New York*, 278, 280, 285–86. *See also* homosexuality
Qui, Paul, 244

race and ethnicity: advertising aimed at Asian Americans, 235–36; Asian American indie rock and, 215–26; Asian Americans and U.S. notions of, 48, 56–57; Asian Americans in reality television, 79; in *Battlestar Galactica*, 198–210; and beauty norms, 304–18; Cambodian Americans and, 111–12; Chinese Americans and, 62–72; complexity of relations involving, 97; digital identity formation related to, 139–49; food blogs and, 151–62; Hawai'i and, 184, 187–88, 191–92, 195; in Hollywood films about Asian Americans, 46–59; Indian Americans and, 228, 230–32, 242n11, 263–74; indie rock and, 215–16; Jordan and Pacquaio and, 35; LA riots and, 89–102; in science fiction, 200, 211n7; Vietnamese Americans and, 175; and virtual fashion, 322–23; workplace relations and, 271–73. *See also* interracial romance; post-racial society; *individual races and ethnicities*
racial branding: Asian American food as vehicle for, 158–60; Asian Americans and, 235–36; Indian Americans and, 228, 232; spelling bees and, 228, 232, 236
racism: against African Americans, 95; against Chinese Americans, 63–64; against Indian Americans, 270–71; against Muslims, 134
radio, 6–7, 124–36
Rafael, AJ, 214
Rafael, Dan, 40
Rafael, Vicente, 347
Rai, Amit, 284, 285
Rain (pop star), 290
Ramírez Berg, Charles, 200
Rana, Junaid, 127
R&B. *See* rhythm and blues (R&B), K-pop and

rap music. *See* Cambodian American rap; hip-hop

The Ravenous Couple (blog), 155

Read, Allan Walker, 230

reality television, representation of Asian Americans in, 78–79

recipes, 154–55, 157

Refugee Act, 107, 122n14

religion, Pacquiao and, 30, 32–33

restaurants. *See* Asian cuisine and restaurants

Return of the Dragon (film), 22

Reyes, Eric Estuar, 335–36

Rhodes, James, 31

rhythm and blues (R&B), K-pop and, 290–93, 297–300

Richter, Linda, 338

Rimer, Sara, 117–19

Ripani, Richard J., 291

Robins, Kevin, 197

Root, Maria P. P., 192

Rose, Tricia, 107, 112

Roun, Tony Auyeth, 118–20

Ryce, Manila, *Thug Passion of the Christ*, 35–39

Ryoo, Jiwon, 298

Sackhoff, Katee, 205

Sa-I-Gu (film), 94–95

sa-i-gu subject, 90, 94–95, 100, 101

Saints Row IV (video game), 321

Saleem, S. M., 127, 129, 131

Saleem, Suriya, 127–29, 131

Sam, Kim Young, 292

Sanneh, Kelefa, 215

Santiago, Arabella, 76

Sayonara (film), 48, 191, 209

science fiction, 8–9, 197–210

Scripps National Spelling Bee, 9, 228–41

Se7en, 290

Seasia, 116–20

Second Life (online game), 321

Secret Identities collective, 143, 150n17

See, Lisa, 65

September 11, 2001 attacks. *See* post-9/11 world

sexuality: of Chinese Americans, 64, 73n18; in Hollywood films featuring Asian Americans, 46–59; of Muslims, 203, 278; non-normative, in *Battlestar Galactica*, 203–4. *See also* homosexuality; queer

SGU Stargate (television show), 199

Shahzad (radio host), 130, 132

Shakur, Tupac, 36

Shanghai, International Settlement of, 19

Sharma, Rekha, 198

Shigeta, James, 4, 46–59, 191

Shinoda, Mike, 214

Shpagina, Anastasiya, 317

Sik, Whang Ing, 24

Silicon Valley, 265–67

Singh, Prerna, 156

Siu, Lok, 145

SKIM (hip-hop artist), 224

Smith, James, 326

Smithsonian Asian-Latino Project (exhibition), 144–45

Smithsonian Asian Pacific American Center, 140, 142, 144, 146, 148–49

Smithsonian Institution, 140–44

software industry, Indian Americans in, 263–74

Song, Cathy, 65

Song, Eugene, 217–18

Song, Min, 94

Sony, 326, 330

soul music, 297–99. *See also* rhythm and blues (R&B), K-pop and

South Asian Americans, and spelling bees, 9, 228–41

South Asians for Justice, 225

South Asian Spelling Bee, 229, 233, 235–40, 243n30, 243n33

Southeast Asian Water Festival, Lowell, Massachusetts, 117–18

Spade, Dean, 344

Spellbound (documentary), 228, 239, 241n1

spelling bees, 9, 228–41

Spigel, Lynn, 249

stars (culture), 3–5

Star Trek (television show), 197, 198, 200

Star Wars (film series), 197

Star Wars: The Old Republic (online game), 328

stereotypes: of Asian American mothers, 65; of Asian American women, 208–9, 220, 316; of Asian character traits, 202; of Asian masculinity, 4, 37–39, 116, 176; in *Flower Drum Song*, 52; food-related, 247–48, 259, 263–74; of IT workers, 273; labor-related, 245, 259. *See also* forever foreigners, Asian Americans as; model minority, Asians as

Stevens, John, 183

stindians, 263–64, 270

street art, 98–100

Sujoe, Ansun, 231

Suk, Yang Hyun, 296

Sung, Wendy, 5

surfing, 187

tabak toyok, 21

Taeyang, 293

Tan, Amy, 63, 65, 69

Tassi, Paul, 329–30

The Taste (television show), 244

Tate, Greg, 98

Taylor, Paul C., 295

techno-Orientalism, 197

Teena Marie, 299

television cooking shows: competition format, 9–10, 244–45, 252–59; cook-along format, 249–51

Tencent QQ, 328

Tequila, Tila, 76–77

Terasaki, Gwen, 56

terrorism. *See* 9/11 attacks; war on terror

Tezuka, Osamu, 315

Thind, Bhagat Singh, 143

Thompson, Robert Farris, 296

Tiger JK, 294

TNP. *See* Tuesday Night Project

TokyoWink, 306

Top Chef (television show), 244, 252, 254, 258

Top Chef Masters (television show), 244

Toteson, Hugh, 241n2

Tourino, Christina Marie, 64

tourism: culinary, 153–54, 173; Hawai'i and, 183–95; in the Philippines, 338

Tran, GB, *Vietnamerica*, 7–8, 165–78, 178n14

Tran, Ky Phong Paul, 46

Transcontinental Railway, 146

transgender, 336, 339–44

transnational flows, 4; Asian food and, 157–58; beauty norms and, 309, 314–17; Cambodian American rap and, 120–21; *Fist of Fury* and, 20; of martial arts, 20–21; radio programming and, 125

Truong, Monique, 177

Tsai, Ming, 251

Tsing, Anna, 40

Tu, Thuy Linh Nguyen, 111, 254, 322

Tuesday Night Project (TNP), 214–15, 221–26

ulzzang style, 309–10, 314

Um, Hae-Kyung, 292, 294

United States: global role of, 201, 210; Hawai'i and the identity and ideology of, 183–95; and Korea, 292; labor and immigration in, 205, 209; nationalism in, 268–69, 272–73, 277; Pakistani criticisms of foreign policy of, 134–35; reflected in *Battlestar Galactica*, 198–210; role of spelling bees in, 230, 232; treatment of Muslims in, 284

Varadarajan, Tunku, 282, 284

Vietnamese Americans, 165–78

Vietnam War, 114

Villard, 175

virtual fashion and shopping, 11, 321–33

visas. *See* H-1B visas

Wadhwa, Vivek, 268

Wagnleitner, Reinhold, 292

Waldman, Ayelet, 61

Walker, Isaiah Helekunihi, 187

The Walking Dead (television show), 199

Walk Like a Dragon (film), 46, 47, 49–52, 58

Wall, Robert, 24

Wall Street Journal (newspaper), 61–62

Wang, Grace, 62, 78–79

Wang, Joe and Heidi, 78

Wang, Oliver, 116, 219, 224

Wang Laboratories, 108

War Brides Act, 52

war on terror, 32–33, 128, 134–35, 201–2. *See also* post-9/11 world

Watanabe, Bill, 223

Waugh, Thomas, 280

Way of the Dragon (film), 22–26

Web 2.0, 74, 76–77, 87n18, 140, 214

Wen, Ming-Na, 199

Williams, Rhonda M., 92

Winant, Howard, 102, 219

Wing Chun kung fu, 20

Wong, Anna May, 3

Woodward, Kathleen, 30

The World of Suzie Wong (film), 209

World of Warcraft (online game), 321, 324, 325

Wu, Alice, 65

Wu, Kevin "KevJumba," 5, 74–86

Wu, Michael, 78–81, 85

Wu, Theresa and Serena, 65

Wu-Tang Clan, 25, 111

Yamaguchi, Kristi, 304

Yamamoto, Hisaye, 65

Yamauchi, Wakako, 65

Yan, Martin, 250

Yan Can Cook (television show), 250

Yang, Gene Luen, *American Born Chinese*, 175–76

Yang, Jeffrey, 61–62

Yellow Fever, 67, 220

Yellow Peril, 63, 203, 231

Yellow Power, 216–17, 223, 226

YG Entertainment, 293, 296, 299
YOMYOMF (YouTube network), 85, 88n28
Yong-pil, Cho, 298
Young, Lee Ji, 299
Young Men's Christian Association (YMCA), 33–34
YouTube: beauty gurus on, 311–14; community formation through, 75–76; crossover to mainstream from, 74–77, 83–86; KevJumba on, 5, 74–75, 82–86
Yu, Dara, 245
Yumpit, Geraldine, 335
Yung, Victor Sen, 244

Zero Dark Thirty (film), 276
Zhao, Xiaojian, 52, 55